JEWISH LAW AS REBELLION

JEWISH LAW AS REBELLION

A Plea for
RELIGIOUS AUTHENTICITY
and Halachic Courage

NATHAN LOPES CARDOZO

URIM PUBLICATIONS
Jerusalem • New York

Jewish Law as Rebellion:
A Plea for Religious Authenticity and Halachic Courage

by Nathan Lopes Cardozo

Index: Shoshana Hurwitz

Copyright © 2018 Nathan Lopes Cardozo

Printed in Israel

First Edition

ISBN 978-965-524-276-8

Urim Publications
P.O. Box 52287
Jerusalem 9152102
Israel

www.UrimPublications.com

Library of Congress Cataloging-in-Publication Data

Names: Lopes Cardozo, Nathan T., author.
Title: Jewish law as rebellion : a plea for religious authenticity and halachic
  courage / Nathan Lopes Cardozo.
Description: First edition. | Jerusalem ; New York : Urim Publications, [2018]
Identifiers: LCCN 2017056908 | ISBN 9789655242768 (hardback)
Subjects: LCSH: Jewish law—Philosophy. | Judaism—21st century. | Judaism
  and secularism. | Judaism and social problems. | BISAC: RELIGION / Judaism /
  Rituals & Practice.
Classification: LCC BM520.6.L67 2018 | DDC 296.1/8—dc23 LC record
  available at https://lccn.loc.gov/ 2017056908

This book is dedicated in honor
of our anonymous friends' 60th birthdays.
May they merit many more years in good health
and may they continue to inspire those around them
with their wisdom and generosity.

*

ARIELLA and CHARLES ZELOOF

Approbations

This latest book by Rabbi Nathan Lopes Cardozo is a *cri de coeur* from the "enfant terrible" of Modern Orthodoxy. He is a rebel fighting for a most worthy cause – to reinvigorate Judaism and infuse it with real spiritual context. He inveighs against the over-codification of Halachah, a sort of pietistic OCD syndrome, which stifles the true spirit of Judaism. He calls for a return to the Talmud and its sources, with its openness, its bewildering variety of opinions, its multifaceted character, its liberality, and its halachic flexibility. This book is the powerful plea of a genuinely pious Jew deeply concerned for our Jewish future. The problems and challenges he presents are real and urgent, requiring creative rethinking on the part of our religious authorities. He is to be admired and congratulated for his courage and the clarity of his vision.

Sadly, he appears to be the lone voice of a tormented prophet battling against the overwhelming forces of the rabbinic establishment. The hope is that his impassioned plea be heard, and he be joined by a powerful chorus calling for a truly holy rebellion, a rebellion against the constrictions of a narrowly-focused and blinkered Orthodoxy, and one that will bring the vision of a new freedom functioning within the parameters of genuine Halachah.

> ❯ Rabbi Daniel Sperber is Professor of Talmud and President of the Higher Institute of Torah at Bar-Ilan University.

*

---

* Approbations are published in the order in which they were received.

This is a collection of highly original essays by an Orthodox person passionately pleading with us to humanize contemporary Jewish law in Israel. While likely too radical at times for some of his readers (including me), no reader can doubt the brilliance, courage, and deep concern that Rabbi Lopes Cardozo displays in these pages for authentic halachic living. A true *avodah l'shem shamayim*.

> ❯ YEHUDA GELLMAN is Emeritus Professor of Philosophy at Ben Gurion University of the Negev.

*

Rabbi Nathan Lopes Cardozo has written a challenging, even provocative book, inviting us to restore the iconoclasm with which Judaism was born as a religion of protest against the status quo. Agree or disagree, you will find yourself thinking hard and deep about the current state of Jewish law and life, and that makes it a work well worth reading – a new chapter in one of the great Jewish traditions: the dignity of dissent.

> ❯ Rabbi Lord JONATHAN SACKS is a British philosopher and scholar of Judaism and was formerly Chief Rabbi of the United Hebrew Congregations of the British Commonwealth.

*

What this exceptional book offers is a rationale for halakhic practice as a discipline of resistance – resistance to the corrupting effect of the ordinary, to the hollowing-out of human behaviour and human awareness that a fast-paced and feverish culture produces. It is full of insights that will challenge and inspire Jews and non-Jews alike: a reminder that Orthodoxy of whatever kind is empty if it does not arise from the deep, radical awareness of the divine imperative to be amazed and thankful in the face of every thing and every experience. Immensely enriching.

> ❯ ROWAN WILLIAMS, Doctor of Philosophy and Doctor of Divinity, is a Welsh Anglican bishop, theologian, and poet. He was formerly Archbishop of Canterbury.

*

What a great pleasure it is to discover this book! What an interesting, creative, and off-beat mind its author has! Where else do you find an Orthodox rabbi so deeply committed to autonomy, chaos, and non-conformity? Lopes Cardozo fully understands the problematics of Halakha, loving and appreciating it from within, but is also able to transcend it and see it from without. This allows him to pose great challenges to the halakhic community. He longs to restore to halakhic decisors the courage and individuality that has been lost in recent centuries. This is terribly urgent in our age, when the ever-tightening reins of spiritual conformity threaten to choke the religious life out of Judaism, alienating so many honest seekers. This man sees it all and speaks of it with great courage. May God bless his efforts and stretch forth the walls of his virtual *bet midrash*!

> ‣ Rabbi AVRAHAM YITZCHAK (ARTHUR) GREEN is Rector and Professor of Jewish Philosophy and Religion at Hebrew College Rabbinical School, Boston.

*

Rabbi Nathan Lopes Cardozo is that rare entity, a seeker who is unafraid to challenge accepted ideas and norms. His *Jewish Law as Rebellion* perfectly embodies his own engagement with tradition. It will inspire any who struggle with Judaism's most basic principles.

> ‣ JAMES KUGEL is Professor of Bible at Bar-Ilan University and Emeritus Professor of Classical and Modern Hebrew Literature at Harvard University.

*

Rabbi Dr. Nathan Lopes Cardozo's insistence that Halakha is meant to "disturb" and that the Jewish people must recover its sense of "strangerhood" restores an ancient prophetic voice to contemporary Jewish discourse. We must hope that this rich collection of his thought will expose his wisdom and challenges to an even wider audience.

> ‣ DANIEL GORDIS received his PhD from the University of Southern California. He is the author of *Israel: A Concise History of a Nation Reborn*, winner of the 2016 Jewish Book of the Year Award.

*

Rabbi Nathan Cardozo's *Jewish Law as Rebellion* is a bold plea for a reinvigorated Torah Judaism, one whose touchstone is critical reflection: on Halacha, on values, on policy, as well as on religious authority and religious authenticity. It is not, R. Cardozo argues, certainty that prompts these values, but rather asking the tough questions, even when altogether satisfying answers are not easily forthcoming. Our emphasis in education has been too much on what to think; not enough on how to think. Rabbi

Cardozo's approach promises a generation of passionate, creative halachic Jews. His book is a must read.

> HOWARD WETTSTEIN is Professor of Philosophy at the University of California, Riverside.

*

Rabbi Cardozo is an independent thinker who reframes conventional pieties with startling clarity. He targets a religious establishment whose conformism has robbed Orthodoxy of meaning. In reminding us that Judaism produced the world's first rebellious religious text, this book is itself a much-needed protest against rabbinic mediocrity and spiritual decline.

> MELANIE PHILLIPS is a British journalist, author, and public commentator. She currently writes for *The Times*, *The Jerusalem Post*, and *The Jewish Chronicle*.

*

One of the most creative and courageous thinkers within the contemporary Orthodox Jewish world, Rabbi Dr. Nathan Lopes Cardozo is brimming with the gift of what Ralph Waldo Emerson termed "Divine discontent." This is reflected in his collection of essays, which powerfully critiques an ossification that has substantially immobilized the dynamic spirit of Halachah and which serves as a compass for its creative liberation.

Anyone who wishes to appreciate both the potential of halachic Judaism as well as the challenges it faces will be greatly enriched by this impressive work.

> Rabbi DAVID ROSEN KSG CBE is the American Jewish Committee's International Director of Interreligious Affairs.

*

Rabbi Cardozo offers a vitally important message for the spiritual and intellectual renewal of Judaism. He challenges and provokes; he makes us think and re-think. More importantly, he demands a response that will revolutionize and re-energize the halakhic way of life. Are we up to the challenge?

> Rabbi MARC D. ANGEL is Founder and Director of the Institute for Jewish Ideas and Ideals.

*

Rabbi Nathan Lopes Cardozo has a unique and inspiring way of exploring Jewish tradition. Without sacrificing intellectual and religious integrity, he challenges us to rethink our relationship to this tradition. Irrespective of a reader's starting point, he or she will be both challenged and inspired.

> › DEBORAH E. LIPSTADT is Professor of Modern Jewish History and Holocaust Studies at Emory University.

*

Rabbi Nathan Lopes Cardozo is a unique intellectual presence in the rabbinical world today. His new book raises profound questions that disturb our complacency and demand the attention of our hearts and minds. To think with him about the challenges he raises is one of the great experiences of modern Jewish thought.

> › SUSANNAH HESCHEL is the Eli Black Professor of Jewish Studies at Dartmouth College.

*

The "spiritual autobiography" of Rabbi Nathan Lopes Cardozo is fascinating reading, also for a European Muslim. The universal significance of loneliness and of togetherness brings us all back to the mystery and identity of the Unity of God. Our differences and our uniquenesses, however, need to be respected as a special gift from our Lord to allow brotherhood and cooperation. So how can we manage unity in diversity? Shall we be obedient to the Divine Law, or rebellious?

Rabbi Nathan Lopes Cardozo seems to provoke us with the science of Halacha, choosing rebellion rather than strict obedience. These days, when bigotry seems to justify violence among some narrow-minded radical Muslims, Rabbi Cardozo's approach can inspire a wise renewal in understanding the deeper meanings of the Law rather than following it only as a technical practice and forgetting the sacred science within the Law.

The challenge we face is to give priority to the goals of our obedience to the Law rather than have obedience to the Law as a goal; to open our hearts and minds to the higher, literal and symbolic teachings of the Law through the guidance of traditional masters. We really do not need "salafi" archaeological slogans, but rather sincere intellectual debate, even between Jews and Muslims.

Maqasid al-shari'ah and the renewal of *ijtihad* are also part of the debate among Muslim scholars. In current times of great confusion, decadence and abuse of religion, Rabbi Cardozo's book inspires us to live up to our social and spiritual responsibilities.

> ❯ Imam YAHYA PALLAVICINI is President of COREIS, the Islamic Religious Community of Italy.

*

A really ingenious, Jewish, spiritual and enlightened mind is rare. And you're lucky if you meet up with it during your lifetime. Nathan Lopes Cardozo's is such a mind. His knowledge of Halacha is undisputed, his almost scientific approach mind-blowing. The first time I met Cardozo was during a Spinoza symposium in Amsterdam. He eloquently pleaded to lift the 17th century *cherem* that was put on the philosopher. This is typical for Cardozo: rebel against narrow-mindedness, especially within the Jewish religious establishment that tends to prefer a status quo over rejuvenation, even when the latter is embedded in Halacha.

Judaism is not a pond with still water. Its origin is rebellion against rigid, stuck ways of being. And it is about *tikun olam*, without fear of science, human nature and evolution. Cardozo brings science, psychology and religion together. That requires a great mind, constantly wondering and curious about why and how. He is a bridge; a great relief for people who wonder why those disciplines must clash so often.

But foremost, a conversation with Lopes Cardozo is a conversation between two human beings, an exchange of questions and observations, like an intense talk between friends. This is what makes Cardozo *ein mensch*. His ideas and opinions are a blessing for anyone seeking truth behind daily Jewish life and beyond, for his lessons are universal.

> ❯ ESTHER H. VOET is the Editor-in-Chief of the Dutch Jewish weekly, *Nieuw Israëlietisch Weekblad* (NIW).

*

For decades, Rabbi Cardozo has embodied the most authentic kind of love for Halacha – a love that is at once admiring and demanding, reverent and critical, committed and questioning. His is an approach that reassures us that Halacha will remain vibrant and viable for thinking Jewish audiences for decades to come. As we were all taught in yeshiva, there is nothing more valued than a "good *kashya*," an insightful question that forces us to rethink, and to explore possibilities that we had never considered before.

We all owe a debt to Rabbi Cardozo for the fantastic *kushyot* that he poses, and the new possibilities he broaches.

> ➤ Rabbi YOSEF KANEFSKY is Senior Rabbi of the B'nai David-Judea Congregation in Los Angeles.

*

For decades, Nathan Lopes Cardozo has been a prophetic voice in contemporary Judaism. Like a prophet, he challenges and criticizes out of love. He punctures complacency and calls us to holy rebellion against conventional religious living, for God's sake.

In this book, we find a remarkable collection of essays. They are the fruit of a lifetime of exploration, of openness to a variety of issues, of integrity in admitting problems and in appreciating the insights of critics. His teachings call us to a deeper relationship with God instead of rote/ritual religious life. They show the way to a redemptive Halakha in place of a by-the-book legalism that lacks compassion and human connection. Every subject that he treats he sees with fresh eyes, makes hitherto unexpected links, and relates to Torah life with unique insights.

Cardozo is an inspiring model of a lifetime of vitality and growth. He became a Haredi Jew and gifted educator, starting from a marginal background. Then he outgrew this way of life because he refused to settle for conventional certainties. Yet he has taken the richness of sources and thickness of practice with him. He uses his remarkable body of knowledge and spirituality to understand and illuminate a much broader swath of life. He explores the resources in Halakha for needed innovation and pluralism. He calls up the availability of older minority views and openings. He pleads for spiritual redirection and humane responsiveness in halakhic rulings, to enable a better life.

Rav Nathan is our guide to religious authenticity, a wise counselor on balancing conflicting moral and religious claims. He is the strategist of bringing healthy change to a system that is trying to maintain its distinctive voice – but has grown too defensive.

We cannot do justice to this wonderful book in a brief review. Among its treasures are appreciation (and critique) of major philosophers, other religions, and important cultural alternatives. Everywhere there are rich passages with food for thought, questions to unsettle us, answers to goad us on to new spiritual heights. Dear reader, before you is an intellectual/

spiritual feast. Taste and see that God is good and that Cardozo's wisdom is the stuff of a better life.

> ❯ Rabbi IRVING (YITZ) and BLU GREENBERG – YITZ GREENBERG is an American scholar and author, and a promoter of greater understanding between Judaism and Christianity. BLU GREENBERG is an Orthodox American writer specializing in modern Judaism and women's issues.

*

The very word 'Halakha' demands movement. It's a dynamic concept that has all too frequently fallen into fixity and inflexibility. For many, it is used as the straightjacket rather than the scaffolding for Jewish life.

Rabbi Cardozo has wonderfully issued this clarion call to all thoughtful Jews – and others – as to the purpose of our tradition. It was not for nothing that God took the Jews out of Egypt before giving us the Torah. The essence of our tradition and our mission is to challenge and provoke. Even our classical 'establishments' were built on, and demanded, debate and disagreement – priest, prophet and king, rabbi versus rabbi. The most triumphant moments of Torah are when Avraham and then Moshe argue with God! *Makhloket l'shem shamayim* is a wonderfully Jewish idea. Perhaps that is why so many have found us so difficult to live with. I fear that might also be Cardozo's fate when some of our authorities and 'leadership' read this book. They will find him hard to live with. After all, in these many glorious essays, he demands generosity of thought, creativity of imagination, kindness of heart and simple *gemilut hasadim* when considering the challenges that Halakha and its standard approaches sometimes generate.

And what is wonderful about his challenge is that no decent thoughtful Jew can put aside these ideas without proper consideration. His scholarship is indisputable; his sincerity evident; his Orthodoxy – if frequently unorthodox – consistent; and his intelligence shines from every page.

This book has the capacity to give new hope in the renewability of the Jewish tradition for this and for every age. Radical and courageous, the rebellion that Rabbi Cardozo seeks has the power to make Judaism fresh and purposeful even in the eyes and hearts of those who have left it behind as sterile and irrelevant. For this reason alone, the book deserves to be read by all, especially by those who think theirs is the only way.

> ❯ CLIVE A. LAWTON OBE JP is co-founder of Limmud, Chief Executive Officer of the Commonwealth Jewish Council, and an international consultant in educational and community development.

Prayer

May it be Your Will, O God, that a mishap shall not come
about through me. And may my readers and I not stumble in
a matter of law or spirit.

Give us the courage to change those things which can and
should be changed.
Give us the serenity of mind and heart to accept those things
which cannot be changed.
And give us the wisdom to distinguish one from the other.

(Based on *The Serenity Prayer* by Reinhold Niebuhr)

"To Boldly Go Where No One Has Gone Before"

Star Trek

*

"We Are Only Human Beings
As Long As We Are Human Becomings"

(Based on an observation attributed to ERNST BLOCH)

Contents

Preface

I have titled this book *Jewish Law as Rebellion: A Plea for Religious Authenticity and Halachic Courage*, because I believe that one of Halacha's main functions is to protest against a world that is becoming ever more complacent, self-indulgent, insensitive, and egocentric. Many people are unhappy and apathetic. They have lost their ambition to live an inspiring life, even though they are surrounded by luxuries that no one could have even dreamed of only one generation ago.

The purpose of Halacha is to disturb. To disturb a world that cannot wake up from its slumber because it actually thinks that it is alive and well. This is not only true of the secular community, but also of many religious communities that have fallen victim to the daily grind of halachic living while being disconnected from the *spirit* of Halacha, which often clashes with halachic conformity just for the sake of conformity. Many religious people convince themselves that they are religious because they are "*frum*." They are conformists, not because they are religious but because they are often self-pleasers, or are pleasing the communities in which they live.

Large numbers of religious Jews live in self-assurance and ease. The same is true of the secular community. Both live in contentment.

My book is a protest against this malady.

As Rabbi Louis Jacobs notes, "Who wants a life of contentment? Religion throughout the ages has been used to comfort the troubled. We should now use it to trouble the comfortable."[1]

*

---

1. Louis Jacobs, quoted in Elliot Jager, "Power and Politics: Celebrating Skepticism," *The Jerusalem Post*, Dec. 4, 2007.

This book contains many essays on Halacha, its philosophy, and the way it functions. They were written over several years and reflect my thoughts, which have developed and sometimes radically changed. As the reader will soon realize, the book presents the theory of halachic chaos while trying to make some sense of it.

I have steered clear of imposing an overall philosophical order and system on Halacha, but have allowed several, often opposing ideologies and methods to represent themselves. *As a result, some essays contradict each other.* This is *deliberate* and is an excellent representation of Judaism itself. Contradictions put us face to face with reality.

Some of the essays were written for scholarly journals, others for lay people. Some are therefore more academic, others more spiritual; some more daring and others more mainstream. With some exceptions, I have used language that the average reader can follow. Too often, books and essays on philosophy and religious issues are geared to an elite group of intellectuals and written in a style that is incomprehensible to most readers. I have tried to avoid this as much as possible, but cannot claim to have always succeeded.

The essays have been subdivided into various categories so as to make for more convenient reading. These categories are somewhat arbitrary, and many of the essays overlap. On a few occasions they are partially repetitious, since they were written over a long period of time. However, the meticulous reader will also soon realize that an earlier-mentioned idea gave birth to a new insight at a later stage.

To repeat an idea in a slightly different way often means that the reader will start to realize that it has meaning and might even be true. In fact, if the author has anything worth saying, that is just what he ought to do. (Oliver Wendell Holmes, Sr., *Over the Teacups*, [1891].)

This is even more true about this book, since it should not be read in one sitting, but rather with intervals, to allow the reader to have its ideas penetrate, leading to contemplation and hopefully to personal transformation.

It is my intention that people of different religious and academic backgrounds will find something of interest in this book, and while every essay may not achieve this goal, my hope is that there is enough material to strike a balance and satisfy most readers. For this reason, too, general concepts in Judaism and Halacha are often briefly explained, even if the explanations will be somewhat superfluous for some readers.

For those interested in further research, the footnotes provide material for further inquiry. It is important to make the reader aware of the fact that the many sources that are mentioned throughout the book do not always prove my point of view. I use them as points of departure; signposts to move beyond what the actual source states. Also note that sometimes the sources argue the opposite point of view. The sources are provided as a reference for further study and to highlight various viewpoints, some in support and some against the claims made in the text.

Wherever possible, full documentation of the sources is included, except for Hebrew books that are widely available, for example in the Bar Ilan Responsa Project. For citations of *teshuvot* (responsa), a *siman* number is provided rather than a page number. For citations of Talmud Yerushalmi (JT), the chapter, halacha, folio, and column number of the Venice 1523 edition are provided. Midrashic works are cited by specific edition for the sake of accuracy, as different editions contain different textual variants. For readers who want to look up the sources, these editions are available in the Bar Ilan Responsa Project. Where a Hebrew-language book or article is cited with an English title, the citation is followed by [Hebrew].

For footnotes that reference citations of English language works, I have followed the Chicago citation style. Thus, author titles such as Rabbi or Dr. are omitted. However, where a note cites Hebrew *sefarim* or Hebrew Torah journal articles and they are authored by a rabbi, I refer to the author with the prefix R. It is likely that there exists a certain amount of discrepancy, and any errors in this matter are solely my oversights, for which I apologize.

I have endeavored to ensure a degree of consistency in the standardization of citations of Hebrew *sefarim*. However, practical considerations such as the existence of multiple editions of works and publications from different time periods make this a difficult, sometimes impossible task.

Translations into English prioritize clarity of meaning and fluency over word-for-word or literal translation. Thus, translations that I have used in this book have been chosen with this consideration in mind and are sometimes adapted for clarity where deemed appropriate.

Transliteration into English – especially of Hebrew book or article titles – follows a broad approach to transcription rather than strict adherence to an academic transliteration style, and preference is given to a rendering that reflects the pronunciation of today's Modern Hebrew. However, where a Hebrew word is commonly transliterated a certain way, I have retained that spelling for the sake of familiarity.

It is difficult to mention all the people who have had a profound influence on my thinking. They are too numerous. Still, I want to name a few because of the significant role they have played in the evolution and development of my thoughts: Franz Rosenzweig; Hillel Zeitlin; Rabbi Avraham Yitzchak ha-Kohen Kook; Chacham Ben-Zion Uziel; Rabbi Chaim Hirschensohn; Rabbi Yosef Mashash; Rabbi David Cohen, the *Nazir*; Rabbi Dr. Eliezer Berkovits; Rabbi Dr. Louis Jacobs; Rabbi Dr. David Hartman; Professor Michael Wyschogrod; Rabbi Dr. Norman Lamm; Professor Yehuda Gellman; Rabbi Lord Jonathan Sacks; Professor Menachem Kellner; and Rabbi Dr. Daniel Sperber. Special mention should be made of Rabbi Dr. Abraham Joshua Heschel, whose ideas greatly influenced the spirit of this book. While I do not agree with some aspects of his theology, he has, together with Rabbi Eliezer Berkovits, been the most influential person on my thinking. Special mention should be made of the journal *Conversations*, edited by my friend Rabbi Dr. Marc D. Angel; *The Jerusalem Post*; *The Times of Israel*; *The Algemeiner*; the *Jewish Journal*; the Israeli Hebrew newspaper *Makor Rishon*; and the Crescas Jewish Educational Center in Amsterdam.

Acknowledgments

There are many people to thank. I begin with my parents, Jacob and Bertha Lopes Cardozo, may their memory be a blessing, who gave me the opportunity to study Judaism and were gracious enough to allow me to become religious while I was still living at home in the Netherlands. My mother made her kitchen kosher so that I wouldn't have to leave or occupy a "kosher corner." My parents made it possible for me to start observing Shabbat and gave me permission to be absent on Saturdays when I was in high school. (See my spiritual autobiography "Lonely but Not Alone," https://www.cardozoacademy.org/thoughts-to-ponder/autobiography-lonely-but-not-alone-ttp-344/.)

My younger brother, Dr. Jacques Eduard Lopes Cardozo, was always supportive of me as I was going my religious way, while he went his own way. His (and his wife's) constant encouragement, to this very day when we are both in our 70s, demonstrates his absolute integrity. Annemarie and their children are a source of great delight to me.

Special mention should be made of my parents-in-law, Grisha and Ro Gnesin z"l who, together with my parents, allowed my wife and me to live in Gateshead, England, which was home to the largest yeshiva and Torah community in Europe. I was able to spend more than eight years in Talmud study, and our two oldest children were born there. It was Gateshead Yeshiva's outstanding teachers, world-renowned talmudists, who laid the foundations of my love for Judaism and learning.

Although I have moved away from some of their ideologies, it was they who made me realize the enormous spiritual potential within Judaism.

My parents and parents-in-law also helped us immensely when our family moved to Israel, where I spent four years in the Mirrer Yeshiva in Yerushalayim and met several eminent talmudists.

The David Cardozo Academy's think tank has been crucial in helping me develop my ideas. The occasionally fierce opposition from members to some of my views, and their tremendous encouragement to step out of the box with some unusual notions and suggestions, always give me much joy. I'd like to make special mention of three Yaels: Yael Unterman, Yael Valier, and Yael Shahar, who have been vital to the think tank's success.

A very big thank you goes to my dear friends Michael and Hila Kagan and Rabbi Yehoshua Looks, for all their support and encouragement.

My dear friend and scholar Yehudah DovBer Zirkind had the responsible, rigorous task of checking all the sources and, when relevant, adding more references and offering insights. I cannot thank him enough for his painstaking work.

Obviously, it is only *I* who bears responsibility for the observations and ideas found in this book.

My secretary, Mrs. Esther Peterman, has been with me for many years. Had she not taken care of all the administrative work at our academy, this book would never have come about. *Toda raba* to her!

Many thanks to Ilana Sinclair of Modi'in, Israel. Ilana has been my right-hand woman in organizing the distribution and exposure of many essays in this book via social media, including Facebook. It is the Abraham & Esther Hersh Foundation that has made this possible. Rony and Toby Hersh have become very close friends. My sincere thanks go to them.

Over the many years, the Spijer Foundation in Holland has financed the David Cardozo Academy and many of my publications. Its founders, the late Aron and Betsy Spijer z"l, were always ardent supporters of my work. The foundation's board members, my friends Dr. Leo Delfgaauw, Dr. Hans Wijnfeldt, and Mr. Eldad Eitje, have been extremely loyal.

The Board of the Israeli Ohr Aaron Foundation, the Boards of the American Friends of the Cardozo Academy in the USA, in Britain, and in Canada have greatly helped me to make it possible to teach and publish. *Chazak u-Baruch* to them!

This book is sponsored by my dear friends Charles and Ariella Zeloof of Herzliya and formerly of London. May they be blessed for all the great work they do for the people of Israel.

Infinite thanks are due to our dear friend Channa Shapiro of Yerushalayim, my dedicated editor who for years has made sure that my essays are written in flawless English. This book would not have appeared without her. The same is true of Chaim Frankel who painstakingly went through the manuscript. Also, many thanks to the editorial staff of Urim Publications. There are no words to express my gratitude.

Some "older" essays were transcribed from oral lectures I gave. Thanks to Amy Heavenrich, Gavin Enoch, and Jake Greenberg.

My dear friends Tzvi Mauer and Moshe Heller, of Urim Publications, were prepared to publish and distribute this book, as they have done with previous books of mine. The distinct advantage of working with them is that the publication of books is not just a financial endeavor to them, but also a mission. This makes working with them a special experience.

Last, but far from least, I thank my wife, Frijda Rachel, who lives with the challenge of being married to me. This is far from an easy undertaking. She has shown and continues to show infinite patience with me even as I spend many hours in my study writing books and essays, only to return home at midnight. We have been married for nearly fifty years, and while we've had health and other challenges to overcome, we have been blessed with many *smachot* and much *nachat* from our children, children-in-law, grandchildren, and great-grandchildren. Thanking them all is totally beyond my reach. Knowing that each and every one of them is a devoted Jew is a source of tremendous joy.

Above all of this, I give thanks to the One above, Who has been exceedingly kind to us.

To Him all praise,
Nathan Lopes Cardozo
Kislev 5777 / December 2017

Biographical Notes

The numerous approbations that I received for this book were written by some of the greatest scholars, educators, authors, leaders, and journalists of our day. Below are their short biographical profiles.

RABBI DR. DANIEL SPERBER is a British-born Israeli academic and rabbi. He earned a doctorate in ancient history and Hebrew studies from University College, London, and is currently a professor of Talmud and president of the Higher Institute for Advanced Torah Studies at Bar-Ilan University, Israel. Rabbi Sperber has published books in Hebrew as well as in English. Amongst them are: *Why Jews Do What They Do: The History of Jewish Customs Throughout the Cycle of the Jewish New Year* (1999) and *A Dictionary of Greek and Latin Terms in Rabbinic Literature* (2012). He is considered a prominent halachic authority in the Modern Orthodox community and has published an eight-volume work, *Minhagei Yisrael: Origins and History* (1991–2013), on the character and evolution of Jewish customs. In 1992 he was awarded the Israel Prize in Jewish Studies.

DR. YEHUDA (JEROME) GELLMAN is emeritus professor of philosophy at Ben-Gurion University of the Negev, Israel. He was a senior fellow at the Hartman Institute for Advanced Judaic Studies, Jerusalem, and a fellow at the Center for Philosophy of Religion at the University of Notre Dame, Indiana. Dr. Gellman has authored a number of books on general and Jewish philosophy, including *God's Kindness Has Overwhelmed Us: A Contemporary Doctrine of the Jews as the Chosen People* (2012) and *This Was from God: A Contemporary Theology of Torah and History* (2016).

RABBI LORD JONATHAN SACKS is a British philosopher, theologian, and scholar of Judaism, and a renowned speaker and moral voice for our time. He served as the chief rabbi of the United Hebrew Congregations of the British Commonwealth from 1991 to 2013. Rabbi Sacks holds sixteen honorary degrees and has authored over twenty-five books, including *Crisis and Covenant: Jewish Thought after the Holocaust* (1992); *The Koren Siddur* (2009); *Not in God's Name: Confronting Religious Violence* (2015); and *The Great Partnership: God, Science and the Search for Meaning* (2011). He was knighted by HM Queen Elizabeth II in 2005.

DR. ROWAN DOUGLAS WILLIAMS, Baron Williams of Oystermouth, doctor of philosophy and doctor of divinity, is a Welsh Anglican bishop and theologian. He was archbishop of Canterbury from 2002 to 2012 and spent much of his earlier career as an academic at the universities of Cambridge and Oxford. He is currently Master of Magdalene College. In addition to writing over thirty theological and historical texts, Dr. Williams is a poet, and his collection *The Poems of Rowan Williams* was long-listed for the Wales Book of the Year award in 2004. Some of the eleven languages he speaks and/or reads are English, Welsh, Spanish, French, German, Russian, Greek, and Biblical Hebrew. He is considered one of the foremost Christian philosophers of our day.

RABBI DR. AVRAHAM YITZCHAK (ARTHUR) GREEN is an American scholar of Jewish mysticism and a neo-Hasidic theologian. He is rector and professor of Jewish philosophy and religion at Hebrew College Rabbinical School, Boston. Rabbi Green received his *semicha* at the Jewish Theological Seminary of America, where he studied privately with Abraham Joshua Heschel. He has authored many books, of which *Radical Judaism: Rethinking God & Tradition* (2010) is said to be his most important theological work. His doctoral dissertation at Brandeis University, Boston, became his book *Tormented Master: The Life and Spiritual Quest of Rabbi Nahman of Bratslav* (1992).

DR. JAMES KUGEL is emeritus professor of Bible at Bar-Ilan University, Israel, and emeritus professor of classical and modern Hebrew literature at Harvard University, Boston. He received his doctorate from City University of New York. Dr. Kugel is the author and editor of more than twenty books and numerous articles on the Bible and its early commentators, focusing on the Second Temple period. In 2001, his book

The Bible as It Was (1997) won the University of Louisville Grawemeyer Award in Religion, and *How to Read the Bible* was awarded the National Jewish Book Award for the best book of 2007. His latest book is *The Divine and the Human: The Great Shift of Belief in the Biblical Era* (2017).

DR. DANIEL GORDIS is senior vice president, Koret Distinguished Fellow, and chair of the core curriculum at Shalem College, Jerusalem. He is a popular speaker and was listed in *The Jerusalem Post* as one of the fifty most influential Jews in the world. Dr. Gordis is the author of eleven books, the latest of which is *Israel: A Concise History of a Nation Reborn* (2016), which won the 2016 Jewish Book of the Year Award. He has written for numerous publications, including *The New York Times*, *The New Republic*, *Moment*, and *Haaretz*. He writes a regular column, "A Dose of Nuance," for *The Jerusalem Post*.

DR. HOWARD WETTSTEIN has been professor of philosophy at the University of California, Riverside, since 1989, and held positions there as chair of the Department of Philosophy and as director of the university honors program. Dr. Wettstein earned his doctorate from City University of New York, and has written extensively on philosophy of language, philosophy of mind, and philosophy of religion. He has written three books – *Has Semantics Rested on a Mistake? And Other Essays* (1991); *The Magic Prism: An Essay in the Philosophy of Language* (2006); and *The Significance of Religious Experience* (2014). He has also co-authored, edited, and co-edited many more volumes.

MELANIE PHILLIPS is a British journalist, author, and public commentator. She used to write for *The Guardian* and *New Statesman*, and currently writes for *The Times of London*, *The Jerusalem Post*, and *The Jewish Chronicle* on social and political issues. She has written numerous books, including *The World Turned Upside Down: The Global Battle over God, Truth, and Power* (2010); her memoir, *Guardian Angel: My Story, My Britain*, which first came out in 2013; and her best-selling *Londonistan* (2006), about the British establishment's capitulation to Islamist aggression. In 1996, she was awarded the Orwell Prize for Journalism, a British prize for political writing of outstanding quality.

RABBI DR. DAVID ROSEN KSG CBE is international director of the American Jewish Committee's department of interreligious affairs.

He served as chief rabbi of Ireland from 1979 to 1985. Before that appointment, he was the senior rabbi of the largest Orthodox Jewish congregation in Cape Town, South Africa, and served as a judge on the local *bet din* (rabbinic court). Rabbi Rosen received a papal knighthood in 2005 for his contribution to Jewish-Catholic reconciliation, and in 2010 he was made a CBE (Commander of the British Empire) by HM Queen Elizabeth II for his work in promoting interfaith understanding and cooperation.

RABBI DR. MARC D. ANGEL is rabbi emeritus of Congregation Shearith Israel, the historic Spanish and Portuguese Synagogue in New York City. He is founder and director of the Institute for Jewish Ideas and Ideals, and editor of its journal, *Conversations*. Rabbi Angel was president of the Rabbinical Council of America, and a member of the editorial board of its journal, *Tradition*. He received his PhD and his *semicha* from Yeshiva University, and also has an MA in English literature from the City College of New York. Among the many books he has authored are *Losing the Rat Race, Winning at Life* (2005) and *Maimonides, Spinoza and Us: Toward an Intellectually Vibrant Judaism* (2009).

DR. DEBORAH E. LIPSTADT is professor of modern Jewish history and Holocaust studies at Emory University, Georgia. She received her PhD in Jewish History from Brandeis University, Boston. Dr. Lipstadt was a consultant to the United States Holocaust Memorial Museum, and in 1994 was appointed by former US president Bill Clinton to the United States Holocaust Memorial Council, on which she served two terms. She is best known as author of the books *Denying the Holocaust* (1993); *The Eichmann Trial* (2011); and *Denial* (2016), previously published as *History on Trial: My Day in Court with a Holocaust Denier* (2005). In 2016, the movie *Denial*, based on her book, was released.

DR. SUSANNAH HESCHEL is professor of Jewish Studies at Dartmouth College. She earned her doctorate in religious studies from the University of Pennsylvania and has received many grants and awards, including four honorary doctorates. Two of her major works of scholarship are *Abraham Geiger and the Jewish Jesus* (1998) and *The Aryan Jesus: Christian Theologians and the Bible in Nazi Germany* (2008). Dr. Heschel is the author and editor of many books and articles, and has also edited, translated, and published numerous works by her father, Abraham

Joshua Heschel, including *Moral Grandeur and Spiritual Audacity: Essays by Abraham Joshua Heschel* (1997) and *Abraham Joshua Heschel: Essential Writings* (2011).

YAHYA PALLAVICINI is imam of the al-Wahid Mosque of Milan, vice president of the Islamic Religious Community of Italy, and an advisor for Islamic affairs to the Italian Minister of Interior. Imam Pallavicini is known as a voice for moderate, democratic Islam, and has strongly denounced violence committed in the name of Islam. He is the author of *Dentro la moschea (Inside the Mosque)*, and was one of the lead authors of "A Common Word between Us and You," a 2007 open letter from Muslim clerics and intellectuals to the world's foremost Christian religious leaders, promoting dialogue between the two in an effort to foster global peace and interreligious understanding.

ESTHER H. VOET is a Dutch journalist and editor-in-chief of the Netherlands' largest Jewish paper, the weekly *Nieuw Israëlietisch Weekblad* (NIW). She worked for the newspaper *De Telegraaf* and for the media company RTL Nederland. From 2009 to 2015, Ms. Voet was director of the CIDI, a Jewish human rights organization that aims to secure the peace and prosperity of the Jewish people anywhere in the world. It is a position that required her to comment publicly on such matters as Holocaust education, Nazi literature, and anti-Semitism.

RABBI YOSEF KANEFSKY has been rabbi of the B'nai David-Judea Congregation in Los Angeles since 1996. During his tenure, he has built B'nai David-Judea into a leading center of Modern Orthodoxy and one of the most dynamic, warm, and respected Modern Orthodox synagogues in the country. He received his *semicha* and a master's degree in Jewish history from Yeshiva University. Rabbi Kanefsky has introduced changes intended to enhance the role of women in Orthodox life and has established social action as a central part of the congregation's activity. He is a past president of the Board of Rabbis of Southern California and a regular contributor to *The Jewish Journal of Greater Los Angeles*.

RABBI DR. IRVING (YITZ) GREENBERG is an American scholar, author, and educator, and one of the most important voices in America's Jewish community. He received his *semicha* at Yeshiva Beis Yosef (Novardok), and earned a PhD in American history from Harvard University. He

taught at Yeshiva University, where he was among the first to introduce the teaching of Holocaust studies into a university curriculum.
Rabbi Greenberg served as the communal rabbi of the Riverdale Jewish
Center while teaching Jewish studies at the City College of New York.
For twenty-three years, he served as founding president of CLAL: The
National Jewish Center for Learning and Leadership. He is a promoter
of greater understanding between Judaism and Christianity. Among his
published books are *For the Sake of Heaven and Earth: The New Encounter between Judaism and Christianity* (2004) and *Sage Advice* (2016), his
commentary on *Pirke Avot*. He is married to writer Blu Greenberg.

BLU GREENBERG is an American writer specializing in modern Judaism
and women's issues. She holds an MA in clinical psychology from City
University of New York and an MS in Jewish history from Yeshiva
University. She is a co-founder and the first president of the Jewish
Orthodox Feminist Alliance, and she chaired the first and second International Conference on Feminism and Orthodoxy. Ms. Greenberg has
served on the boards of many organizations, including Project Kesher
and U.S. Israel Women to Women. At the forefront of her struggle today is solving the issue of women whose husbands refuse to grant them
a *get* (Jewish divorce document). Her best-known books are *On Women
and Judaism: A View from Tradition* (1981) and *Black Bread: Poems, After
the Holocaust* (1994). She is married to writer and scholar Irving (Yitz)
Greenberg.

CLIVE A. LAWTON OBE JP is a British-Jewish educator, broadcaster,
and writer. He co-founded Limmud and now serves as their senior
consultant. He is a lecturer at the London School of Jewish Studies,
chief executive officer of the Commonwealth Jewish Council, and an
international consultant in educational and community development.
In 2016, he was appointed OBE (Officer of the British Empire) by
HM Queen Elizabeth II for his services to the Jewish community. Mr.
Lawton has been involved in the development of Holocaust studies,
and was vice-chairman of the Anne Frank Educational Trust, UK. He
is a published author and an editor of children's books and young adult
books, including *Matza and Bitter Herbs* (1986) and *The Story of the
Holocaust* (1999).

Jewish Law (Halacha) as Rebellion

It is time to start thinking big about Halacha. Great opportunities are awaiting us and too much is at stake to let them pass by. For too long, Halacha has been jailed in compartmentalized and awkward boxes. It is time to liberate it.

Most religious Jews are not aware that Halacha has nearly become passé. They believe it is thriving. After all, Halacha is very "in" and there are more books on this subject than ever before. Despite this, it lacks courage. We have fallen in love with – and become overwhelmed by – an endless supply of all-encompassing but passive halachic information, which does not get *processed* but only *recycled*. We have access to a nearly infinite amount of information via the Internet, books, journals, and pamphlets, providing us with all the knowledge we could ever dream of. The problem is that this easily accessible information has replaced creative thinking. It has expelled the possibility for big ideas, and we have grown scared of them. We only tolerate and admire bold ideas when they provide us with profit-making inventions – when we feel our empty pockets – but not when they dare challenge our hollow souls. We do not discuss big ideas because they are too abstract and ethereal.

Novelty is always seen as a threat. It carries with it a sense of violation; a kind of sacrilege. It asks us to think, to stretch our brains. This requires too much of an effort and doesn't suit our most important concern: the need for instant satisfaction. We love the commonplace instead of the visionary, and therefore do not produce people who have the capacity to deliver true innovation.

It is only among some very small, secular fields that we see staggering ideas emerging (Hawking and black holes, Aumann and game theory). In

the department of Halacha, with only few exceptions, we rarely find anyone who even comes close to suggesting something really new. This is all
the more true within Orthodox Judaism. While in ages past, discussions
within Halacha could ignite fires of debate, we are now confronted with
an increasingly *post-idea* Halacha. Provoking ideas that would boggle our
minds are no longer "in." If anything, they are condemned as heresy. Since
they cannot easily be absorbed into our self-made halachic boxes, and they
don't bring us the complacency we long for, we stick to the mainstream
where we can dream our mediocre dreams and leave things as they are.

THE RETREAT OF CREATIVE THINKING

Most of our yeshivot have retreated from creative thinking. We encourage
the narrowest specialization rather than push for daring ideas. We are
producing a generation that believes its task is to tend potted plants rather
than plant forests.

We offer our young people prepared experiences in which we tell them
what to think instead of teaching them *how* to think. We rob them of the
capacity to learn what thinking is really all about. The plethora of halachic
works, which educate them in the minutiae of the most intricate parts
of Jewish Law, hardly generate the inspiration for new ideas about these
laws. In fact, they stand in the way. There is no time for anyone to process
all the information even if they want to. But instead of seeing this as a
problem, they and their teachers have turned it into a virtue.

And that is exactly the point. We are faced with two extremes: either
our youth walk out on or maintain a lukewarm relationship with Jewish
observance, or they become so obsessed by its finest points that they are
incapable of seeing the forest for the trees and they consequently turn into
rigid religious extremists.

What we fail to realize is that this is the result of our own educational
system. In both cases, young people have fallen victim to the disease of
information for the sake of information.

Information is not simply to *have*. It is there to be converted into
something much larger than itself; it is there to produce ideas that make
sense of all the information gathered in order to move it forward to higher
latitudes. Information is not there to be possessed, but to be *comprehended*.

Jewish education today is, for the most part, producing a generation
of religious Jews who know more and more about Jewish observance,

but think less and less about what it means. This is even truer of their teachers. Some are even talmudic scholars, but these very scholars don't realize that they have drowned in their vast knowledge. The more they know, the less they understand. Just as a young child may think it is an act of kindness to lift a fish out of an aquarium and "save" it, so these rabbis may be choking their students while thinking they are providing them with spiritual oxygen. Doing so, they rewrite halachic Judaism in ways that are totally foreign to the very ideas that it truly stands for. They are embalming Halacha while claiming it is alive, because it continues to maintain its external shape.

Fewer and fewer young religious people have proper knowledge of the great halachic arbitrators of the past. They know little of their weltanschauung. And even when they do, the ideas of these great thinkers are presented to them as information, instead of as challenges to their own thinking or as prompts to the development of their own creativity. This is a tragedy. Our current halachic, spiritual, and intellectual challenges cannot be answered by simply looking backward and giving answers that once worked, but are now outdated.

THE QUEST FOR CERTAINTY PARALYZES THE SEARCH FOR MEANING

Instead of new theories, hypotheses, and great ideas, we get instant answers to questions of the utmost importance, offered via a wide variety of self-help books, the authors of which seem to claim that their halachic information came directly from Sinai. Trivial, simplistic, and often *incorrect* information replaces significant ideas. The information is reduced to a catchline – thus too brief and unsupported by proper arguments – yet still presented as "the answer." By delivering "perfect" answers, which fit nicely into the often underdeveloped philosophies of their authors, everything is done to crush the questioning of halachic conclusions. *The quest for certainty paralyzes the search for meaning.* It is *uncertainty* that is the very stimulus impelling man to unfold his intellectual capacity. Every idea within Halacha is multifaceted – filled with contradictions, opposing opinions, and unsolvable paradoxes. The greatness of the Talmudic Sages was that they shared with their students their own struggles and doubts and their attempts at solving them, as when Bet Hillel and Bet Shammai, Rava and Abaye debated major halachic problems; their fierce disagreements rooted in their outlook on life and how they saw Judaism.[1] Students were made privy to their teachers' inner lives, and that made their discussions exciting. The teachers created tension in their classes, waged war with their own ideas, and asked their students to fight them with knives between their teeth. They were not interested in teaching their students final halachic decisions, but instead asked them to take them apart, to deconstruct them so as to rediscover the questions. These teachers realized that not all halachic paradoxes can be solved, because life itself is full of paradoxes. They also realized that an answer is always a form of death, but a question opens the mind and inspires the heart.

It is true that this approach is not without risk, but there is no authentic life choice that is risk-free. Nothing is worse than giving in to the indolence and callousness that stifles inquiry and leaves one drifting with the current. Such an approach shrinks the universe of the Halacha to a self-centered and self-satisfying ideological ghetto, robbing it of its most essential component: the constant debate about the religious meaning of life and how to live in God's presence and move to higher levels.

THE GREATEST PROOF OF JUDAISM'S DECLINE IS THE PRODIGIOUSLY LARGE NUMBER OF LIKE-MINDED RELIGIOUS JEWS

Outreach programs, although well intentioned, have become institutions that, like factories, focus on mass production and believe that the more people they can draw into Jewish observance, the more successful they are. That their methods crush the minds of many newcomers who might have made a major contribution to a new and vigorous Halacha is of no importance to them. The goal is to fit them into the *existing* system. That their outdated theories make other independent minds abhor Judaism and Halacha is a thought they do not seem to even entertain. To them, only *numbers* count. How many people did we make observant? Millions of dollars are spent to create more and more of the same type of religious Jew. Like the generation of the Tower of Bavel, in which the whole world was "of one language and of one speech,"[2] we are producing a religious Jewish community of artificial conformism in which independent thought and difference of opinion is not only condemned, but its absence is con-

---

1. *Eruvin* 13b.
2. *Bereshit* 11:1.

sidered to be the ultimate ideal. We have created a generation of yes men. We desperately need to heed what Kierkegaard said about Christianity: "The greatest proof of Christianity's decay is the prodigiously large number of [like-minded] Christians."[3]

Insight has been replaced with clichés, flexibility with obstinacy, and spontaneity with habit. What was once one of the great pillars of Judaism – the esteemed value of spiritual, intellectual, and moral dissent – has become anathema. Instead of teaching the art of audacity, we are now educating a generation of kowtowers.

There is social ostracism of any kind of healthy rebellion against the conventional. The famous Orthodox rabbi, Eliezer Berkovits, was ignored when he argued that Halacha had become defensive; the master thinker Abraham Joshua Heschel's understanding of Halacha is completely disregarded by Orthodoxy; Charedi yeshivot pay no attention to Rav Kook.

INTELLECTUAL DISHONESTY

Above all, we see dishonest attempts to portray halachic fundamentalism as a genuinely open-minded intellectual position, while in truth it is nothing of the sort. Great visions of the past are misused and abused. Today we are seeing many people taught that they must imitate so as to belong to the religious camp. Spiritual plagiarism (a term used by Heschel) has been adopted as the appropriate way of religious life and thought.

It is true that there are still dissidents within the world of Halacha today – and they are growing in number. There are even some yeshivot and institutions that dissent, but the great tragedy is that these places speak in a small voice, which the religious establishment is unable to hear. Instead, the establishment puts its weight behind the insipid and the trivial, and has fallen in love with the uncompromising flatness of mainstream institutions; places that yield large numbers of students and offer instant answers to people who find themselves in religious crisis.

Original halachic Jewish thinkers today fall victim to the glut of conformists. While these thinkers challenge conventional views, they remain unsupported and live lonely lives because our culture writes them off. Rather than saying yes to new halachic ideas, which we are in desperate

---

3. M.M. Thulstrup, "Kierkegaard's Dialectic of Imitation," in *A Kierkegaard Critique*, ed. H.A. Johnson and N. Thulstrup (NY: Harper, 1962), 277.

need of, the conformists pander to the idol worship of intellectual and spiritual submission.

Most talmudic scholars don't realize that the authors whose ideas they teach would turn in their graves if they knew their opinions were being taught as dogmas that cannot be challenged. They wanted their ideas tested, discussed, thought through, reformulated, and even rejected, with the understanding that no final conclusions have ever been reached, could be reached, or even should be reached. They realized that matters of faith should remain fluid, not static. Halacha is the practical upshot of living by unfinalized beliefs while remaining in theological suspense. Only in this way can Judaism avoid becoming paralyzed by its awe of a rigid tradition or, conversely, evaporate into a utopian reverie.[4]

Parents today who are worried by their children's lack of enthusiasm for halachic Judaism do not realize that they themselves support a system that systematically makes such passion impossible.

THE NEED FOR VERBAL CRITICS

What today's Halacha desperately needs is verbal critics who could spread and energize its great message. It needs halachic Einsteins, Freuds, and Pasteurs who can demonstrate its untapped possibilities and undeveloped grandeur.

The time has come to deal with the real issues and not hide behind excuses that ultimately will turn Judaism into a sham. Our thinking is behind the times, and that is something we can no longer afford. Halacha is about bold ideas and discovering solutions which nobody ever thought of. Its goal is not to find the final answer, but to inspire us to honestly search for it. The study of Halacha is not only the greatest undertaking there is, but also the most dangerous, since it can so easily lead to self-satisfaction and spiritual conceit. The leashing of our souls is easier than the building of our spirit.

What we need to do is search for the Halacha as it was in its embryonic form, before it was solidified into the great halachic codifications such as Rambam's *Mishne Torah* or Rabbi Yosef Karo's *Shulchan Aruch*. We must return to the great ideologies of Halacha and its many varied opinions, as found in the Talmud and other early sources, and develop the Halacha

---

4. See Walter Kaufmann, *Critique of Religion and Philosophy* (Princeton, NJ: Princeton University Press, 1958), 268.

in ways that can inspire the soul and address the varied spiritual needs of modern man.

TO EMULATE REMBRANDT

We need to emulate Rembrandt, the great Dutch painter who, unlike all other painters of his generation, used the raw material of Holland's landscape to perceive hidden connections – linking his preternatural sensibility to a reality that he was able to transform, with great passion, into a new creation. He found himself in a state of permanent antagonism with his society, and yet he spoke to his generation and continues to speak to us because he elevated himself to the point where he could see the full dimensions that art could address, which nobody else had discovered.

Just like art, one cannot *inherit* Halacha and one cannot just *receive* the Jewish Tradition. One must fight for it and earn it. To be halachically religious is to live in a state of warfare. The purpose of art is to disturb; not to produce finished works, but to stop in the middle, from exhaustion, leaving it for others to continue. So it is with Halacha. It still has scaffolding, which should remain while the building continues.

I am not advocating revisionist positions, presented just for the sake of being novel or to justify certain behavior. History has shown that such approaches do not work and often lack the genuine religious experience. We should not be overanxious to encourage innovation in cases of doubtful improvement. But the time has come to rethink Halacha and its goals and methods as it is taught in many traditional places.

A NEW KIND OF YESHIVA

We are in need of a radically different kind of yeshiva: one in which students are confronted with serious challenges to Halacha and its weltanschauung and learn how to respond; where they become aware that it is not certainty, but doubt, that gets you an education; where it is not rabbinic authority that reigns supreme, but religious authenticity. A yeshiva where the teachers have the courage to share their doubts with their students and show them that Judaism and Halacha teach us how to live with uncertainty, and *through* that uncertainty to be deeply religious people. Students need to learn that Halacha, like life, is the art of drawing sufficient conclusions from insufficient premises (Samuel Butler). A reasonable probability is the only certainty we can have. No doubt there will be fierce arguments, but we should never forget that great controversies are also great emancipators.

Broad change is not just window dressing, and it can be painful. It is liberating and refreshing, but comes with a price. Without it, though, not only is there no future for Halacha; there is also no purpose.

TO DELIBERATELY CREATE AN ATMOSPHERE OF REBELLION

One of the great tasks of Jewish education is to *deliberately* create an atmosphere of rebellion among its students. Rebellion, after all, is the great emancipator. We owe nearly all of our knowledge and achievements not to those who agreed, but to those who differed. It is this virtue that brought Judaism into existence. Avraham was the first rebel, destroying idols, and he was followed by his children, by Moshe, by the prophets, and by the Jewish people.

What has been entirely forgotten is that the Torah was the first rebellious text to appear in world history. Its purpose was to protest. It set in motion a rebel movement of cosmic proportions, the likes of which we have never known. The text enumerates all the radical heresies of the past, present, and future. It calls idol worship an abomination, immorality an abhorrence, the worship of man a catastrophe. It protests against complacency, self-satisfaction, imitation, and negation of the spirit. It calls for radical thinking and drastic action without compromise, even when it means standing alone, being condemned and ridiculed.

All of this seems to be entirely lost on our religious establishment. We are instructing our students and children to obey, to fit in, to conform, and not to stand out. We teach them that their religious leaders are great people because they are "all-right-niks" who would never think of disturbing the established religious and social norms. We train them to view these leaders as the ideal to be emulated. But by doing so, we turn our backs on authentic Judaism and Halacha, and convey the very opposite of what Judaism is meant to project.

By using clichés instead of the language of opposition, we deny our students the excitement of being Jewish. It is both the excitement resulting from the realization that there is a need to revolt and take pride in it, no matter the cost, as well as the excitement at the awareness that they are part of a great mission for which they are prepared to die, knowing that it will make the world a better place because *they* are the real Protestants.

When we teach our children to eat kosher, we should tell them that this is an act of disobedience against a consumerism that encourages human beings to eat anything as long as it tastes good. When we go to synagogue, it is a protest against man's arrogance in thinking that he can do it all by himself. When couples observe the laws of family purity, it is a rebellion against the obsession with sex. By celebrating Shabbat, we challenge our contemporary world that believes our happiness depends on how much we materially produce.

THE MEDIOCRITY OF RELIGIOUS TEACHING

As long as our religious educators continue to teach Jewish texts as models of approval instead of manifestations of protest against the mediocrity of our world, we will lose more of our young people to that very mediocrity.

Halacha, in its essence, is an act of dissent, not of consent. Dissent leads to renewal. It creates loyalty. It is the force that compels the world to grow.

INSTABILITY

One wonders why we Jews, throughout thousands of years of our history, were never able to develop into a stable, secure nation. We had to deal with so many obstacles: being deprived of our homeland for nearly two thousand years; experiencing difficulties living with each other; being few in number; and being the target of a constant onslaught of accusations and calls challenging our very right to exist – all unparalleled in world history. Even today, after the re-establishment of our Commonwealth – the State of Israel, with its mighty power and exceptional accomplishments – we remain a nation in a constant state of uncertainty, never sure what the next day will bring, confronted with one crisis after another.

This emerges as a major paradox, considering the nation's remarkable capacity to be constantly on the brink of extinction, yet, to not only survive, but to rejuvenate itself in a most powerful way. Historians and anthropologists are hard put to comprehend how we not only live on, but we outlive our enemies, draw the world's attention with our achievements, and contribute to humankind in a manner that is significantly far out of proportion to our numbers.

The shifting sands on which all of Jewish history is based makes us wonder whether this paradox is not, in fact, essential to the very existence of the Jewish people.

THE STRANGER IN OUR MIDST

There is one commandment and halacha that, unlike any other in the Torah, is almost endlessly repeated. It instructs us to be concerned about the welfare of the stranger in our midst.[5] According to one opinion in the Talmud, this commandment appears forty-six times in the Torah.[6] Since no other commandment even comes close to such numerous repetitions, we must conclude that we are looking at *the core of the mystery of Jews, Judaism, and Halacha.*

Of great importance is the fact that we are asked to look after the stranger because of our own experience in Egypt. Here we are confronted with a crucial aspect of a halachic moral imperative. The demand of what is seemingly the most important of all commandments, *to care about the stranger*, can only have sufficient authority when it is substantiated through the appeal to personal experience.

It indeed does not take much effort to realize that all of Jewish history is founded on strangerhood. Avraham, the initiator of Judaism, was called upon to become a stranger by leaving his home and country to find his Jewish identity. Early Jewish history relates the story of a nomad people who even after they reached their destination, the Jewish land, were compelled on numerous occasions to leave that land and live once again as foreigners. They were forced to live for hundreds of years "in a land that is not theirs,"[7] namely Egypt, and it was under those circumstances that their identity was formed. It was only sporadically that Jews actually lived in their own homeland. Even the Jewish *raison d'être*, the Torah, was not given "at home," but in a desert, an existential experience of "foreign-er-hood." It is as if all of the Torah's commandments, without exception, find their meaning, justification, and fulfillment only once one knows and experiences what it means to be a stranger. More recent Jewish history, of the last nearly two thousand years, once again found Jews living as foreigners in other people's lands.

---

5. See, for example, *Shemot* 23:9, "Do not oppress a stranger. You know how it feels to be a stranger, for you were foreigners in Egypt."

6. *Bava Metzia* 59b. See *Talmudic Encyclopedia*, s.v. "ona'at ha-ger," 1:345–346 and s.v. "ger," 6:277–278.

7. *Bereshit* 15:13.

THERE CAN ONLY BE MORAL HOPE AS LONG AS MAN IS SOMEHOW UNSETTLED

What the foreigner lacks is security; a feeling of home and existential familiarity. Paradoxically, it is this deficiency that creates the climate in which man can be sensitized to the plight of his fellow men. *It leads to the realization that there can be moral hope only as long as man is somehow unsettled.* The human being's quest for security will obstruct his search for meaning and purpose, while his lack of security will impel his moral powers to unfold. It is clearly this fact that underlies the ongoing repetition of the commandment to look after the stranger "because you were strangers in Egypt."

What this means is that for a nation to maintain sensitivity and concern for "the Other," it must continue to live in some form of strangerhood. It must never be fully secure, and must constantly be aware of its own existential uncertainty. As such, the Jew is to be a stranger. Only in that way can he become a moral beam of light to the nations of the world; a mission that above anything else is the reason for his Jewishness. The Torah is a protest against humans feeling overly secure, for it is aware that the world will become a completely insecure place once people begin to feel too much at home and consequently forget their fellow man.

We Jews must live between eternal existence and insecurity, even as we reside in our own homeland.

The upheavals in recent Israeli Jewish history, which deny the Jewish people stability and security, may well be a message to return to a much greater sensitivity toward the stranger and fellow man. *Jews must realize that God fashioned them into a people of archetypal foreigners, in order to enable them to live by the imperatives of the Torah.* We need to understand and internalize that nearly all problems in society result from seeing "the Other," including one's own fellow Jew, as a stranger. Most people cannot perceive what it means to be a stranger and how far it extends, unless they themselves experience it on some level. "For a crowd is not company; and faces are but a gallery of pictures; and talk but a tinkling cymbal, where there is no love."[8] Most men are alone, surrounded by many; and man suffers his most difficult moments when by himself, standing in a crowd.

---

8. Francis Bacon, *The Essays or Counsels, Civil and Moral* (CreateSpace Independent Publishing Platform, 2016), 46.

TO TROUBLE THE COMFORTABLE

This awareness is the bedrock of Halacha. It wants Jews to be an eternal nation because this lack of definite security is the great paradox that makes a truly moral Jewish society possible. Halacha is a protest against too much familiarity with this world, because familiarity breeds contempt, causes complacency, mediocrity, and a lack of authenticity. The function of Halacha is not just to comfort the troubled, but above all to trouble the comfortable (Louis Jacobs). It teaches us that something great is demanded of us, to rebel against spiritual and religious plagiarism, to never become aged and outmoded in one's search for real life, and to warn us against the fallacy of expediency.

BOREDOM

Psychologists tell us that one of man's greatest enemies today is boredom. Sometimes, when reading a paper or popular journal, watching television or a DVD, using an MP3 or iPod, or just listening to the old-fashioned radio, we are confronted with the most absurd manifestations of dullness and apathy. Believe it or not, there are people who spend their time rolling around Europe in a barrel, and couples who dance the salsa for hours upon hours in order to break a record. Others seek entry into the *Guinness World Records* by developing the stunning art of eating more ice cream than any human since the days of prehistoric man.

What is boredom? It is a disorder that has stricken our modern world as a result of our wishes being too easily and too quickly satisfied. Once the urge has been fulfilled, we immediately feel the pressure of new urges because we cannot live without them. We are like deep-sea fish. We thrive on atmospheric pressure, and without it we are lost. Since Western man is easily able to satisfy most of his wishes, he begins to look for absurd pursuits to satiate his urges.

Our sages make a very interesting point when they say a man's character can be uncovered in three different ways: *be-kiso, be-koso, u-ve-ka'aso.* By his pocket; is he a miser or a spendthrift? By his cup; how does he hold alcoholic intake? And by his temper; how does he control himself when provoked? But according to one of the sages, there is a fourth test: *af be-sachako* – also by how he plays, i.e., *how he spends his free time.*[9]

---

9. *Eruvin* 65b.

One of the great blessings of our day is that more and more young people realize that there is more to life than having a good time. Many of them are showing a keen interest in matters of the spirit. Lectures on religion and philosophy in famous universities and other places of learning are becoming more and more popular. Young people are looking for existential meaning and a high-quality spiritual mission. It is here that Halacha has to tap in and show that it is able to dare to respond to this challenge. By showing that it has a wealth of different ideas, and even opposing rulings, it is able to fascinate many young people who live and love pluralism. Just like poetry, Halacha must become an expression of excited passion, and it can only do so by causing continuous spiritual earthquakes accompanied by eternal fever, which will throw young people off their feet in total surprise.

In Israel we see a large number of secular young men and women interested in studying Talmud, Halacha, Midrash, and Jewish philosophy in their attempt to understand what it means to be a Jew and what Judaism has to offer the world.

Most interesting is the fact that young people are finding their way back to Judaism in rather unconventional ways. Official outreach programs are losing their grip on Israeli society. They are replaced by a new phenomenon: Jewish self-discovery. It is not uncommon to see young, bareheaded men with long hair, earrings, and *tzitzit*;[10] others eating kosher, but never entering a synagogue; young women lighting candles on Friday afternoon without observing Shabbat, praying with great fervor and going off to a dance party. There are even committed atheists who will enthusiastically join prayer events. And women, whose dress code perhaps leaves much to be desired, sincerely kissing *mezuzot* before entering a shopping mall or gym.

Surely not all of this is a sign of maturity – no doubt in certain cases it is superstition; still, what we observe is people searching for a sense of authenticity.

NO TO RELIGIOUS PLAGIARISM

It is an aversion to religious plagiarism that keeps these people out of mainstream Judaism and the conventional Halacha. By paving their own

---

10. Ritual fringes knotted on each corner of a four-cornered garment, which religious Jews wear under their shirts as a remembrance of God and His commandments. See *Bamidbar* 15:37–41.

way, they develop a fresh approach to what Judaism is *really* all about –
being open to new adventures. They are keenly aware that one cannot
passively inherit Judaism and its vital companion, Halacha; they realize
that one needs to discover it on one's own.

Spiritually, nothing can be worse than trying to fit these people into
mainstream Judaism and conventional Halacha. The religious establishment could make no greater mistake than to interfere in this development
and start giving advice. All it can do is be there to help when asked. By
trying to force its views on these people, it will uproot the seeds that have
been carefully planted.

What the religious establishment needs to realize is that Halacha itself has generally fallen victim to boredom. Rituals and prayers are often
mechanical and do not touch the soul. Today, show and ceremony must
be minimized in Judaism. Ceremonies are for the eye, but Judaism is an
appeal to the spirit. The only biblically required ceremony in today's synagogue service is the blessings of the priests, and even then the congregation is asked to close its eyes![11]

In biblical days the Halacha was astir while the world was sleeping.
Today the world is astir while the Halacha is sleeping. Only when it wakes
up and starts to challenge our society with novel ideas and rulings will
it once more be the vital mover of Jewish life. It must be prepared to
look inward, challenge its own verdicts, and once again understand that
its main function is to protest and rebel.

We are in desperate need of bold ideas that will place the Halacha in
the center of our lives and make us receptive to God's presence through a
daring *new* encounter with Him. Let it be heroic. Not staid and comfortable, but painful and hard-won; a deep breath in the midst of the ongoing
conflict ever-present in the heart of humankind.

To forget this is to betray Judaism.

---

11. See Abraham Joshua Heschel, *I Asked for Wonder: A Spiritual Anthology*, ed. Samuel H.
Dresner (NY: The Crossroad Publishing Company, 1983), 87.

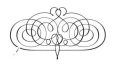

One

THE NATURE OF HALACHA

Chapter 1

Halacha as Deliberate Chaos

Chaos is God's signature when He prefers to remain anonymous. Halacha is the chaotic way through which God wants the Jew to live life, according to strict and structured rules that seem to be part of a well-worked-out system.

Upon careful analysis, however, it becomes evident that Halacha consists of "arbitrary" laws, which on their own can make a lot of sense on a religious, ritual, or social level, but which are difficult to understand as an overall consistent weltanschauung with halachic methodology applied to them.

Many prominent thinkers have tried to impose logic or systematic structure on these laws, but they have been forced to admit that their overall systematic philosophy of Halacha doesn't fit into the very structure of Halacha. This prompts them to put forth sometimes farfetched and unconvincing arguments that make sense only within an entirely different classification, or by means of arbitrary reasoning that they would normally reject out of hand.

Austrian-British philosopher Karl Popper, when discussing the logic of science, said:

> Science is not a system of certain, or well-established, statements; nor is it a system which steadily advances towards a state of finality. Our science is not knowledge: it can never claim to have attained truth, or even a substitute for it. . . . We do not know: we can only guess. And

---

* With thanks to my students Anne Gordon and Yael Shahar for their observations.

our guesses are guided by the unscientific, the metaphysical (though biologically explicable) faith in laws, in regularities which we can un-cover – discover. . . . The old scientific ideal of *episteme* – of absolutely certain, demonstrable knowledge – has proved to be an idol. The de-mand for scientific objectivity makes it inevitable that every scientific statement must remain tentative forever.[1]

In his preface to *Realism and the Aim of Science*, Popper writes:

As a rule, I begin my lectures on Scientific Method by telling my students that scientific method does not exist.[2]

Almost paradoxically, he writes two pages later:

I dislike the attempt, made in fields outside the physical sciences, to ape the physical sciences by practicing their alleged "methods" – mea-surement and "induction from observation." The doctrine that there is as much science in a subject as there is mathematics in it, or as much as there is measurement or "precision" in it, rests upon a complete misunderstanding.[3]

Anyone who reads halachic literature – particularly responsa – will quickly realize that while some basic principles of interpretation (mainly found in the Talmud) are at work, there is chaos regarding how to understand them in terms of ideology, weltanschauung, and even the practical application of Halacha.

Halachic expert Professor Aaron Kirschenbaum, in his essay "Subjec-tivity in Rabbinic Decision Making," refers his readers to a remarkable book written by British scholar Rabbi Dr. Louis Jacobs, *A Tree of Life: Diversity, Flexibility, and Creativity in Jewish Law*, "in which he catalogues innumerable changes in the Halacha – drastic modifications as well as moderate adjustments. These changes are so varied – in subject matter, in geographic distribution, in historical period – that one is at loss to delin-eate the precise parameters of halachic development."[4]

---

1. Karl Popper, *The Logic of Scientific Discovery* (London: Routledge, 1992), 278, 280.
2. Karl Popper, *Realism and the Aim of Science* (New York: Routledge, 1999), 5.
3. Ibid., 7.
4. Aaron Kirschenbaum, "Subjectivity in Rabbinic Decision Making," in *Rabbinic Authority and Personal Autonomy*, ed. Moshe Z. Sokol (Northvale, NJ: Jason Aronson, 1992), 87.

One of the main reasons for this is that much depends on the personality, emotional makeup, and weltanschauung of the halachic arbiter. His personal circumstances, as well as where and in what era he lives, makes all the difference. No objectivity can ever be achieved, because humans – no matter how clever – cannot escape their own soul forces, and even the environmental influences that they subconsciously internalize. Moreover, the type of halachic training the arbiter has received, the religious values in which he has been steeped, and even his secular education, all play a major role.

Many would argue that this is far from ideal. After all, how can a person gain an accurate understanding of the Divine Will when they are hampered by their subjective emotions, desires, philosophies, and circumstances?

But within the context of classical Judaism, all of this is considered a blessing. For people to be human and reach out to the Divine, they must maintain their humanness, and having emotions and desires is exactly what makes us human. Were we to relinquish those feelings (clearly, an impossibility), we would cease to be human beings and the Halacha would no longer have any meaning for us since it was intended for humans, not for angels (or robots). This is what is meant by the Talmud: "The Merciful One said: Do it [construct the Sanctuary] and in whatever manner you are able to do it, it will be satisfactory."[5]

Furthermore, if Halacha were to operate by clearly determined boundaries and criteria, it would not survive. Studies have shown that in ensuring the survival and productivity of an idea, movement, lifestyle, or philosophy, biological and unconscious dynamics are much more successful than agenda-driven organizations and ideologies.[6] Clearly-stated platforms and goals cannot develop and expand in ways that are conducive to real-life scenarios. They are too confining to solve the many problems that we humans are asked to deal with. Overall strategies often create stagnation. Flexibility for free association produces progress.

Within religious thought and experience, there is the awareness that we must allow God to enter via what appears to be chaos and chance. Were everything to be worked out and predictable, we would close the door on

5. *Bechorot* 17b. See *Ohr Yisrael* (Vilna: Yehuda Leib Metz, 1900), 87. (Selected writings of R. Yisrael Salanter and his disciples.)

6. See Matt Andrews, Lant Pritchett, and Michael Woolcock, "Doing Problem Driven Work" (CID Working Paper no. 307, Harvard University, 2015), http://bsc.cid.harvard.edu/files/bsc/files/doing_problem_driven_work_wp_307.pdf.

God and therefore on real life. Chaos is the science of surprises of the nonlinear and unpredictable. It teaches us to expect the unexpected.

This does not mean that anything goes and we can dispense with rules. That would cause a breakdown of society. What it means is we must allow for openings in the prevailing system, enabling the unpredictable to enter. Anything that rejects our conviction that all is predictable and bound by absolute laws is the *sine qua non* for a vigorous life. Certain things must be left to chance in order to solve problems that we are unable to predict or resolve in conventional ways. They cannot and should not be forced into a carefully worked out plan. We can't always make accurate predictions, but we can suggest probabilities.

This is true also because, as Kurt Gödel's incompleteness theorem has proven, in any axiomatic system, if the system is consistent, it cannot be complete, nor can the consistency of the axioms be proven within the system, since the system itself is "part of the problem." We can only know something to be true when regarded by an observer outside the system. While one cannot compare Gödel's incompleteness theorem – which deals with mathematics and number theory – to the world of Halacha, we can surely use it to gain some insight into its nature. In Halacha, too, we find what appears to be inconsistencies and a lack of completeness.

It is for this reason that Halacha has developed on the basis of case law and not overall well-worked-out ideologies. It is *sui generis*. Much depends on circumstances, the kind of person we are dealing with, local customs, human feelings, and sometimes trivialities. God, as Abraham Joshua Heschel explains, is concerned with everydayness. It is the common deed – with all of its often trivial and contradictory dimensions – that claims His attention. People do not come before God as actors in a play that has been planned down to the minutest detail. If they did, they would be robots and life would be a farce.

One of the most remarkable aspects of Orthodox Halacha is that it is almost an open market. Any person with halachic knowledge can write and state whatever they believe is true, knowing full well that others could refute their arguments. They must surely have all the relevant sources at their fingertips, but they are completely free to use the information in a creative way, so long as they adhere to the *masoret*, an unwritten and undefined tradition going back thousands of years. Some will view the *masoret* as a minimal and almost fundamentalist observance, and others will view it as a maximal and highly flexible tradition, which allows for much innovation.

Their common ground is their view of this tradition as a river that flows through an often rocky terrain, with many unexpected turns, but which never dries up. These arbiters would never forsake the river. Some will subtly alter its course, pushing against the river's shore in an attempt to widen it, while others would never dare. But not one of them would suggest creating an altogether new river. If that were to happen, all would be lost.

Most of these actions, or lack of them, are not deliberately planned, but are largely unconscious reactions which the halachic arbiter may not even be aware of. There is a deep trust in this process while nobody really knows what the process involves. There's no agenda (or should be no agenda), and that's exactly why it remains alive and successful.

This is also why in Orthodox Judaism there are generally no "Halacha committees," as we find in Conservative Judaism. While in the olden days there was a Sanhedrin – a supreme rabbinical court that was given authority over the functioning of Jewish Law in the Jewish State – it deliberately left many loopholes, and rulings had to then be made by local rabbinical courts or individual rabbis. Once the ancient Jewish State ceased to exist, the Sanhedrin was dissolved. This may quite well have been a blessing, since a centralized legal body would have become an obstacle in a scattered Jewish world that could only survive if the theory of "halachic chaos" would take the upper hand.

In modern times, the leading halachic authorities decide major cases independently. They are not voted in or appointed by a commission, but they spontaneously become accepted as the main arbiters, with no official declaration made. It is the circumstances, which appear in a chaotic way, that suddenly bring a halachic authority to prominence. It may be that others are better qualified to take on the task, but they never make it because the community looks the other way for reasons it may never know. It might be the arbiter's personality, a specific trait, or just being in the right place at the right time that makes them stand out. It could be that one unusual and daring ruling does the trick, and it is probably true to say that the halachic arbiters themselves are taken by surprise to suddenly be at the center of the halachic community.

It is no doubt absolutely essential that they have all talmudic and halachic literature at their fingertips, but that is not what makes them prominent. They must develop a creative, versatile, and somewhat chaotic mind, able to make connections that no one has ever seen or thought about, and be willing to come up with unprecedented ideas. Unconscious

and turbulent forces must be at work. If arbiters have a wealth of encyclopedic knowledge but are unable to develop it, they cannot fill the role of
posek (halachic authority). They must also be flexible enough to allow for
the unpredictable to enter the halachic conversation.

Not only do we see a considerable amount of chaotic halachic literature, published by numerous authorities, which seems to lack consistency
and order, but we may even find contradictions in the various writings of
one halachist. This doesn't mean that the writer lacks a particular line of
thought and some basic principles; it just means that within these norms
almost everything is an open market.

I believe this is the reason why the Conservative movement, with all
its good intentions and significant scholarship, was unable to grasp the
imagination of many halachic authorities. It is not the lack of knowledge,
but rather the over-systematization that is responsible for this. Once there
is too much of a unified weltanschauung and agenda, Halacha loses its
vitality. The multitude of attitudes, worldviews, chaotic thinking, and
sometimes wild ideas, through which the greatest halachic authorities
freely expressed their opinions, is what kept the Orthodox halachic world
alive. In some sense, and even almost paradoxically, Orthodox Halacha
is less fundamentalist than Halacha in other movements within Judaism.

None of this should surprise anyone. When looking into the Talmud,
which is the very source of Halacha, we find a range of opinions so wide,
and often radical, that it is almost impossible to find any sense of order.
There's a reason why the Talmud is compared to a sea in which storms
create unpredictable waves and turbulence. The revealed beauty of this
natural phenomenon is what attracts people to gaze at the sea for hours
on end. It reflects their inner world, which thrives only in the presence of
tension, paradox, and chaos.

This may be related to another phenomenon in authentic Orthodox
Judaism. Before Rambam (Maimonides), Judaism did not really have a
theology – there were no universal, accepted beliefs that were codified
or dogmatized. While Judaism certainly has beliefs, they are flexible and
open to interpretation. Belief in God and the divinity of the Torah, for
example, are fundamental. But the myriad interpretations of these beliefs
are so at variance with one another that we don't see any real consistency.
However, once Rambam appeared on the scene in the eleventh century
and categorized these beliefs into clear-cut statements through his Thirteen Principles of Faith, Judaism became systematized and dogmatized,
losing one of its strongest assets: a religion without a fixed theology.

It is surprising that Rambam, who was perhaps the greatest of all Jewish philosophers, was the very same man who codified and straight-jacketed Jewish law and beliefs in ways that are completely unprecedented in classical Judaism. It's even more astonishing when we realize that this was done by an independent thinker who went his own way and seemed to have cared little about what his opponents thought of him or his ideas.

Rambam also left us his magnum opus, *Moreh Nevuchim – The Guide for the Perplexed*, which was his major and ongoing contribution, not only to Jewish philosophy, but to general philosophy as well. It is surprising that this book, written by one of the most renowned methodologists ever, is for the most part a disorganized work. It looks like a turbulent storm in which the reader must make order out of all the chaos. But to anyone who reads this work carefully, it's as clear as day that this chaos is deliberate. It even seems that Rambam, who worked five years on it, first drafted a completely orderly work and then deliberately disorganized it. By doing so, he challenges readers to use their own minds and, instead of passively reading the book, become active partners in its creation. Rambam thus shows his genius as well as his brilliant teaching skills.

Perhaps there is some kind of systematic theology behind all this, which the author wants readers to discover on their own, and which he therefore hides behind *deliberate* chaos.

We almost get the impression that Rambam wanted to compensate for his unusual ideas, philosophy, and sometimes unprecedented halachic rulings by becoming a harsh codifier and dogmatist who did not allow for any deviation from "normative" Judaism, while at the same time sending the message that Judaism really can't be systematized.

In doing so, however, he caused a crisis in Judaism which is still with us and which has created major obstacles for the future of a vigorous Judaism. While his *Mishne Torah* is an ingenious example of rigorous codification written in a beautiful, poetic, and straightforward Hebrew, and while the same is true of his Thirteen Principles of Faith, which are uncompromising and highly dogmatic, one really wonders whether Rambam himself believed in these principles and always followed his own rulings. It's one of the great riddles in the history of Judaism.

Still, the Thirteen Principles of Faith have been accepted as accurate readings of what Judaism is all about. The Orthodox community has certainly embraced them as a *sine qua non*, not to be challenged (with minor exceptions as far as the *Mishne Torah* is concerned), and considered the ultimate representation of Jewish law and belief. The reason this is not the case with *Moreh Nevuchim* is not because there is opposition to dogmatism in today's Orthodox community. Rather, it is because of the Aristotelian-Greek flavor that is found throughout this work, which many feel compromises genuine Judaism. (Moreover, most Orthodox readers are unfamiliar with philosophy and don't know how to read *The Guide*.)

The task of today's halachists and philosophers should be to reverse this phenomenon and allow Halacha to once again be what it has always been: an anarchic, colorful, and unequaled musical symphony that requires room to breathe. Only a dynamic system of Halacha can guide the Jewish people and the State of Israel to a promising future. This is not just a matter of semantics. It is of crucial importance, because it will be impossible for the State of Israel to exist without being deeply influenced by Halacha. The eminent Jewish philosopher Sa'adia Gaon said, "Our nation is a people only by virtue of our Torah."[7]

This is as true today as it was in the past. All attempts to define the Jewish people otherwise have utterly failed, no matter how many thinkers and sociologists have tried.

Nevertheless, a system of Halacha that cannot be true to itself, but is constantly plagued by dogmatism, stagnation, and systematization, will cause not only its own downfall, but also that of the Jewish people and the Jewish State.

In my opinion, Halacha is in need of more "chaos" or free rein. It must allow for more ways to live a halachic life unbounded by too many restrictions of conformity and codification. It must make room for autonomy on the part of individuals, to choose their own way once they have undertaken to observe the foundations of Halacha. Acceptance of minority opinions will have to become a real option, and some rabbinical laws must be relaxed so that a more living Judaism will emerge.[8] While some people need more structure than others, in this day and age we must create halachic options that the codes such as the *Mishne Torah* of Rambam and the *Shulchan Aruch* of Rabbi Yosef Karo do not provide.

Surely those who prefer to live by the strict rules of the codes should continue to do so. For some, these rules are actually a necessity – even a religious obligation – since this may be the only way they can experience God. But they should never become an obstacle to those who are unable

---

7. Sa'adia Gaon, *Emunot ve-De'ot*, chap. 3.
8. See chap. 2.

to adhere to them. Labeling these new approaches "non-Orthodox," or "heresy," is entirely missing the point.

I wish to be clear: I am not advocating Reform or Conservative Judaism which, as I stated earlier, have paradoxically become overly structured or agenda-driven. They lack sufficient "chaos" to make them vigorous.

While there is great beauty in attending synagogue three times a day to pray, we clearly see that much of it has become mechanic – going through the motions, with no or little religious experience. Yes, it's better than not being involved in any prayer at all, but the price we pay is increasing by leaps and bounds. It is pushing many away. Codification is the best way to strangle Judaism. By now, Orthodox Judaism has been over-codified and is on its way to becoming irrelevant.

This is made evident by the fact that in Israel more and more people are staying away from Orthodox Judaism, while becoming increasingly involved in Jewish studies and ritual. What Judaism needs is depth, God-consciousness, and religious experience, which is not offered by the codes, but is certainly provided by a living, vibrant practice of Halacha.

Two

THE CONTEMPORARY CRISIS
OF HALACHA

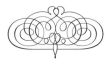

Chapter 2

The Future, Image, and Spirit of Halacha
Unconventional Thoughts in Relation to Autonomous Religiosity

INTRODUCTION

It is with great hesitation and trepidation that I write this essay. I do not want to be misunderstood. I am in love with Judaism, Rabbinic Tradition, and Halacha. I regard them as holy, and they are at the very core of my existence. Nonetheless, I am concerned about the future of Judaism and its impact on our young people.

This essay is an emotional appeal to our religious leadership, and should be read in that spirit. It is *not* an academic paper, citing many sources and raising intellectual arguments; rather, it is written out of deep *concern*, and should be viewed as an honest attempt to deal with some serious problems which plague the contemporary Jewish religious community. It is written in sweat and blood. My intention is not to spread discontent, but to help Orthodox Judaism move forward in an age which is radically different from that of our forefathers.

I teach Jewish philosophy. I am confronted daily with countless young Jews who search for an authentic Jewish religious way of life, but are unable to find spiritual satisfaction in the prevalent halachic system as practiced today in most ultra- or Modern Orthodox communities. For many of them, typical halachic life is not synonymous with genuine religiosity. They feel that Halacha has become too monotonous, too standardized, and too external for them to experience the presence of God on a day-

---

* An earlier edition of this essay was originally published in *Conversations* 7 (Spring 2010): 66–82.

to-day basis. Beyond "observance," they look for holiness and meaning. Many of them feel there is too much formalism in the halachic system and not enough internal meaning; too much obedience and not enough room for the individualistic soul, or for religious spontaneity. More and more sincere young people express these concerns, and many of them are deeply affected by their inability to live a conventional halachic life.

Since they sincerely long for the opportunity to *experience* Halacha, I struggle to find a response to this acute, growing predicament. The solution must simultaneously acknowledge that a genuine Jewish religious life cannot exist without being committed to the world of Halacha. This existential tension greatly influenced the content of this essay. My observations are therefore not written from the perspective of a halachist, but from the perspective of a deeply concerned Jewish thinker, who wants young people to be authentically religious while living a halachic life which is meaningful to *them*. The following paragraphs suggest a new insight into the world of Halacha and its practical application.

Surely there are many arguments which can be brought against the contents of this essay, some of which I myself can point out. However, the purpose of this essay is to get people thinking, not to claim the definitive truth of my observations and suggestions.

I am fully aware that the views expressed may not be palatable to most bona fide and respected *poskim* (halachic authorities). My analysis and suggestions will probably not carry their approval. I hope only to act as a catalyst so that *some* halachic authorities and Jewish thinkers will take my suggestions seriously and be prepared to discuss them. They are nothing more than thoughts which came to mind when contemplating and discussing these issues with students.

It is essential that the reader realizes my intention is not to simplify Judaism by making it more compatible with the progressive spirit of our age. Nor do I seek to make Judaism easier and more user-friendly by finding leniencies and short cuts. I do not believe that *this* is at the heart of the problems Judaism faces today.

What is vital is whether or not Judaism is able to offer the Jew a divine mission, transforming the modern Jew into a holy, religiously inspired being, who embodies the very essence of Torah in modern society. Judaism needs to be infused with greater spiritual vitality and religious vigor. This is what so many young people are searching for today.

In order to achieve this, the spiritual dimensions of Judaism need a lot more attention. This may require application of aggadic (non-legal) inspirational sentiments *in* halachic decision-making.[1] No doubt many formal *poskim* will object to this approach, based on the notion that aggadic and halachic material should be separated. Nonetheless, I believe that if we wish to keep Judaism alive for the many people who seek different paths to Jewish religiosity, this approach must be carefully considered. Once additional spiritual dimensions are infused into the world of Halacha, *and the very image of Halacha is seen in a different light*, young, searching people will be able to find the Jewish religious life which they seek. This may require going beyond the conventional *klalei pesika* (rules of decision-making) which were used in the past. This approach is *not* meant to undermine the conventional ways in which Halacha works; rather, to find a way to inspire many young people who seek to find themselves in halachic Judaism.

The observations and suggestions brought here are based on the belief that while Halacha has a stiff and formal side, it also includes a cry for personal religious creativity, a call for human nobility, and a demand for devotion and *kedusha* (holiness).

THE PROBLEM OF CODIFICATION

Over the last five hundred years, famous rabbinic leaders have called to limit the overwhelming authority of Rabbi Yosef Karo's *Shulchan Aruch* and Rambam's *Mishne Torah*.[2] They felt that these works do not reflect authentic Judaism and its halachic tradition.[3] The reason is obvious. These

---

1. For a comprehensive study on the definition and role of Aggada in Jewish Tradition, see Berachyahu Lifshitz, "'Aggadah' and Its Role in the History of the Oral Law," *Annual of the Institute for Research in Jewish Law* 22 (2001): 233–328 [Hebrew]. On the relationship between Halacha and Aggada, see Yair Lorberbaum, "Halakhah and Aggadah," in *In God's Image: Myth, Theology, and Law in Classical Judaism* (NY: Cambridge University Press, 2015), chap. 3.

2. For an excellent overview of the halachic codification literature, see Menachem Elon, *Jewish Law: History, Sources, Principles*, trans. Bernard Auerbach and Melvin J. Sykes (Philadelphia: Jewish Publication Society, 1994), 3:1149–1452. The following essays in his book are particularly relevant to our discussion: Regarding Rambam's codification, see "Critical Reaction to Maimonides' Codificatory Methodology," 3:1215–1229. Regarding the codification of the *Shulchan Aruch*, see "The Codifactory Literature: Reactions to the Shulchan Aruch, and its Final Acceptance," 3:1367–1422. See also Elon, "Codification of Law," in *Encyclopaedia Judaica*, ed. Michael Berenbaum and Fred Skolnik, 2nd ed. (Detroit: Macmillan Reference USA, 2007), 4:765–781; Elon, "Meni'im ve-Ekronot be-Codifikatsia shel ha-Halacha," in *Hagut ve-Halacha: Sefer ha-Kinus ha-Shenati le-Machshevet ha-Yahadut*, ed. Yitzchak Eisner (Jerusalem: Ministry of Education and Culture, 1968), 75–119.

3. For a history of opposition to the *Shulchan Aruch*, see Chaim Tchernowitz (Rav Tzair), *Toledot ha-Poskim* (NY: The Jubilee Committee, 1947), 3:73–137. For a list of numerous sources on the authority of the *Shulchan Aruch* and its detractors, see Hanina Ben-Menahem, Neil S. Hecht, and Shai Wosner, ed., *Controversy and Dialogue in Halakhic Sources* (Jerusalem: The Institute of Jewish Law, Boston University and The Israel Diaspora Institute, Jerusalem, 2002), 1:513–559 [Hebrew]; Yoel Schwartz, *Ha-Shulchan Aruch ve-Nosei Kelav* (Jerusalem: Devar Yerushalayim,

great codes of Jewish Law are very un-Jewish in spirit. They present Halacha in ways which oppose the heart and soul of the Talmud, and therefore of Judaism itself. They deprived Judaism of its multifaceted halachic tradition and its inherent music. It is not the works *themselves* which are the problem, but the ideology which they represent: *The ethos of codifying and finalizing Jewish Law.*

This problem has taken on formidable proportions in our day. There is more Jewish learning today than in the last two thousand years. More and more young people dedicate themselves to a life of *shemirat ha-mitzvot* (Torah observance). This should be cause for great optimism. What more could we want in an age of extreme secularism?

However, it is hard to deny that this commitment reveals a worrisome side-effect. It exposes elements of an artificial Judaism suspended in time, which has been rewritten in ways which detrimentally oppose its very living nature.

A careful read of modern Jewish Orthodox literature reveals that many authors misunderstand the nature of Jewish Law. Much of this literature is dedicated to extreme and obsessive codification, which goes hand in hand with a desire to "fix" Halacha once and for all. The laws of *muktza*[4], *tevilat kelim*[5], *tzeniut*[6], and many others are codified in much greater detail than ever before. These works have become the standard by which the young, growing, observant community lives its life. When studying them one wonders whether our forefathers were ever really observant, since such compendia were never available to them and they could never have known all the minutiae presented today to the observant Jew. *Over the years we have embalmed Judaism while claiming it is alive because it continues to maintain its external shape.*

The majority of halachic literature today is streamlined, allowing little room for halachic flexibility and for the spiritual need for novelty. For the most part, the reader is encouraged to follow the most stringent view without asking whether this will actually help her or him in their *avodat ha-Boreh* (service of the Almighty) according to her or his distinct personality. The song of the Halacha, its spirit, weltanschauung, and mission

---

1995). On the problem of deciding Halacha based on the summarized rulings contained in the *Mishne Torah* and *Shulchan Aruch*, see Meir Berkovits, "Pesika mi-Toch Sifrei Kitzurim: Iyun be-Darko shel ha-Rambam," *Shana be-Shana* (1995): 390–420.

4. Laws pertaining to the moving of objects on Shabbat.

5. Laws pertaining to utensils that are used for food preparation or consumption, which need to be immersed in a *mikva*, a ritual bath.

6. Laws pertaining to modesty.

are entirely lost in this type of literature. When the student tries to look beyond these works (seeking spiritual music), he is often confronted with a dogmatic approach to Judaism which entirely misses the mark. *We are plagued by over-codification and dogmatization.*

The obsessive attempt to *codify* Jewish *beliefs* also contradicts the very nature of Judaism. Jewish beliefs are constantly being dogmatized and halachicized by rabbinic authorities, and anyone who does not accept these rigid beliefs is no longer considered to be a real religious Jew. A spirit of *finalization* has taken over Judaism.

THESE AND THOSE ARE THE WORDS OF THE LIVING GOD

One of the Talmud's greatest contributions to Judaism is its indetermination, its frequent refusal to lay down the law.[7] Talmudic discussions consist primarily of competing positions, often lacking a clear decision on which view is authoritative. The reason is obvious: *There should not be one.* The well-known talmudic statement "Elu ve-elu divrei Elokim Chaim" (These and those are the words of the Living God)[8] supports this position. Halachic disagreement and radically opposing opinions are of the essence. There is a profound reason for this principle. The Torah, which is the word of God, can only be multifaceted. Like God Himself, it can never fit into a finalized system, for it is much too broad in scope. Every human being is different; the Torah must therefore be different to each one of them, showing nearly infinite dimensions and possibilities. *This is one of the most fascinating aspects of Jewish Tradition, making it strikingly distinct from the religions of the world.*

In an illuminating discourse, Rabbi Shlomo Luria, Maharshal (1510–1574) states:

> One should never be astonished by the range of debate and argumentation in matters of Halacha. . . . All these views are in the category of "these and those are the words of the Living God" as if each one of them was directly received by Moshe at Sinai. . . . The kabbalists explained that the basis for this is that each individual soul was present at Sinai and received the Torah by means of forty-nine *tzinorot*, spiritual channels. Each one perceived the Torah from his own perspective

---

7. See also Leon Wiener Dow, "Opposition to the 'Shulhan Aruch': Articulating a Common Law Conception of Halakha," *Hebraic Political Studies* 3, no. 4 (2008): 352–376.

8. *Eruvin* 13b.

in accordance with his intellectual capacity as well as the nature and uniqueness of his particular soul. This accounts for the discrepancy in perception inasmuch as one concluded that an object was *tamei* (ritually impure) in the extreme, another perceived it be absolutely *tahor* (ritually pure), and yet a third individual argues the ambivalent status of the object in question. All these are true and authentic views. Thus the sages declared that in a debate among the scholars, all positions articulated are different forms of the same truth.[9]

Maharshal's observations go to the heart of Judaism. There is no such thing as a fixed Halacha which is identical for all. Surely there are objectives which need to be achieved: namely, the fulfillment of God's commandments. *But there are no passive recipients.* Each person receives the Torah individually, according to his or her own personality and exceptional circumstances.

In fact, one could argue that ideally no written text should have been given at Sinai, since no two people are able to read the same text in an identical way. The meaning of the text is dependent to a large extent on the reader, and is therefore not a fixed reality. The fact that a text was even given at Sinai is in itself a compromise. Even if a text *should have* been given, *a priori*, it should have been in as many versions as there are Jews since Sinai. This did not happen; only one text was revealed. This was due to the fact that there was a need for unity and affiliation among Jews, sharing the experience of a divine text in a bond of togetherness, shaping a Chosen People that would carry the word of God to the world. There was a need for a *grundnorm* through which Jews would be able to discuss the word of God and share it wherever they go. Above all, a fixed text was necessary to facilitate discussion, not agreement. In this way it would stay alive, infinitely enhancing new possible interpretations and unique insights.

It could even be argued that not all Jews were in need of the same mitzvot (sing. mitzva – Torah commandment). It was only for the sake of comradeship and for the common destiny of the Jewish people and their mission to the world that they all *had* to commit themselves to *all* of the mitzvot. As Rabbi Mordechai Yosef Leiner of Izbica (1801–1854) states, although not every Jew is in need of every prohibition in the Torah, "he is

---

9. *Yam shel Shlomo*, introduction to *Bava Kamma*.

still obligated to heed and suffer this prohibition for the sake of his fellow Jew."[10]

THE NATURE OF HALACHA

Halacha is the practical upshot of unfinalized beliefs, a practical way of life while remaining in theological suspense. In matters of the spirit and the quest to find God, it is not possible to come to final conclusions. The quest for God must remain open-ended to enable the human spirit to find its way through trial and discovery. As such, Judaism has no catechism. It has an inherent aversion to dogma. Although it includes strong beliefs, they are not susceptible to formulation in any kind of authoritative system. It is up to the talmudic scholar to choose between many opinions, for they are all authentic. They are part of God's Torah, and even opposing opinions "are all from one Shepherd."[11]

Halacha transforms the fluid liquid of Jewish beliefs into a solid substance. It chills the heated steel of exalted ideas and turns them into pragmatic actions. The unique balance between practical Halacha and unfinalized beliefs ensures that Judaism will not turn into a religion which is paralyzed in awe of a rigid tradition, or evaporate into a utopian reverie.

Still, it would be entirely wrong to believe that the need for practical application of Halacha has anything to do with absolute truth. Practical Halacha is in principle only *one way* to act. It carries authority only as far as the practical implementation of the Halacha is concerned. Even when practical Halacha must be decided upon, the heat of debate *must* stay alive. Jewish beliefs are like arrows that dart to and fro, wavering as though shot into the air from a slackened bowstring. Halacha must reflect this. While Halacha is more straight and unswerving, it must adhere to the unequivocal truth that even opposing halachic opinions are "all the words of the Living God," and each of them carries the *potential* to become practical Halacha.

CRITIQUE ON RAMBAM AND RABBI YOSEF KARO

As mentioned earlier, several outstanding talmudists have argued that Rambam's *Mishne Torah* and Rabbi Yosef Karo's *Shulchan Aruch* starved

---

10. *Mei ha-Shilo'ach* 1:29 on *Bereshit* 22:12.
11. *Chagiga* 3b.

Jewish Law of this very spirit. Rambam eliminates all references to the basis of his rulings and almost entirely ignores even the existence of dissenting and minority opinions. On the occasion where he does refer to them, he seems to express a negative attitude, as if he would like to save Judaism from this embarrassment.[12]

Although less extreme, Rabbi Yosef Karo also states his rulings in the *Shulchan Aruch* in general language without mentioning sources or other opinions. It is true that he first authored the *Bet Yosef* in which he brings many opinions and citations, so one might argue that he did not want his *Shulchan Aruch* to become a distinct and self-contained work. However, the fact is that once he authored this work, it quickly assumed this very status. It would be hard to argue that the author did not foresee this possibility.

MAHARSHAL, MAHARAL, AND RABBI CHAIM BEN BETZALEL

Three early authorities were deeply concerned about this development: Rabbi Shlomo Luria, known as Maharshal (1510–1574); Rabbi Yehuda ben Betzalel Loew, known as the Maharal of Prague (1520–1609); and Rabbi Chaim ben Betzalel (1530–1588), brother of the Maharal.[13] Each in his own way attacked the *Mishne Torah* and the *Shulchan Aruch*, claiming they were anti-talmudic and therefore anti-halachic. Maharshal accused Rambam of acting "as if [he] received it [the *Mishne Torah*] directly from Moshe at Mount Sinai who received it directly from Heaven, offering no proof."[14] Directing his attack toward Rabbi Yosef Karo's *Bet Yosef*[15] in which the author follows the majority opinion of three Sephardic authorities (Rif, Rosh, and Rambam), Maharshal asked how the author had the right to do so. Did Rabbi Yosef Karo receive such a tradition going back to the days of the sages?

Maharshal goes on to state that the *Bet Yosef*'s entire enterprise is dangerous. Those who study it will come to believe that what Rabbi Yosef Karo wrote has finality, and even "if a living person would stand in front of

---

12. See *Mishne Torah, Hilchot Mamrim* 1:3–4.

13. See Dow, "Opposition to the 'Shulhan Aruch'," 352–376. See also Shlomo Glicksberg and Shlomo Kassierer, "The Halakhah and Meta-Halakhah Codification Debate: Rabbi Chaim ben Bezalel and the Maharal of Prague," *Jewish Studies* 49 (2013): 157–191 [Hebrew].

14. *Yam shel Shlomo*, introduction to *Bava Kamma* and introduction to *Chullin*.

15. It is possible that Maharshal never saw the *Shulchan Aruch*, at least at the time when he authored his *Yam shel Shlomo*. The first edition of the *Shulchan Aruch* was published in 1565, about nine years before Maharshal's passing.

them and exclaim that the Halacha is different, citing excellent arguments or even an authoritative received tradition, they will pay no heed to his words."[16]

Rabbi Chaim ben Betzalel adds that people will fail to realize that this current authority is "just one person among many." Moreover, such codes lead to intellectual laziness. People will no longer study the Talmud in their reliance on these works. They can be compared to a pauper who collects alms from wealthy people and shows off his riches. At first it seems that he is indeed rich. After all, he has food and clothing. But in truth this is illusory, for all he has are the items he collected. Similarly, one who studies only these codes and rules does not know the ins and outs of the talmudic debates which preceded them.[17]

Rabbi Chaim ben Betzalel warns of yet another danger. How can one ever know whether the law as stated in the *Mishne Torah* or *Shulchan Aruch* is applicable to a particular situation? Such matters are in a state of flux. A minor change may require a radically different response. Even more daring is his observation that since the "[Torah] is no longer in Heaven"[18] and halachic matters must be decided upon by human beings, it is possible that the same halachic authority may see things differently today than he did yesterday. As such, he may *rule* differently today than he did yesterday. This is not a shortcoming or inconsistency. It is all part of the principle that "Elu ve-elu divrei Elokim Chaim."

Maharal adds that the rabbi can only rely on his own intellect: "And even when his wisdom leads him to err, he is nonetheless beloved by God as long as he has used his best reasoning. And this person is by far preferred to the person who determines the Halacha from within one work, without knowing the reason, walking like a blind person along the way."[19]

These authorities agree that the Talmud alone should be the source of halachic decision-making. All declare that the concern "that there will be many Torahs in Israel"[20] has no bearing on this matter. It is not the multitude of halachic opinions which creates the danger of many Torahs; it is the rejection of the Talmud as the authoritative text to decide on halachic issues which presents this danger. In fact, it is codification which causes the problem of many Torahs in Israel, since it no longer requires the *posek*

---

16. *Yam shel Shlomo*, introduction to *Chullin*.
17. Introduction to *Vikuach Mayim Chaim* (Amsterdam: Shlomo Propes, 1712), section 7.
18. *Bava Metzia* 59b.
19. *Netivot Olam, Netiv ha-Torah*, end of chap. 15.
20. *Sanhedrin* 88b.

to return to the various opinions stated in the Talmud! The Talmud embodies Judaism in its most authentic form. It is the validity of opposing opinions as part of God's Torah which actually makes Judaism vibrant and true to its own spirit. It is from the Talmud itself that the rabbi needs to decide the law, taking into account all the different opinions.

No doubt Rambam and Rabbi Yosef Karo had the best of intentions. They wanted to create common ground and felt that a unified codification would make that possible. Both felt that their fellow Jews needed a streamlined Judaism in which nearly nothing was left to imagination. As Rambam's Thirteen Principles of Faith gave Judaism an appearance of a dogmatic religion, so do the *Mishne Torah* and the *Shulchan Aruch*. These two main codified works introduced a foreign element into Judaism. Looking back, we can see that they caused a misrepresentation of the *nature* of Jewish Law and its spirit. They set in motion an entire genre of halachic literature which is un-Jewish in spirit. The result was a severely false impression of Judaism, which became the *cause célèbre* for attacking Judaism as a religion of stern rigidity. Spinoza's *Tractatus Theologico-Politicus* is a typical example of this. He saw Judaism in terms of obsessive legislation.[21]

By all means, we should continue to study the works of Rambam and Rabbi Yosef Karo and possibly even live by their directives. But we should be careful not to create an impression that there are no alternative ways. We must make our young, searching people aware that Halacha is much more than what these works represent. Above all, we should see these works as sublime commentaries on the Talmud. Specifically, Rambam's *Mishne Torah* offers us profound insights into how his genius mind read and understood the Talmud. It is in *this*, and not in his attempt to codify Jewish Law, that Rambam made his greatest contribution to Jewish learning. Ultimately, it is only through the discussions in the Talmud that we, with the help of our rabbis, should decide how to live our religious lives.

JUDAISM IS AN AUTONOMOUS WAY OF LIVING

The question we now need to ask is how to bring Judaism back to its original authentic "self" in which the halachic tradition of *elu ve-elu* is once more recognized and applied. Can we reactivate this concept in order to

---

21. See Benedictus de Spinoza, *A Theologico-Political Treatise*, chaps. 3, 4, 13, in *The Chief Works of Benedict de Spinoza*, trans. R.H.M. Elwes (London: G. Bell and Sons, 1883), vol. 1.

bring new life into the bloodstream of Judaism for those young people who are in dire need? Surely the principle of *elu ve-elu* is not a blank check that means anything goes. The principle should only be implemented if it will stimulate greater commitment to Jewish religious life while simultaneously responding to the many drastic changes which have taken place in our modern world. The need for human autonomy as well as spirituality and meaning, which are sought by so many young people, will have to be addressed.

We must realize that Judaism is an autonomous way of life. While the need for conformity within the community must constantly be taken into consideration, ultimately man is expected to respond *as an individual* to the Torah's demands. Each human being is an entire world, and no two human beings are identical in their psychological make up, religious needs, or experience of God. One encounters God as an individual.

What, after all, is the purpose of my existence if not to relate to God differently than my neighbor? To imitate what others do in their service of God is to demonstrate that there is no reason for me to have been born. The overwhelming need for human distinctiveness is demonstrated by the fact that no Jew received the Torah or heard the voice of God at Sinai in a similar way, as Maharshal observed. The need for more halachic autonomy is not for the sole purpose of adapting Judaism to the spirit of modern times, but also to make Judaism more authentic and true *to its own spirit*. While the necessity for communal conformity often made it difficult for Judaism to emphasize the need for personal autonomy, the difficulty experienced by so many young people today may propel this matter to the forefront of our concern.

DIFFICULT QUESTIONS

In light of the abovementioned observations, I wonder whether we can reintroduce the great talmudic debates in a way which will reshape Judaism into its original multifaceted and colorful self, so that the young, searching Jews of today will fall in love with it. Should we perhaps permit and even encourage people or communities to decide *themselves* which of the many opinions in the Talmud they would like to follow?

To answer this question we surely must move beyond the conventional way in which Halacha has been applied throughout later generations. In many ways the question is not only a halachic one; it is also one of *hashkafa*, ideolology. We need to mine for new paths to Jewish spirituality, and the world of Aggada may be able to help us. While it is not at all clear where issues of Halacha end and where matters of *hashkafa*, Aggada, and spiritual needs which influence halachic thinking begin, it is necessary to enter into a new halachic way of thinking; one which has rarely been used, but is clearly part of the world of the Talmud. This is the concept of multiple truths within God's Torah. In our modern world, the *spirit* of Halacha as a multifaceted living tradition becomes extremely relevant. Conventional rules on how to reach a halachic decision may have to incorporate more spiritual requirements and expectations. However, this can be done only as long as they are rooted in the Talmud and do not violate the underlying *principles* of halachic debate as disclosed by *elu ve-elu*. The debate regarding whether individuals can decide on their own which opinion in the Talmud they would like to follow is of utmost importance.

HALACHIC SCHOLARS AND RELIGIOUS CRISIS

The great halachic scholars of today and tomorrow will have to decide whether we are permitted to implement this idea. Will they be prepared to sincerely consider these questions? Are they equipped with enough knowledge about our world – the moral, spiritual, and *religious crisis* in which so many young people find themselves – to handle this matter? Do they fully understand the central place that human autonomy occupies in today's society and in *authentic* Judaism?

Do they connect enough with the religious melody of Halacha to even see the need for these questions? They can easily reject these questions as irrelevant, unacceptable, non-kosher, or even heretical; but this won't do. Too much is at stake. The existential predicament of humankind at large and the Jewish people in particular is so great that rejection of these problems will ultimately distance many fine Jews from the Jewish Tradition and *shemirat ha-mitzvot*. This distance is a result of our *poskim* being inflexible, where, in my opinion, our own tradition may allow for a display of elasticity.

Ignoring the growing need of so many young, intelligent, searching people for an autonomous approach to a *personal* halachic life is no longer possible. Great courage is required to even raise these questions, let alone give answers. What is needed is sincere willingness to think out of the box.

HALACHIC PROBLEMS

At first glance, it seems that many halachic principles might bar the possibility of reintroducing the concept of *elu ve-elu*. The Talmud includes minority opinions concerning *dinei de-Rabbanan* – Rabbinic Law (as opposed to Biblical Law). This is the category which urgently necessitates dealing with issues of spirituality and established Halacha. Generally, minority opinions are not meant to be followed. The reason is obvious: allowing people to re-enact these opinions would have a destructive impact on the Jewish community and its need for uniform and normative behavior. "So as not to fragment the Torah into many Torahs."[22]

But what if following minority opinions would only *increase* the love for and adherence to Torah Law (*de-Oraita*) by many fellow Jews? Many of the rabbinic laws are fences for the distinct purpose of *preventing* people from violating Torah Law, but what if they produce the *opposite* result, the absolute rejection of Torah Law? Today, many of these rabbinic laws keep people *out* instead of inviting them *in*. They are not conducive to the spirituality longed for by many people trying to observe Torah laws. What if some of the minority, rejected opinions would be more conducive to the observance of Torah Law? This is specifically true about rabbinic laws which affect the individual. These matters require great spiritual investment on an individual level. Would it not be wiser in these cases to encourage the implementation of minority opinions as recorded in the Talmud instead of dismissively prohibiting them and simply standardizing the majority opinions?[23]

BET SHAMMAI AND BET HILLEL

I wonder whether such an approach would be valid when dealing with the ritualistic controversies between Bet Shammai and Bet Hillel. Halacha unequivocally follows Bet Hillel in nearly all cases, and under normal

---

22. *Sanhedrin* 88b.

23. The question of the permissibility of following minority opinions in halachic matters is a complicated one. See *Talmudic Encyclopedia*, s.v. "halacha," 9:255–263; Nathaniel Helfgot, "Minority Opinions and their Role in Hora'ah," *Milin Havivin* [Beloved Words] 4 (2010): 36–60; Yitzchak Sheilat, "Semicha al Da'at Yachid be-Sha'at ha-Dechak," in *Berurim be-Hilchot ha-Rayah*, ed. Moshe-Zvi Neriah, Aryeh Stern, and Neriya Moshe Gutel (Jerusalem: Bet ha-Rav, 1992), 451–476; Ro'i Siton, "Ha-Im Nitan Lismoch al Yachid be-Sha'at ha-Dechak," *Torat ha-Chaim* 1 (Cheshvan 2012): 30–38; Daniel Sperber, *The Path of Halakha* (Jerusalem: Ruben Mass, 2007), 217–221 [Hebrew].

circumstances it is forbidden to abide by the opinions of Bet Shammai.[24] However, the reason is not entirely clear.[25] In fact, it seems there were cases in the past where following Bet Shammai's ruling was even encouraged.[26] Whatever the reason, would it be permitted to follow the opinions of Bet Shammai when some people feel more connected to this view?[27] After all, many of these differences of opinion are not just legalities or academic disputes; they are, above all, differences in approach to religious life.[28] Would it not be more in the spirit of Bet Shammai and Bet Hillel to allow people this choice, now that religious commitment in a secular society is of an entirely different nature than it was in earlier days?

IGNORING MINORITY OPINIONS

Moreover, would the Talmud allow us not only to ignore *majority* opinions, but *minority* rabbinic opinions as well, if the result was people keeping the Torah laws? Undoubtedly many rabbinic laws make it easier to observe Torah laws, but what if people feel confined by these laws which deny them the spirit of, say, what prayer or Shabbat is all about? In many instances it is not clear whether a law is *de-Oraita* (biblical) or *de-Rabbanan* (rabbinical), and in such cases one cannot take any chances. But where we know for a fact that they are *de-Rabbanan*, would this be permitted? After all, human beings are most complex. Freedom in one area often leads to greater commitment in another.

If, arguably, practical Halacha would indeed allow us to ignore even a minority opinion, this would be true only in exceptional circumstances (*be-di'avad*) and for specific individuals. It should never be encouraged as a new way of dealing with religious crisis in which *whole communities* of people long for autonomy while genuinely searching for religious commitment. Indeed, in pre-mishnaic and talmudic times many of these rabbinic laws did not yet exist, and people made their own decisions on how to ensure that they would not violate Torah Law or how to give meaning to their relationship with God through their own prayers or other rituals.

---

24. See *Berachot* 11a, 36b; *Eruvin* 6b, 13b.
25. See *Yevamot* 14a.
26. *Berachot* 53b.
27. On ruling according to Bet Shammai vs. Bet Hillel, see *Talmudic Encyclopedia*, s.v. "halacha," 9:281–283.
28. See, for example, R. Eliyahu Eliezer Dessler, *Michtav me-Eliyahu* (Jerusalem: Kiryat Noar, 1963), 2:120–122, concerning the question whether one should light all eight candles on the first day of Chanuka (Bet Shammai) or only on the last day (Bet Hillel).

There were no prayer books,[29] and it seems that it was strictly forbidden to write down any prayers.[30] Is it not possible that we need a similar approach today?

PERSONALIZING BLESSINGS, PRAYERS, AND SYNAGOGUE SERVICES

Could people adopt other versions for *berachot* (sing. *beracha* – blessing), such as those discussed in the Talmud but not codified in practical Halacha?[31] Would the Talmud really object to people formulating their own *berachot* if it was more meaningful to them?[32] When people complain that some of the official *berachot* and prayers seem irrelevant; that these *berachot* and prayers are of such beauty that they are unable to absorb their magnificent meaning and therefore feel hypocritical when saying them; or, that the constant reciting of the *same berachot* and prayers no longer allows for saying them with religious fervor, is there not some truth to their claim?

After all, was it not the purpose of the sages to formulate these religious texts in order to inspire us to sincerely praise and thank God? Is it not preferable for people to say different prayers when this goal would be better served? Needless to say, certain spiritual-religious requirements would have to be preserved.

Could various types of synagogue services be created in which alternative prayers and rituals are offered from which people can choose? *Minhagim*, rituals, and other traditions are most important and should not be taken lightly. They have greatly contributed to Judaism. But what if people desperately need to express their religious devotion in a different way? Just as it is possible for a rabbi to make a halachic decision one day and a different one the next, because he sees matters differently, could this not also apply to the praying human being? What if this would help create a more genuine religious experience?

These questions and others are of the greatest importance if we want to revitalize Judaism in the hearts of many people.

---

29. *Mishne Torah, Hilchot Tefilla* 1:3–4.
30. See *Shabbat* 115b.
31. On the issue of modifying the text of the *berachot*, see *Mishne Torah, Hilchot Berachot* 1:5; *Hilchot Kriat Shema* 1:7; *Talmudic Encyclopedia*, s.v. "berachot," 4:298–299. For a detailed study of this topic, see Daniel Sperber, *On Changes in Jewish Liturgy: Options and Limitations* (Jerusalem: Urim, 2010).
32. See *Berachot* 40b; *Tosefta Berachot* 4:4–5; JT *Berachot* 6:2, 10c.

HORA'AT SHA'AH

In this vein, perhaps we should look to halachic concepts which deal with circumstances where the suspension of a particular law will "bring back the multitudes to religion and save them from general religious laxity."[33] Such concepts might include *hora'at sha'ah*,[34] the need for temporary suspension of a law; *le-migdar milta*, improvement of a particular matter; and *et la'asot la-Shem*, a time to act for God.

As the great talmudic sage Resh Lakish remarked, "There are times when the suspension of the Torah may be its foundation."[35] These concepts usually refer to short-term deferments, and are generally limited in scope. However, there have been cases in Jewish religious history where matters have been changed on a long-term basis, and in some instances were never revoked. In fact, these principles have even been used for totally contradictory religious needs, depending on the *hashkafot* of the communities in question who were at their wits' end trying to ensure the survival of Judaism in modern times. Modern examples can be found in Rabbi Samson Raphael Hirsch's concept of *Torah im Derech Eretz*; the Chatam Sofer's opposition to general culture; the Chafetz Chaim's permissive ruling about intensive Torah education for young women; and the rabbinic prohibition in certain circles concerning women's prayer groups. All of these were a *response to an acute crisis*, whether *le-kula* or *le-chumra*, permissively or restrictively. They probably can't be included in the *strict* definition and parameters of *hora'at sha'ah*, but they clearly carry its character and were accepted as such by different communities. They are all "*hora'at sha'ah*-like."

To avoid any misunderstanding, I reiterate that in no way am I suggesting that we do away with parts of Judaism, or deny the divinity of the Torah and the importance of Rabbinic Law. The reverse is true. My observations and suggestions flow forth from a deep love and appreciation for what Halacha is all about. It is out of love for the word of God which came down to us at Sinai that this idea was born.

---

33. *Mishne Torah, Hilchot Mamrim* 2:4.

34. On *hora'at sha'ah*, see *Talmudic Encyclopedia*, s.v. "hora'at sha'ah," 8:512–527; Shlomo Rosenfeld, "Gidrei Hora'at Sha'ah," *Mi-Ma'ayan Mechula* 2 (Adar 1996): 9–14.

35. *Menachot* 99.

POSTSCRIPT

It is not the changes *themselves* which will bring young people what they are looking for. It is important that such changes create a new *image* of Judaism and Halacha. They will set Judaism and Halacha in a positive light and will ensure that Judaism is again understood as a living organism which is averse to dogmatism, finalization, and obsessive codification. The tradition of *elu ve-elu* must again stand at the center of Judaism's overall religious philosophy. The call for human autonomy as a condition for deep religiosity together with profound commitment to the word of God is crucial.

It is impossible to discuss any of these issues without a deep commitment to *Yirat Shamayim*, the Awe of Heaven. No motive other than *Yirat Shamayim* may guide us. It is this same *Yirat Shamayim* which *forces* us to ask these questions and propose possible solutions. Denying their urgency would be a serious dereliction of our duty as religious Jews.

My suggestions in this essay are only proposals by an educator who wants Judaism to become much more meaningful to many young people who are otherwise unable to connect. No doubt some of the suggestions are fraught with risk, but no spiritual search is risk-free, and by shutting the door to all error we risk blocking the chances for greater love and commitment to Judaism. I am fully aware that some readers will suggest that my proposals are too radical while others will say that I did not go far enough. This again would be in the tradition of *elu ve-elu*.

These observations have nothing to do with making Judaism easier so that people can be *more lax* in their observance. The reverse is true. I believe that Judaism may have to be made more difficult in order to become more meaningful. Simply making it user-friendly, by introducing all sorts of leniencies, will not bring young, serious people closer to its message. After all, they expect sweat, challenge, and discomfort in order to accomplish great achievements in university studies, music, sports, and martial arts. They are well aware that to conquer these disciplines they need to fight, not be entertained. It is the very need to exhaust themselves that gives them the satisfaction of accomplishment.

Living a genuine Jewish life is hard work, and the revisions I suggest require hard work. Young people must be sure they are familiar enough with talmudic texts to make the autonomous decisions they seek. Our young people will only value Judaism when it is at least as challenging and demanding as all the other disciplines they study. In fact, it may need to be *more* challenging, since it is a lifelong involvement which requires constant attention even to the sanctification of daily trivialities. There are no short cuts. *For many of them Judaism will become a joyful experience because it demands sweat and discipline while its reward is deep meaning and a strong notion of mission and holiness.*

I recognize that the road to implementation of these ideas is not simple; nonetheless the route must be drawn out before we can begin this journey. My intention is not to suggest a new halachic way of living for all Orthodox Jews. Those who are deeply inspired by their religious commitment in accordance with well established traditions should definitely continue on their path. If we come to implement some of these suggestions, we must never forget that we do not discover new lands by losing sight of the shore from which the journey had begun. I do hope, however, that my observations will bring them new insights as well, and help them realize how beautiful and dynamic Judaism really is. They should ask themselves whether the issues expressed have not a direct bearing on their own religious lives.

THE WAKEUP CALL TO ORTHODOXY

What the leadership of Orthodox Judaism needs to realize, above all, is that the internal danger is greater than the external threat of secularism. Judaism must renew itself, or face decline. The greatest problem Judaism faces is lack of belief in itself. Orthodox Judaism must stop being defensive and looking over its shoulder. It should strengthen itself by looking to its great talmudic resources and rebuilding itself accordingly. Only when it reappears as a dynamic living tradition, averse to all finalization and dogmatization, will it become the great passion of all Jewish people.

May *Ha-Kadosh Baruch Hu* grant us insight.

Chapter 3

Needed: Redemptive Halacha
How Halacha Must Transcend Itself

Some time ago, I had a long talk with my only brother, Dr. Jacques Eduard Lopes Cardozo, sixty-nine years old and two years my junior. We spoke about our early years, growing up in our parents' home in the Netherlands. Although we were children of a mixed marriage (Jewish father, non-Jewish mother), we took a keen interest in Judaism. Our father was a very proud Jew, and our mother was raised in a strong Jewish cultural milieu in Amsterdam, where she felt completely at home. If not for her "Jewishness," my father would probably not have married her. In fact, our mother was in many ways more Jewish than some members of my father's family, who were halachically Jewish but completely disconnected. I decided to do *giyur* (conversion to Judaism) at the age of sixteen, and my mother followed suit many years later.[1] After twenty-seven years of married life our parents remarried, this time by the same rabbi who officiated at my wedding three months later. Both weddings took place in the famous Esnoga, the Portuguese Synagogue in Amsterdam.

This put my brother in a very strange position. From then on, all members of his immediate family were Jewish, and while he did not have the halachic status of a Jew, he continued to feel very Jewish. This was, to say the least, an atypical Jewish family.

---

* An earlier edition of this essay was originally published in *Conversations* 23 (Autumn 2015): 29–44.

1. See Nathan Lopes Cardozo, "Lonely but Not Alone: An Autobiography by a Jew Who Should Never Have Been," *Conversations* 16 (Spring 2013): 1–35. Available online at https://www.cardozoacademy.org/thoughts-to-ponder/autobiography-lonely-but-not-alone-ttp-344/.

During our conversation, my brother referred to a particular Pesach Seder that I conducted at our parents' home when I was about seventeen. An incident took place that profoundly shocked him and caused one of the most painful moments in his life. Fifty years later, with great emotion and tears in his eyes, he told me that he had taken a bottle of kosher wine to pour for our many guests. He felt very much a part of the Jewish Tradition, and immersed himself in this religious experience, wanting to participate fully. After all, those who had left the bondage of Egypt that very night and would cross the Reed Sea a few days later were also *his* ancestors! But instead of realizing my brother's enormous religious dedication to that experience, I snatched the wine bottle from his hands and told him he should not touch it since he was not Jewish, and that when a non-Jew touches the wine, according to Jewish Law it could be cursed. The latter statement proved my complete ignorance. As a newcomer to Judaism, I had been told that the Halacha determines that non-Jews should not touch our wine, and I probably concluded that this meant the wine would be cursed. Our sources state nothing of the sort. The only thing indicated is that the wine is no longer permissible to drink (and according to some opinions it is forbidden to derive benefit from it).[2]

My brother froze, and then sat down without uttering a word.

A man of great integrity and now a dental surgeon of fame, my brother told me that to this day he is deeply hurt by the incident and, although he forgave me for what I had done, he could not emotionally make peace with it. Not only because he considered himself to be very Jewish and could not imagine that this law would apply to *him*, but also because he could not believe that such a law would be part of this beautiful tradition called Judaism, which he dearly loved.[3] My gut feeling tells me that this incident played a huge role in his decision not to convert, though he came very close to doing so.

Although I studied for more than twelve years in Charedi (ultra-Orthodox) yeshivot, which are hardly, if at all, concerned with the non-Jewish world, I admit that I may be more sensitive than others about matters

---

2. See *Shulchan Aruch, Yoreh De'ah* 123:1 (note the dispute between R. Yosef Karo and Rema); *Mishne Torah, Hilchot Ma'achalot Asurot* 11:4.

3. Once my brother told me about this incident, I realized there are other laws as well that are very disturbing, such as *bishul akum* (the prohibition of eating food that was cooked by Gentiles), the saving of non-Jews on Shabbat, the institution of the "Shabbos goy," and the prohibition of doing a favor for a non-Jew. This is not the place to discuss each one of them, but it will become clear to the reader that all of these laws or customs are the result of circumstances that prevailed in ancient times, and they should no longer apply today.

relating to non-Jews. After all, how could I not be? My own background, as well as my brother's situation, forces me to confront this issue on an almost daily basis.[4] At the same time, I am fully aware of the fact that more and more thinking religious Jews are becoming highly uncomfortable with this and similar laws, and are asking why these rulings are necessary. What is it about non-Jews that makes kosher wine that they have handled forbidden for us to drink?

NON-JEWS

During the almost forty years that I have been living in Yerushalayim, I have discussed this law with yeshiva students, both Charedi and Dati Leumi (Modern Orthodox). Most of them were born in Israel and have had almost no exposure to non-Jews besides the Arab population. When I challenge them and ask whether they are uncomfortable with this law, and whether they feel that it is discriminatory and perhaps racist, they do not understand my question. Their usual argument is straightforward: Since, according to Judaism, non-Jews are secondary inhabitants of this world, and most, if not all, are anti-Semitic, they should definitely not touch our wine. On top of that, it is their task to serve the Jews, and the law makes it clear who are the servants and who are the masters. When I tell them that billions of non-Jews around the world are living in countries where they never meet a Jew and therefore cannot serve Jews, their response is either complete silence or that these non-Jews have nothing to live for and are sadly unable to fulfill their mission on earth. When I press them further and ask whether they believe that God treats all His creatures fairly, and whether His failure to allow these non-Jews to fulfill their mission would not highly compromise this belief, they are dumbfounded. Their astonishment increases when I explain that since there are so few Jews and there are billions of non-Jews, it would mean that every Jew would have a few thousand non-Jews as servants, and that I wonder whether this would not be a little overdone! Moreover, doesn't our tradition teach us that one of the functions of the Jewish people is to aid Gentiles and be concerned about their spiritual and physical welfare?[5]

---

4. Human subjectivity is a major factor in halachic decision-making. See Aaron Kirschenbaum, "Subjectivity in Rabbinic Decision Making," in *Rabbinic Authority and Personal Autonomy*, ed. Moshe Z. Sokol (Northvale, NJ: Jason Aronson, 1992), 61–91.

5. It is true that certain sources, many of them kabbalistic, seem to point out that non-Jews should serve the Jews, but such notions are much debated and not generally accepted. These beliefs may be the result of historical developments. When the Talmud states that Gentiles will

YAYIN NESECH

Surely some readers will argue that when I snatched the wine bottle from my brother's hand, I did the right thing halachically. After all, this law appears in the *Shulchan Aruch*: One may not drink kosher wine that was handled by a non-Jew. This prohibition is called *isur yayin nesech* or, more accurately, *isur maga nochri*[6] – loosely translated as the prohibition of using wine that has been handled by a non-Jew, meaning the bottle is not only touched but moved as well.[7] The law applies only when the bottle has already been opened.[8]

The big question is: How did this law ever become a part of Judaism?

Looking into the history of this prohibition, we can clearly see that the reason why the early Talmudic Sages forbade the drinking of wine after it was handled by a non-Jew is that most non-Jews of that time were idol worshipers.[9] This worship is identified with evil and immoral behavior, not much different from that of the Nazis, or the terrorists of today. In fact, the same law applies to a wicked Jew; we are also forbidden to drink wine that *he* handled.[10]

---

serve the Jews in the messianic age, it means they will do so voluntarily, out of respect for the Jews, but not because it is their duty. See *Yeshayahu* 49:22–23; *Eruvin* 43b and the commentary by R. Yosef Chaim of Baghdad, *Ben Yehoyada* (Jerusalem, 1898–1904), vol. 2, 6a. See also Nathan Lopes Cardozo, "On Jewish Identity and the Chosen People," in *Between Silence and Speech: Essays on Jewish Thought* (Northvale, NJ: Jason Aronson, 1995), chap. 3. For an excellent survey of a vast array of diverse Jewish attitudes toward non-Jews, see Alan Brill, *Judaism and Other Religions: Models of Understanding* (NY: Palgrave Macmillan, 2010). See also Menachem Kellner, *Maimonides on Judaism and the Jewish People* (Albany, NY: SUNY Press, 1991) and Kellner, *They Too Are Called Human: Gentiles in the Eyes of Maimonides* (Ramat Gan: Bar Ilan University Press, 2016) [Hebrew].

6. See *Shulchan Aruch, Yoreh De'ah* 123:1.

7. See *Shulchan Aruch, Yoreh De'ah* 124:10–11, 17–18. Wine that has merely been touched by a non-Jew is not prohibited. *Maga* means handling. Two actions have to take place: touch and movement. When a non-Jew touches the bottle without intent, the wine is permitted for the purpose of drinking.

8. See R. Yosef Chaim of Baghdad, *Ben Ish Chai, Second Year, Parashat Balak*, 11.

9. For a general overview, see *Talmudic Encyclopedia*, s.v. "yayin shel goyim," 24:330–496. See also the following three works by Haym Soloveitchik: *Yenam: Sachar be-Yenam shel Goyim al Gilgula shel Halacha ba-Olam ha-Ma'aseh* (Tel Aviv: Alma, 2003); *Ha-Yayin Bimei ha-Benayim: Yayin Nesech [Wine in Ashkenaz in the Middle Ages: Yayin Nesech – A Study in the History of Halakha]* (Jerusalem: Zalman Shazar Center for Jewish History, 2008) [Hebrew]; "Can Halakhic Texts Talk History?," *AJS Review* 3 (1978): 153–196.

10. The wicked Jew is usually identified as a *mumar* (an apostate or renegade Jew), one who deliberately rejects Judaism and violates its demands. For the criteria establishing who is considered a *mumar*, see *Talmudic Encyclopedia*, s.v. "yayin shel goyim," 24:395–397. Nowadays, many authorities are of the opinion that this term no longer applies, since it is not malice that motivates him but ignorance, as well as the lack of revealed divine providence, which would convince him of the Torah's truth. See *Chazon Ish* on *Yoreh De'ah, Hilchot Shechita* 2:16, 28. See also R. Ya'akov Ettlinger, *Binyan Tzion ha-Chadashot*, no. 23; R. David Zvi Hoffmann, *Melamed le-Ho'il, Orach*

PROTEST

It is clear, then, that the motive for this prohibition was one of the great principles behind Judaism: *protest*. Protest against the kind of abomination that was an integral part of idol worship. The sages wanted to ensure that Jews would never come close to this sort of behavior or to these kinds of people, and as a protest they forbade the drinking of wine that had been handled by them. It reminds me of the Dutch, who, after World War II, refused to have anything to do with Germans, or even bring German-made products into their homes. It was taboo.

It is important to understand that the sages were not so much concerned with idol worship *per se*. Had idolatry not led to such excessive abominations, they would most likely not have made such an exacting decree concerning wine. What really prompted them to issue these rulings were the accompanying loathsome immorality and abhorrent acts, particularly gluttony and orgies.[11]

FAMILIARITY

Yet another reason for this prohibition is that drinking wine[12] with non-Jews increases familiarity, which could then lead to intermarriage and assimilation.[13] It seems, though, that the proscription was more formal

---

Chaim, no. 29; R. Ovadia Yosef, *Yabia Omer*, vol. 1, *Yoreh De'ah*, no. 11; R. Yitzchak Yosef, *Yalkut Yosef, Orach Chaim*, 329:1 n1.

11. Some of my halachic "opponents" may claim that I am overstating the case of wickedness and immorality as the reason for the law concerning *yayin nesech*, when the main reason for the prohibition is the fear that the wine was used for idolatrous libations. However, this seems to me incorrect. What really bothered the Torah and the sages about idol worship were the abominable, immoral acts that were inherent to paganism. Under those circumstances, ethical monotheism could never succeed and flourish. This view is based on the approach of the medieval sage R. Menachem ha-Me'iri regarding the issues of religion, morality, and idolatry. See, for example, *Bet ha-Bechira* on *Avoda Zara* 26a. Much literature has been published on Me'iri's understanding of the Gentile world. See David Berger, "Jews, Gentiles and the Modern Egalitarian Ethos: Some Tentative Thoughts," in *Formulating Responses in an Egalitarian Age*, ed. Marc D. Stern (Lanham, MD: Rowman and Littlefield, 2005), 83–108. See also Marc B. Shapiro, "Islam and the Halakhah," *Judaism* 42, no. 3 (Summer 1993): 332–343. Whether or not ongoing compulsive libations actually took place is a matter of dispute. See Sacha Stern, "Compulsive Libationers: Non-Jews and Wine in Early Rabbinic Sources," *Journal of Jewish Studies* 64, no. 1 (2013): 19–44. See also *Sanhedrin* 63b.

12. The prohibition against non-Jewish wine is only one instance of more thoroughgoing measures that the sages enacted to prevent intermarriage. These include prohibitions against consuming food cooked by non-Jews, bread baked by non-Jews, the initial prohibition against non-Jewish oil that was later revoked, and non-Jewish milk and cheese, etc. For a general overview, see *Talmudic Encyclopedia*, s.v. "chatnut," 18:362–366.

13. See *Shabbat* 17b; *Avoda Zara* 36b. It is most revealing that several commentators on the Tal-

than practical, since other drinks, even alcoholic, are not included in this prohibition.[14] In the olden days, wine was by far the most popular alcoholic drink, and was used specifically in religious settings. The fact that a person could become intoxicated and lose control increased the possibility that boundaries between Jews and non-Jews would be blurred. The sages decided to apply this law only to *bona fide* wine, not to kosher wine that was pasteurized or cooked (known in halachic literature as *yayin mevushal*), because once wine was boiled[15] it was no longer used for idol worship and therefore no longer considered "real" wine.[16] The fact that the *beracha* of *boreh pri ha-gafen* (the blessing made over wine) is still recited over *yayin mevushal*,[17] and that it remains an alcoholic drink that could still lead to familiarity in social settings,[18] clearly indicates that this law is mostly formal.

While too much familiarity is still one of the primary causes of assimilation, one can hardly argue today that drinking wine plays any serious role in this unfortunate situation. Religious Jews would not marry non-Jews even if they would drink wine with them, while those who run the chance of assimilating are the ones who don't care about this law. So what does this prohibition really accomplish? It would seem that its only claim is to remind us Jews of our special status.

AN ONTOLOGICAL VIEW OF NON-JEWS?

Over the years, however, this law has taken on a life of its own. It has created a psychological condition among many religious Jews that exceeds

---

mud were at one time not concerned about mixed marriages, since the non-Jews prohibited such marriages. See *Chiddushei ha-Ramban* on *Avoda Zara* 35b; *Talmidei Rabbenu Yona*, ibid.; *Levush*, *Yoreh De'ah* 123:26; *Turei Zahav* on *Shulchan Aruch*, *Yoreh De'ah* 123, no. 18; *Talmudic Encyclopedia*, s.v. "chatnut," 18:362–363.

14. It should be noted, however, that there is also a prohibition against drinking non-Jewish beer. However, this prohibition is not as stringent and categorically forbidden as wine, and in many instances it is permitted. See *Avoda Zara* 31b; *Mishne Torah*, *Hilchot Ma'achalot Asurot* 17:10; *Shulchan Aruch*, *Yoreh De'ah* 114:1-2; *Talmudic Encyclopedia*, s.v. "chatnut," 18:362–368.

15. See *Avoda Zara* 30a. For a discussion on when wine is considered to be *yayin mevushal*, see *Ran* on *Avoda Zara* 30a; *Shulchan Aruch*, *Yoreh De'ah* 123:3; R. Moshe Feinstein, *Igrot Moshe*, *Yoreh De'ah* 2, no. 52 and *Yoreh De'ah* 3, no. 31.

16. On whether boiled wine is permitted for *Kiddush*, see *Shulchan Aruch*, *Orach Chaim*, 272:8.

17. This is subject to a dispute among halachic authorities. Some authorities maintain that on boiled wine the blessing of *boreh pri ha-gafen* is still recited, while other authorities maintain that *she-hakol* is recited. See *Tur*, *Orach Chaim*, 272; *Talmudic Encyclopedia*, s.v. "yayin," 24:254–255.

18. However, the sages did prohibit social drinking with non-Jews even where no wine is drunk at all, and attending a non-Jewish feast. It is beyond the scope of this article to discuss all the details and nuances pertaining to this law. See *Mishne Torah*, *Hilchot Ma'achalot Asurot* 17:10; *Tur*, *Yoreh De'ah* 112; *Shulchan Aruch*, *Yoreh De'ah* 152:1.

by far what the sages wanted to accomplish. Since the law was never officially abolished, it created an *ontological* view of non-Jews as the practice expanded to include all non-Jews, and not just idol worshipers. No matter what their beliefs regarding this issue, non-Jews became by definition idol worshipers and depraved people; this is their very nature, and they cannot escape it. This view on the part of many religious Jews is not conscious and deliberate, but it is deeply ingrained in the Jewish religious psyche. It points to a kind of Jungian archetype. What this means is that many religious Jews believe not only that the law concerning wine should not be changed, but also that non-Jews are not meant to and are unable to change. After all, this law must reflect Judaism's authentic view of non-Jews. In other words, there is nothing wrong with the Jewish Tradition for still applying this law. On the contrary, there is something wrong with the non-Jewish world for changing and no longer fitting the description that the Jewish Tradition attributes to them.

While all this may sound very foreign to those living in *chutz la-Aretz* (the Diaspora), this view is widespread in Israeli religious communities, whether Charedi or Dati Leumi, with few exceptions.[19]

This attitude is tragic and extremely dangerous. It completely contradicts one of the most important teachings of the Jewish Tradition; that man – both Jew and Gentile – can and must change. In fact, this belief is not only a misrepresentation of Judaism; it is the very antithesis of all that Judaism stands for. If non-Jews will always be looked upon as idol worshipers, no matter how far behind they have left that world, then Jews cannot be a light unto the nations, nor do they have anything to offer them. That would mean that Judaism was doomed to fail from the start.

WHY A JEWISH NATION? *HEILSGESCHICHTE* AND GOD

To understand the danger of this unfortunate development, we need to take a broad look at Judaism and its vital mission. Several questions come to mind. Why does the world need a Jewish nation and what is its purpose? Why do the Jews need to be separate, and why is assimilation seen as one of the most destructive forces within Judaism throughout the ages? What lies at the very core of Judaism?

While many opinions prevail, there are some basic beliefs concerning

---

19. I refer here to native Israelis, not to those who came on aliyah from Western countries. See the most disturbing observations by R. Moshe Sternbuch in *Teshuvot ve-Hanhagot*, vol. 3, no. 317. See p. 242 below.

the very existence of the Jewish people and their mission. With perhaps the exception of Rambam,[20] all the classic Jewish philosophers claim that the ultimate reason for Israel's existence is to be part of the unifying thread in a kind of *Heilsgeschichte* (redemptive history). Its purpose is to move humankind forward on its spiritual journey both to full recognition of God as the ultimate Master of all existence and to supreme ethical behavior. This noble role demands exemplary conduct on the part of the Jews. To fully understand this, we must realize that God is not merely the Creator and God of the Universe, but primarily the God Who is deeply involved in human history. God is not a philosophical idea advanced by Greek philosophers, totally separate from and beyond all human existence. He is an almost touchable Being Who dresses Himself in human emotions to make His point known to humankind.

> God appears to experience all the human emotions: love, anger, involvement, indignation, regret, sadness, and so on. By so doing, He gives the seal of divinity to the very essence of our humanity. He implicitly says to man: "You cannot know what is above and what is below, but you can know what is in your hearts and in the world. These feelings and reactions and emotions that make up human existence are, if illumined by faith and rationality, all the divinity you can hope for. To be humane is to be divine: as I am holy, so you shall be holy; as I am merciful, so you shall be merciful." Thus, there is only one kind of knowledge that is open to man, the knowledge of God's humanity.[21]

God, then, becomes a specific and historic Personality. He becomes a player in the history of man, together with all the players in the human race. This makes Him the most tragic Figure in all of human history, because He cannot appear in His authentic form, which would require Him to be far beyond all human limitations and characteristics. Would He do so, He would be meaningless to humankind. He must appear in opposition to His very Self. Not as a philosophical idea beyond all human resemblance, but as a Redemptive God within history. This means that

---

20. See David Hartman, *Israelis and the Jewish Tradition: An Ancient People Debating its Future* (New Haven, CT: Yale University Press, 2000).

21. Yochanan Muffs, "A Jewish View of God's Relation to the World," in *The Personhood of God: Biblical Theology, Human Faith and the Divine Image* (Woodstock, VT: Jewish Lights Publishing, 2005), 171.

He had to become a God of compromise for the sake of man's limitations. Precisely for that reason He often fails in His ultimate goals. He *has* to fail so as to connect with man. His objective is to allow man to fail so that redemptive history becomes a reality. Nothing can be redeemed if all is perfect.

To achieve His goal, God requires a specific people who are destined to carry out the redemptive nature of history. Universal ideas cannot be relied upon, because they are impersonal, and what is impersonal is beyond history. Furthermore, an impersonal entity cannot carry a commitment, a moral assignment; for if *all* are committed to a particular mission, there is no one to be persuaded and therefore no mission to implement. Redemptive history then becomes impossible.

More important, however, is that the God of history can work only within time and space. This allows for a personal encounter with Him solely in the context of life and history. And only in that way can there be a mission of redemptive and God-centered history. It is through particularism that this universal mission can be accomplished.

And yet, those who are called on to carry out this mission must have an element of universality and eternity. They cannot be completely distinct, as that would lead them to becoming self-absorbed and unable to redeem and help humankind on its spiritual journey. So, paradoxically, this group must to some degree be ahistorical. It must be unique and incapable of being sociologically or ethnologically categorized. It cannot belong to a particular race, culture, or even a conventional religious denomination. Nor can it be a nation in the traditional sense of the word. It must transcend all these definitions and represent something that is a mystery, an anomaly and even a contradiction, so that it can stand at the center of history. Through its uniqueness, all of human history must be expressed. It has to carry the true history of humankind in a world that has an origin and a divine goal. This group of people, then, must identify with all of humankind while remaining separate.

NOT A NATION, A RACE, OR A RELIGION

Only "Israel" fits this description, for Israel is neither a race nor a nation nor a religion in the conventional sense. It violates all the criteria that "race," "nation," and "religion" stand for. Indeed, it is religion that determines its nationality, and it is nationality that determines its religion, while both concepts are a far cry from its essence. It includes members of all races, and everyone can join to become a genuine child of Avraham and Sara.

In addition, there is such a wide range of language, culture, and belief among Jews that no definition of these terms can accurately describe this unusual people. Yet the Jews do represent a surviving historic continuum, identifiable but consisting of constantly shifting groups.

This perplexing notion of "redemptive history" stands at the very core of the mission of Jews and Halacha. For Halacha to be meaningful and eternal, it must be *redemptive* Halacha, constantly deriving its vitality and its guidelines from this notion. Redemptive history must move forward in order to be redemptive, and Halacha must therefore move with it. Once it has accomplished a certain goal, it must abandon the means by which it achieved this goal and move to the next stage of its redemptive goals. If, instead, it adheres to the means by which it achieved its goal, it undermines itself and becomes destructive. Instead of being redemptive, it becomes confining and harmful, turning progress into regression and reversing everything that it wants to achieve.

COUNTERPRODUCTIVE

It is for this reason that the law of *yayin nesech* is counterproductive. *Its objective has already been achieved.* It fulfilled its purpose and has become obsolete. As long as a good part of the non-Jewish world was deeply committed to idol worship and abominable acts, it was important and made a powerful point. But since by now a very large percentage of humankind has abandoned idol worship, is no longer dedicated to repugnant deeds, and has accepted values such as human rights, equity, and equality, we can no longer ignore these developments and look the other way.

In fact, by continuing to observe this law, we deny that Judaism has had a powerful influence on our world. As a protest movement in the face of great evil, it has done extremely well. Many of its redemptive goals have been fulfilled. Franz Rosenzweig's thoughts on this subject have been right on the mark. He points out that it is not so much Judaism *itself* that is directly responsible for these achievements.[22] It required a more extroverted monotheistic religion to take on its ideals and expose them to the world. This, says Rosenzweig, is what Christianity did. With all its

---

22. Franz Rosenzweig, *Briefe* (Berlin: Schocken, 1935), 100, quoted in Jacob Agus, *Modern Philosophies of Judaism* (NY: Behrman's Jewish Book House, 1941), 194.

mistakes and anti-Semitic overtones, it paradoxically made monotheism into a powerful force throughout the world, and many Jewish values are now well known, while conventional idol worship has ceased to exist. Rosenzweig adds that Judaism gave birth to Christianity for this *very* purpose, and Christianity can only fulfill its purpose if Israel is in its midst. It must take its inspiration from Israel. It cannot stand on its own feet. Christian philosopher and theologian Paul Tillich suggested that there would always be a need for Judaism because "it is the corrective against the paganism that goes along with Christianity."[23]

That is the reason why there is no point in continuing to observe a law that forbids non-Jews to touch our wine.

To argue that idol worship is still alive and well and that there is still a lot of evil around is missing the point. First of all, it is questionable whether idol worship is indeed still around. Hinduism and Buddhism may very well not fall into this category, and even if they would, they are not prone to immorality and evil.[24] Secondly, evil behavior is no longer acceptable by any law-abiding society. This is the indirect result of Judaism's influence on civilization. In fact, Judaism introduced many other ethical laws that are not found in the Torah itself. The redemptive qualities, which the law of *yayin nesech* symbolizes, have finished their job.

The same is true about assimilation, which is no longer affected by the law of *yayin nesech*. Now that there are so many other alcoholic drinks that are not forbidden after they've been touched by non-Jews, the law is meaningless. If anything, we should forbid non-Jews to touch whiskey, or beer. But to do so would be ineffective. If we want to fight assimilation, we need totally different strategies. Assimilation has undergone a shift and it can be countered only by ideology. To believe that the law of *yayin nesech* still has anything to do with preventing assimilation is to bury one's head in the sand.

THE NEED FOR SEPARATION

For Jews to remain separate, other strategies will have to be developed. It will require a novel attempt to stir a strong feeling of mission among our youth, combined with a very compelling ideology and education that

---

23. From an unpublished manuscript by Paul Tillich quoted in A. Roy Eckardt, *Christianity and the Children of Israel* (NY: King's Crown Press, 1948), 147.

24. See Alon Goshen-Gottstein and Eugene Korn, ed., *Jewish Theology and World Religions* (Oxford: Littman Library of Jewish Civilization, 2012), 263–316.

would be irresistible. Paradoxically, as long as this law exists, it sends a message that the mission rooted in the concept of redemptive history is a fake, and an effective ideology cannot be developed. So the law, which should be building a strong, compelling Jewish identity, in fact does the reverse.

HALACHIC AUTHORITIES AND *YAYIN NESECH*

My position has been alluded to by several Sephardic halachic authorities. As is well known, Rabbi Menachem ha-Me'iri (1249–1316, Provence) already stated his opinion that non-Jews in the Western Hemisphere are moral people who have left idol worship behind them. He therefore concluded that many discriminating talmudic laws concerning non-Jews are no longer applicable.[25] He was clearly a believer in redemptive Halacha. However, Me'iri did not go so far as to abolish the law of *yayin nesech*. The person who came closest to doing so was none other than Rema (1520–1572), Rabbi Moshe Isserles, the foremost Ashkenazic commentator on Rabbi Yosef Karo's *Shulchan Aruch*. He brings a view that if a *ger toshav* (a non-Jewish resident of Israel) touches a bottle of wine, it is still permitted to drink that wine. Whether or not today's non-Jew, who is no longer an idol worshiper, fits the definition of a *ger toshav* is a matter of debate.[26] Another great halachic authority who came very close to doing this was the eminent Rabbi Yosef Mashash (1892–1974), who served as rabbi in Algeria and Morocco, and was later Chief Rabbi of Haifa. He was one of the most daring halachic authorities of our days. Dr. Marc B. Shapiro writes about Rabbi Mashash:

> He defends drinking alcohol which contains wine that had been handled by Muslims. He quotes a responsum by an earlier Moroccan rabbi who even permitted drinking the wine itself – [Rabbi] Messas didn't go this far – and who had justified this decision as follows: "There is no unity [of God] like the unity found in Islam; therefore, one who

---

25. See n11 above.
26. See *Shulchan Aruch, Yoreh De'ah* 124:2 and especially 124:24. See also *Shu"t ha-Rema*, ed. Asher Ziv (Jerusalem: Chemed, 1970), no. 124, where R. Moshe Isserles is *melamed zechut* (judges favorably) those who drink wine produced by non-Jews. See also the sources cited in Marc B. Shapiro, *Changing the Immutable: How Orthodox Judaism Rewrites Its History* (Oxford: Littman Library of Jewish Civilization, 2015), 95–99.

forbids them to handle [wine] turns holy into profane by regarding worshippers of God as worshippers of idols, God forbid."[27]

Even more revealing is the observation by Dr. Shapiro that Rabbi Shmuel Yehuda Katzenellenbogen of Venice (1521–1597), the leading Italian halachic authority of his time, drank non-Jewish wine himself and so did other Orthodox well-known rabbis.[28]

DEFENSIVE HALACHA AND THE WAITING MODE

But there is more. The famous philosopher, talmudist, and halachic expert Rabbi Eliezer Berkovits argues that over the last two thousand years Halacha has become increasingly defensive.[29] It has had to deal with aggressive anti-Semitism, as Judaism and Jews were constantly attacked in the Diaspora. Under those circumstances, rabbinical authorities built many walls between us and the Gentiles. This was very understandable; it was the only way to survive. But it also meant that Halacha became stagnant. It couldn't develop naturally because it had to constantly look over its shoulder to make sure that Jews wouldn't be affected by the non-Jewish world whose practices and ideologies might oppose Jewish ethical values. It had to ensure that in no way, neither directly nor indirectly, would Jews be influenced by or support non-Jewish idolatrous traditions and immoral acts. During all of these two thousand years in exile, Halacha was forced into a "waiting mode", in anticipation of redeeming itself when Jews would again return to their homeland and live in freedom.

While Rabbi Berkovits does not discuss the issue of *yayin nesech*, it is very clear that the law prohibiting it originated under these circumstances.

THE WAITING MODE HAS COME TO AN END

But times have changed. The "waiting mode" has come to an end. Halacha's longtime dream, to liberate itself from its defensiveness and fear, is

27. Marc B. Shapiro, "Rabbi Joseph Messas," *Conversations* 7 (Spring 2010): 100–101. See R. Yosef Mashash, *Otzar ha-Michtavim*, vol. 1, nos. 454, 462 and *Mayim Chaim*, vol. 2, *Yoreh De'ah*, no. 66. Rabbi Mashash expresses a similar opinion concerning *bishul akum* (kosher food cooked by non-Jews). See also R. Ovadia Hadaya, *Yaskil Avdi*, vol. 1, *Yoreh De'ah*, no. 4.

28. Shapiro, *Changing the Immutable*, 96–97.

29. See Eliezer Berkovits, *Ha-Halacha, Kocha ve-Tafkida* (Jerusalem: Mossad HaRav Kook, 1981), translated and abridged in English as *Not in Heaven: The Nature and Function of Halakha* (NY: Ktav, 1983), chap. 4.

slowly being fulfilled in our own days! The Jews' situation has drastically changed, specifically since the establishment of the State of Israel. We no longer have to be defensive, as we were in the ghettos. The State has given us our long-awaited independence. We run our own affairs and are no longer afraid of the anti-Semitic world. If attacked, we will strike back. And just as the Jewish State has freed the Jews from defenselessness by building a powerful army with tens of thousands of soldiers and the most sophisticated weaponry, which has made the Israeli army into the world's best, so must Halacha abandon its fear, take a courageous, assertive approach, and make a radical turnabout.

Instead of fearing the corrupt influence of the non-Jewish world, we should now show ourselves and the world the enormous spiritual and moral power of Judaism. Instead of building high walls around us, we should create transparent partitions. It's time for the world to be awestruck by the power of Judaism. It's time for exposure, and the export of Jewish spirituality and ethics. The world needs it. The world is ready for it. Jews would find great meaning in religious Judaism, and non-Jews would be astonished and impressed. Assimilation will not come to an end by enacting laws rooted in fear and weakness, but by a halachic ideology of strength and courage. Judaism has more than enough strength to face head-on the many negative powers that surround us, and win the war. Yes, there will be victims, as we have in any Israeli war, but war can only be won if you take that risk, no matter how painful. Today's weak approach creates more victims, by far.

TO FIGHT FOR A MISSION

Even more important is the fact that all of this will have an immediate effect on our own youth. Judaism will be something people want to be part of. It will once again become a mission to fight for and be proud of.

One of the great tasks of Jewish education is to *deliberately* create an atmosphere of rebellion among its students. Rebellion, after all, is the great emancipator. To paraphrase English writer Charles Caleb Colton (1780–1832): We owe almost all our knowledge and achievements not to those who agreed, but to those who differed. It was this quality that brought Judaism into existence. Avraham was the first great rebel, destroying idols, and he was followed by his children, by Moshe, and by the Jewish people.

THE TORAH WAS THE FIRST REBELLIOUS TEXT

What has been entirely forgotten is that the Torah was the first rebellious text to appear in world history. Its purpose was to protest. It set in motion a rebellious movement of universal proportions second to none.[30] The text includes all the heresies of the past, present, and future. It calls idol worship an abomination, immorality a scandal, and the worship of man a catastrophe. It protests against complacency, imitation, and negation of the spirit. It calls for radical thinking and radical action, without compromise, even if it means standing alone and being condemned or ridiculed.

This reality seems lost on our religious establishment. We are teaching our students and children to obey, to fit in, to conform, and not to stand out. We teach them that their religious leaders are great people because they don't want to rock the boat. They would never think of disturbing the established religious or social norm. But these teachers don't realize that they are teaching a tradition of protest, and if they want to succeed they must communicate that message.

REBELLIOUS JUDAISM

By using clichés instead of the language of opposition, we deny our students the excitement of being Jewish. Excitement, after all, comes from the knowledge that you make a difference, and you take pride in that fact, whatever the cost. It comes from being aware that you are part of a great mission for which you are prepared to die, knowing that it will make the world a better place.

When we tell our children to eat kosher, we need to tell them that this is an act of disobedience against self-indulgence, by which human beings are prepared to eat anything as long as it tastes good. When we go to synagogue, it is a protest against man's arrogance in thinking that he can do it all himself. When young couples are asked to observe the law of family purity, it is a rebellion against the obsession with sex. The celebration of Shabbat must be taught as an enormous challenge to our contemporary world, which believes that happiness depends on how much we can produce.

As long as our religious teachers continue to teach Jewish texts as models of approval instead of manifestations of protest against the mediocrity

---

30. See Introduction.

of our world, we will lose more and more of our young people to that very mediocrity.

Judaism is in essence an act of dissent, not of consent. Dissent means renewal. It creates loyalty. It is the stuff that world growth is made of.

But all of this can be achieved only if we re-establish Halacha as an ideology and practice by which courage and determination will lead to great pride and a strong feeling of mission.

BACK ON TRACK

We must now make sure that Halacha can once again develop in its original, innovative way and come back to itself. We don't need to reform or update it. We need to simply take it back to the point where it had to turn against its own self because of our *galut* (exile) experience, and we must get it back on track. We have to cut off the many foreign branches that have for centuries concealed its ancient roots. It requires a purifying process so as to bring it to complete spiritual fulfillment.

Yes, it has to be done slowly, with great care, and in a way that doesn't harm the core. I haven't the slightest doubt that we'll discover a beautiful canvas with many diverse but harmonious colors that will deeply impress our fellow Jews and make Judaism irresistible.

DE-CODIFICATION

To achieve this goal, we have to de-codify Jewish Law and dispense with the official codes of law by which Judaism was able to survive in past centuries. Codification stagnates.[31] While it was necessary in order to overcome the enormous challenges of exile, it has now become an obstacle, outdated and unhealthy, which to a great extent now blocks the natural development of Halacha.

Jewish Law must move and grow, taking into account various developments in our world and giving them guidance. And that can happen only if it is fluid and allows for a great amount of flexibility, which codification cannot offer. Certainly, some conformity is necessary, such as in the case of civil law. But unlike non-Jewish codifications, Jewish Law is foremost a religious and spiritual tradition. As such, it can never be translated into immutable rules to be applied at all times, under all conditions, and

---

31. See chap. 2 for an elaborate treatment of this issue.

for everyone, without considering the personal, religious, and practical components. These elements vary drastically, as can be seen by the many differing and even opposing opinions in the Talmud, which the sages were not only aware of, but seem to have actually encouraged.[32]

PROPHETIC HALACHA

What we need now is innovative *prophetic* Halacha, dedicated to the great, authentic, ethical mission of the Jewish people as conveyed by the prophets, and combined with the demands of the Torah. The prophets preached a rare combination of particularism and universalism. They strongly advocated Jewish particularism, so as to keep the Jews separated from the rest of the nations. But they always viewed this in terms of universalism.[33] There was a need for a central driving force, full of spiritual and moral energy, that would enable the Jews to inspire all of humankind and be "a light unto the nations," conveying the oneness of God and the significance of justice.

*

We must continue to be different and marry only among ourselves, or with those who have joined our people. We should make our own wines and not drink those produced by our Gentile friends, because wine is a sacred drink that needs to be sanctified by the beliefs of different religious communities. I would even suggest that each monotheistic religion produce its own wine, since it is not the liquid itself that is sacred, but the winemaker's intentions that have suffused the wine.

It is nonsensical to believe that the world would be a better place if all differences would be eliminated. Distinctiveness is a most important aspect of our society. It gives it color and allows people to belong. But it should not lead to a form of separation, which serves no real goal and is the outgrowth of something that was meant for a different time.

---

32. See *Eruvin* 13b.

33. See, for example, *Shemot* 19:5–6, *Yeshayahu* 42:6. See Cardozo, *Between Silence and Speech*, chaps. 3 and 5.

YAYIN NESECH AND ANTI-SEMITES, TERRORISTS AND SELF-HATING JEWS

Should the law of *yayin nesech* be abolished altogether? Definitely not! We should not drink kosher wine that has been handled by anti-Semites, terrorists, rapists, financial swindlers, men who refuse to grant divorces to their wives, self-hating Jews, and the like.

After all, the purpose of the law is to protest, not to discriminate.

It is high time that the rabbis consider revisiting this ancient law and adapting it to our new reality.

My brother would agree.

Chapter 4

The Dangling Bridges of Halacha
Making Rules Where Rules Should Not Exist

AUTHENCITY AND PURE BUTTER

One of the strongest longings of human beings today is for authenticity. We want to be ourselves, or to become ourselves. We admire children's spontaneity, because they do not yet know how they "ought to be." They are still impulsive and natural.

More and more, we distrust "objective" information because it is distant from our inner lives. It reasons too much and makes us forget what our *real* lives are all about. It has straight-jacketed us into the mainstream. What we want is to recapture and hold on to genuineness. Otherwise we choke. We even need to purchase pure butter and natural foods without artificial additives. We have been overwhelmed by the artificiality in our lives, and we crave authenticity.

The more we are suffocated by this disingenuousness, the more our emotional relationships with ourselves and others require space, because we have learned that neither science nor modernity can offer us a spiritual sanctuary. They are unable to teach us the stuff of life. Science is a shell surrounding what is real.

THE LONGING FOR CANDLELIGHT

In our complicated existence we are still romantics searching for candlelight instead of simply using electricity. But even romanticism has succumbed to rules. It began prescribing its own set of laws and decided how authenticity should be expressed in art and even music. Suddenly we were introduced to ambiguity.

Place Alexander Pope's *An Essay on Man* next to the poetry of the romantics and you discover the difference. Poetry becomes suggestive rather than literal. In the knowledge of this ambivalence we recognize that the world is not really what it appears to be. As in Plato's world of Ideas, we discover a world much more real than its mirror image, which we mortals consider to be our world.

And so it is with us. We are not who we appear to be. We long to be ourselves, attentive to our subconscious and unconscious spiritual urges and experiences. But we are limited, bound by pressures and needs that we cannot escape because they are inherent to the outer world we live in. They make this world possible, and consequently unbearable to live in as untainted and real human beings.

And so we recognize that authenticity reflects a paradox. What, after all, is it? Is it dealing with our inner lives, or is it our sincere attempt to live in the outer world? Or maybe both simultaneously?

Perhaps we human beings are genuine, but we also play the part of being genuine. We may be good, but we love to impress others with our goodness; and we don't know where one ends and the other begins. There is artificiality in authenticity.

L'HOMME SAUVAGE AND L'HOMME CIVILISÉ

To use a French expression, we have cast aside *l'homme sauvage*, the natural, wild, and free man, and replaced him with *l'homme civilisé*, the civilized man of today. We have become estranged from ourselves, abandoning the paradisiacal purity of the natural man. Through the incessant "ought to" education of norms, the childish innocence has systematically been suffocated and ultimately destroyed. We are caught up in social conventions and behavior patterns. So, real love, friendship, and even good citizenship are frustrated.

The ideal of authenticity is like Adam and Chava's before eating of the fruit in the Garden of Eden. Once one has bitten into the fruit of genuineness, artificiality emerges. Then man is in need of laws to restrain him so that he may survive, but his inner self pays the price. We, like millions of other people, sit in front of our computers that have opened new worlds for us but have made it more difficult to see the other. And so we long for more contact . . . more love . . . more human trust.

But within this lies an aspect of narcissism as well – the yearning to be with ourselves. This longing clashes with the needs of the other, social conditions, family, and society at large.

So, does real life not include social tradition and the "ought to," despite the tension between authenticity and the needs of the society? It is this constant paradox that we must accept, however difficult it may be. Real life is the clash between our inner needs and our outer conditions. To choose one and reject the other is no longer life. To be sure, all this is the irony of our existence, but it should not be confused with cynicism. Since the time of Adam ha-Rishon (the first human being), it is the acceptance of paradox that gives life substance.

HALACHA AS PARADOX

Halacha is built on this paradox; it is the impetus behind its call for authenticity as well as for the norms and behavior patterns it dictates even when they do not agree with the inner human being. Halacha is full of seeming contradictions that sometimes cause us deep frustration. One day it asks for inner authenticity; the next day it demands conformity. It refuses to inform us why in one case it asks for a genuine, personal inner experience, while in another it disturbingly demands compliance with rules and standards.

The great halachists battle over what should have priority, because they themselves are part of the "problem." Since they are human beings, not angels, they reflect all the dimensions of human limitation and are therefore highly competent to decide on matters of Halacha, because Halacha deals *only* with a life of paradoxes and constraints.

Great halachists do not possess absolute knowledge. They are not scientists who deal with impartial conditions. They deal with human life. And once they or others start to believe that they are infallible, they have left the world of Halacha and succumbed to radical inauthenticity. It is for this reason that God gave the Torah to man. *Torah lo ba-Shamayim hi* – the Torah is no longer in Heaven.[1] Halacha is and needs to be unfinalized, since life can never be perfect. It is unable to conclusively solve all problems because this world is a place where romanticism and its own artificial rules clash with the external conditions of society. Life consists of tradeoffs: equality vs. liberty; justice vs. mercy; kindness vs. truth.[2]

All Halacha can do is offer guidelines when absolute answers do not exist. But it converts arbitrary solutions into demands, because loyalty to

---

1. *Bava Metzia* 59b; *Temura* 16a.
2. See Ramin Jahabegloo, *Conversations with Isaiah Berlin* (London: Halban, 2007), 142–143.

these guidelines needs to become part of the worship of God. It is God who set up this ambivalence and demands from man to live under these conditions.

Halacha makes rules where rules should not exist, but need to exist lest chaos ensue. But it is these very rules that create unsolvable problems that are inherent to our existence.

THE NEAR COLLAPSE OF HALACHA

In trying to ask for both religious authenticity and conformity, Halacha nearly collapses in its attempt to satisfy both, and consequently builds bridges that dangle loosely and are then declared by Halacha to be castles of security. Halacha is constrained by man's need to look after his own spiritual wants: the playfulness and innocence of the child in all of us – our real I – and the fact that we have consumed the "fruit" and must now conform because we could not deal with the tree.

It is this balancing act that becomes beautiful once the Divine Will declares it holy and teaches us that life's absurdity has meaning.

Chapter 5

Halacha and the Inadequacy of Jewish Dogma

Judaism is experiencing a great renaissance these days, something we can rejoice over. Today we are blessed with a great number of highly unusual Israeli "secular" programs where completely non-religious young men, informally dressed and sporting long hair with no *kippot*, bend over the Talmud and Midrash trying to rediscover their Jewish roots; where young women in trousers and sleeveless blouses try to unlock the secrets of Jewish mysticism or get excited about a talmudic debate between Abaye and Rava, two ancient talmudic sages. They live it and can't get enough of it; some do nothing else but study these sources all day.

There is a plethora of new Jewish ideas floating around within these circles, and one can only marvel at the creativity of these young people, though one may not always agree with some of the conclusions they reach. There is great open-mindedness, and it is becoming clearer and clearer that secular Israelis will be much more careful than their grandparents were about scoffing at the Jewish Tradition. They are aware that this Tradition is more profound than their predecessors had ever thought it to be. Not only is there greater respect for the Jewish Tradition, but many young people realize that Judaism is more versatile and multifaceted than they had ever imagined; that it is as yet untapped and has so much to offer, far beyond what has been discovered until now.

Strangely enough, this phenomenon goes hand in hand with an increase in rigidity within mainstream Orthodox circles – not only in the ultra-Orthodox, but even in some Modern Orthodox communities, although there are definite exceptions in both.

While these people show enormous dedication to Judaism and an immense longing to be deeply religious, we find a frightful closing of the mind. All that counts is the careful fulfillment of every halachic requirement without asking: Why? What is the significance of Halacha? What does it mean to be religious?

HALACHA AS RESPONSE

One of the main reasons for this is that Halacha is no longer seen as a *response* to the search for meaning in people's lives. The image of Halacha as a rigid tradition has taken the upper hand. Completely unawares, these devoted communities have reduced Judaism to definitions, laws, codes, and dogmas. While their love for Judaism is undisputed, they are not aware of how it cannot be squeezed into any of these categories. It is like trying to fit the ocean into a bathtub.

Halacha cannot be restricted to absolute definitions, because no law – and certainly not Halacha, which guides the Jew in every aspect of his life – will ever fit into a rigid code; but more than that, it is a *way of living* accompanied by deep emotions, a strong religious experience that can never be achieved by just observing laws, and no law can ever encompass it.

PLATO

In one of Plato's earliest dialogues, *Charmides*, the philosopher discusses the question: what is temperance? After offering several definitions, which all prove inadequate, he has Socrates exclaim: "I have been utterly defeated and have failed to discover what that is to which the imposer of names gave this name of temperance. . . the impossibility of a man knowing in a sort of way that which he does not know at all."[1] Plato's own words are: "It [philosophy] does not at all admit of verbal expression like other studies, but, as a result of continued application to the subject itself and communion therewith, it is brought to birth in the soul on a sudden, as light that is kindled by a leaping spark, and thereafter it nourishes itself."[2]

Indeed, to define words such as "good," "love," and "holy" is impossible. Any attempt to do so not only limits them, but actually makes them

---

1. Plato, *Charmides*, in *The works of Plato, Vol. 4: Charmides, Lysis, Other Dialogues and the Laws*, trans. Benjamin Jowett (NY: Cosimo Classics, 2010), 44.
2. Plato, *Letters*, Letter 7, 341C, in *Plato in Twelve Volumes*, vol. 7, trans. R.G. Bury (Cambridge, MA: Harvard University Press, 1966).

meaningless, since one removes their most essential component. The best part of beauty is that which a picture cannot express.

As with other religions, teachers of Judaism have often attempted to raise the foundations of religion to the level of clear utterances, dogmas, and creeds. Yet, such endeavors cannot be more than *indications*, an attempt to convey what cannot be adequately expressed.

To argue that they are the definite fundamentals of faith is to undermine authentic religious faith. It would be like arguing that musical notes are the fundamentals of music. They are not; they are only directions for the musician to follow, showing the way, but they are never *das ding an sich*, the thing itself.

THE DANGER OF DOGMA

Judaism is in perpetual danger of giving priority to concepts and dogmas and forfeiting the primacy of the inexpressible dimensions of religious insights. Doctrines and creeds should never become screens; they can only function as windows into a world that is beyond definition. Dogmas in the hands of man often turn into expressions of clerical authority setting down a fixed set of principles without an existential search for genuine faith.

Despite the fact that such an approach has been tried by some of the greatest Jewish thinkers, it has never succeeded, because Judaism is not the outcome of a doctrine, but rather of concrete events, actions, and insights of a people who experienced an encounter with God, which cannot be transmitted in absolute verbal expression. One can inherit dogmas and fundamentals of faith, but faith itself can only be discovered in the light of one's soul. It is a moment in which all definitions end, and any attempt to come to conclusive articles of faith can only yield stifling trivialities that become suspended in the heart of the man of real faith. Genuine Judaism can only be understood in its natural habitat of deep faith and piety, in which the Divine reaches *all* thoughts.

Even if dogma has a purpose, it can never function as a substitute for faith, but only as an aspect of faith, just as music is much more than what a musical note can ever convey.

FREEZING AWE AND UTOPIAN REVERIE

For Halacha to be a response to man's search for meaning, it must make space for a non-dogmatic philosophy of Judaism. It must encourage dialogue concerning all basic Jewish beliefs and show how it is the practical upshot of these unfinalized beliefs; a practical way of halachic life while staying in theological suspense.

Only in this way can Judaism be saved from freezing in awe of a rigid tradition, or evaporating into a utopian reverie. Judaism is the art of encountering God in all dimensions of life. As such, it includes all that man does, feels, says, and thinks.

Still, unlike the arrows of Jewish belief that dart hither and thither, wavering as though shot into the air from a slackened bow string, Halacha is straight and unswerving. It is a place to stand on, solid bedrock. But it must reflect that it consists of fluid that is somehow transformed into a solid substance. It needs to chill the heated steel of exalted ideas and turn them into pragmatic deeds. In that way, it can combine the infinite dimension with the finite deed.

But this can only work once the Halacha is experienced by the Jew through a weltanschauung of tremendous depth. He needs to know that behind any halachic act there is profound spiritual quality, which provides him with spiritual growth. It allows the unseen to enter into his world and the metaphor to become tangible. Halacha alone is unable to provide insight into the quality of a halachic act. To make this known, the religious person must learn how to struggle with the great thought processes, debates, and spiritual upheavals within the Jewish Tradition.

Those who want to start Jewish education with absolute certainties will end up with doubts; but those who start in doubt will become more and more convinced of its truth.

To all those who want to convince us that Judaism consists of unambiguous and all-inclusive definitions, we respond with a resounding no.

HALACHA IS NOT ABOUT LAW BUT ABOUT GOD

It is this undefined element of Judaism that many young secular people are beginning to discover. While they may not yet fully understand the need to incorporate Halacha into their own lives, they are laying the foundation for a healthy Judaism, which will hopefully bring them to a deeper appreciation of Halacha. It would be a significant endeavor if the Orthodox establishment would give this much more attention, and rediscover that Halacha is not about law, but about living in the presence of God. Perhaps it should listen to some of the voices in the secular community while the latter is on its way to discovering Judaism. All of us may benefit.

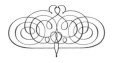

Chapter 6

The Expulsion of God in Halacha

When trying to understand Halacha's failure to inspire many Jews in modern times, we need to recognize that not only has it been flattened by over-codification and stagnation due to its being out of touch with the spiritual needs of modern man, but it has also, paradoxically, exiled God.

Halacha has been disconnected from a conscious awareness of God. Today, halachic living ignores Him. When living our "religious" lives we are more concerned about the specifics of Halacha than we are about our existential relationship with God. No doubt this is partially the fault of the halachic process itself. Even the sages in the Talmud, when discussing halachic issues, rarely mention God in their conversation, making these discussions very legal and often dry in a religious sense. The reason for this is obvious. There was no need to mention God in all these debates because they were thoroughly touched by His presence, just as water touches every part of our body while we are swimming. One does not have to mention water when completely immersed in it. God was the magnificent background music to anything the sages felt and said. In their view, God was a challenge, not a mere notion. They had a trembling sense of the "here-ness" of God. They realized that they were more known by God than God could ever be known by them.

WHERE IS GOD MENTIONED IN THE RESPONSA? NEVER!

In modern times, this religious experience is lost on us. We study Talmud and Halacha in ways that have been deeply affected by the secular environment in which we live. God-consciousness is no longer a priority. The majority of us are no longer God-intoxicated. Most, if not all of our halachic authorities have also fallen victim to this sad situation without even being aware of it. They decide on halachic matters while God is not actively present. This does not mean that they do not believe in God or that they have no *Yirat Shamayim*, but it does mean that they are not stirred by His presence while dealing with halachic issues. How often is God mentioned in *sheilot u-teshuvot* (rabbinic responsa)?

One needs to have a religious experience while deciding the Halacha. Rabbis do not realize that one can only render a halachic decision while simultaneously experiencing the wonder of life, the astonishment of existence, and the marvel of Judaism. Halacha can be lived and decided upon only when we ask the question: How are we able to – indeed, how do we even dare to live in His presence?

Halacha is a protest against taking life for granted. One of its aims is to make us aware that there is no commonplace, no moment of insignificance, and no deed of triviality. Halacha is the attempt to undo the attitude of everydayness, but it can only work when we are fully conscious of this impediment and realize that there is no way to understand the meaning of Halacha unless we make this goal our primary concern. If the *posek* does not realize that this is the function of Halacha and that this should be his ultimate goal when making a decision, his attempt to lay down the Halacha is futile.

RELIGIOUS SELF-DECEPTION

The problem we face is not realizing that halachic living may become, if it hasn't already, a form of *avoda zara* (idol worship). When we think that by following halachic demands we will automatically draw closer to God, we are guilty of self-deception.

We do not understand that we often use Halacha as a way to escape Him. Living a halachic life is not what brings us close to God. That can only happen through the development of our God-consciousness. It must come from awe – from radical amazement, as Abraham Joshua Heschel called it. Only then is the Halacha able to develop and deepen these notions.

This, however, is no longer part of Jewish education. We have allowed the spirit of Halacha to be flattened and have incorporated this dullness into the way we teach our children. We have made Judaism common instead of an astonishing experience. No wonder many of our young people drop their Judaism!

Only after we have cultivated this God-awareness can we start speaking about proper halachic observance, the goal of which is to take this cognizance and introduce it into every level of our lives. The fact that we see an unhealthy emphasis on rituals, but a disregard for matters that relate to ethical standards, proves our point.

Violence, a severe dislike for non-Jews, and financial corruption within certain segments of the religious community, all of which are not even properly and fiercely condemned by some influential rabbinical authorities, are the obvious results of this escape from God in the name of Halacha.

If religious Jews would really experience the awesome presence of God, how would it be possible for them to engage in these practices? Is it not most remarkable that rabbis who suggest slight changes in Jewish rituals for the sake of greater religious devotion are condemned as heretics and non-Orthodox, while the so-called Orthodox Jews who violate major tenets on the ethical side of Judaism are still considered to be Orthodox?

WHY ARE YOU RELIGIOUS?

When conversing with yeshiva students, I often ask them how many years they have spent learning in yeshiva and how many *masechtot* (talmudic tractates) they have studied. Once they tell me that they have mastered a good portion of the Talmud, I ask them what they would answer if a secular Jew or a non-Jew would ask them why they are religious. Nearly all of the students react with total indignation and are completely taken aback by this question. They have no answer.

When I ask them how it is possible that after so many years of intensive study of religious texts they are still incapable of responding, the answer I usually hear is that they have never thought about these questions, nor have their teachers ever discussed these matters with them. Topics such as religion, God, and the meaning of life are taboo in many yeshivot. The half-hour spent on *mussar* (ethical) literature is, for the most part, nothing but lip service. These topics are treated like *chukat ha-goyim* (the ways of the non-Jews), and too inferior for Jews to discuss. They are certainly seen as inferior to the legalities of Talmud study. On several occasions I have challenged their teachers or *Roshei Yeshiva* (the heads of rabbinical academies) about this. Most of them, although not all, avoided my questions by telling me that more Talmud learning or "another *Tosafot*" (classic commentary on the Talmud) would do the trick.

They were sincerely convinced that this was the solution to the problem. When I showed them the inadequacy of such an answer and kept pressuring them, it became crystal clear that they themselves were deadly scared of these topics.

GOING OFF THE *DERECH?* SURE!

The policy was to ignore these issues and bury one's head in the sand. When their students abandon yeshiva and, in today's parlance, "go off the *derech*" (abandon halachic observance), the teachers are totally surprised. But is this not obvious? What else should we expect?

God's voice needs to be heard rising from the text, but we have long stopped teaching our students to hear it. It has been replaced with ceremonies, "observance," and *chumrot* (stringencies), but not with holy deeds. God is of no importance unless He is of supreme importance, said Heschel.

In fact, many yeshivot will skip – and not without pride – all non-halachic texts in the Talmud, such as the aggadot (talmudic legends, folklore, and religious/spiritual insights), which in fact deal with the most important dimension of halachic living – the religious transformational purpose of the Halacha. By ignoring these texts, they are sending a message to their students, not only that this part of the Talmud is inferior, but that authentic religiosity is of little value.

Teachers do not seem to realize that although Halacha may be able to inform man how to act in any given situation, it cannot provide insight into the quality of a given act, nor can it provide a sense of spiritual change that is the result of the performance of, or adherence to, a specific dictate. The power of aggadic and other non-halachic material is in preventing mechanical observance and freeing man's spirit, as well as in suggesting what one's religious aspirations should be all about. Halacha is only the minimum of these religious aspirations. Religious non-halachic material allows the unseen to enter the visible world and was formulated to give man the ability to go beyond the realms of the definable, perceivable, and demonstrable.

THE FAILURE OF THE BRISKER APPROACH

Methods such as the Brisker approach to Talmud learning[1] – today immensely popular in many yeshivot – have in fact made this experience nearly impossible. While *chakirot* (conceptual inquiries concerning talmudic concepts) and even *pilpul*[2] may give spice to the discussion, they are unable to draw the students' attention to the existential meaning of what, religiously, needs to be accomplished through their engagement with these texts. This is a tragedy of the first order, for which Orthodoxy pays a heavy price. Precisely that which needs to be its most important goal has been totally dismissed and buried under the weight of halachic discourse.

Another most important issue, which should be central to halachic conversation, is the Jews' obligation to be "a light unto the nations." The Jewish people have been called upon by God to be the instrument through which He enters into the lives of all people. The universal purpose of *Am Yisrael* is to inspire and to transform. This has serious consequences for how Halacha should be applied and, above all, how it should be taught. Almost no halachic authority seems to make this a central point when dealing with halachic issues.

Most of Halacha is decided by focusing solely on the exclusive needs of the Jewish people. Universalistic issues are ignored. While some profound Chassidic thinkers, and people like former Chief Rabbi Avraham Yitzchak ha-Kohen Kook, dealt with these issues when writing non-halachic works, I can think of only Chacham Ben-Zion Uziel, the former Sephardi Chief Rabbi of Israel, who incorporated the universalistic mission, as expressed by the prophets, in his halachic decision-making.[3]

Most present-day Halacha is self-centered and often created under the pressures of our *galut* experience and defensiveness, instead of being a

---

1. A highly analytic – nearly mathematical – approach to the talmudic text, developed by the venerable R. Chaim Soloveitchik (1853–1918) of the town of Brisk.

2. See Mordechai Breuer, "Pilpul," in *Encyclopaedia Judaica*, ed. Michael Berenbaum and Fred Skolnik, 2nd ed., (Detroit: Macmillan Reference USA, 2007), 16:161–163. Originally it was a systematic approach, often involving an intricate halachic discussion, which later was carried to extremes and resulted in excessive hairsplitting. One is reminded of the words of the Maharal of Prague, R. Yehuda ben Betzalel Loew (1520–1609), who claimed that those who see the essence of study in sharp-witted *pilpul* show disrespect to the Torah and are spending their time erroneously, and would do better to learn carpentry. See Maharal's commentary *Derech Chaim* on *Pirke Avot* 6:7.

3. See Marc D. Angel, *Loving Truth and Peace: The Grand Religious Worldview of Rabbi Benzion Uziel* (Northvale, NJ: Jason Aronson, 1999).

powerful cry of protest against the tediousness of our modern world.[4] What is urgently needed is prophetic Halacha.

Indeed, one of the most serious complaints made by young, searching Jews when they study Halacha is that there is an absence of the notion of mission and concern for the rest of humankind. This flattens the Halacha in ways that do great damage to its very image.

The contents of this essay are only the tip of the iceberg. Left unchecked, mainstream halachic Judaism will become more and more irrelevant in the years to come, except for a small but growing community of religious Jews. The more the latter will dedicate their lives to Halacha, the more the rest of our people will be detached from it, for the very reasons the religious Jews get more involved: the stabilization of and self-satisfaction with halachic living.

Halacha has become a platitude instead of being a great spiritual challenge. Our thinking is behind the times.

---

4. See Eliezer Berkovits, *Ha-Halacha, Kocha ve-Tafkida* (Jerusalem: Mossad HaRav Kook, 1981).

Three

THE MEANING AND MYSTERY
OF HALACHA

Chapter 7

The Ideal and Idyllic
A View of Halacha as Musical Notes

INTRODUCTION

A young scholar completed his learning of the entire Talmud for the third time. Full of enthusiasm, he ran to tell his teacher the good news. "Rabbi," he announced proudly, "I've just been through the whole Talmud for the third time."

"That's wonderful," replied his teacher. "But let me ask you one question. How many times has the Talmud been through you?"

This story encapsulates the tension of living a halachic life and simultaneously being spiritual and spontaneous. We all know that Jewish religious life is defined by observance of Halacha – a specific set of rules that dictate the dos and don'ts of our behavior. The scope of Jewish Law is all-encompassing, covering every aspect of life from business to diet to interpersonal relations, and while it can be argued that Jewish Tradition includes certain articles of faith, nevertheless the person defined as a religious Jew is the one who lives – or at least tries to live – by the rules and regulations of Jewish Law. Jews may feel proud to be Jewish, they may relate to Judaism culturally, or they may find intellectual stimulation in certain aspects of the Jewish Tradition, but acting "Jewishly" ultimately boils down to one thing: observing Halacha.

The problem with this definition is that many of us feel it is a mistake to so narrowly circumscribe Judaism in this way. Why, after all, does being a religious Jew have to be defined by observance of Jewish Law? Many people are spiritually inclined and would like to consider themselves religious, but find that the mundane practicalities of Jewish Law run counter to the development of spirituality. They question what happened to all the lofty emotional and spiritual elements of life that religion is supposed to help us experience. There appears to be little emphasis on emotive expression, on the contemplation of the metaphysical, or on delving into the transcendent within halachic living. Judaism seems to glorify only *deeds*.

Judaism's emphasis on the deed raises a further issue. The demand for conformity that is inherent in Judaism's focus on regulating behavior impinges on our modern sensibilities; it contradicts our perception of ourselves as independent-minded, mature, and progressive individuals who are capable of making our own decisions. We do not feel that we need to be told how to tie our shoes[1] or when to wash our hands, yet the Halacha seems to assume that we cannot make these types of decisions for ourselves.

There is hardly a single act in our daily routine that does not fall within its purview. It seems we are being told we must relinquish our own ideas in favor of rote compliance. Where, then, is there room for individuality and the spiritual expression that is unique to each and every soul?

Even for those who do accept upon themselves the obligation to live by these rules, and see spiritual value in them, the minutiae of Jewish Law can too easily destroy its mystique. Just thinking about the sheer number of commandments can become burdensome. There are 613 mitzvot in the Torah, but as Rambam writes, even these are only the roots.[2] Each mitzva then branches out into tens or even hundreds of halachot, leaving us with a code of thousands upon thousands of laws, each telling us something else to do or not to do. The extent of Jewish Law can make even the most devout Jew feel bound by fetters.

What is the purpose of all these laws? Why are there so many of them, and how are we supposed to relate to them properly? Are we meant to be like the young scholar of our story, who finds satisfaction in the simple performance of the laws and the fulfillment of his duties, or rather, as his rabbi seems to intimate, should we be striving for a more spiritual transformation that will make us into nobler and more dignified individuals? Herein lies the tension. Are we supposed to go through Judaism, or is Judaism supposed to go through us?

---

1. See *Shulchan Aruch*, *Orach Chaim* 2:4.
2. Rambam, introduction to *Sefer ha-Mitzvot*. See also R. Avraham, brother of the Vilna Gaon, *Ma'alot ha-Torah* (NY: Shulsinger Bros., 1946), 5–7.

Although we can be sure that this problem existed from the moment that Moshe received the Torah at Sinai ("We shall do and hear"), it was Paul of Tarsus, in the New Testament, who identified the problem and consequently sought to wage war on Halacha. He, and later, his many followers, were convinced that humanity cannot approach God through the merit of their deeds. What was needed, rather, was purity of the heart, and absolute faith. The secret to salvation lay within the emotional dimension of human existence, the apostle claimed. All the good deeds in the world won't help, because God judges what your heart feels, not what your body does.

Paul claimed that because Judaism failed to recognize this basic fact, it actually failed as a religion altogether, and had nothing left to offer humankind. According to Paul, Judaism's insistence on adherence to Halacha was actually its undoing.

Later on, others also sought to break away from traditional Judaism on the basis of this complaint. The movement for Reform Judaism lodged their objection during the nineteenth century, and followed through by doing away with many of the mitzvot. This was not only done so as to make Judaism more compatible with modern life, but also because they believed that traditional Judaism missed the spiritual and spontaneous dimension. The Reformers wanted to emphasize Jewish ethical and spiritual imperatives, as well as the keeping of those mitzvot that have "kept the Jewish people" – however those may be defined – but they argued that all other mitzvot could and should be done away with. As with Christianity, the change was viewed as transforming Judaism from a cult of action to a religion of feeling and freedom.

SPINOZA'S CRITIQUE

Secular philosophers have also written about this problem. Their arguments were spearheaded in the seventeenth century by none other than Baruch Spinoza, who hailed from the Jewish Spanish-Portuguese community in Amsterdam. Although he had been raised as a Jew, Spinoza broke away from his ancestral roots. He was one of modernity's first true "free thinkers" in that he was neither bound by a tradition, nor by any particular religious conviction.

Of all modern thinkers, Spinoza is most famous for his rejection of

Jewish Law. His complaint, however, was not unique. As many others did before and after him, he viewed Judaism as a kind of religious behaviorism that idolizes outward action at the expense of inner devotion. He lamented that the ultimate goal of the religious Jew seemed to be mere conformity to the minutiae of the law. Spinoza claimed that Judaism had no space for "lofty speculations nor philosophical reasoning." He continued, "I should be surprised if I found [the prophets] teaching any new speculative doctrine which was not commonplace to those Gentile philosophers."[3] He believed that "the rule of right living, the worship and the love of God was to them [the Jews] rather a bondage than the true liberty."[4]

Thus ran Spinoza's critique of Judaism. Since he penned those words, almost every secular philosopher who has had something to say on the subject of Judaism has echoed his criticisms. Immanuel Kant even went so far as to claim that Judaism is "eigentlich gar keine Religion" (actually not a religion at all).[5]

RELIGIOUS FREEDOM

Despite these naysayers, there remains a flipside: those who have seen the virtue in this very aspect of Judaism. It was the eighteenth-century Jewish philosopher Moses Mendelssohn who praised Judaism for not being a revealed religion, but rather a revealed law. "The spirit of Judaism," wrote Mendelssohn, "is freedom in doctrine and conformity in action."[6] Judaism offers flexibility. If you are a rationalist, study Talmud, Rambam's *Moreh Nevuchim*, and *Mishne Torah*, his code of Jewish Law. If you lean toward mysticism, be a Chassid. If your bent is metaphysics, find an outlet in Kabbala. But the flexibility ends where your deeds begin – your actions may not depart from Jewish Law.

As we have seen, those like Paul and Spinoza read the situation differently. They claimed that Judaism offered "freedom" in these matters simply because it had no clear spiritual path to offer. Instead of directing the soul heavenward, it bound the body earthward. Hence Mendelssohn's liberty was Spinoza's bondage.

---

3. Benedictus de Spinoza, *A Theologico-Political Treatise*, chap. 13, in *The Chief Works of Benedict de Spinoza*, trans. R.H.M. Elwes (London: G. Bell and Sons, 1883), vol. 1.

4. Ibid., chap. 2.

5. Immanuel Kant, *Die Religion innerhalb der Grenzen der blossen Vernunft* (Berlin: Akademie-Ausgabe: 1914), 6:125.

6. Moses Mendelssohn, *Jerusalem*, chap. 2, quoted in Abraham Joshua Heschel, *God in Search of Man: A Philosophy of Judaism* (NY: Farrar, Straus and Cudahy, 1955), 322.

YIRMIYAHU'S PROCLAMATION

Beyond the actual delineation of hundreds of mitzvot that we find in the Torah, there is a dramatic, even shocking episode in the book of *Yirmiyahu* (Jeremiah) that seems to support this interpretation of Judaism's unwavering focus on law to the exclusion of connecting to the Divine. The prophet Yirmiyahu, who is considered to be the author of *Echa* (Lamentations), lived at the time of the destruction of the First Temple and was the period's main seer of doom. The Jewish people had gone astray, and the ultimate punishment was about to come – the destruction of the Temple and exile to a foreign land. It was Yirmiyahu's tragic task to try to convince the Jews to repent.

With a bitter and broken heart, he chastised the Jewish people at God's behest, speaking for Him: "Oti azavu ve-Torati lo shamaru" (They have forsaken Me and neither do they observe My Torah).[7]

When we pay close attention to the words of Yirmiyahu's rebuke, there is something strange about them. If the Jewish people had abandoned God, of course they must have done so by discarding the Torah. One could hardly have the one without the other. So why is there a doubling of the rebuke here? What is the difference between abandoning God and forsaking His Torah? This apparent textual anomaly led the Midrash to seek a deeper meaning to Yirmiyahu's words – a reinterpretation of his prophecy. What he was really proclaiming, says the Midrash, was this: "Halevai Oti azavu ve-Torati shamaru" (Would that they forsake Me and keep My Torah).[8] It seems that God would rather have the Jews keep the Torah than maintain their belief in Him!

Could this possibly be the ultimate statement of Judaism? Be an atheist, be an agnostic, even believe in another religion, but as long as you observe the mitzvot you are considered a good Jew? If that's truly what Yirmiyahu was saying, then those who criticize Judaism for its obsession with human acts are, in fact, correct. How can Judaism be a religion if it makes no more demand on its adherents than to just do what it says to do? No belief, no feeling – just action. If that is the case, then Kant was right after all – Judaism is not really a religion!

---

7. *Yirmiyahu* 16:11.
8. *Echa Rabba*, Buber ed., *Petichta* 2; JT *Chagiga* 1:7, 66c.

BE HOLY

Anybody who studies Judaism seriously will see that there is more to Judaism than just observing the mitzvot. It is too simplistic to claim that God merely expects the Jew to perform certain actions by rote. The mitzvot have a certain ideology behind them, an aim to which they are constantly driving those who observe them. So what is this much sought-after but enigmatic goal?

When we look into the Torah, one goal seems to stand out among all the others: holiness, or *kedusha*. Over and over again in the Torah, God implores the Jews to be holy. One example is what the Torah says concerning the mitzva of wearing *tzitzit* (ritual fringes on a four-cornered garment): "In order that you will remember and perform all My commandments and you will be holy unto your God."[9]

Clearly the point is that performing this physical act, wearing *tzitzit*, is supposed to make men holy. Judaism has its own unique understanding of holiness. In order to appreciate it, we must banish any preconceived notions that come to us from other sources. That said, the Jewish concept of holiness is admittedly difficult to define without oversimplification. Like love and beauty, we can only really tell what it is when we experience it. While the Torah itself fails to give us a definition, we could perhaps make the following suggestion: Holiness is that which a person experiences when he or she lets God into their thoughts, feelings, and actions (Heschel). The experience is ineffable but highly recognizable for those who experience it. It is a powerful encounter with the Creator. It leads to an internal transformation that brings with it both elation and elevation.

No doubt, many people would like to be holy. The only question is how to achieve this goal. It is often maintained that one can reach it by utilizing some kind of meditation. While Judaism does have a tradition of meditation, and both Chassidism and the Kabbala hold it in very high regard, it is not a major aspect of Jewish Tradition. Nowhere in the Torah does God say, "If you want to be holy, go and meditate."

The Torah does, however, give instructions on how to become holy. We've already seen one of them, above, regarding the wearing of *tzitzit*.

Here's another: "For I am the Lord your God, you shall sanctify yourselves and you shall become holy, for I am holy and you shall not defile

---

9. *Bamidbar* 15:40.

yourselves . . ." What makes us unholy? Continues the Torah: ". . . by [eating] any creeping creature that crawls on the ground."[10]

The Torah is making a most unusual, even strange claim. It is telling us that if we want to be holy, then one of the ways to achieve this goal is by avoiding eating creeping creatures. At other instances the Torah forbids the eating of impure animals, such as swine. It seems to imply that by refraining from consuming these creatures, one will be sanctified to God. In general, the dietary laws are seen as ways to become holy.

The only problem is that it's very difficult to see the connection between keeping kosher and being holy. History is full of examples of Jews who kept kosher – entire villages and towns of them – but it would be hard to claim they were *all* holy people.

As said, we believe that holiness is about recognizing God in everything and experiencing Him with everything. In seeking holiness we are supposed to try to be like God and draw ourselves close to Him. How could all this possibly be accessed merely through our physical actions, through such simple things as the food we eat?

THE CONFLICT BETWEEN THE BODY AND THE SOUL

To answer this seeming paradox, we need to ask a question: What is the relationship between the body and soul? And let us pose this question not only to Judaism, but also to two other important traditions: Christianity and the Western-philosophical tradition. In this way we can sharpen our understanding of Judaism by way of comparing and contrasting it with other ways of thinking.

Nearly all traditions agree that humankind possesses both body and soul, and that we strive to find an expression for our souls, to feel its imprint on our being. However, this task too often proves a challenge, as the desires of the body can thwart the loftier aims of the soul. How to resolve this conflict between the body and the soul is the principle objective of nearly every major philosophy of life. How we live, what we live for, and how we relate to the world around us, all depends on our answer to this question, and the answer varies depending on the tradition.

The following summaries concerning Christianity and the Western philosophical tradition, will, of necessity, contain some generalizations. They are presented here with the utmost respect, with no intention of

10. *Vayikra* 11:44.

downplaying the breadth or scope of these traditions; I am aware that they encompass a wide range of beliefs and ideas. Nevertheless, there are common threads and patterns. In a broad sense then, what do these traditions teach about how to resolve the conflict between the body and the soul?

THE CHRISTIAN APPROACH

Christianity, as represented by Paul and major theologians such as Thomas Aquinas and St. Augustine, offers a very distinct answer to our question.

When it came to the body/soul conflict, the Church fathers claimed that resolution was simply beyond human capacity. Body and soul are engaged in a constant struggle, and neither can reach any satisfaction through that which the other desires. In order to advance spiritually, traditional Christianity claims that one must completely subdue the body. Save your soul, said the Church fathers, because you cannot save your body – it is too attached to the pleasures of this world. The ideal lifestyle mandated by this outlook was internally very consistent. Christian leaders and monks were expected to take vows of celibacy and poverty, and to separate themselves from worldly affairs. Since there was no way of sanctifying the body, it simply had to be ignored, at least as much as possible.[11]

The classical Christian position seems quite pessimistic. There is no hope of resolving the conflict between body and soul. However, from the perspective of our experience, this view is quite realistic. How often do we struggle with the desires of the body going against our more lofty aspirations? The Church fathers were certainly on the mark when they recognized that this is, indeed, a significant problem. They also recognized that not all Christians would be able to achieve the total subjugation of their bodies, and therefore allowed some space for bodily needs, such as a sexual relationship, but only within marriage. However, this was definitely seen as a compromise of the ideal.

THE WESTERN-PHILOSOPHICAL APPROACH

The Western-philosophical tradition has a very different approach. Here it is correct to consult the father of this tradition, the philosopher Socrates. Socrates' philosophy has been made known to us mainly through the writings of Plato and Xenophon, his students. It is clear from these

---

11. See Aquinas, *Summa Contra Gentiles*; Augustine, *Sermones post Maurinos reperti*.

writings that Socrates also struggled with the question of body and soul and how to resolve the conflict between them. He was certainly not a materialist who relegated humanity to the sphere of earthly matters. Rather, he grappled with the issue of how the human being might best live his life, both spiritually and physically.

The method Socrates taught to resolve the body/soul conflict is a two-step process. The first step is to follow a path of intellectual discovery in search of the "good life" – the proper way by which all are supposed to live. Once the mind, the seat of the soul, has discovered this truth, all that remains to be done is to inform the body about it. At this point, the body will be so overwhelmed by the beauty and depth of the truth presented to it by the intellect, that it will follow its advice more or less automatically. Socrates therefore prescribed a life of philosophical investigation, and put great faith in the ability of education to raise humanity's moral standards. The world he envisioned was ruled by philosopher kings who were so conquered by their own enlightenment that the dictates of the body simply would not hold any sway, the body having become a willing slave to the insight of the intellect.[12]

But if Christianity is realistically pessimistic, Socrates was unrealistically optimistic. The flaw in his hopeful but rather naive reasoning is not too difficult to demonstrate. Imagine someone who wanted to become a gold-medal Olympic swimmer but had never before set foot in a pool. Socrates' advice would probably be to tell him to go to a university; not to its pool, but to its library. "Learn as much as you can about swimming," Socrates would tell him. "Really become an expert in the subject, and then inform your body about it." Now imagine that our friend proceeds to follow Socrates' advice, earns his BA in dog paddle, and then goes on to do a master's in advanced breaststroke. Ultimately, he defends his doctoral thesis, which is entitled, "Sink or Swim: Toward a New Theory of Recreational Buoyancy." He has a doctorate in swimming, but what would happen when our professor actually gets in the pool? He is more likely to drown than he is to win any race!

Training our body to do that which our mind knows to be true is unfortunately not as easy as Socrates made it out to be. The most convincing argument will fail to move the stubborn sinner, because we do not automatically do what is right just because we know it to be so. The body, with

---

12. For a discussion, see Eliezer Berkovits, *God, Man, and History: A Jewish Interpretation* (Middle Village, NY: Jonathan David, 1959), chap. 10.

all its complex drives and desires, offers strong resistance to the counsel of the soul.

THE JEWISH APPROACH

Judaism's response to both these traditions is that while there is much to say for each, both are wrong because they are too radical.[13] The truth lies somewhere between the two extremes advanced by the Church fathers and Socrates. Judaism agrees with Christianity that the struggle between body and soul is very problematic; however it is not hopelessly insoluble. But whereas Western philosophy maintains that we can easily resolve this conflict, Judaism counters that it is not quite so easy. The task of training the body in the ways of the soul, of sanctifying the body and its desires, presents perhaps the most difficult challenge known to human beings. It may indeed take an entire lifetime to achieve, but it is not impossible.

What then is Judaism's answer to this dilemma? If it can indeed be done, how do we make the body receptive to the conditioning of the soul? Judaism claims, first of all, that the body and the soul are not completely separate entities. Rather, the human being consists of a composite of the two, within which it is difficult to tell where one ends and the other begins. The body and the soul constantly interact with each other. Therefore, whatever a person thinks or feels will be reflected in their actions, and conversely, everything that a person does will influence their thoughts and emotions (Heschel).

It is this latter point that is most crucial for understanding how people work. How do actions influence the spirit? The idea here is that external actions awaken the internal being. Our deeds create a mentality; they infiltrate our subconscious mind in ways that ultimately shape who we become. Whereas good intentions and nice feelings will not necessarily produce morally correct behavior, if you behave "correctly" you will eventually come to feel the right feelings and think the right thoughts.

The reason Judaism stresses the importance of law, and places so much emphasis on the conformity of action, is *not* because it believes human beings' deeds to be the sum total of their existence, but rather because deeds are the key to all the other facets of their being. As the Torah makes clear when it tells us, "You are to know this day and place it upon your heart that

---

13. For further explanation, see Berkovits, *God, Man, and History*, chaps. 11–12.

the Lord He is God,"[14] spiritual growth starts with intellectual realization, but it does not end there. What we experience is a process of "becoming real" with our knowledge, of truly making it a part of us. That transformation only comes about through one means: action. For Judaism, once a person performs "holy deeds," holiness enters one's very being.

SPIRITUAL CHANGE THROUGH PHYSICAL ACTION

Once, on a visit to America, I was sitting in my hotel lobby minding my own business when I was approached by two men who wanted to know if I was a rabbi. When I told them that I was, without asking for any further credentials, they proceeded to tell me their story. The two men were Vietnam War veterans and they had a question that they specifically wanted to ask a rabbi, because so far no one else had been able to help them.

Both men had been raised in America with strong Christian values, particularly as regards the sanctity of human life. As they were growing up, they had never thought of hurting a fellow human being. Certainly they never imagined ever killing anyone. So you can imagine their terror when, upon being sent into battle in Vietnam, they were given orders to kill the enemy. Nothing could have been so incongruous with their upbringing or so repulsive to their very natures.

At first they resisted their orders. But under the duress of their commanding officers, they were eventually forced to comply. The first time, it was torture for their souls. The contradiction between their beliefs and their actions was almost physically painful. They felt they would never be able to live with themselves again. But after a short while, the killing got easier. Too easy. Even enjoyable. Things deteriorated to the point that murder became a game to them. They would even compete to see who could kill the most; so far had they fallen.

As they stood before me, they admitted with heavy hearts that they had lost all feeling for the sanctity of human life. The sensitivity they had felt in their youth toward others had not returned to them once they had re-entered civilization. They admitted to me that they felt as though they could kill anybody on the street and not feel an ounce of regret. What they wanted me to teach them was how to get that feeling back; the feeling that life is holy and not to be violated. Their spiritual leaders and psychologists had not been able to help them – could I?

---

14. See *Devarim* 4:39.

I did not give them Socrates' advice. All the books on philosophy, psychology, and poetry would not help them regain that lost feeling of compassion. Neither did I tell them that their mission was hopeless. I gave them, rather, the advice that Judaism offers. I told them to get involved with helping others, to do *acts* of lovingkindness – what we call *chesed*. "Volunteer in a hospital or an old age home," I advised. "Just start *doing* things for others and you will slowly begin to recognize life's sanctity once more. The deeds will create a new mentality and bring out the thoughts and emotions that you did not even know were hiding there."

In this way I could offer these men a means to try to reverse the process that they had already undergone. Actions had desensitized them, and only by action could they regain what was lost.

ONE'S HEART IS DRAWN AFTER ONE'S ACTIONS

The same is true of all mitzvot, not just *chesed*, acts of kindness. Performing a mitzva is not merely a religious rite or a symbolic act. When we perform the mitzvot, we *become* them. If at the outset the heart and mind are not engaged, by performing the actions the appropriate thoughts and feelings will be aroused. These acts slowly begin to mold our consciousness around the ideas that they seek to impart. Each act closes the gap between what we are supposed to do and that which we are supposed to be.

This is essentially the advice given by *Sefer ha-Chinuch* (The Book of [Mitzva] Education), usually attributed to Aharon ha-Levi of Barcelona (probably 13th century), as its author expounds upon Judaism's philosophy of action:

> Know that a person is influenced according to his actions. His heart and all his thoughts are [drawn] after his deeds in which he is occupied, whether good or bad. Thus, even a person who is thoroughly wicked in his heart, and every imagination of the thoughts of his heart are only evil the entire day – would he arouse his spirit and set his striving and his occupation with constancy in Torah and mitzvot, even if not for the sake of Heaven, he would veer at once toward the good, and with the power of his good deeds he would deaden his evil impulse. For after one's actions is the heart drawn.[15]

---

15. *Sefer ha-Chinuch*, mitzva 16.

At first the body will not naturally take to the conditioning of the soul, but after an initial push, the external actions will eventually strengthen the internal feelings. These feelings will then gain more control over the actions that gave rise to them in the first place, in an escalating spiral of spiritual enhancement. Ultimately the body will conform to the demands of the soul.

Obviously this is easier said than done, and it is difficult to believe that it will happen automatically. If the human spirit is not open, or if it somehow denies the development of these feelings, they may not be able to have an effect on the actual psyche. It is only when there is an openness and a desire for such a change that a deed can have its effect. Of course, while there may be laws, there is no ritual to ensure that one will pay one's taxes instead of evading them. But by constantly acting in an honest way in all matters, and doing acts of kindness toward one's fellow man, one creates a mentality whereby it will become more and more difficult to evade one's taxes.

One is reminded of William James' observation: "Could the young but realize how soon they will become mere walking bundles of habits, they would give more heed to their conduct while in the plastic state. We are spinning our own fate, good or evil, and never to be undone."[16] Habit is capitalized action. It becomes conscience. As Henri Bergson said, "It is then right to say that what we do depends on what we are; but it is necessary to add also that we are, to a certain extent, what we do, and that we are creating ourselves continually."[17]

INTERNALIZING THE MEANING BEHIND THE MITZVOT. THE "AS IF" ATTITUDE

There is a famous story told about a holy Chassidic rebbe. His students were so impressed with his level of piety that they assumed he must fast several times a week. Seeking to follow in his footsteps, they approached their rebbe and asked him, "Our master, our teacher, how many times a week do you fast?" The rebbe turned to them with surprise. "Why, none," he said. "I do not fast at all." "Then how many times a year do you fast?" they asked. "I'm sorry," said the rebbe, "you did not understand me. I do not fast at all – ever!" The students were taken aback. They had no doubt

---

16. William James, *Principles of Psychology* (London: Macmillan, 1891), 1:127.
17. Henri Bergson, *Creative Evolution*, trans. Arthur Mitchell (NY: Random House, 1944), 9.

that at the very least, as Jewish Law requires, the rebbe must be fasting on Yom Kippur, the Day of Atonement, and on Tisha be-Av, the national day of mourning for the destruction of the Temple and other calamities in Jewish history. It could not be that they fasted on these days and their holy rebbe did not.

Reading the confused looks on their faces, the rebbe began again. "Let me explain," he said. "Do not get me wrong. I certainly do not eat on Yom Kippur, and neither do I eat on Tisha be-Av. But it is not because I am *fasting* on those days. I just do not eat and drink on those days! On Yom Kippur there is *no time* to eat. I am too busy praying and trying to repent for my sins. Who has time to eat? And on Tisha be-Av, a day on which so many calamities happened, I simply have *no appetite*. Who could eat on such a day? So, you see, I never fast."

There is a commandment not to eat on Yom Kippur or Tisha be-Av, but that is only so that we can become aware that we would not be *able* to eat or drink if we realized the true awesomeness of these days. The fact that many of us *would* be able to eat and drink on these days requires a law forbidding us to do so.

But if we truly understood that we have only one such special day a year on which to gain atonement and purification, drawing ourselves ever closer to God, we would hardly entertain the notion of squandering the time with a meal. And if we were able to perceive the depth of tragedy behind the events that transpired on Tisha be-Av, then we would honestly be too upset to stomach any food.

So, the Torah and our sages respectively tell us to act *as if* we have no time to eat or *as if* we have no appetite on these days. They do so based on the understanding that after some time practicing acting in this way, we will begin to internalize the meaning of the action. As the Talmud says, "Mi-toch she-lo lishma, ba lishma,"[18] – the performance of the deed without the proper intention will eventually lead to the performance of the deed with the proper intention. The Torah tells us to do the mitzvot so that we do not come to see spirituality as something external to us. We are called on rather to internalize it, by first doing. Once we start performing the mitzvot, we begin to *think* the mitzvot, we begin to *feel* the mitzvot. Ultimately, as the holy rebbe was trying to teach his students, we *become* the mitzvot.

---

18. *Pesachim* 50b. For further understanding of this talmudic principle, see R. Chaim of Volozhin, *Nefesh ha-Chaim*, gate 3, section b, chaps. 2–3.

Besides this, there is also an educational message: The fact that the Torah requires an external deed such as fasting teaches human beings that they should really reach higher and dream of the day when there will no longer be a need for a command to fast, but that fasting will naturally follow from their very beings. Would the Torah not command this, they would not be aware that they should even aspire to such a dream.

CREATIVITY THROUGH CONTROL

Now we are able to understand the necessity of having so many positive commandments – our actions guide us toward the realization of their inner meanings. But what we have yet to explain is why Judaism places so many restrictions on our behavior as well. Granted that our thesis, reversed, also holds true: destructive actions guide the soul toward a corrupt character. But there is more to it than that.

When I was growing up, people used to say that if you wanted to be creative all you had to do was "let go." It was assumed that the way to unleash creativity was to shed all limitations and "go with the flow." But reality proves otherwise. Most of the time, letting go only makes us less focused and more confused. The range of options overwhelms us. The truth about creativity is that it is not born out of the chaos of a lack of boundaries, but rather from the devotion of discipline. True creativity is, as Abraham Joshua Heschel once said, "an emotion controlled by an idea."[19] It is the ultimate triumph of form over undeveloped matter.

I remember as a schoolboy in Amsterdam being taken to see the paintings of the Dutch artist, Rembrandt van Rijn. My teacher at the time was fascinated by a certain painting of his and took us to the museum to see it. The painting happened to be a portrait of the prophet Yirmiyahu crying over the destruction of the Temple. The teacher did not discuss the meaning of the painting. Rather, he instructed us to look closely at the hair on Yirmiyahu's head. As I moved my face as close as I could to the painting, I was stunned by how real it looked. Rembrandt had painted each and every hair individually, each strand a creation of its own. It literally looked alive, as if it were growing before my eyes.

Can you imagine what it might have been like to sit with Rembrandt in his studio, watching him paint such a portrait? Watching each tedious stroke of his tiny paintbrush, you could be forgiven for thinking he was

---

19. Heschel, *God in Search of Man*, 300.

not doing anything at all. What control he must have had, what restraint! Certainly he could never have created that masterpiece just by letting go. Only a master of the trade, with an incredibly skilled and disciplined hand, could have painted such an astonishing work. It was Rembrandt's control that facilitated his creativity. Limitations, far from being a hindrance, are what allow us to focus our creative potential.

The artist who perhaps most epitomized this concept of creativity was the great composer Johann Sebastian Bach. Those who carefully study his music will discover that Bach dealt with music as Judaism deals with law. Bach was totally traditional in his approach to music. He adhered strictly to the rules of composition as understood in his day, and nowhere, in any of his works, do we find any deviation from these rules. But what is most surprising is that the volume of Bach's musical output was not only unprecedented, but, above all, his compositions were astonishingly creative. According to many, he was the greatest composer of all time. After carefully listening to his *St. Matthew Passion*, anyone with a background in music would readily admit that it is one of the most sophisticated compositions ever written within the Western tradition of classical music.

What we discover is that the restrictions Bach imposed upon himself – to keep to the traditional rules of composition – allowed him to become the author of outstandingly innovative music. It was from within the "confinement of the law" that Bach was able to burst out with unprecedented creativity. What Bach proved more than anything else was that it is not by novelty alone that one reaches the heights of human creative potential, but by the capacity to plumb the depths of that which is already given. Bach's works were entirely free of any innovation, but utterly original.

To work within the constraints and *then* to be utterly novel – that is the ultimate sign of greatness. That is what Johann Wolfgang von Goethe, the great German poet and philosopher meant when he said: "In der Beschränkung zeigt sich erst der Meister, / Und das Gesetz nur kann uns Freiheit geben" (It is in limitation that the master really proves himself, and it is [only] the law which can provide us with freedom).[20] Bach, then, was a "legal" giant of the first order. He realized that the adoption of a well-defined system does not force one to forfeit spiritual profundity. On the contrary, the defined system gives expression to the greatest spiritual potential.

---

20. Johann Wolfgang von Goethe's sonnet "Natur und Kunst, sie scheinen sich zu fliehen" ("Nature and Art, they go their separate ways") in *Was wir bringen* (Tübingen: J. C. Cotta, 1802).

EVERYONE IS UNIQUE

Music has more to teach us about how to relate to our tradition. This lesson is drawn from a personal encounter I had a number of years ago. A neighbor of mine in Yerushalayim is a music teacher. In the summer, when all the windows are open, the sounds of his violin would enter my home. They were uninvited, but certainly not unwelcome; on a hot summer's eve I found refreshment in the grace of these free concerts.

One summer, he was instructing his pupils in a particular section of one of Mozart's violin concertos. As teachers do, he taught it over and over again. I listened to him play that piece so many times that, by summer's end, I must have known it by heart.

Some time later, as chance had it, I saw an advertisement for a concert: the violinist Yehudi Menuhin was to perform the very same symphony. I thought to myself, *Wonderful. I'll go and hear Yehudi Menuhin play, and I'll even be able to correct him if he makes any mistakes.* So I went to the concert, but I returned very disturbed. Menuhin's rendition of Mozart's concerto did not sound remotely like the piece that my neighbor had been playing all summer. I simply could not understand. The notes were the same, but the music was completely different.

I decided to seek out my neighbor and ask him to explain this strange phenomenon to me. Was it the instrument that made it sound different, or perhaps the concert hall acoustics, or was I just entirely mistaken?

He told me that actually it was all very simple. "What you heard," he explained, "was a completely different piece of music." "But it wasn't," I assured him. "The program said that it was the same symphony that you were playing." "It might have been the same violin concerto," he said, "but it certainly was not the same piece of music. You see, when I play Mozart, I take Mozart's notes and play Mozart. But when Yehudi Menuhin plays, he plays Menuhin and borrows the notes from Mozart."

It was for this reason, he went on to tell me, that someone like Yehudi Menuhin would never get bored of playing the same piece of music over and over again. When one is truly creative, it is never the same piece twice. The notes may be the same, but the vibrations and the music will always be new and unique each time.

LA-MENATZE'ACH (FOR THE CONDUCTOR)

Around 3,300 years ago, a unique symphony was composed for an ensemble of no less than two million people. Its Composer invited His conductor into His chamber at the top of Mount Sinai. It was at this apex of history that God handed over to Moshe the masterful score upon which the Jewish people were to play the music of life. God taught him exactly how it needed to be played, not a note more and not a note less. But the vibrations, intonations, interpretations of these notes were up to the musicians standing at the foot of the mountain. "We will do, and we will hear"[21] means that "one hears in the doing."[22] And although the divine voice spoke the same words to all, nobody heard the same musical sounds because this depended on the kind of soul each one had.

Every Jew is a musician. They play their spiritual music on a musical instrument called Halacha. We have been given the notes and it is left to us to bring them alive. If we seek creativity, the notes are anything but a burden. They are, rather, a guide. And while it may be easier to just play whatever comes to mind, ultimately we have to step back and listen to the sounds we are making. Sitting down at the piano, if one hand plays the music of Mozart while the other just slaps at the keys randomly, we can be sure that the overall effect will sound less than melodic. Sticking to the notes on the sheet might prove difficult, but in the end it is the only way to make real music. Far from being restrictive, it will facilitate the release of the most robust creativity.

What critics of Judaism did not comprehend when they criticized Jewish Law was that rules, when deeply contemplated and internalized, become the impetus for a special kind of creativity and spirituality, never to be found by those who reject such limitations. As any student of Jewish Law can testify, the study of Halacha and a life lived according to its teachings is one of the most creative of all human endeavors.

THE SIGNATURE IN THE CORNER

So, what did Yirmiyahu mean when he said to the Jewish people that it is better to be an atheist who observes the Torah than a true believer who does not? Let us listen to the words of the Midrash in full: "Would that

---

21. *Shemot* 24:7.
22. Franz Rosenzweig, *On Jewish Learning*, ed. N.N. Glatzer (Madison: University of Wisconsin Press, 1955), 122.

they forsook Me but still observed My Torah, since by engaging with it, the light that lies therein will bring them back [to Me]."[23]

God need not worry if we disregard Him, as long as we still observe His mitzvot. Somehow He knows that if we continue to perform these deeds, we will eventually come back to Him. It is inevitable that we will be drawn to seek out God just by following the dictates of the Torah.

How long can you play God's music without actually meeting Him? Do you have to be a trained artist to appreciate sublime beauty? Walk up to a painting in a museum and, whether or not you recognize it as a Rembrandt, you will recognize the genius of the one who created it. We first judge art by the depths of its aesthetic appeal, and only then do we look for the artist's signature in the corner.

God saw that performing the mitzvot would bring out such a beautiful expression of our true selves that we would want to know who it was who told us to live by them. And once we reach that point, how much longer will we remain atheists or agnostics?

Human beings' hearts are drawn after their actions. What one does will ultimately be what one is. In the realm of spiritual growth, action takes precedence because it alone is the medium of personal transformation. But not all actions produce the same effect. Halacha is the musical score that molds our actions into a symphony of the divine.

We may start by borrowing notes that perhaps we would not ourselves have written, but when we play them with compassion, the sounds they make will soon resonate within us. And at the moment when we start to hear the music of our own souls issue forth, there can be no doubt that its Composer was also our Creator. Critics of Judaism, like Paul or Spinoza, simply do not understand that Judaism's "obsessive" emphasis on Halacha is the very route to man's spirit and feelings.

---

23. *Echa Rabba*, Buber ed., *Petichta* 2; JT *Chagiga* 1:7, 66c.

Chapter 8

Halacha as the Art of Amazement

INTRODUCTION

In the way that man observes the world and interacts with it, he reveals one of the most surprising and impressive sides to all of human existence: the faculty of appreciation. When walking through a landscape he can be overwhelmed by its beauty. Wondering at the sky, standing at the seashore, or viewing the sunset, he becomes aware of an inner, uplifting experience that he cannot verbalize. Enjoying the music of Mozart, Beethoven, or Paganini, man can be lifted to unprecedented heights. Through the constant search for beauty, harmony, conformity, and so forth, man confirms his unique place in this universe. But even in the "small moments" of man's life, he shows an unusual appreciation for his surroundings. When choosing the interior of his home or the color and style of his clothes, he will carefully select colors, patterns, and specific combinations. Many hours, if not days and months (or years), are spent on this endeavor. For most people this is far from a waste of time, but rather a deep emotional need that enriches their lives.

Things must "go well," flow into each other, and create a picture of great harmony, tranquility, and beauty. One blotch of paint will not inspire us, but a certain combination of them definitely does. One musical note is boring, but the flowing of many of them within a certain pattern will make a symphony that can bring thousands of listeners to exaltation. Art collectors will pay large amounts of money to become the owners of paintings

* An earlier edition of this essay was originally published in Nathan Lopes Cardozo, *Between Silence and Speech: Essays on Jewish Thought* (Northvale, NJ: Jason Aronson, 1995), 151–163. Reprinted by kind permission of Jason Aronson.

that are often no larger than a few square centimeters. Some paintings are valued at millions of dollars and are viewed by hundreds of thousands of human beings, who are often prepared to travel long distances to view them. The world of haute couture has, for hundreds of years, produced an infinite amount of elegant (and not so elegant) garments of all kinds and fashions. Instead of man tiring of all these efforts and getting bored, he is deeply involved in all this, searching for every possible new way to make sure that beauty and novelty will always be with him.

HOW DID WE GET LIKE THAT?

Let us ask: How did we get like that? Rudolf Otto and many others have already made us realize that we cannot adequately explain why we enjoy music or fall in love with a painting or the seashore.[1] Indeed, what is there about beauty that makes it beautiful? What is there so great about a van Gogh, or the music of Beethoven? Is there not a certain absurdity to all this? How is it that we can hear more than one musical note at a time? And why is it that we do not just hear the different notes together, but also apprehend them as a unity? We somehow grasp them. We are conscious of the music and its beauty. There is indeed a faculty called appreciation. But what is this faculty made of? The American philosopher G.N.M. Tyrrel, writing about "reading," reminds the reader of this most miraculous faculty of the human being:

> A book we will suppose, has fallen into the hands of intelligent beings who know nothing of what writing and printing mean, but they are accustomed to dealing with the external relationships of things. They try to find out the laws of the book, which for them mean the principles governing the order in which the letters are arranged. . . . They will think they have discovered the laws of the book when they formulated certain rules governing the external relationships of the letters. That each word and each sentence expresses a meaning will never dawn on them because their background of thought is made up of concepts which deal only with external relationships, and explanations to them means solving the puzzle of these external relationships. . . . Their

---

1. See Rudolf Otto, *The Idea of the Holy*, trans. John W. Harvey (NY: Oxford University Press, 1958).

methods will never reach the grade of significance which contains the idea of meanings.[2]

Why do we associate sounds with meaning? How is it that meaning-less shapes are capable of triggering within us the concept of meaning? Perhaps the most outstanding example of man's mysterious nature is the experience of love. If we could imagine a creature from outer space looking at the human body, what would he see? Probably one of the most repulsive creations walking around in the cosmos. "Deformed" organs such as protrusions of flesh hanging on both sides of some kind of round-ness or enlarged balloon on top of the human body. In the middle of this oval shape, called a head, there is another extension placed between two items of glass, and below, a hole into which man disposes of all sorts of substances (which by outer space standards may have a most offensive taste!). Legs and arms will be described in most uncomplimentary terms. Most astonishing of all would no doubt be the fact that these "monstrous" creations fall in love with each other, fight wars because of jealousy, and like to have intimate relationships that result in producing even more of these unsightly creatures. Why, indeed, do we not consider music an ab-horrent experience, a Rembrandt painting the ravings of a hideous human creativity, or lovemaking a most repulsive act?

AMAZEMENT

This, in fact, touches on the very core of religion and the problem of secu-larism. Western civilization has a very specific approach to life. It is highly pragmatic. Matters are basically seen from a purely utilitarian point of view. Everything is measured by result-getting standards. What matters is whether things "work." Humans have become tool-making creatures for whom the world is a gigantic toolbox for the satisfaction of their needs. Satisfaction, luxury, and pleasure are man's goals. Everything is calculated, and there is supreme faith in statistics.

This has caused possibly the greatest problem of our times: the tragedy of existential indifference, missing out on exactly that which is no doubt the most exciting side of life – the *mysterium tremendum* that lies behind all existence, behind every move man makes, behind every human expe-

---

2. G.N.M. Tyrrel, *Grades of Significance* (London: Rider, 1930), quoted in E.F. Schumacher, *A Guide for the Perplexed* (London: Harper Colophon, 1977), 42.

rience. It is in the invisible part of life that the real flow of life runs; that which the five senses cannot grasp or touch. But modern man takes notice of what surrounds him and tells himself that everything will be explained. Man looks to the skeleton but does not see the content and the essence. Maurice Nicoll describes this very well when he discusses the fact that humans cannot even see themselves or their fellowmen:

> We can all see another person's body directly. We see the lips moving, the eyes opening and shutting, the lines of the mouth and face changing, and the body expressing itself as a whole in action. The person *himself* is invisible. . . . If the invisible side of people were discerned as easily as the visible side we would live in a *new humanity*. As we are, we live in visible humanity, a humanity of appearances. . . . All our thoughts, emotions, feelings, imaginations, reveries, dreams, fantasies are *invisible*. All that belongs to our scheming, planning, secrets, ambitions, all our hopes, fears, doubts, perplexities, all our affections, speculations, ponderings, vacuities, uncertainties, all our desires, longings, appetites, sensations, our likes, dislikes, aversions, attractions, loves and hates – all are themselves invisible. They constitute "*oneself.*"[3]

Nicoll insists that while all this may appear obvious, it is not at all overt:

> It is an extremely difficult thing to grasp. . . . We do not grasp that we are invisible. We do not realize that we are in a world of invisible people. We do not understand *that life before all other definitions of it, is a drama of the visible and the invisible.*[4]

When I plant grain, my main interest is that it is alive and not dead. But that life I cannot see, touch, or smell. An unconscious cat, even though still alive, is not a real cat until it regains consciousness. This is what philosophers call "inner space." The matter itself, however, is mysterious. "Analyze, weigh and measure a tree as you please, observe its form and function, its genesis and the laws to which it is subject, still an acquaintance with its essence never comes about."[5] What strikes us with total

---

3. Maurice Nicoll, *Living Time* (The Netherlands: Eureka Editions, 1998), 3–4, quoted in Schumacher, *A Guide for the Perplexed*, 33.

4. Nicoll, *Living Time*, 5, quoted in Schumacher, *A Guide for the Perplexed*, 33.

5. Abraham Joshua Heschel, *Man Is Not Alone: A Philosophy of Religion* (NY: Farrar, Straus and

amazement is the realization that what lies within our reach is actually beyond our grasp; there is something about the qualitative aspect of nature that is totally beyond our comprehension. Everything is more than the sum total of its parts. One is aware of it, but it is beyond description or comprehension. Even the very act of thinking baffles thinking: the most incomprehensible fact is that one can comprehend altogether. That which one can apprehend, one cannot comprehend. That which one takes account of, cannot be accounted for! "The search of reason ends at the shore of the known. We sail because our mind is like a fantastic sea shell and when applying our ear to its lips, we hear a perpetual murmur from the waves beyond the shore."[6] And only through the awareness of this mystery does man start to live. Only then can one experience what real life is all about. The beginning of happiness lies in the understanding that life without the awareness of mystery is not worth living. Why? Because all life really starts in wonder and amazement! Being struck by the impenetrable mysterium of all being, the soul becomes reawakened. As if struck by fire, man is taken by a radical amazement. *This is the beginning of all genuine religion.* Because of man's astonishment with the world and himself, he recognizes the masterly hand of God. He ponders over the grandeur and sublimity of God. When seeing God as the foundation of all mystery, he starts to feel Him in his bones, in all that he does, feels, thinks, and says! As has been said, the tendency to take everything for granted and the indifference to the sublime is the root of all irreligiosity. It is a path toward the secularization of the world. *Religion is a protest against taking things for granted.* It is the art of living in amazement.

HALACHA AND MYSTERIUM

To be aware of the total mystery of all matter, to feel it, to breathe it, is obviously not an easy task. To become aware of the great secret behind all being is no doubt an art. How does man capture the notion of wonder and amazement and inject this into one's very life? Some people sense these qualities at distant intervals, in extraordinary events, but can one capture it in every moment? This, I would suggest, is only possible by capturing the mysterium and transforming it into a way of living. This is the purpose of the Halacha: to experience the mysterium in and through

---

Giroux, 1951), 6.
    6. Abraham Joshua Heschel, *God in Search of Man* (NY: Farrar, Straus and Giroux, 1983), 47.

commonplace deeds. Halacha is the art of revealing the nonhuman side, the meta-human side, the divine dimension through the medium of every human act. Halacha is there to teach us that our humanity is utterly inexplicable, that man should stand trembling before God. Judaism teaches that proper deeds lead to correct and true thinking. Deeds create mentality: the actual deed of killing creates a mentality to kill, the distribution of charity creates a mindset to care for one's fellow. Likewise, certain deeds have the power to make man walk through life in the awareness of the mysterium behind all human existence.

By giving deeds a certain direction, they become sensitized to the notion of mystery. By living according to Halacha, we hold back and allow for a moment of reflection. It creates a mindset not to take anything for granted, but to become amazed by the very deed that follows. The dietary laws make man take notice, while eating, of the very wondrous existence of food, by making a *beracha* on the miracle of eating. It stalls a deed, giving it an opportunity to transcend being a commonplace act and to become a higher deed. It causes a new, profound reflection on life. Consequently, it provides for a different and more dignified way of living. It makes man take notice of his deeds and his life and ask, why am I acting? What is the meaning of a human act and, therefore, of life?

What is there in the human deed that it should be the main carrier of this message? Is action the most important manifestation of human life? Why is philosophical reflection without the deed not good enough? Did not the Greeks contemplate the mystery of life without the Halacha? Does one really have to act, so as to know?

It is in the deed that man meets himself. In deeds man becomes aware of what his life is really all about: the power to harm, to wreck, and to destroy, but also the possibility of deriving joy and bestowing it upon others, of relieving or intensifying one's own and other people's tension. The deed shows man who he really is and not what he would like to be. Here his own self is exposed: what man does not dare to think, he shows in his deeds. The "real" heart of man is revealed in his deeds. Man may have lofty ideas but behave like a criminal. History teaches that noble ideas are no guarantee for noble deeds. And since God provided man with a world in which noble deeds are by far the most powerful ways to build and fashion this world, it is the deed that counts. No noble thought ever changed this world for the better if it did not become a noble deed. Metaphysics is not known for giving birth to noble deeds. But even when philosophical speculation would conduce man to act nobly, it would slowly evaporate into thin air if it did not go hand in hand with a firm and continuous commitment to a pragmatic deed. It is the deed that upholds the thought.

It should be added that such an approach will only bear fruit when these deeds are constantly repeated. No human deed will leave its mark if done only once. To become effective it must grow into some kind of a habit as the result of its having rooted itself in the deep consciousness of a person. Things continually done come to be done subconsciously.

Habit is capitalized action. Habit becomes conscience. For this reason alone Judaism sees the deed as the key to teach humankind to recognize the mysterium. By way of rituals, blessings, and so on, often done in a habitual way and becoming second nature, people will subconsciously open themselves up to the experience of amazement. Obviously, this is no guarantee. Deeds, even when they carry the potential to reveal the mysterium, do not automatically result in a greater awareness. This will always depend on the person's consciousness. Only when someone wills it to happen will the subconscious mind activate this potentiality.

What it does, however, is to lay the subconscious foundation of this awareness, so that if a person should wish to capitalize on it, they may – thus enabling them to realize the wondrous aspect of human existence. In other words, a halachic life is not a guarantee that one will become consciously aware of the need to be amazed. One can live a halachic life without any notion of amazement. But what is important is that the Halacha gives us the option so that if one wants, one can achieve amazement, since this plants in the subconscious the seed for amazement. We turn our subconscious mind into an instrument that will take notice of the mysterium.

Halacha makes man aware of the uniqueness of time. It is in time that man meets God. Every second that passes by is never to return. This makes time extremely precious. Consequently, it must be handled with the greatest of care. It teaches man that there are no insignificant moments or deeds. Whatever is done by man is to be done within the framework of an encounter with God. This requires that every deed be done with the awareness that one stands before the Lord of the Universe and that every little matter, however unimportant in the eyes of man, counts. It is done in the presence of the King!

A NEW AWARENESS

The aim is to infuse purely subjective emotions, needs, and desires with a new awareness – one that otherwise is almost congenitally foreign to the entire component of the human personality. The religious system of Judaism, which disciplines the Jew in every situation all through life, establishes habitual patterns of bodily reaction and conduct that testify to an acute awareness of an order of reality that is not of the body. In this sense it liberates us from taking things for granted. This liberating act is a means, not a guarantee that it will result in a higher consciousness of amazement.

When a Jew is overcome with nausea at the sight of non-kosher food, such a reaction is not natural; it is not in keeping with the laws of normal human experience. The reaction shows the awareness of some outside will that his personality has acquired. In a sense, the nausea reflects the partial transformation of the natural desire for food into the desire for that which is beyond man. It has often been said that Halacha requires mechanical, ritual performances. What is more important, the conscious worship of the mind or the quasi-automatic performances of the body? This is a question based on an utterly mistaken conception of the human personality.

The human being is made of body and soul. The body cannot worship consciously, and the mind is incapable of serving by way of ritual. The human being is not only body or soul; he is the result of both and therefore in need of serving God in a way that corresponds to the body as well as to the soul, each according to its own nature. On the level of the soul, the relationship to God is spiritual and conscious, but there is no place for action. On the level of the body, there is no place for "conscious" worship. It can only be materialized into action. Only a combination can lead to an appropriate result.

In the deed, the mitzva is the union of the two. The mitzva is never only thought, nor is it a mere reflex action. The mitzva is a deed that is of the spirit and of the body at the same time. The subconscious conditioning toward the will of God and the *mysterium tremendum* is brought about by continuous conscious suggestion. Halacha is designed to make our lives compatible with our sense of the mysterium. What counts is not if it is compatible with common sense or the "obvious," but if it is compatible with that which is unspoken. What it wants to accomplish is to bring together the passing with the everlasting, the momentary with the eternal.[7] And only through the human deed, transformed into a mitzva, will it

---

7. Abraham Joshua Heschel, *Between God and Man: An Interpretation of Judaism from the Writings of Abraham Joshua Heschel*, ed. Fritz A. Rothschild (NY: Free Press Paperbacks, 1997), 183.

accomplish that task – to bring eternity into that person's life, to redeem God's power in every human experience, to discover divinity within one-self. Once it has done so, it is capable of turning every human deed into a mitzva.

TO DESERVE[8]

The fact that we are capable of taking action, building, investigating, and enjoying, and are aware that we can only take account of these abilities, but cannot account *for* them, challenges us with another unavoidable question: Do we deserve these faculties? No normal person is without some regard for truth, beauty, and love. But can we make any claim on them? The shattering truth is that we do not deserve them. Nobody ever earned the right to love, to enjoy. No one ever obtained these faculties through their talents or abilities. They are gifts, not rewards earned. We experience countless things and not one of them is truly earned. This is most embarrassing! We eat from Somebody's table without giving it a thought. Our first concern should be: Do I deserve all this? How can I make myself worthy of it all? Indeed, how will we respond to all these undeserved gifts? Without response there is no dignity! Love obligates; we must react by discharging our debts to God. Only through that will we gain dignity. This is another aspect of halachic life. By living in ac-cordance with Halacha, we acknowledge God's ultimate gifts. We find and recognize God's fingerprint on every single thing. By honoring God's power in this world, we sanctify all our deeds and become worthy of life!

Love becomes law in the life of the beloved. To become aware that he is the recipient of genuine love, man imposes upon himself disciplines – the dos and the don'ts – that make him worthy of this love. This is, in fact, the hallmark of the mature human being. God's love becomes God's commandment. Moral consequences follow, not without struggle and dif-ficulties, not without the constant need to revise and rethink. With hard work, the heavens open and this awareness of the mystery becomes man's experience.

---

8. See Dudley Weinberg, *The Efficacy of Prayer* (NY: Jewish Chautauqua Society, 1965), re-printed in Jakob J. Petuchowski, *Understanding Jewish Prayer* (NY: Ktav, 1972), 121–137.

Chapter 9

Religious Authenticity and Wonder in and Beyond Halacha

INTRODUCTION

Things that are alive constantly move and grow. Organic matter that fails to grow, shift, and move, decays and eventually dies. So it is with the human being. A man or woman who does not strive to grow and transform him or herself, who does not live with passion and excitement, is one who is not fully living. Such people merely exist and survive on our planet. Like all of God's creations, they must experience seasons of their souls – cycles of change and renewal.

Jewish philosophy sees God primarily as the constant Creator. As we say in the morning prayers, "Every day He (re-)creates the works of the beginning." And since human beings are "created in the image of God,"[1] it follows that they, in their essence, must also be creators. A person who is not constantly engaged in creative endeavors denies his or her nature.

The role of religion is to facilitate the blooming of the soul, and to prevent the human being from descending into spiritual stagnation. Genuine religion should implant a consciousness in human beings that helps them actualize their creative energy, thus allowing them to emulate their Creator at the highest level. One of the most powerful ways that religions accomplish this critical goal is by training their followers in the art of wonderment.

---

1. *Bereshit* 1:27.

VEILED LOGIC

In a fascinating passage in the Torah concerning Moshe's descent from Sinai, we learn about one of his most remarkable initiatives:

> When Moshe descended from Mount Sinai, with the Tablets of Testimony in Moshe's hands; as he descended from the mountain, Moshe did not realize that the skin on his face became radiant when he spoke to Him. Aharon and all the Children of Israel saw Moshe, and behold! Moshe's skin had become radiant; and they feared to approach him. Moshe called to them and they came to him – Aharon and all the princes of the assembly – and Moshe spoke to them.
>
> After that, all the Children of Israel would approach, and he would command them regarding everything that God had spoken to him on Mount Sinai. After Moshe finished speaking to them, he placed a veil on his face. When Moshe came before God to speak with Him, he would remove the veil until his departure, and then he would leave and recount to the Children of Israel what he was commanded. And the Children of Israel would see Moshe's face – that the skin of Moshe's face was radiant. Moshe would put the veil back on his face until he came to speak with Him.[2]

What was the purpose of this veil? Why did Moshe need to hide his radiance? It seems that Moshe concealed his shining face when he spoke with the people. This would make sense since the people, and even his own brother Aharon, were afraid to approach him. The glow from Moshe's face overwhelmed and paralyzed the people who beheld it. As such, one might conclude that the main purpose of the veil was to allow the people to be close to Moshe without fear or intimidation.

A deeper analysis of the text, however, suggests a very different reading. A second look reveals that Moshe actually removes the veil in the presence of *Bnei Yisrael* (the Children of Israel), and puts it back on his face only *after* speaking with them. The Italian preacher Rabbi Azaria Figo (1579–1647), in his classical work *Bina le-Itim*, provides a fascinating insight into this episode.[3] What was God's intention when he caused Moshe's face to become illuminated? Moshe did not need to be convinced of the fact that

---

2. *Shemot* 34:29–35.
3. *Bina le-Itim*, sermon no. 28.

he had received the word of God. Therefore, the rays of light emanating from Moshe's face must have conveyed a necessary message to the people regarding Moshe's religious integrity, authenticity, and authority. Above all, Moshe's incandescent countenance was meant to invoke a religious *joie de vivre* in the hearts of the Jewish people, and to thoroughly energize them with spiritual verve.

The radiance allowed the Jewish people to be newly inspired every time they looked at the face of their leader and teacher. The supernatural glow ideally would have kept the Jews in a permanent state of religious amazement. This was critical since God communicated His word through Moshe over a period of time. Thus, Moshe's face reminded the people of the source of the commandments, and ensured that they received God's laws with the right attitude. The awe they felt while listening to a human being whose face was alight with spiritual energy allowed them to experience each communication as if it were the first – with a sense of novelty and excitement. God's messages captivated them completely, as Moshe delivered the Word in all its nuanced complexity.

Of course, we all know that human beings can become desensitized to astonishing stimuli very quickly. How many of us still marvel at our ability to speak to our friends via cell phone? How many of us are awed each time we profit from the convenience of the Internet? So too, if the people saw Moshe walking around the camp with a radiant face all the time, the effect would have worn off. Only by revealing his face sporadically, on special occasions, could the phenomenon continue to astonish, as it did when Moshe first came down from the mountain. For the radiance to stay radiant, it had to be hidden. Familiarity breeds contempt!

So when Moshe walked through the camp, he wore his veil.[4] In this way, the people never got the chance to become desensitized to the experience of hearing communication originating from the Creator of the Universe, nor did they doubt their teacher's legitimacy.

THE TEMPLE GATES

The prophet Yechezkel saw the following vision concerning the third and future Temple:

---

4. It seems that Moshe's mask was a kind of hair-thin covering which did not completely hide his face.

And on the *Mo'adim* (Festivals) when the *amei ha-aretz* (common people) came before the Lord (in the future Temple) – whoever enters by the northern gate to bow low shall leave by the south gate, and whoever enters by the south gate shall leave through the northern gate. They shall not go back through the same gate by which they came in, but shall go out by the opposite one.[5]

Rabbi Yosef Yavetz (c. 1440–1505), in his classic commentary on *Pirke Avot*, asks what purpose it served to have people enter and leave through different gates. He writes, "God was particular that man should not see the same gate [of the Temple] twice. Lest he see the gate as he sees the door of his house."[6]

If people became overly familiar with the House of God, it would cease to serve one of its most valuable purposes. The Temple invoked in man a sense of great wonder. While inside the Temple, the Jewish people witnessed many miraculous occurrences that sensitized them to the hidden miracles manifested in their everyday lives.[7] This sensitization process began with the Temple gates.

An object we observe twice, especially within a short span of time, already begins to lose its aura. In spiritual matters, this presents a serious problem. Since even a second encounter carries the seeds of familiarity and ultimately boredom, one should (for the sake of his connection with the Creator of the Universe) try never to see anything more than once. Of course, the best way to combat this problem, since we obviously must all traverse the same paths many times as we go about our routines, is to see things always with a new eye and a sharper understanding. Since we cannot provide ourselves with an ever-new environment to stave off our mental weariness, we must change our perception and ourselves so that we notice new aspects, details, and depths in the things we've seen on numerous occasions before. The Temple was the ultimate worldview elevator; after being inside, it was virtually impossible not to see the world in a completely new light.

Rabbi Yosef Yavetz sees this issue at the center of the Golden Calf incident.[8] Somehow the Israelites got too familiar with Moshe and became

---

5. *Yechezkel* 46:9.
6. R. Yosef Yavetz, *Perush Masechet Avot* (Warsaw: Yitzchak Goldman, 1880), 11 on *Pirke Avot* 1:4.
7. See *Pirke Avot* 5:5.
8. Yavetz, *Perush Masechet Avot*, 11.

desensitized to his unprecedented greatness and religious authenticity. They therefore desired a new spiritual conduit and believed erroneously that they could generate it themselves. This attempt to replace Moshe was their very undoing. Had they made themselves into deeper perceivers of reality instead, they would have recognized that below the surface, their leader Moshe was a spiritual giant. Precisely because the Jewish people failed to appreciate what they already had, God blessed Moshe later with his astonishing facial radiance.

Not only did the people take Moshe for granted, the community also lost their awe of God. In a sense, the Golden Calf was also an attempt to replace God with a new and therefore more exciting spiritual entity.[9]

FREQUENT MIRACLES

In his *Michtav me-Eliyahu*, Rabbi Eliyahu Eliezer Dessler discusses the modern world's conception of the phenomenon we call "nature." He explains that modern man, as a rule, has come to believe that the laws of nature are fully explainable by science. This, however, is a mistake, and both religious thinkers and also many great scientists agree that science is in fact extremely limited in its explanatory powers. According to Rabbi Dessler, the laws of nature do not really exist as such, but are only indicative of the way the universe interacts with the human perceptual apparatus.[10]

Moreover, what we perceive as hard and fast laws of nature are actually the result of God's miraculous re-creation of the world in every moment. It is *frequency* that leads us to put our faith in the laws of nature. After all, how do we discover these laws? When we observe a phenomenon enough times and see that it repeats itself constantly and consistently, we form a belief that this is the way the world behaves. But what we really observe in such cases is the frequent repetition of a miracle.

If, during the course of human history, only a single comet had ever streaked across the night sky, we would be as much astonished by that anomaly as we are by the splitting of the Reed Sea in Moshe's days. Likewise, if we witnessed a constant repetition of the Reed Sea parting on a regular cycle, we would ultimately conclude that splitting oceans are part

9. For a full explanation of this issue, see Nathan Lopes Cardozo, *Between Silence and Speech: Essays in Jewish Thought* (Northvale, NJ: Jason Aronson, 1995), chap. 1.

10. See R. Eliyahu Eliezer Dessler, *Michtav me-Eliyahu* (Jerusalem: Kiryat Noar, 1963), 1:177–183.

of the natural course of events, and as such we would explain the phenomenon within the framework of some newly derived natural law. And
such is the case with all natural laws, that they do not really explain the
underlying causes for anything. Rather, they simply describe in a logical
way the regular processes that happen around us.[11]

SCIENCE IS TENTATIVE

Professor Karl Popper (1902–1994), one of the great philosophers of
science in the twentieth century, draws attention to the fact that the laws
of nature are not reducible to elementary experiments, as far as logic is
concerned. The reason is that we can never test our theories completely.
The truth of the statement that *"all* copper conducts electricity" really
depends on our ability to check *all* the copper that exists in the universe.
Clearly then, within all statements of natural law, there is some element of
faith involved. Popper writes regarding scientific knowledge that:

> Science is not a system of certain, or well-established, statements; nor
> is it a system which steadily advances towards a state of finality. Our
> science is not knowledge: it can never claim to have attained truth, or
> even a substitute for it. . . . We do not know: we can only guess. And
> our guesses are guided by the unscientific, the metaphysical (though
> biologically explicable) faith in laws, in regularities which we can un-
> cover – discover. . . . The old scientific ideal of *episteme* – of absolutely
> certain, demonstrable knowledge – has proved to be an idol. The de-
> mand for scientific objectivity makes it inevitable that every scientific
> statement must remain tentative forever.[12]

In a dramatic statement, the famous scientist Max Planck (1858–1947)
provides us with a completely different and equally important viewpoint
on what scientific inquiry essentially is:

> The feeling of wonderment is the source and inexhaustible foun-
> tainhead of the desire for knowledge. It drives the child irresistibly

---

11. It has been argued that the Big Bang theory would on the basis of the above not be "scientific" since it lacks frequency. Scientists have however argued that the theory is based on the fact
that one is able to trace this moment back because of the physical effects it had on the universe,
which we continue to experience. In that sense it does rely on frequency.

12. Karl Popper, *The Logic of Scientific Discovery* (London: Routledge, 2002), 278, 280. See also
chap. 1.

on to solve the mystery, and if in his attempt he encounters a causal relationship, he will not tire of repeating the same experiment ten times – a hundred times – in order to taste the thrill of discovery over and over again. . . . The reason why the adult no longer wonders is not because he has solved the riddle of life, but because he has grown accustomed to the laws governing this world picture. But the problem of why these particular laws, and no others, hold, remains for him just as amazing and inexplicable as for the child. He who does not comprehend this situation, misconstrues its profound significance, and he who has reached the stage where he no longer wonders about anything, merely demonstrates that he has lost the art of reflective reasoning.[13]

DOGMATIC FALLACY

The surest way to suppress our ability to understand the meaning of religion is to take our world for granted. Likewise, one of the most important tasks of genuine religion is to protest against such an attitude. Modern man has fallen into the trap of believing that everything can be explained. Even if he doesn't understand what he perceives around him (e.g., light, life, death, weather patterns, etc.), he has faith in the power of science to reveal, order, and master nature. Since he believes that all enigmas can be solved, modern man considers amazement to be a function of primitive ignorance. Few people fully understand the fallacy of this worldview.

The history of European thought, even to the present day, has been tainted by a fatal misunderstanding. It may be termed the Dogmatic Fallacy. The error consists in the persuasion that we are capable of producing notions which are adequately defined in respect to the complexity of relationship required for their illustration in the real world. Canst thou by searching describe the universe? Except perhaps for the simpler notions of arithmetic, even our most familiar ideas, seemingly obvious, are infected with this incurable vagueness. Our right understanding of the methods of intellectual progress depends on keeping in mind this characteristic of our thoughts . . . During the medieval epoch in Europe, the theologians were the chief sinners

13. Max Planck, *Scientific Biography and Other Papers*, trans. Frank Gaynor (NY: Philosophical Library, 1949), 91–93.

in respect to dogmatic finality. During the last three centuries, their pre-eminence in this habit was inherited by the men of science.[14]

Life is only worth living when one lives in wonder, because consciousness of existence and all its mysteries elevates and gives meaning to our experience. Science and reason cannot explain anything to its core. Physics can tell us about the Big Bang, but not *why* the Big Bang occurred or *why* it happened. And so too for all the other "whys." Why is life propagated through the union of sperm and egg? Why are there seven colors in a rainbow? Why are things this way and not any other? To ask the deeper "why" is to wonder. And humankind was given a superior mind in order to spend life in a perpetual state of wonderment. With a little concentration, people can and must reach the recognition that everything, without exception, is baffling, including the very fact that they can be baffled. Even the act of thinking should amaze us. Our ability to reason scientifically is a complete mystery, which of course implies that those who faithfully believe that science will one day develop a complete theory of everything have "lost the art of reflective reasoning."

A *BERACHA* IS A STATEMENT OF ASTONISHMENT

To remain in the state of appropriate wonderment, we must develop a capacity to look deeper and deeper, so that we can always find something new in everything we encounter. Without developing our ear for music, we become bored at hearing a composition for the second and third time. One does not gain a greater appreciation for a painting by simply staring at it. In Judaism, we hone our ability to perceive the transcendent in our everyday reality by making a *beracha* whenever we partake of food or drink. Jews make *berachot*, which are statements of astonishment and recognition of the remarkable and amazing complexity that surrounds us, whenever we see a new fruit tree, wear a new garment, smell a pleasant fragrance, etc.[15]

The *beracha*, when said with concentration and feeling, ensures that we experience each day as something entirely new. Even when Jews relieve themselves, they afterward take time to thank God for giving them such a well-functioning body. This is indeed one of the most important goals

---

14. Alfred Northern Whitehead, *Adventures of Ideas* (NY: Macmillan, 1933), 185.
15. See chap. 10.

of traditional Jewish practice: to experience spirituality in commonplace deeds.

In a remarkable observation, the rabbis declared: "Redemption and the earning of bread [earning a living] may be compared to each other. There is [as much] wonder in earning bread as there is wonder in redeeming the world." Just as the earning of bread takes place every day, so too redemption takes place every day, because fundamentally, redemption means the revelation of an underlying reality which has yet to be noticed by humanity. But Rabbi Yehoshua ben Levi added: "The earning of bread is as difficult as the division of the Reed Sea," because to him, the daily repetition of a miracle is as impressive as the one-time miracle of the splitting of the Reed Sea.[16]

THE MYSTERIUM

Such an attitude should, however, not become a cushion for the lazy intellect. Just because our ability to understand reality is necessarily limited does not mean that we shouldn't seek to know all we can. Where analysis is possible, we must analyze. And where doubt is legitimate, we must doubt. All the while, though, we must remain cognizant of the fact that ultimately, we all reside within a great mysterium.

Immanuel Kant (1724–1804), in his masterpiece *Critique of Practical Reason*, expresses a similar point:

> Two things fill the mind with ever new and increasing admiration and awe the more often and the more steadily we reflect on them: the starry heavens above, and the moral law within. . . The countless multitudes of galaxies annihilates, as it were, my importance as an animal creature, which after it has been for a short time provided with a vital power (one knows not how) must again give back the matter of which it was formed to the planet it inhabits, a mere speck in the universe. The second, on the contrary, infinitely elevates my worth as an intelligence by my personality, in which the moral law reveals to me a life independent of animal-nature, and even of the whole sensible world – at least so far as may be inferred from the destination assigned

---

16. *Bereshit Rabba*, Vilna ed., 97:3; cf. *Pesachim* 118a.

to my existence by this law, a destination not restricted to conditions and limits of this life, but reaching into the infinite.[17]

COERCED BY SINAI

The Talmud[18] relates a serious dilemma the Children of Israel encountered when they received the Torah at Mt. Sinai. The incident is one of the most difficult parts of the Talmud to comprehend, and commentators throughout the ages have struggled with its meaning.

In anticipation of God's revelation, the Children of Israel "placed themselves at the mountain."[19] The Talmud, an extremely exacting grammarian when it comes to God's words, states that in reality the text does not say that they placed themselves *at* the mountain, but rather *under* (*tachtit*) the mountain. The unusual phraseology gives rise to an allegorical interpretation. The sages suggest that God "took the mountain and turned it on its top," and threatened the Israelites. "If you accept the Torah [and its commandments], then you will live, but if you do not, there will be your burial place" – right under the mountain!

The talmudic sage, Rabbi Acha bar Ya'akov, makes a surprising observation that creates major theological problems. Rather than just accept that God, who is the Lord of the Universe, can make any condition on his human creations, Rabbi Acha bar Ya'akov responds to this story with great consternation. "From here we must deduce a strong objection against the very giving of the Torah!" Rashi here explains that forcing the Israelites to accept the Torah could be considered unjust and morally objectionable. Why would God force the Jewish people into a religious commitment under duress? Is the Torah not a covenant? And does its status as covenant not imply that both parties should freely agree to its terms without any kind of coercion?

This observation however begs the question: Is *obedience* to God not at the very root of religious life? Why would Rabbi Acha bar Ya'akov, who spent his entire life trying to understand and obey God's directives for humankind, object to God forcing His will on the Jews at Sinai? We could ask an additional question: Why does God, who created the universe, and

---

17. Immanuel Kant, *Kant's Critique of Practical Reason and Other Works on the Theory of Ethics*, trans. Thomas Kingsmill Abbott, 4th revised ed. (London: Longmans, Green and Co., 1889), 260. Translation slightly modified.

18. *Shabbat* 88a.

19. *Shemot* 19:17.

gave man his role in it, need to establish a covenant to get people to do His will? Why give us any choice in the matter at all?

The most surprising part of the whole discussion is the Talmud's response to Rabbi Acha bar Ya'akov. After agreeing with the rabbi's objections, the Talmud says that the matter was rectified many hundreds of years later at the time of Mordechai and Esther (in the Purim narrative), when the Jews, after being saved from Haman's plot, accepted the Torah out of their own free will, thus rendering our covenant with God fully legitimate and in good faith from all sides.

BOREDOM AS COERCION

Lying beneath this give-and-take is our original problem of boredom and the need to experience a sense of wonder. After exiting Egypt in a barrage of miraculous plagues, and then witnessing the splitting of the Reed Sea, and eating manna, and experiencing a whole host of supernatural phenomena, the Israelites were not in the best position to really appreciate the profundity of the giving of the Torah at Sinai. Revelation for that generation was the status quo. And so, Sinai becomes a paradox.

On one level, God's entrance into the physical world in such an all-encompassing way totally overwhelmed the Israelites, so that they felt as though they were forced to accept the Torah. On another level, they were desensitized to an extent, and thus lacked the capacity to recognize each divine word as a unique expression of God's greatness. There was a deficiency of enthusiasm for the Torah and its commandments, which implies that they did not accept it as *completely* free beings. Receiving the Torah as a free-will choice does not mean having an option to refuse (because that is simply not an option), but rather to recognize the mitzvot as a source of tremendous joy and wonderment.

In the days of Mordechai and Esther, when open miracles no longer took place, the Jews were able to appreciate fully the wondrous way in which they were saved. They stood in awe of God since their normal existence was so routine. As such, the miracle of their salvation affected them like the radiance of Moshe's face affected their ancestors years before. Ironically, those who witnessed more, saw less; and those who witnessed less, actually saw more.

The Jewish custom to wear masks on Purim, when Jews celebrate the miracle of their salvation from Haman's genocidal plot, is therefore not unfounded. By concealing our faces, we remind ourselves of the need to see miracles hiding behind commonplace events. Metaphorically, on Purim, we don the veil that Moshe wore.

FUTURISTIC WONDER

For Judaism to remain a religion of wonder, we must keep an eye on the future. All living is living into the future, but of course no future is completely open. The events to come are deeply rooted in the past. Judaism, like most religions, has a strong tendency to celebrate the past. After all, the Jewish people's greatest glories and triumphs took place many centuries ago. It is only logical that Jews cling to these events. A Judaism without historic memory is therefore inconceivable.

Jewish practice must remind us that God created (symbolically) the world in six days, and that He rested on the seventh. It must focus on Avraham's remarkable personality, on the Israelites' miraculous Exodus from Egypt, and obviously on its most transcendent moment – the giving of the Torah at Sinai. Since our tradition derives from events that took place in the past, there is a strong urge to place the emphasis in Judaism on the past. And yet to do so would be to misconstrue the very essence of our religion. However significant the past may be, its value lies primarily in its ability to inform the future. To stay genuine, the epic Jewish experience must be relived, now and in the future, giving birth to exciting elements that continue to create wonder and anticipation.

Observant Jews, therefore, never memorialize their great history. Rather, they celebrate the events of their people's distant past *as if* they took place in the present day. During Pesach, the Jew sits at the Seder table and tells the story of the Exodus from Egypt in such a way that he or she re-experiences it. He is obligated to create an atmosphere in which he and his family feel as though they themselves were slaves in Egypt and are now able to enjoy freedom. The famous Chassidic saying that Pesach is not so much a festival about how the Jews got out of Egypt, but how Egypt and its mentality gets out of the Jews, beautifully illustrates the point. Halachically, Pesach has to be experienced in a way that transcends history and thereby illuminates the present.

Pesach is also a celebration of the future and the messianic times to come, since in its essence, Pesach is the festival of redemption. This is one of the great secrets of Judaism's success. Our traditions allow us to travel through time, realizing a history that has yet to take place. Religious Jews live in a constant state of anticipation and wonder. On Shabbat, while sitting at home in a state of peace, without the need to do any work, they experience a taste of what the messianic days will be like, when everyone will sit "under their own vine and under their own fig tree."[20] On Sukkot, they live under the open sky in an unstable structure, the sukka, to experience another aspect of the messianic age, when we will all have total clarity about the fact that it is God who provides for our security. Miracles that are already celebrated, but have not yet taken place, will always stay new and cause wonder.

WITHDRAWAL

It is here that we find problems in the contemporary Jewish religious situation. Over the years, Judaism has shifted to a Tradition-centric religion, focusing primarily on the past and ignoring the promise of a better or messianic future. Without an eye on its redemptive goal as a global spiritual revolutionary movement, Judaism has become somewhat withdrawn from the world. This is most apparent when we compare stories of the great sages with the situation today. Many stories in the Talmud demonstrate how much the sages were involved in their communities. They dwelled in inns, conversed with the peasants, learned with the simpletons. They were involved in commerce, even politics. Of course, they dedicated many years of their lives to intensive learning, during which they sometimes withdrew from society, but always with an intention to return. Traditionally, withdrawal was seen only as a means.

The great Chassidic rebbes interacted with the common man, became farmers, cut wood, and looked after babies when their mothers had to leave home. This was not just due to their intense love for humanity, but also because they realized that one must be involved in day to day life to stay religiously fresh. At the same time, they understood that retreat could be useful for meditation, after which they could return with a greater sense of wonder. Through withdrawal, they were able, like Moshe, to remove the masks of complacency and see the world with wonder, always from different points of view. This allowed them to be highly successful leaders. They were able to move Judaism in a direction of renewal and vibrant life, something which their Lithuanian counterparts, who developed the Mussar movement, did not accomplish to the same extent. While the Mussar movement, with its emphasis on character development, stayed a small

---

20. *Micha* 4:4.

movement, Chassidut moved millions of Jews and created empires based on lively religious experience.

EXPECT THE UNEXPECTED [21]

For Judaism to stay vibrant, it must develop an atmosphere that fosters creativity. Without growth and creative energy, religions fall away into obscurity. Everything in this world that remains static, ultimately decays. Judaism must always be open to the unexpected. This, after all, is the deepest manifestation of the awareness of God's living presence. To embrace the potential for upheaval means recognizing that so long as God runs the world, nothing is predictable. Such an attitude properly reflects the reality of God's involvement in the world.

Jewish history is full of unexpected moments coming from unexpected settings at the most unexpected times. Redemption does not spring from where we seek it, but often from situations where we expect it the least. For example, Moshe, our redeemer, stuttered. Who would ever have imagined that he would become the leader responsible for bringing down the mighty Egyptian Empire? Moshe's background logically should have caused him to side with Pharaoh in his fight with the Jews. After all, Moshe was raised by Pharaoh's daughter in Pharaoh's own home, and received a thoroughly Egyptian (i.e., anti-Jewish) education. Who would ever think that such a man would rise to become the redeemer of Israel? So too, the mashiach (the messiah), our ultimate redeemer, may not come as the result of a natural process, but as a sudden interference of God in the natural order of things. The mashiach can come in the blink of an eye, when the world least expects him. This is the wonder of the mashiach, an element that Judaism must surely maintain if it wants to stay alive to witness its fruition.

AUTHENTIC NOVELTY

Although there is a very real need for religions to be able to see things in a new way, one must be wary of novelty for its own sake. One of the greatest tragedies in modern Jewish life is that the call for novelty often has little to do with authentic religiosity. Most of the time, changes are introduced for

---

21. See Michael Wyschogrod, *The Body of Faith: God in the People Israel* (Northvale, NJ: Jason Aronson, 1983), chap. 6.

the sake of social accommodation. The Reform movement, and to a lesser extent Conservative Judaism, were often much more motivated by social and economic factors than by the need for renewed Jewish spirituality. While we will not deny that some of its spokesmen were concerned about a perceived lack of spirituality in traditional Judaism, most of the social changes in Judaism have arisen from a desire to partake in the pleasures of Western culture and to gain entrance to the country club that is "modernity."

Reading the history of German Jewry in the nineteenth century, it is clear that Reform Judaism became a new option *after* many Jews (in pre-war Germany and other European countries) had already abandoned traditional Judaism. The Reform Movement served as a retroactive justification *de jure* of what had long been the case *de facto*. As such, it did not add anything of real substance to Jewish spiritual life, which is clear from the fact that it has produced very few enlightened *religious* leaders. Neither did it create a spiritual movement, as was the case with the early Chassidim.

DIVINE REVELATION AND WONDER

Many modern thinkers argue that revelation is an impossibility. They explain away the events recorded in the Torah by claiming that our forefathers misconstrued natural phenomena as revelation due to their simple way of thinking and their lack of philosophical and scientific knowledge. A deeper look, however, may reveal a very different picture.

Scientific reasoning, while tremendously important, also has a downside. As mentioned before, scientific inquiry depends on laws that necessarily exclude the possibility for exceptions. Nature's general constancy is what allows for scientific inquiry, and for its results to be so powerful. But, revelation is revelation only insofar as it demonstrates an existence beyond the consistent order of things. For revelation to serve its purpose (i.e., to make a big impression on those who experience it), it must be extraordinary and preferably unprecedented. And so it is the "nature" of revelation to elude scientific inquiry. The moment it can be repeated or understood, the miracle loses much of its significance.

Still, we must be able to trust that what we experience in such moments is real. Unfortunately, authentic revelation lacks resemblance to other kinds of experience, and since we are trained to think in terms of categories and sameness, we adopt a Western worldview in which the extraordinary is impossible. Revelation is not so much rejected because of any proper logical reason, but rather because our minds have been indoctrinated to believe that what cannot be replicated should not be taken seriously. But this is a logical fallacy. Just because something cannot happen again does not give us a reason to claim that it could not have happened. For example, there will never be another person like you in the world, with the same genetic information and life experiences. Yet, you exist. You, and every other human being you see, are walking, talking proofs that one-time-only events can and do happen.

MIND CLOSING

Belief in revelation depends on our openness to wonder. The *a priori* rejection of revelation, based on the fact that it cannot be proven via scientific investigation, is not a sign of progressive thinking, but rather of an intellectual and spiritual stagnancy. It is too easy to be lulled into a sense that the well-defined laws and ordered progression of events constitute all that reality has to offer. In the meantime, we become mentally shut off from what can happen suddenly and without precedent. Because our forefathers were still open to the possibility of unexpected occurrences, they therefore had little reason to doubt the possibility of revelation on a grand scale. It was not their intellectual primitivism, but their open-mindedness – their willingness to see what was, rather than what they expected or understood – which gave them the capacity to wonder, and therefore to trust their belief in revelation.

NOVELTY AND LAW

Novelty poses a problem for law. The application of law would be much easier if the world was stagnant and consisted of more limited variety and endless repetition. The real difficulty arises when situations change radically, because suddenly the established precedents fail to provide enough relevant insight to make definitive judgments. In such cases, the lawmakers are forced to become creative. Such a situation exists now for the Orthodox Jewish world. There have been profound changes in the state of the world and in world Jewry since the emancipation, and even more so since the Holocaust and the establishment of the State of Israel. These changes demand creative thinking in order to render judgments on unprecedented halachic issues.

In the past, many halachic decisions were made locally. With the re-entrance of Jews into world history through the emancipation and the establishment of a Jewish State, halachic authorities were thrust into a new era, which forced them to rule on decisions of life and death on a national level. This was never before the case in the Diaspora. The halachic arguments in Israel over whether or not to relinquish parts of the so-called West Bank for security reasons, is a good case in point. Such a profound shift in such a short time span means that in some cases the law has not entirely caught up with the street. As a result, we find that it is possible to find convincing proofs for completely opposing views, which augments the confusion, especially in matters of national importance.

SPIRITUAL CRISIS AND HALACHA

Even so, the greatest problem in the Jewish world today is its haunting spiritual crisis. Unfortunately, spiritual crises are the most difficult to quell, as they concern life in its totality, and therefore demand a response that provides a personal course of action and thought, which will necessarily transcend the inherent limitations of a purely legalistic approach. A solution to our spiritual crisis must allow the unseen to enter the visible world, giving man the ability to go beyond the realms of the definable, perceivable, and demonstrable. The answer lies in our ability to cultivate wonder. But over the years this part of the Jewish Tradition has been increasingly neglected, ignored, and even denigrated.

A large percentage of the Talmud is composed of Aggada, the non-legal side of the Jewish wisdom tradition. The spiritual grandeur of the aggadic text, its magnificent understanding of Jewishness and Jewish history, and its keen insight into the nature of religion and the religious personality, are precisely what would reinvigorate the Jewish world. Unfortunately, the majority of conventional yeshivot do not focus on these sections of the Talmud. The result is that our most talented youth emerge from the yeshivot unable to guide the vast majority of Jews. In addition, many of these higher Jewish learning institutions have become sapped of real religious fervor since they do not incorporate the weltanschauung set forth by the Aggada. This is regrettable since one can often understand the depths of Halacha and ensure its proper application *only after* one has an awareness of the deeper messages developed in the world of the Aggada.[22]

22. See Nathan Lopes Cardozo, *The Written and Oral Torah: A Comprehensive Introduction,*

HALACHIC THEOLOGY

We see in Tanach that when King David and the later kings had to decide on national matters, they were guided both by Halacha and also by an understanding of Judaism as a way of life based on a theology in which God remains extremely active. Deeply religious concerns weighed heavily in their thought processes in political matters (i.e., the state and its security). Of course, for the Jewish kings, statecraft was a means to bring the people of Israel closer to God. And this is really the point – that the leaders of our distant past were able to integrate fully the implementation of Halacha with the spiritual growth and aspirations of the nation. Halachic decisions helped connect our people with God's Divine Presence. Israel's legal affairs were simultaneously (on a deeper level) journeys into the highest spiritual realms, generating spiritual breakthroughs in which the world and God came a little closer, which in turn aroused feelings of religious amazement and fervor. In this way the Halacha stayed fresh, and was therefore able to deal with new issues and unprecedented circumstances.

In our days, halachic authorities should perhaps call upon Jewish religious thinkers to help them integrate the experience of wonder and universal Jewish values into their decision-making process. Their halachic rulings would then emanate from a broader and more inclusive base. Pluralism for its own sake is not necessarily a good thing. In this case, however, the participation in halachic discussion of a wide variety of highly sophisticated and broad-thinking people of many different stripes could add legitimacy to the judge's final ruling. This would ensure that halachic decisions are more widely accepted among Jews from across the entire spectrum of religious observance. The Jewish people as a whole will come to feel that the halachic decisions coming down from its leaders are as wise as they can possibly be, which is probably the most we can ask for.

Halachic decisions must be made in the spirit of a living covenant, with the recognition that each judgment serves as a link in the ongoing rejuvenation of God's word. The Halacha should guide us in our attempts to manifest God's will while we live in a constantly changing world that continues to astonish us.

(Northvale, NJ: Jason Aronson, 1989), 167–191.

Chapter 10

The Protest of a *Beracha*

In our contemporary world it is difficult to continue being surprised. Our educational system (with exceptions) has been teaching us for several decades that everything must make sense and nothing can be left to intellectual randomness. Scientific knowledge with its emphasis on order and consistency, together with the study of human behavior and its insistence on universal psychological patterns, have hijacked our minds and convinced us that basically there is no place for astonishment.

Many of us still live with an awareness of the notion of surprise. But we have convinced ourselves that this is nothing but the result of our limited understanding and knowledge of our world. If we would have complete knowledge and insight, every phenomenon would turn into a predictable and completely cohesive fact.

No doubt our willingness to accept this view relates to our fear of confronting the many metaphysical and moral-philosophical implications which do not fit into such a weltanschauung.

This attitude has sabotaged our minds and hearts. Instead of realizing – as the great explorers and teachers of science do – that with the expansion and evolution of scientific knowledge comes a greater recognition of the inescapable mysterium behind all existence, the average human being has instead convinced him/herself that all is explainable and "under control."

To a very great extent this has led to the secularization of our worldview. The desire to escape the recognition of *mysterium tremendum* has played a trick on the minds of even the most intelligent of people. Convincing themselves that the laws of nature explain "the above and beyond" in totally rational terms, they have lost the insight which allows them to see that such laws are purely descriptive and cannot provide any ultimate explanations in the existential sense. Frequency, the basis for the estab-lishment of the laws of nature, is not a final elucidation. It can tell us what to expect, and in this sense it is a powerful tool; indeed, we can live our lives in a consistent way only because of these frequency-based laws. But it cannot give us any insight into the ultimate "why."

As philosophers of science have constantly emphasized, science does not involve itself in ontology, epistemology, or that which is beyond the experiential.

Religion in general, and the Jewish Tradition in particular, have warned us that we must avoid the stagnancy of our minds. It teaches us that we must be able to grasp an insight before it is frozen into ordinariness and reduced to something else. No greater danger exists to man's spiritual condition than stereotyping views and insights. The art is to discover the unprecedented in that which is common; to stop in the middle of a thought before it becomes ordinary and cold.

I believe that with this in mind, our sages introduced the notion of a *beracha* before we eat, drink, and involve ourselves in religious or even "common" activities. All such human activities are dangerous once they no longer provoke astonishment.

With every morsel or sip, we need to remind ourselves of the inscruta-bility of such deeds. We must capture them in their freshness before they become imprisoned.

A *beracha* is the Hebrew way of saying Wow! When we say "Baruch Ata Hashem . . ." (Blessed are You, God, for providing us with. . .), we make it clear to God and ourselves that we have not fallen victim to the ordinary, and that our hearts are able to climb beyond the average.

As such, it is a protest against the dullness of the human mind and heart.

Chapter 11

To Be a *Posek* Is to Be a Halachic Poet

THE TASK

Few of us are aware that Jewish observance and our dedication to Halacha do not make us religious Jews. They are departures, but never arrivals. Much hard work is needed before one gets a sense of what it means to be genuinely religious. And most of us will never make it. That in itself is not a tragedy. The tragedy is when we do not even strive to get there, but live a life of religious mediocrity, convincing ourselves that since we go to synagogue and are meticulous about every halacha, we are therefore religious. In no way should we look down on these commitments; after all, they are most important. But integrity demands of us to admit that these things alone do not make us religious. The same is true about our rabbis. They may be great halachic authorities, but whether or not they are men of God will depend on factors that far transcend the world of classic Halacha. Only when they incorporate these factors into their halachic lives can we claim that they are *Gedolei ha-Dor*, the great ones of our generation.[1]

To be religious is to experience spiritual moments of such rapture that they cause your body to figuratively burst open, liberating the soul that you thought you had lost and restoring it to your body as something entirely new, causing a revolution in your mundane life. Only when that happens can one enter the world of religiosity and decide on unadulterated Halacha.

---

1. See chap. 13.

WORD PAINTING

There is a technique in writing called word painting. It differs from the way most of us write in that it paints an image in the reader's mind. It does not merely state a description, such as "the grass was green and the heavens were blue." Rather, it recognizes that some matters strike us as beautiful, not because of aesthetics – when colors match or the symmetry is perfect – but because they make a deep psychological impression on us due to the mood or the value they embody. Word painting uses rich, evocative words that accurately portray the images in the reader's mind. Descriptions such as these and the emotions they evoke can mollify many ugly moments we human beings have to endure. Only after experiences such as these can one access genuine religiosity and be ready to give a real *psak din*, an authentic halachic decision.

It was Rainer Maria Rilke (1875–1926), the inimitable German poet of Jewish descent, who gave expression to this. When asked what it takes to compose a single verse, he wrote:

> Ah! but verses amount to so little when one writes them young. One ought to wait and gather sense and sweetness a whole life long and a long life, if possible, and then, quite at the end, one might perhaps be able to write ten lines that were good. For verses are not, as people imagine, simply feelings (those one has early enough) – they are experiences.
>
> For the sake of a single verse, one must see many cities, men, and things. One must know the animals, one must feel how the birds fly and know the gesture with which the little flowers open in the morning. One must be able to think back to roads in unknown regions, to unexpected meetings and to partings one had long seen coming; to days of childhood that are still unexplained, to parents whom one had to hurt when they brought one some joy and did not grasp it (it was a joy for someone else); to childhood illnesses that so strangely begin with such a number of profound and grave transformations, to days in rooms withdrawn and quiet and to mornings by the sea, to the sea itself, to seas, to nights of travel that rushed along on high and flew with all the stars – and it is not yet enough if one may think of all this. One must have memories of many nights of love, none of which was like the others, of the screams of women in labor, and of light, white, sleeping women in childbed, closing again. But one must also have

been beside the dying, must have sat beside the dead in the room with the open window and the fitful noises. And still it is not enough to have memories. One must be able to forget them when they are many, and one must have the great patience to wait until they come again.

For it is not yet the memories themselves. Not till they have turned to blood within us, to glance, and gesture, nameless, and no longer to be distinguished from ourselves – not till then can it happen that in a most rare hour the first word of a verse arises in their midst and goes forth from them.[2]

And so it is with the world of Judaism and Halacha. Halacha is the practical expression of discovering the infinite within the finite. To grasp the world of religiosity, or the real essence of Halacha, it is not enough to know all of the Written and Oral Torah. One must also see how the birds fly and the flowers blossom; one must sit by the bed of the dying, watch the stars, and have unexpected meetings. Because all of these are a *living* commentary on the Text. Only then, and not a moment earlier, have we entered *olam she-kulo Torah*, a world that is completely Torah. Only then can we have a notion of what it means to be religious and know the art of how to decide on God's Halacha.

---

2. Rainer Maria Rilke, *Rilke on Love and Other Difficulties*, ed. John J.L. Mood (NY: W.W. Norton & Co., 1975), 112–113. With thanks to my dear friend and family member Sid Tenenbaum of Yerushalayim who brought this passage to my attention.

Chapter 12

The Divine Word is Deadly
Only a Melody Can Rescue It

Rabbi Azaria and Rabbi Acha said in the name of Rabbi Yochanan: When, at Mount Sinai, the Israelites heard the word "Anochi" ("I" – the first word of the Ten Commandments), their souls left them, as it says: "If we hear the voice of God any more, we will die."[1] It is also written: "My soul departed when He spoke."[2] Then the Word went back to the Holy One, blessed be He, and said, "Lord of the Universe, You live eternally and Your Torah lives eternally, but You have sent me to the dead. They are all dead!" Thereupon, the Holy One, blessed be He, sweetened the Word for them. . . . Rabbi Shimon bar Yochai taught: The Torah which God gave to Israel restored their souls to them, as it says:[3] "The Torah of the Lord is perfect, it restores the soul."[4]

It may perhaps be argued that this midrash, like no other text, encapsulates the essence of Judaism and its dialectic nature. The tension between Jewish Law and the near hopelessness of man to live by it, survive it, and simultaneously obey it with great fervor, is what is at the very core of Judaism's complexity.

The Divine Word is deadly and causes paralysis. The Word, wrought by fire in the upper world, is unmanageable and wreaks havoc once it descends. Its demands are not of this world; it belongs to the angels. The Word therefore comes to naught once it enters the human sphere, since

---

1. *Devarim* 5:22.
2. *Shir ha-Shirim* 5:6.
3. *Tehillim* 19:8.
4. *Bamidbar Rabba*, Vilna ed., 10:1; *Shir ha-Shirim Rabba*, Vilna ed., 1:2, section 4.

there is no one to receive it. All have died before the Word is able to pronounce its second word. How then can it delight the living soul?

The answer is: sweetness. It has to have grace and therefore must be put to music. The problem with the Word is that it carries the possibility of *literal-mindedness*,[5] which takes the word for what it is, robbing it of its inner spiritual meaning. The language of faith employs only a few words in its own spirit. Most of its terms are borrowed from the world in which the Word creates physical images in the mind of man. But the Divine Word needs to be heard, not seen. To hear is to perceive what is beyond the utterance of the mouth. To live with the Word is to discover the ineffable and act on it through the direction of the Law. The mitzvot are founded on the appreciation of the unimaginable, but they become poison when performed only for the sake of the deed.

> Rabbi Shefatia said in the name of Rabbi Yochanan: If one reads the Torah without a melody, or repeats the Mishna without a tune, of him Scripture says:[6] "So, too, I gave them statutes that were not good and laws by which they could not live."[7]

Death refers also to those who do mitzvot in an improper manner. The full impact of Torah and mitzvot comes only when, while performing them, one realizes their great value and gives them their proper due honor.

The function of music is to connect the Word with Heaven. It is not so much the music that man plays on an instrument or sings, but the music of one's soul, which is externalized through the use of an instrument or song. It leads man to the edge of the infinite and allows one to gaze, just for a few moments, into the Other. Music is the art of word exegesis. While a word on its own is dead, it is resurrected when touched by music. Music is the refutation of human finality (Heschel). As such, it is the sweetness that God added to His Word when the Word alone was wreaking havoc. It is able to revive man when he dies as he is confronted with the bare Word at Sinai. Life without music is death – poignantly bitter when one realizes that one has never really lived.

There is little meaning in living by Halacha if one does not hear its grace. It is not a life of halachic *observance* that we need, but a life of hala-

---

5. See Abraham Joshua Heschel, *God in Search of Man: A Philosophy of Judaism* (NY: Farrar, Straus and Cudahy, 1955), 179.

6. *Yechezkel* 20:25.

7. *Megilla* 32a.

chic *living*. Observance does not propel man to a level of existence where he realizes that there is more to life than the mind can grasp.

Jewish education has often been founded on the Word *before* it turned to God to be sweetened. As a result, there are many casualties, and a large part of our nation has been paralyzed.

It is the great task of Jewish educators and thinkers to send the Word back to God and ask Him to teach us how to sweeten it.

Four

HALACHA AS PROTEST

Chapter 13

The Death and Birth of the Halachic Expert
One Should Listen to Bach, Mozart, or Beethoven
Before Ruling on a Halachic Problem

INTRODUCTION

Filling the position of *Posek ha-Dor*, the leading halachic arbiter of the
Jewish people, has become an almost hopeless undertaking in our complicated and troubled times. We are told he must be someone possessing
halachic knowledge greater than anyone else's. The *Posek ha-Dor* must
be totally imbued with Torah knowledge; he has acquired Torah values
and refined his character to such a degree that he embodies and is thus
qualified to offer *Da'at Torah* (an authentic and authoritative Jewish view
on all matters). *Da'at Torah* is seen as quasi-prophetic and thereby beyond
reproach.[1] The *Posek ha-Dor* has to decide on issues of life and death,
literally and figuratively. He must make judgments about political matters
– especially in and concerning the Land of Israel – which are so complicated that they are nearly beyond anyone's grasp. People insist that this
person must have wisdom that surpasses anything ordinary mortals could

---

1. The concept of *Da'at Torah* is highly questionable and in fact incompatible with Jewish
Tradition. Too many rabbis whose *Da'at Torah* is accepted contradict each other in many pro-
found and disturbing ways, which makes a farce of the whole idea. See the highly critical article
by Lawrence Kaplan, "Daas Torah: A Modern Conception of Rabbinic Authority" in *Rabbinic
Authority and Personal Autonomy*, ed. Moshe Sokol (Northvale, NJ: Jason Aronson, 1992), 1–60.
For a general overview of the doctrine of *Da'at Torah*, see Alfred S. Cohen "Daat Torah," *Journal
of Halacha and Contemporary Society* 45 (Spring 2003): 67–105; Benjamin Brown, "Jewish Political
Theology: The Doctrine of Da'at Torah as a Case Study," *Harvard Theological Review* 107, no.
3 (2014): 255–289. See also the series of lectures and accompanying source sheets by Rabbi
Anthony Manning entitled "Da'at Torah and Rabbinic Authority," 2017, http://www.rabbiman
ning.com/index.php/audio-shiurim/daat-torah/. I would suggest that there is something we can
call *Ruach ha-Torah*, according to which differing opinions are stated which are all rooted in
diverse readings of our traditional rabbinic literature. This is a beautiful example of *elu ve-elu*.
See *Eruvin* 13b.

ever dream of. He is asked to singlehandedly decide on matters that will affect hundreds of thousands of religious Jews, and by extension, millions of secular Jews. This is most dangerous.

TO BE A *POSEK HA-DOR*. IS IT POSSIBLE?

The establishment of the State of Israel cast all Jews around the globe into a new world order and created a need for pioneering religious leadership and a completely new kind of halachic arbiter. Social and economic conditions as well as ideologies have changed radically, creating major upheavals in Jewish life. As a result, unprecedented circumstances have arisen that need to be translated into reality. The question is whether the *Posek ha-Dor* will grasp these opportunities and turn them into major victories so as to inspire people. Developments in the rabbinical world show that we no longer have such extraordinary people. Most of the time, halachic authorities have withdrawn, living in denial and continuing to believe that the world has not evolved and nothing of substance has happened that requires an altogether new approach.

Today, halachic authorities need to lead religious Jewry through a new world order. They must realize that their views will affect Jews as well as Gentiles, for their voices will be heard far beyond the Jewish community, transmitted via the media. Their observations may cause ridicule and even anti-Semitism if they misrepresent Judaism and Jewish Law. Rather unfortunately, this has happened on more than a few occasions.

The *posek* has to understand that he may be called upon to give guidance to an often extremely secular and troubled world that is in great need of hearing the words of a Jewish sage. His decisions must reflect the imperative that we Jews are to be a light unto the nations – a light that must shine everywhere. It is no longer possible to focus on the often narrow world of Orthodoxy and look down on or ignore the secular and Gentile world.

IS THE HALACHA STILL EXCITING AND ENNOBLING?

Most Jews today are no longer observant, nor are they even inspired by Judaism. To them, it has become irrelevant and outdated. The reasons for this tragedy are many, but no doubt a major cause is the failure to convey Halacha as something exciting and ennobling, like the music of Bach, Mozart, or Beethoven. Only when a Jew is taught *why* Halacha offers him or her the musical notes with which to play the soul's sonata, will he or she then be able to hear its magnificent music.

Just as great scientists are fascinated when they investigate the properties of DNA or the habits of a tiny insect under scrutiny, so should even a secular Jew be deeply moved when encountering the colors and fine subtleties of the world of Halacha.[2] But does the *posek* realize this, and does he know how to convey that message when he deals with halachic inquiries?

THE CURSE OF NEARSIGHTEDNESS

Many religious Jews are nearsighted and in dire need of a wider vision. Is making sure that a chicken is kosher all that there is to kashrut? Or, are the laws of kashrut just one element of a grand weltanschauung that defines the mission of the People of Israel; a mission whose importance surpasses by far the single question of a chicken's kashrut? Such inquiries are but one small component of a larger question concerning the plague of consumerism and humankind's obsessive pursuit of ever-increasing comfort. Should the *posek* who is asked about the kashrut of someone's *tefillin* (phylacteries) not ask that person: "And what about the kashrut of your much-too-expensive and ostentatious car?" After all, the *posek* needs, foremost, to be an educator. Hard-line narrow rulings will not create the future for a deeply spiritual Judaism.

The first requirement of a *posek* is to live in radical amazement and see God's fingers in every dimension of human existence, including the Torah, Talmud, science, technology, and above all in the constant changing of history, which may well mean that God demands different decisions from those of the past. Today's halachic living is severely impeded by observance having become mere habit. As Abraham Joshua Heschel put it so beautifully:

> Indeed, the essence of observance has, at times, become encrusted with so many customs and conventions that the jewel was lost in the setting. Outward compliance with externalities of the law took the place of the engagement of the whole person to the living God.[3]

---

2. See Abraham Joshua Heschel, *The Earth Is the Lord's: The Inner World of the Jew in East Europe* (NY: Farrar, Straus and Giroux, 1978), 62–63.

3. Abraham Joshua Heschel, *God in Search of Man: A Philosophy of Judaism* (NY: Farrar, Straus and Cudahy, 1955), 326.

Over the years, this problem has become exacerbated because everything in Judaism has been turned into a halachic issue.

UNKNOWN LANDSCAPES

The future *posek* must reverse this crisis. He can do so only if he is touched by something much larger than himself. It is entirely impossible to *pasken* (render a halachic ruling) when his own soul is cold and all he does is go by the book. He must live the Divine, and the Divine must emerge from his decisions. To paraphrase Heschel: The *posek* must feel more than he understands in order to understand more than he grasps. He must touch Heaven while standing with both his feet on the ground, similar to what takes place when one hears the music of Bach, Mozart, or Beethoven and suddenly feels that he is taken on a journey to unknown landscapes. I would even suggest that some *poskim* should actually listen to this kind of heavenly music while contemplating halachic problems presented to them. It will broaden their minds and hearts, and they will see a world emerging that opens halachic possibilities they never contemplated before. They will sense God's presence, because music sets the soul free and evokes in us wonder about who we are and what we live for. As Swiss Protestant theologian Karl Barth once wrote, "Whether the angels play only Bach in praising God, I am not quite sure; I am sure, however, that *en famille* they play Mozart."[4]

NO LEGALISM

It is the *posek*'s task to ensure that Judaism is not identified only with legalism. There is an entire religious world *beyond* Halacha – one of Aggada, philosophy, deep emotional experiences, devotion, and often unfinalized beliefs. Shouldn't these be part of the process of deciding how Halacha is to be applied? The task of Halacha has always been to ensure that Judaism does not evaporate into a utopian reverie, a superficial spiritualism. But the facts on the ground suggest something entirely different. Judaism has developed in a way that has destroyed the delicate balance between law and spirit, and it has turned into a type of sacred behaviorism. Halacha is supposed to be the practical upshot of even unfinalized beliefs. Judaism

---

4. Karl Barth, "A Letter of Thanks to Mozart," from the Round Robin in the weekly supplement of the *Luzerner Neuesten Nachrichten*, Jan. 21, 1956. This is also quoted in "Selections From Barth's Writings," *New York Times*, Dec. 11, 1968.

was never supposed to become a religion that is paralyzed in its awe of rigid tradition. It is a fluid liquid that must be transformed into a solid substance so as to enable the Jew to act. It must chill the heated steel of exalted ideas and turn them into pragmatic deeds without allowing the inner heat to cool off entirely.

Halacha is the midwife that assists in the birth of not only answers but also profound spiritual questions created by that very halacha. As such, we must ensure that the *Posek ha-Dor* does not turn into someone who gives automatic answers on the spot. Instead, he should walk the person through a landscape in which these questions are properly discussed.

THE WIFE OF THE *POSEK*

It is high time that a group of women, particularly the wives of *poskim*, be deeply involved in certain halachic decisions when they touch on emotions and social conditions that they may understand better than the *posek*/husband. Why do we almost never hear about the wife of the *Posek ha-Dor*, her wisdom, and especially the sacrifice entailed in being married to such a great man who is needed by so many and who often has little time for his own family?[5]

Today's *Posek ha-Dor* is often absolutely sure of the truth of his religion, but not informed or aware of the many challenges today's world presents to religious faith and Judaism. How could such a person be able to understand the many issues of people who live in religious doubt?

Furthermore, the *posek* must sincerely appreciate the plight and pain of the confused teenager, the Jewish Ethiopian, the bereaved parent, the struggling religious homosexual, the child of a mixed marriage with only a Jewish father, and even the Christian or Buddhist who has an affinity for Judaism and asks for guidance.

THE NEED FOR ADVICE

Is there anyone in this world who has all the qualities necessary to single-handedly rule on these matters? It is entirely unfair and extremely danger-

---

5. ArtScroll Publications did publish a book about the wife of Rabbi Chaim Kanievsky, well-known leader and halachic authority in Israel's Charedi community: Naftali Weinberger, Naomi Weinberger, and Nina Indig, *Rebbetzin Kanievsky: A Legendary Mother to All* (NY: Mesorah Publications, 2012). But this is a drop in the bucket to what should and could be done, and it is entirely unclear whether Mrs. Kanievsky was involved in any halachic decision-making.

ous to ask *one* person, however pious and wise, to adequately respond to all these issues. It requires teamwork with fellow rabbis and teachers who may not be as learned in Halacha but are much more familiar with many of the problems of which the *Posek ha-Dor* may not be aware. The *Posek ha-Dor* should be advised by a team of highly experienced professionals – psychologists, social workers, scientists, and even poets and musicians – before giving a ruling, so as to prevent major pitfalls. Halacha should be decided by consensus (as was once the case with the Sanhedrin) instead of by one person, even if he is the greatest. Centralized authority has become a dangerous matter. It may be wise to allow people, with some guidance, to decide on their own after having heard all the halachic views and spiritual dimensions of their question.

NEW TORAH IDEAS AND NOT THE VATICAN

Poskim should encourage new Torah ideas and shun the denunciation of those books that try to bring religion and science together in harmony. Instead of banning them, as the Vatican used to do in former times, they should encourage these works. In the last few years, powerful rabbis have tried to prevent books from being published, or have condemned them, because they did not agree with their content, claiming them to contain heresy. In their ignorance, they tried to ban them and their authors, causing a terrible *chillul Hashem* (desecration of God's name) after secular newspapers were informed of these condemnations and ridiculed them, since they indicated a total lack of scientific knowledge on the part of those who signed and endorsed these bans. Some of these great rabbis should stop the banning and instead learn to offer scientific and philosophical solutions to possible conflicts between Torah, science, and philosophy. But to do so, they need to acquire enough knowledge! What is the point of labeling certain ideas as heresy when one does not have the knowledge to understand the issues involved? In any case, bans and inquisitions have no place in Judaism.

The *Posek ha-Dor* must have shoulders broad enough to carry and appreciate different worldviews, including Zionist, non-Zionist, ul-tra-Orthodox, and Modern Orthodox. And he must ensure that all these denominations feel his impartiality and his allowance of space for their varied ideologies. Perhaps he could even have an open ear for Reform and Conservative Judaism and realize that many of their adherents are serious about their religion, even though he would not agree with these movements. And when he disagrees, he should be sophisticated enough to explain why he indeed differs.

A true *posek* should visit women's shelters, speak personally with abused women and children, and perhaps periodically deny himself food and drink so that he feels the real horror of poverty and rejection. Unless he is a very sensitive soul, he should perhaps get himself hospitalized and spend time observing and even experiencing the lives of people who are incapable of leaving their beds. They are in the hands of doctors and nurses who do not always deal with their patients in an adequately compassionate manner, whether due to lack of time, insensitivity, or some other reason. He should also carefully listen to the complaints, problems, and frustrations of the medical staff.

THE *POSEK* SHOULD GO INTO EXILE

Before dealing with the question of *agunot*[6] and the refusal of husbands to grant their wives a *get* (writ of divorce), it would perhaps be a good idea for the *posek* to leave his wife for a period of time (with her consent, of course) and live in total loneliness, so as to understand what it means to live in utter silence and have no life partner.

Above all, it is the *Posek ha-Dor*'s responsibility to narrow the serious gap between the ultra-Orthodox and the rest of Israeli society, and to come up with creative halachic solutions that will boggle the minds of all branches of Jewry.

Poskim must be people who will propose unprecedented solutions for the status of the tens of thousands of non-Jews with Jewish roots living in Israel. They must ensure that courses on Judaism are so attractive that Halacha becomes irresistible. They should instruct their students to welcome these people with open arms, knowing quite well that otherwise we will be confronted with a huge problem of intermarriage in Israel, which threatens the very existence of the Jewish State.

The *posek*'s farsighted and long-term view must ensure that major problems, such as the exemption of yeshiva students from army service, will be resolved once and for all.

Over nearly two thousand years of exile, Jewish Law has developed into a "waiting mode" in which it has become the great "Preserver of the

---

6. An *aguna* (pl. *agunot*) is a Jewish woman who is chained to her marriage because her husband is missing or refuses to give her a get.

Precepts." It has been protective and defensive, and mainly committed to conformity, in order to ensure the survival of Judaism and the Jews who were surrounded by a non-Jewish, mostly hostile society. It became a "galut Halacha" – an exilic code – in which the Torah sometimes became overly stultified. It may have worked in the Diaspora, but it can no longer offer sufficient guidance in today's world and in Israel.[7]

The State of Israel is the great catalyst for this new situation, which we have not experienced during the past two thousand years. Consequently, we are in dire need of "prophetic Halacha," in which not only the rules of Halacha are applied, but also the perspectives of our prophets who spoke of burning social and ethical issues. This should be combined with a melodious spiritual resonance that introduces new points of view on genuine and deep religiosity.

Isn't it time to leave the *final* codification of Jewish Law behind us; to unfreeze Halacha and begin reading between the lines of the Talmud to recapture Halacha's authentic nature?

TO BE A CONDUCTOR OF AN ORCHESTRA

To be an arbiter of Jewish Law is to be the conductor of an orchestra. It is not coercion, but persuasion that makes it possible for the other to hear the beauty of the music and to accept a halachic decision, just as one would willingly listen to the interpretation of a conductor – because one is deeply inspired.

To be a *posek* means to be a person of unprecedented courage; one who is willing to initiate a spiritual storm that will shake up the entire Jewish community. A storm that will free conventional and codified Halacha from the sandbank in which it has been stuck. In a revolutionary shift, *poskim* should lead the ship of Torah, in full sail, right into the heart of the Jewish nation, creating such a shock that it will take days, weeks, or even months before it is able to get back on its feet. With knives between their teeth, like the prophets of biblical days, these great halachic arbiters, of impeccable and uncompromising conduct, should create a religious uproar that will scare the moral wits out of both secular and religious Jews and weigh heavily on their souls.

---

7. See Eliezer Berkovits, *Ha-Halacha, Kocha ve-Tafkida* (Jerusalem: Mossad HaRav Kook, 1981).

TO BE FEARED AND TO BE LOVED

Poskim should not be "honored," "valued," or "well-respected," as they are now. As men of truth, they should be both feared and deeply loved. Jews of all backgrounds should be shaking in their shoes at the thought of meeting them, while simultaneously being incapable of staying away from their towering, fascinating, and above all, warm personalities.

Halachic decision-making is a great art. The *posek* should never forget that he is the soil in which the Halacha is to grow, while the Torah is the seed and God is the sun.[8]

We are in need of decentralized rabbinical authority in which many more rabbis will have a personal relationship with their flock and consequently be able to respond to the often difficult and very personal questions their followers are asking. There are no longer such unusual great rabbis who know the art of reading people's minds and hearts without having a personal relationship with them. This was exactly the point that Yitro made when he told his son-in-law Moshe Rabbenu to appoint ministers "as leaders of thousands, leaders of hundreds, leaders of fifties, and leaders of tens."[9] Only the major cases would be brought to a giant authority like Moshe. But alas, such leaders no longer exist.

We should be very thankful that we witness the disintegration of rabbinical authority in our days. Nothing could be worse for Judaism and the Jewish people than having rabbis who are admired as great spiritual halachic leaders when for the most part they are not. We will witness, slowly but surely, the rise of a completely new rabbinical world, which will give us more reason to be proud Jews and live a spiritual halachic life. Yes, it will take time – but it will surely happen.

Perhaps our future rabbis should first listen to the heavenly music of Bach, Mozart, and Beethoven, after which they will be able to render a *truthful* halachic decision. It might do wonders!

---

8. Heschel, *God in Search of Man*, 274. See Samuel H. Dresner, *Heschel, Hasidism, and Halakha* (NY: Fordham University Press, 2002), 108.

9. *Shemot* 18:21.

Chapter 14

Oh, That I Could Take Off My *Kippa!*

I need to be honest. I am contemplating taking off my *kippa*. Why, you might ask? I no longer want to be observant. Observance, for me and for many young people, has become irrelevant. It has been used by large sections of religious Jews to live in self-assured ease. Their religion is part of their contentment.

But who wants to live in contentment?

Religious observance has become a tool to comfort the troubled. But it is time that religion is used to trouble the comfortable.[1]

And that is my problem.

Sure, living an observant life and conducting oneself in a manner that is consistent with Halacha is certainly a crucial component of Judaism; but it is *not* what makes me religious. To be religious is to allow God entry into my thoughts, my deeds, what I see and feel. It is to have a constant, intense awareness of living in His presence, seeing His fingerprints everywhere, and living up to that awareness.

Halacha is really a constant reminder, an appeal to be attentive to Him, even in the midst of our day-to-day mundane affairs. It is meant to teach us that even our trivialities need to become holy and be worthy of God, so that our common deeds reach Heaven.

But is that still the case today? Does it accomplish that goal?

Halacha is the external garment of an inner spiritual process that should be stimulated by those very halachic acts. For that to occur, much more has to be accomplished. To become religious is to face opposition, even from oneself – to dare, to defy, and even to doubt.

---

1. See Introduction.

The way to reach God is through spiritual warfare, and all we can hope for is to catch a glimpse of His existence. It is an ongoing challenge. As the Kotzker Rebbe once said, if you cannot win, you *must* win. Only a pioneer can be heir to a religious tradition. Faith is contingent on the courage of the believer.

This is the task of Halacha – to teach us how to confront ourselves when standing in the presence of God, and to never give up, even against all odds. *To be worthy*.

But for many observant Jews, including myself, religion means living in security and peace of mind. This is the "dullness of observance," a religious conditioning that often turns genuine religiosity and the experience of God into a farce. People are more afraid of Halacha than they are in love with God and Judaism. Halacha is a challenge to the soul, not its tranquilizer.

I now realize that my *kippa* is one of the main reasons for my failure to be religious. I want to put my *kippa* on, but I understand that to do so I need to take it off. I don't want to *wear* it. I want to *put it on* as a daring religious act, a declaration to God that I wish to live in His presence. Not as a spiritual condition, but as an act of elevation, moral grandeur, and boldness.

The problem is that my *kippa* no longer carries this message. Its main purpose should be to disturb and to wake me up, but every morning when I put it on, it quickly disappears into my subconscious. It is always on my head, and therefore, never there.

When I first became interested in Judaism and seriously considered giving it a try, I began covering my head when I went to synagogue and when I ate. I even dared to sit with my *kippa* when having a snack with my non-Jewish friends from the Gymnasium, the high school I attended in Holland. There was no one else there of Jewish descent besides my dear brother and perhaps one other person.

I was very conscious of my *kippa*. I needed to take it off so that whenever I'd put it on again, I'd feel it on my head. This was a majestic experience. It made me proud, and I was filled with awe. My *kippa* reminded me that there was Someone above me. Yes, it existentially unsettled me. It made me wonderfully uneasy. But what a magnificent and exalted feeling! Living in the presence of God! I think I was a bit afraid of it. My hands trembled as I would put my *kippa* on. Not because of what my non-Jewish friends would say (they were most sympathetic), but because of what I would feel. What a responsibility and privilege!

Now, more than fifty-five years later, I am so used to my *kippa* that I have developed a love-hate relationship with it. In fact, I realize that I lost it many years ago, the moment I decided to wear it all the time. It is no longer on my head to remind me of Him. It just sits there, a meaningless object, having little to do with my attempt to be religious. It has simply disappeared from my life.

So I find myself in the midst of a "reversed cover-up," a depressing situation. It is most painful, and no rabbi or psychologist can help me. Most don't even understand what I am talking about.

Deep down I know the remedy. I need to take it off, to stop wearing it and just occasionally put it on again. Only then would l again recognize it as my friend. I would feel inspired, as it would remind me once more that Someone is above me and that it is a privilege to live in His presence. It would help me to be truly religious and not merely "observant." If I would take off my *kippa*, it would once more come to life, as when I tried it in my youth. I would have a relationship with it and would begin loving it again. Oh, what a sweet thought!

But, can I do it? Halachically, there is really no problem. There are enough opinions to allow me to walk around bareheaded without ever needing to put on a *kippa*.

True, Rabbi Yosef Karo (1488–1575) rules in his *Shulchan Aruch*[2] that one should not walk more than four *amot*[3] with his head uncovered. But none other than the Gaon of Vilna (1720–1797) takes issue with this ruling,[4] basing his view on the fact that the only reference in the Talmud for covering one's head is the *personal* pious practice of Rav Huna,[5] who never walked more than *dalet amot* (four *amot*) with his head uncovered. The implication is, therefore, that this was never legislated as a universal halachic obligation.[6] It should be one's personal spontaneous expression, out of reverence for God.

---

2. *Shulchan Aruch, Orach Chaim* 2:6.

3. Four *amot* is the equivalent of about six feet, but it translates most accurately as personal space.

4. *Biur ha-Gra, Orach Chaim* 8:2.

5. *Kiddushin* 31a.

6. It is well known that many Orthodox rabbis of the past did not wear a head covering. In the Orthodox school in Frankfurt am Main, established by Rabbi Samson Raphael Hirsch (1808–1888), the students sat bareheaded when they studied secular subjects. Rabbi Dr. David Zvi Hoffmann (1843–1921), the German halachic authority of international repute, told the following story. When he came with a head covering to visit Rabbi Hirsch, the latter told him to remove it since it would be seen as a sign of disrespect. (Interestingly, the Gaon of Vilna was of the opinion that one *should* wear a head covering when visiting a *Gadol ha-Dor*.) Some maintain that Rabbi Hirsch himself wore a wig and may not always have covered his head with a *kippa*. For

The Talmudic Sages clearly had in mind that our souls be greatly aroused when we don a *kippa*. After all, *that* is genuine piety. But now that it has become an "obligation," it has begun to lose this very quality. And while our ancestors, who were great soul-people, may have been spiritual enough to gain inspiration from it even when it became an imperative, most of us no longer feel any such uplifting experience. How many among us can claim that a feeling of piety grows within us when we wear our *kippa* all the time?

Alas, instead of the *kippa* assisting us in being genuinely religious, it has now become an obstacle. It is counter-productive. We need to dispose of it so that we can put it on again as a deeply spiritual act.

But what will my grandchildren and great-grandchildren say when I will have stopped wearing my *kippa*? What will happen to *their* religiosity? Will they – who have been raised in a deeply observant society, where removing one's *kippa* is an act of heresy and a sign of blatant secularism – ever understand what I had in mind? Will they become more religious when they see my head bare and only occasionally covered? Or, will they conclude that I no longer take Judaism so seriously, and they can follow suit? It scares the life out of me to think of the consequences. They may see my act as one of rebellion against what I love most: Judaism. Will it help when I tell them my reasons? Will they ever understand the notion of becoming more religious by taking *off* their *kippa*? I shudder at the thought.

But I worry not only about my grandchildren. My students and friends might also misunderstand my decision and as a result may adopt leniencies in their commitment to Judaism.

Will they use *my* decision to justify taking off *their kippa* when it "bothers" them, or when it's more pleasant to walk bareheaded, or when they don't want to be known as too Jewish? Will they understand that the difference between us is that they want to take it *off* while I want to put it *on*?

The story does not end here. Today, the *kippa* is a powerful symbol of Jewish identity, which is not to be underestimated. It is a statement of Jewish pride, courage, and commitment to living with a mission. And if there's anything I want, it's to be a proud Jew! So, shall I leave it on despite my objections?

How difficult my choice is, especially now that it has become customary

---

an informative study, see Dan Rabinowitz, "Yarmulke: A Historic Cover-up?," *Ḥakirah* 4 (Winter 2007): 221–238.

for Israeli criminals to wear *kippot* while standing trial, so as to make a good impression on the judges. Do I want to "walk in the path of sinners" and "sit in the company of scorners"?[7] As Cervantes would say, "Tell me what company thou keepest and I'll tell thee what thou art."[8]

I still recall, with fondness, the days when those wearing *kippot* were known to be upright people.

So what shall I do? I don't know. Perhaps the solution is to wear a *kippa shkufa* (a transparent *kippa*), which no one but the Lord of the Universe can see. But would that help me in my search for religiosity?

I need to be bareheaded while wearing it all the time. Who would have thought that something as simple as a *kippa* would become a religious problem of considerable magnitude?

None other than Baruch Spinoza said that "all noble things are as difficult as they are rare."[9] Was he speaking about his former *kippa*? A *beracha* on his head!

---

7. *Tehillim* 1:1.
8. Miguel de Cervantes, *Don Quixote*, part 2, chap. 23.
9. Benedictus de Spinoza, *Ethics*, part V, prop. XLII, note.

Five

BETWEEN *FRUMKEIT* AND RELIGIOSITY

Chapter 15

Spinoza's Blunder
and Noach's Misguided Religiosity

In his *Tractatus Theologico-Politicus*, Baruch Spinoza (1632–1677), the famous Jewish "philosopher apostate," launches one of his most outspoken attacks on Judaism. Not mincing words, he accuses it of demanding obsessive and outrageous obedience:

> The sphere of reason is . . . truth and wisdom; the sphere of theology is piety and obedience. . . .
>
> Philosophy has no end in view save truth: faith . . . looks for nothing but obedience and piety. . . .
>
> Scripture . . . does not condemn ignorance, but obstinacy . . .[1]

In contrast, he argues, Jesus sought

> solely to teach the universal moral law. . . . the Pharisees [who were the Sages of Israel], in their ignorance, thought that the observance of the state law and the Mosaic law was the sum total of morality; whereas such laws merely had reference to the public welfare, and aimed not so much at instructing the Jews as at keeping them under constraint.[2]

---

1. Benedictus de Spinoza, *A Theologico-Political Treatise*, chaps. 15, 14, in *The Chief Works of Benedict de Spinoza*, trans. R.H.M. Elwes (London: G. Bell and Sons, 1883), vol. 1.

2. Ibid., chap. 5.

These are serious words from a great thinker, and we need to ask ourselves whether his observations are correct or not. Is Judaism indeed a religion whose primary purpose is to force people's obedience to its demands and keep them under control?

I WOULD HAVE BROKEN DOWN THE ARK

Britain's former Chief Rabbi Lord Jonathan Sacks cites a most remarkable midrash, which I believe challenges Spinoza's critique while simultaneously proving his point.[3]

Commenting on Noach's reluctance to leave the ark after the Flood, the midrash makes the following biting comment:

> Once the waters had abated, Noach should have left the ark. However, Noach said to himself, "I entered with God's permission, as it says, 'Go into the ark.'[4] Shall I now leave without permission?" The Holy One, blessed be He, said to him, "Is it permission, then, that you are seeking? Very well, then, here is permission," as it is said: [Then God said to Noach] "Come out of the ark."[5] Rabbi Yehuda bar Ilai said: "If I had been there, I would have broken down the ark and taken myself out."[6]

There can be little doubt that this midrash confronts Spinoza's critique head-on. It seems to express a lack of patience with submissive religiosity that stifles human autonomy, action, innovation, and responsibility. It warns against the type of religiosity that is self-serving and dangerous, a concept best described by the untranslatable Yiddish/German word *frumkeit*. This refers to an artificial, superficial form of religious behavior, which in our days has become synonymous with the authentic way of Jewish religious living. Instead of agreeing with this sort of piety, the midrash bitterly attacks it as an escape mechanism and lack of *genuine* religiosity.

---

3. Jonathan Sacks, *Covenant & Conversation: A Weekly Reading of the Jewish Bible; Genesis: The Book of Beginnings* (Jerusalem: Maggid Books, 2009), 44.
4. *Bereshit* 7:1.
5. *Bereshit* 8:16.
6. *Midrash Tanchuma*, Buber ed., *Noach* 14.

NOACH'S RELIGIOUS SELF DECEPTION

In our story, Noach is described as a man who lives in self-deception, believing that he has reached the pinnacle of religiosity while in fact he is unknowingly pretending. There is nothing dishonest about him. Noach, in all sincerity, believes that no man should make a move unless God tells him to do so. There is no place for religious initiative. There is only obedience. What he does not realize is that this attitude will wreak total havoc. It is *the* recipe for continued flooding, the termination of all human life, and consequently the elimination of the possibility for genuine religiosity. More to the point, it is exactly what God does *not* want. The great biblical message is that God wants man to be His partner in Creation, not His robot.

What does Noach say when God informs him that He will destroy the world? What does he say when God commands him to build the ark and then enter it together with his family and the animals?

Nothing!

Why? Because Noach is very *frum*, religious, and won't challenge God. Who is he to do so? And so he enters the ark with a clear conscience. He is brave, obedient, and feels very good about himself. No doubt Noach prays *Shacharit*, *Mincha*, and *Arvit* daily. Surely he eats kosher and observes Shabbat, but only because God tells him to do so. He obeys the letter of the law and will never go beyond the divine demand.

What Noach does not grasp is that he is hiding behind his own misplaced religiosity. It is most convenient and carries no responsibility. All is in the hands of God. His argument is straightforward: If God decides that the world has to come to an end, how can man dare to interfere? Who is he to know what is right or wrong? There must be only obedience.

THE ARK IS A GHETTO GETTING US MORALLY AND RELIGIOUSLY DROWNED

The ark is a marvelous place – it is comfortable, there is no need to steer it, and nothing to fear. It floats on its own; one need not know where it is going. It has no sails for man to adjust to the winds. He just sits on his deckchair and waits for what will come.

The ark is a ghetto, both physically and mentally. It has no windows other than one on the roof allowing a view of Heaven.[7] One cannot even look outside to see what's going on around it and hear the cries of millions who are drowning and desperately crying for help. No, the walls are too thick to hear any noise coming from outside. The ark is a highly secure place – an oasis in the storm of human pain and upheaval. True, inside the ghetto man has his tasks. Noach has to look after his family as well as feed the animals and take care of them. But that is all because he is *commanded* to do so. Nothing is done beyond his religious obligations. Noach is the *homo religiosus* par excellence. His is the ark of total obedience, and it is against this type of religious personality that Spinoza correctly protests.

But this is not the authentic religious *Jewish* personality. What would Avraham, the first Jew in history, have done? From reading his life story, it is clear that he would have refused to go into the ark. He would have fought God, telling Him that it is unjust to drown all of humankind. He would have contested God's decision, as he did in the case of the evil men in Sedom and Amora. And if God would have forced him into the ark, he would not have waited an extra moment to get out. He would have stood at the edge and destroyed the ark as soon as he saw land, just as Rabbi Yehuda bar Ilai would have done.

Avraham, like Rabbi Yehuda bar Ilai, proves Spinoza wrong. Noach does not represent genuine religiosity. Yes, many religious Jews believe that it is only in obedience that one must live one's religious life. But that is not what the first Jew and authentic Judaism are all about. Judaism is a covenant between man and God, in which man is co-creator. God orders him to take action beyond His commandments. He is asked to build the world with the ingredients that God supplied at the time of creation. And when God destroys the world, it is man's task to restore it.[8] He is obligated to storm out of the ark, protest, and start rebuilding.

A MEASURE OF WHEAT AND A BUNDLE OF FLAX

But God demands even more of man. He is also asked to be a partner in the creation of the Torah:

---

7. See *Rashi* on *Bereshit* 6:16; *Bereshit Rabba*, Vilna ed., 31:11.

8. See Nathan Lopes Cardozo, "God is Unjustifiable" (Thoughts to Ponder 250), *David Cardozo Academy*, April 18, 2010, https://www.cardozoacademy.org/thoughts-to-ponder/god-is-unjustifiable-ttp-250/.

Once I was on a journey, and I came upon a man who went the way of heretics. He accepted the Written Torah but not the Oral Torah. He said to me: The Written Law was given to us from Mount Sinai; the Oral Law was not given from Mount Sinai. I said to him: But were not both the Written and the Oral Torah spoken by the Almighty? Then what difference is there between the Written and the Oral Torah? To what can this be compared? To a king of flesh and blood who had two servants and loved them both with perfect love. And he gave them each a measure of wheat and a bundle of flax. The wise servant, what did he do? He took the flax and spun a cloth. Then he took the wheat and made flour. He cleansed, ground, kneaded, and baked the flour, and set it on top of the table. Then he spread the cloth over it and left it until the king would come. But the foolish servant did nothing at all. After some days the king returned from a journey, entered his house, and said to them: My sons, bring me what I gave you. One servant showed him the wheaten bread on the table with a cloth spread over it, and the other servant showed the wheat still in the box, with a bundle of flax upon it. Alas for his shame, alas for his disgrace! Now, when the Holy One, blessed be He, gave the Torah to Israel, he gave it only in the form of wheat for us to extract flour from it, and flax to extract a garment.[9]

Man, then, is asked to be the constant co-creator of the Torah, making it more and more beautiful.[10]

Spinoza's view is dangerous and misleading. It has done great harm to Judaism's image. According to Hermann Cohen, one of the great German Jewish philosophers of the nineteenth century, Spinoza is unwittingly responsible for much anti-Semitism.[11] Many Jewish sources prove beyond doubt that Judaism imposes great responsibility on the religious Jew. There is no hiding behind obedience. The truth is that those who are exclusively submissive are only partially in control. Obedience means taking action; it is not merely subjugation.

Judaism is fully aware of the fact that that no law can prevent or solve

---

9. *Seder Eliyahu Zuta*, Friedmann ed., 2.

10. See pp. 290–296 below.

11. See Hermann Cohen, *Jüdische Schriften*, ed. B. Straus (Berlin: C.A. Schwetschke & Sohn, 1924), 3:290–372 (especially 363, 371); translated into English as *Spinoza on State & Religion, Judaism & Christianity*, trans. Robert S. Schine (Jerusalem: Shalem Press, 2014), xviii, 29, 51, 54–55, 59. See also Franz Nauen, "Hermann Cohen's Perceptions of Spinoza: A Reappraisal," *AJS Review* 4 (1979): 111–124.

the enormous life challenges that even the most religious Jew encounters.[12] To identify Judaism as a kind of sacred rote behavior, which does
not require any autonomous human action, is missing the point entirely.
The detailed elaboration of the law in Talmudic Tradition should not be
confused with a simplistic conception of the human condition. Judaism
constantly repudiates formalism because it often leads to a perverse form
of religiosity. In fact, it warns against becoming a degenerate within the
framework of the Torah.[13]

RELIGION IS WARFARE

Spinoza's assessment of the Jewish religious personality is entirely mistaken, but is clearly rooted in all the religious Noachs of our world.[14] It is
a warning to many religious Jews who know nothing other than what we
may call *negative* obedience as opposed to *positive* obedience. Instead of
asking great rabbis to solve all our problems, we should never forget that
Judaism teaches us to stand on our own feet and make our own decisions.
Of course, living one's religious life in this manner is not without risks,
but there is no authentic life choice that is risk-free. Religion, said the
Kotzker Rebbe, is warfare.[15] It is a fight against indolence and callousness
that stifles personal responsibility.

Our religious lives should be inspired by the spirit of the Torah, but it
should never develop into an obsessive form of subjugation, which the
Torah abhors. We must make sure we do not turn into "ark-niks," getting
drunk out of guilt once we leave our ark and see the havoc we could have
prevented.

---

12. See *Sukka* 52a.

13. See *Ramban* on *Vayikra* 19:2.

14. Spinoza's attitude toward the Jewish religion may quite well have been influenced by
the teachers of the Spanish Portuguese community in seventeenth-century Amsterdam, who
expelled him. Their rigid understanding of Judaism, possibly shaped by the ideology of the
Catholic Church from which they had just escaped, impelled the *ma'amad* (the lay leadership of
this community) to take drastic steps against Spinoza. Still, the ban was very mild compared to
the auto-da-fé of the Inquisition. See Antonio Damasio, *Looking for Spinoza: Joy, Sorrow and the
Feeling Brain* (Orlando, FL: Harcourt, 2003).

15. See Abraham Joshua Heschel, *A Passion for Truth* (NY: Farrar, Straus and Giroux,
1973), 183.

Chapter 16

Mitzvot, *Minhagim*, and Their Dangers

Every morning, the Jewish male covers himself with a *tallit*, a prayer shawl which has at its four corners long *tzitzit* (threads), in which certain religious beliefs are represented.[1] (This *tallit* should cover the entire upper body and not just be used as a shawl around one's neck.)[2] The proper way to don the *tallit* is first to cover one's head with it, while keeping the face uncovered. Next, one takes the corners of the garment and moves them over the left shoulder.[3] A common practice is to throw these corners with some force so as to make sure that the *tzitzit* will reach the back of the human body. Obviously, this should be done with care, making sure the person standing behind does not get hit by your *tzitzit* in his face or eyes. Unfortunately, this happens all too often in synagogues. At such a moment, a religious tragedy takes place of which many worshipers do not seem to be aware. In their attempt to fulfill a mitzva, they are, in actual fact, transgressing the law of being concerned about the welfare of one's neighbor.

On other occasions, we find worshipers running to kiss the scroll of the Torah when it is removed from the *Hechal* (*Aron ha-Kodesh*, synagogue ark). In order to get there as fast as possible, or to make sure they will get close enough to be able to kiss it, they often push people aside or step on their feet. It would have been better if they had stayed where they were.

The Talmud calls such an act a "mitzva ha-ba be-avera" ([fulfilling] a commandment which comes with a transgression).[4] In such a case, the

---

1. See *Bamidbar* 15:37–41.
2. See *Shulchan Aruch ha-Rav, Orach Chaim* 8:8; *Mishna Berura, Orach Chaim* 8:3; *Shulchan Aruch, Orach Chaim* 10:10–11.
3. See *Mishna Berura, Orach Chaim* 8:4.
4. *Berachot* 47b; *Sukka* 30a; *Bava Kamma* 94a.

mitzva has turned into an irreligious act and has lost all meaning.

One of the *minhagim* (religious customs) observed by the Ashkenazi community before Yom Kippur is the custom to *shlog kappores.* This is a custom mentioned by Rema, one of the most important commentators on the *Shulchan Aruch* of Rabbi Yosef Karo (who actually condemned the practice), and regarded as the main and decisive authority for Ashkenazi Jewry.[5] The *minhag* of *"kappores shloggen"* is to take a live chicken and wave it around one's head as a kind of symbolic atonement for one's sins throughout the previous year. (It is reminiscent of the atonement sacrifices in the Temple, although not a replacement for these sacrifices.)

The obvious intent of the code is to do this very carefully, so that the chicken does not get hurt or scared. There is, after all, a law which states that it is absolutely forbidden to cause any unnecessary pain and anguish to an animal or any other creature; this biblical prohibition is called *tza'ar ba'alei chaim.*[6]

Not uncommon is the sight of people, in their eagerness to fulfill this custom, picking the chicken up and mercilessly waving it around, scaring the chicken and often hurting it. Sometimes the chickens are kept in small plastic boxes, within a confined space, without adequate food or water. One wonders how these people can enter Yom Kippur in the right frame of mind. They seem to convince themselves that this mitzva will earn them even more merit in the eyes of the Almighty. I wonder if this does not invoke rather a different response from the Heavenly Court.

Perhaps it is time for kosher consumers to no longer just look for *glatt kosher*[7] supervision, but also for *"mercy glatt."* Too many animals are raised in inhumane conditions. While it will be difficult to change these conditions, and meat may become more expensive, rabbinical authorities should consider this possibility. Consumption of kosher meat from animals which are raised in these inhumane conditions, is, in the eyes of the Jewish Law, a contradiction in terms.

When asked if he was a vegetarian for health reasons, Isaac Bashevis Singer replied, "Yes, for the chicken's health."

---

5. *Shulchan Aruch, Orach Chaim* 605.

6. *Bava Metzia* 32b. For a discussion, see Immanuel Jakobovits, *Jewish Medical Ethics* (NY: Bloch Publishing Company, 1967), 102–103 and 297–298 nn30–37.

7. The term *glatt kosher* originally referred to certain stringent rules relating to kashrut of meat, mainly observed by Sephardim. Nowadays, the term encompasses many other stringencies which relate to other kosher food as well. See Yehuda Herzl Henkin, *Equality Lost: Essays in Torah Commentary, Halacha, and Jewish Thought* (Jerusalem: Urim, 1999), 145–148.

Chapter 17

Chumrot, Religious *Frumkeit*, and Religiosity

Self-imposed severities have become part and parcel of the religious Jewish community of today. Many people feel the need to express their religious devotion to God through the acceptance of stringencies which conventional Jewish Law does not in actual fact require. They observe Shabbat more strictly; they make sure that they only eat *glatt kosher*; they use the largest measurements for their *Kiddush* cup or, in the case of some married women, cover their hair not once, but twice.

No doubt there is room for stringencies within Jewish Law. It may even be argued that it would be healthy and prudent if every human being would have his or her specific mitzva to which they would devote extra attention.[1]

In earlier days, the Torah introduced the *Nazir* law, which states that a person who feels the need to deny himself certain pleasures is permitted, and even encouraged, to do so.[2] Sometimes, people have to sort out their religious priorities, and they feel that they can only achieve this goal when they abstain from certain liberties, the practice of which would tempt them beyond the border of the permissible.[3]

What many religious people today seem to forget is that striking the right balance will not be achieved by excessive forms of abstinence, but by modest behavioral changes accompanied by some measure of slight discomfort. In the case of the *Nazir*, the Torah requires abstinence from

---

1. See *Shabbat* 118b.

2. See *Bamidbar* 6.

3. For a broad overview of this topic, see Sara Epstein Weinstein, *Piety and Fanaticism: Rabbinic Criticism of Religious Stringency* (Northvale, NJ: Jason Aronson, 1997); Yehuda Levi, "Laudable, Boorish, and Heretical *Chumroth* (Stringencies)," in *Torah Study: A Survey of Classic Sources on Timely Issues*, trans. Raphael N. Levi (Jerusalem: Feldheim, 2002), 114–134.

certain alcoholic drinks, and to leave the hair untrimmed and the beard unshaved. Nothing more. According to Mishnaic Tradition, this should not last longer than thirty days.[4] It seems to be warning us that longer periods of abstinence will be counterproductive.

Most interesting is the fact that at the end of this thirty-day period, a sin offering has to be brought by the very individuals who took these stringencies upon themselves.[5] Besides this, when the period is over, the Nazirite is *commanded* to drink wine.[6] *This means that the abstinence from permitted pleasures requires atonement because such stringencies are in fact, and under normal circumstances, prohibited.*[7] The only reason why such restrictions are permitted for short periods is that they will result in the possibility of enjoying these pleasures at a later stage, in a way which is part of one's religious experience, i.e., as a human being who is able to enjoy the gifts of the Almighty.[8] And this is the reason why the Nazirite is told to drink wine. The Nazirite must, after the period of abstinence, be able to drink wine in the proper, elevated way. It is not the abstinence from wine and other alcoholic drinks which is a major achievement, but the art of enjoying them in the right spirit and with the correct intentions. This is a much greater achievement.

It should be made clear that this is only true when the Torah permits the use of these delights. Drug abuse would not be considered permitted pleasures, since use of these drugs may lead to a kind of addiction from which few, if any, are able to free themselves. They are detrimental to the mental and physical health of the human being. Ultimately they destroy the capacity to enjoy life in the higher sense of the word.

Still, sometimes certain stringencies are nothing less than a form of escape – a mechanism for self-deception. They are used to hide a lack of proper observance in other religious matters, and are often used to cloak unethical behavior. When people do wrong in their relationship with their fellowman, but hide behind their insistence on *glatt kosher* food, we face a deliberate and vulgar misuse of the concept of *chumrot* (sing. *chumra* – stringency). (Asking for *glatt kosher* food while sitting in jail for

---

4. According to *Mishna Nazir* 1:3, an ordinary acceptance of *nezirut* lasts no longer than thirty days.

5. *Bamidbar* 6:13–21.

6. *Bamidbar* 6:20.

7. See *Sifrei Bamidbar*, Horowitz ed., section 30; *Nedarim* 10a. For a more positive view of the Nazirite, see *Sifrei Zuta*, Horowitz ed., on *Bamidbar* 6:8; *Ta'anit* 11. See also the sources cited by Steven Fraade, "The Nazirite in Ancient Judaism (Selected Texts)," in *Ascetic Behavior in Greco-Roman Antiquity*, ed. Vincent L. Wimbush (Minneapolis: Fortress Press, 1990), 213–233.

8. See JT *Nedarim* 9:1, 41b.

having committed a criminal offence is tantamount to asking, after one has murdered both parents, for dispensation on the grounds that one is an orphan.)

The Talmud recounts the story of a scholar by the name of Eliezer Ze'era who wore black shoes (uncommon in those days) as a sign of mourning for the destruction of Jerusalem. The sages considered this an act of arrogance. They felt that he was trying to show off, so they put him in jail![9]

On another occasion, the sages opposed a "very religious" person who refused to follow a lenient ruling which they had decided on, and nearly excommunicated him.[10]

A story has been told that a rabbi once came to see the famous Jerusalem sage and halachic authority, Rabbi Shlomo Zalman Auerbach. He asked him if a certain *chumra* that was practiced in his community had any foundation in Halacha, or simply belonged to the world of religious fancy. The sage responded that there was no foundation for such a stringency, and advised the rabbi to tell his community to repeal this practice. Several weeks later, the Jerusalem sage met the rabbi and asked him if he had told his community to stop practicing this mistaken *chumra*. The rabbi turned to the sage and said half-jokingly, "No, it is a leniency which my congregation cannot live with. . .[11]

9. *Bava Kamma* 59.
10. *Bava Kamma* 81b.
11. See "Kuntres Netivot Shlomo," *Yeshurun: Me'asef Torani* 15 (2005): 540.

Six

HALACHA: BETWEEN UTOPIAN VISION AND REALISTIC POSSIBILITIES

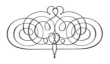

Chapter 18

Why the Kashrut Laws Were Given So Late

Nothing brings to light more about a book than its beginning, and the Torah is no exception. As such, the opening remarks of Rashi to his biblical commentary should prove most instructive. Asks Rashi, "Why does the Torah start with the narrative of creation? If the Torah is meant to be a guide for how to live the best possible life, it should rather skip to the first law delivered to the Jewish people as a whole: 'And this month shall be the first of months.'"[1] With this simple question, Rashi opens up a Pandora's box of other questions about the Torah's intent. Is it a historical narrative, relaying to us the moral message of our ancestors' successes and failures? Or is it rather a code of law, coming to teach us precisely which acts evoke God's blessings and which provoke His ire? No sooner do we focus on one of these aspects than we are confronted by the other. So here lies the problem: One cannot neatly divide the Torah between its didactic and legalistic elements. True, the first book and a half of the five Books of Moshe consist mainly of narrative, but from that point on the program switches back and forth, creating a dynamic interchange of law and lore.

THE EARLIER AND THE LATER

Whenever we attempt to figure out why any given portion appears precisely in the place that it does, we find ourselves most perplexed. Is this the correct location for this law or story? Would it not have made more

---

1. *Rashi* on *Bereshit* 1:1.

sense elsewhere? How does it relate within this particular context? Since the author of the book is none other than the Creator of the Universe Who designed the human body and set the planets in their orbits and Who is perfect and omniscient, it follows that each word and letter of His manifesto should fit into a logical, organic pattern.

Questions regarding the organizational structure of the Torah have become the stock-in-trade of biblical commentary. It is not uncommon to find the greatest of our commentators asking how a certain section relates to that which came before it, or why this or that particular law seems to have been written out of place. All in all, no one seems quite content with the order of the Torah as we have it before us. And rightly so, because no matter how you slice it, the Torah at first glance does not seem to follow the type of logical progression that we would expect from the greatest book of all time.

To add to the confusion, the proposed answers to these difficulties branch off into many far-ranging philosophical disputes, rather than provide any consensus. We even find disagreement about such a fundamental issue as whether the Torah is bound to a chronological pattern at all or not. Some maintain the view that "en mukdam u-me'uchar ba-Torah" (there is no *before* or *after* in the Torah).[2] Even according to them, however, this rule may sometimes be circumvented. But if the Torah may depart from a historical sequence, when exactly will it conform to the rule of order and when will it not? What meta-principles dictate the deviations from the natural timeline?

Before attempting to answer these questions, I would like to consider yet another question. It may seem innocuous enough at first, but once pondered it may open up for us new and daring vistas of thought which will draw us to make some provocative conclusions as to the purpose of the mitzvot and the nature of man.

TIP OF THE ICEBERG

The question, originally put forward by the renowned Italian scholar Rabbi Ovadia Seforno (c. 1470–c. 1550), is concerned specifically with kashrut (Jewish dietary law), and also with *taharat ha-mishpacha* (Jewish family purity laws).[3] These laws seem to arrive too late in the biblical

---

2. See *Talmudic Encyclopedia*, s.v. "en mukdam u-me'uchar ba-Torah," 1:647–649.

3. Seforno discusses his general approach in considerable detail in the introduction to his commentary to the Torah.

narrative, appearing for the first time in the book of *Vayikra*, the third of the five books of the Torah. Why in fact do these mitzvot, so essential to Jewish living, not find their place earlier in the text? We would probably expect their introduction in the book of *Shemot*, along with so many other basic laws of Judaism. There we find the Ten Commandments as well as the *mishpatim*, which together form the basis of Jewish civil law. But where are the laws of kashrut? Where are the laws of family purity? The Torah almost treats them as after-thoughts. Or perhaps even worse. Perhaps the late-game introduction of these laws intimates to us that they are problematic.

But this is really only the tip of the iceberg. Once we start asking questions like these, we can go on and on. Let us ask yet another: Why was the Torah itself given so late in history? Jews had been around for hundreds of years before the revelation at Mount Sinai. Why didn't God present the Torah to the first Jews; Avraham, Yitzchak, and Ya'akov? True, the forefathers kept many of the mitzvot, but they did so only on a voluntary basis, as a result of their own derivations about the spiritual reality, and not because they had been commanded to do so by God. Only much later in Jewish history do we find mitzvot actually coming to us by way of divine decree. One might logically infer that the earlier generations simply did not need the Torah. But if the Torah is the eternal Truth – the blueprint of creation – then surely its statutes must have timeless relevance? What is the Torah if its message has temporal limitations?

BREAKING POINT

Much of the discussion of the Torah's chronological sequencing revolves around a singular event in Jewish history. As such, this pivotal event must be our point of departure for the journey into the world that Rabbi Ovadia Seforno wants us to enter. The episode to which I refer is the *Chet ha-Egel*, the Sin of the Golden Calf.

A mere forty days after the Creator of the Universe revealed Himself with the words, "I am the Lord, your God,"[4] the Jewish people sank into sinful idolatry. Moshe had ascended to Heaven to receive the Tablets of the Covenant, but he tarried too long for the eager masses waiting at the foot of the mountain. After forty days and forty nights, many assumed that Moshe had simply ceased to exist as a physical being and would not

---

4. *Shemot* 20:2.

be returning to them. In their desperation, the people turned to Moshe's brother, Aharon, asking him to make them an idol to compensate for the loss of their leader. As a golden calf emerged from the blazing fire, those taken in by its charm declared, "These are your gods, O Israel."[5] The shocking contrast between this spiritual nadir and the exalted heights they experienced just forty days before could not be any starker.

As difficult as it is to make sense of the Sin of the Golden Calf (and we will explore its significance), what proves even more difficult to understand is the debate over when it took place. As mentioned, in the historical progression of events, it took place exactly forty days after the Jewish people received the Torah. The question, though, lies within the text itself: Is the story of the Golden Calf ordered sequentially with regard to the other events recorded before and after it, or not?

This question takes on special significance in relation to God's command to build the *Mishkan*,[6] the Tent of Meeting that would later become a prototype for the Temple. Was this command issued prior to the *Chet ha-Egel*, as we find clearly indicated in the sequence of the text of the Torah before us, or is the Torah's presentation of these events entirely out of order? Did the instruction to build the *Mishkan* actually come after the sin? While this line of inquiry may sound academic, the consequences of its resolution ripple through the entire foundation of Jewish thought.

THE DISPUTE

The timing of the command to build the *Mishkan* vis-a-vis the *Chet ha-Egel* is the subject of a major dispute among the classical commentators. Ramban holds that the command took place long before the sin – that it was actually decreed shortly after the revelation at Sinai.[7] After forging a covenant with God and agreeing to be His treasured nation, it was only fitting for the Jews to have a place where God could rest His presence amongst them. From this sanctuary God would speak with Moshe and issue forth mitzvot for the Jewish people. We see, therefore, that according to Ramban, the *Mishkan* held an intrinsically necessary function, essential to Jewish belief and praxis.[8]

Rashi, however, takes an altogether different approach. We find that the

---

5. *Shemot* 32:4.
6. *Shemot* 25:8.
7. See *Ramban* on *Shemot* 35:1.
8. *Ramban*, introduction to *Shemot*.

Torah refers to the *Mishkan* as *Mishkan ha-Edut*, a sanctuary of testimony. But to what did the *Mishkan* testify? Rashi explains that the *Mishkan* testified to the fact that God had forgiven us for the Golden Calf.[9] After threatening to destroy the Jewish people for worshiping it, the very command to build the *Mishkan* gave testimony to the fact that God desired to draw close to us once again.

Against Ramban's protests, we hear Rashi's opinion clearly stating that the *Mishkan* came into conception only *after* the *Chet ha-Egel*. Had the Jewish people not built the Golden Calf, we would never have needed a *Mishkan*.

A NEW WORLD ORDER

Rabbi Ovadia Seforno follows Rashi's line but takes it one step further. In a way, Seforno arrives at the logical conclusion of Rashi's hypothesis – that the institution of the *Mishkan* represented a much more fundamental transformation.

The Torah introduces the command to build the *Mishkan* with the following words: "Make Me a sanctuary so that I may dwell among you. Just as I have shown you, the structure of the *Mishkan* and the structure of its vessels, so shall you do."[10]

Here, Seforno makes a most fascinating comment:

> So shall you do in order that I [God] may dwell among you [Israel], speaking with you and accepting your prayers and the service. But not as the matter stood before the *Chet ha-Egel*, as it had been said previously, "in *any* place . . . I will come to you."[11]

After the sin, we only have one place to seek God in a very intimate way: the *Mishkan*. But it had not always been that way. Earlier in our history, we could seek God in any place, and He in turn would come to us. Not only did we not need the *Mishkan*, but neither would we have needed the Temple in Yerushalayim. Even Yerushalayim itself would never have risen to any special significance. Were it not for the Sin of the Golden Calf, the whole world would have been a Temple, the entire universe a

---

9. *Rashi* on *Shemot* 38:21. See also *Rashi* on *Shemot* 31:18, 33:11.
10. *Shemot* 25:8–9.
11. *Seforno* on *Shemot* 24:18.

Yerushalayim. Since God is everywhere, we really should be able to serve Him in the most profound way anywhere at all.

One can easily see, therefore, that prior to the *Chet ha-Egel*, Judaism was of an entirely different essential nature. The religion was decentralized, and perhaps even more open and free-spirited. One needed no pilgrimage to any holy site. Every home was a temple and every corner a possible place of worship. Perhaps most astounding of all, this is the way it would have remained! Were it not for the sin of the *Egel*, we would never have been given limitations on our service of God.

But the situation changes drastically after the *Chet ha-Egel*. God, to be sure, is still everywhere, but our service now requires constraints, becoming bound within an all-too-specific realm. The *Mishkan* can offer us a symbol of God's omnipresence, drawing our awareness toward that lofty realization, but we no longer have the freedom to act as if we really live on the plane of that elevated consciousness. From now on we may serve God only in the precise place and in the meticulous manner in which He instructs us. Hence our need for a *Mishkan*, a Temple, and a Holy City.

HOLDING ON TO TIME

Reflecting back on all that has been said, one cannot help but wonder why the Sin of the Golden Calf should have necessitated such a radical alteration in the method of our divine worship.

The first point to explore must be the sin itself, because, at least at face value, it really appears to make no sense at all. How could a people who had just witnessed a divine revelation turn around such a short time later and serve an idol? They had heard the word of God telling them, "Do not make a graven image."[12] How could they have doubted that their actions would meet with anything other than the Creator's full wrath? Nevertheless, our people sinned, falling from the heights of revelation to the depths of idolatry within the span of a mere forty days.

So implausible and paradoxical is this event, that a surface-level understanding simply cannot hold water. The experience of revelation was too awe-inspiring, too overpowering for such a turnabout to be comprehensible without deeper analysis.

Only when we see the metaphysics behind the story of the Golden Calf do we get an understanding of how the Jewish people could behave in

---

12. *Shemot* 20:4.

such a seemingly fickle manner. And in fact, it turns out that the two events – the revelation and the idolatry – rather than contradicting one another, are actually entirely complementary, like a particle and a wave. On a deeper level of reality, the *Chet ha-Egel* issues forth as the direct and logical consequence of the Sinai experience. Built into that very experience came a need, a desire, to build the *Egel*. As absurd as it sounds, the revelation of God actually led in a rational, causal progression to the sin.

How does this work? The answer is actually rather simple: It is one thing to experience direct spiritual revelation, but it is quite another to hold on to it. Spirituality is not difficult to experience, especially when one is confronted from the outside by the Deity. Anyone can receive revelation if God chooses to bestow it. The challenge lies in maintaining that degree of inspiration once the moment of encounter has passed. Inspiration comes in a momentary high, but living the rest of one's life with the awareness granted in that fleeting moment often proves to be an exponentially more difficult challenge. Passing that inspiration on to the next generation is, of course, even more difficult. The revelation certainly made an impression, but, like with all experiences, Sinai too fades from consciousness with the passing of time. How then to preserve the effect of the greatest event in all of human history? To let it pass would have been a tragedy of the highest order. The Jews at Sinai understood this problem, and therefore came up with a plan. They knew that the nature of experience is ephemeral, so they devised a way to hold on to Sinai permanently, both for themselves and for all future generations. Their solution was what we call the Golden Calf.

SYMBOLIC SINAI

In reality, the Jews did with the Golden Calf what we all do whenever forced to grapple with an abstract concept: we make a model. When the true grasp of an idea evades us, we seek tangible substitutes for the intangible. That is why it is not uncommon to find scientists utilizing models to understand the most intangible elements of our world, such as the structure of the atom or the curvature of space-time. Likewise, this explains why the rabbis of the Talmud always discussed concrete legal cases or taught philosophical ideas by way of metaphor. We humans need models to perceive abstract concepts.

We all experience moments of breakthrough. At these times, as when lightning flashes in pitch darkness, we are shown a brief glimpse of the hidden. But the impact of such experiences is all too fleeting. Therefore, if we wish to recreate the inspiration, we will need something to remind us of it. A model provides just such a tool. It helps us tap into the lofty awareness we once grasped in totality but that has now dissipated into a mist of ambiguity. A frozen model serves as a medium to transform the esoteric and metaphysical into more user-friendly, human terms. As such, it provides the key for concretizing the transitory impressions left by our transcendent experiences.

The Jews felt that they could never live in the higher world, relating so abstractly to the absolute awareness of God's existence. As such, they sought to translate their experience of revelation into more tangible, palatable, and transmittable terms. The alternative, they thought, would have meant losing the experience forever. After a while, they themselves might have fallen into disbelief about whether or not the revelation had actually taken place. How much more so the Jews in later generations! Therefore, in an attempt to capture their experience for posterity and to eliminate the potential for doubt, the Jews fashioned the ultimate memento.

THE *EGEL* UNCOVERED

It may prove difficult for us today to appreciate why a statue of a baby cow would be the most effective symbol for the most sublime experience in human history. The Golden Calf does not seem to us to capture the essence of divine revelation. However, this lack of understanding comes from our crude translation of the Torah's term *Egel ha-Zahav*. Translating this phrase as "Golden Calf" cheapens its meaning immeasurably. We must look deeper into its symbolism to truly understand what the *Egel ha-Zahav* was really all about.

To the Jews at Sinai, the *Egel* represented a metaphysical reality – an abstract demonstration of God's dominion over creation. In fact, we find that when the prophets experienced the height of divine inspiration, the image of a calf was always part of their vision. The revelation recorded in the prophecy of Yechezkel, known as the *Ma'aseh Merkava* (the Working of the Chariot), relates the deepest of kabbalistic secrets about the relationship of the Creator to His creation. Not surprisingly, the *Egel* plays a prominent role in that vision, described as one of the four images engraved on God's "chariot."[13] While a full analysis of this topic is beyond

---

13. *Yechezkel* 1:7.

the scope of these pages, we must nevertheless appreciate that whatever its ultimate meaning, the *Egel* is certainly neither simple nor absurd.

Hence we come to relate to the *Egel ha-Zahav* in a completely new light. Much more than a mere idol, it was a symbol representing a metaphysical reality in the upper worlds. As a model, it served to invoke the spirit of revelation to all those who viewed it. The *Egel* became a realistic and pragmatic attempt to capture the Sinai experience. It was a tool for the preservation of revelation.

THE DISTINCTION

While all this helps to explain how the Jewish people could have come to build the Golden Calf, what now escapes our understanding is why it was viewed as such a sin. God protests the making of the calf in the strongest terms, threatening to destroy the Jews and to create in their place a new people out of Moshe's progeny.[14] But in light of what we now know to be the intent behind the *Egel*, what was actually so wrong about making it?

What makes this even more difficult to understand is the fact that inside the *Mishkan*, which God Himself commanded us to build, we find another *Egel* of sorts. The only difference between the *Egel* and the symbol used in the *Mishkan* is that this time the graven image takes the form of two children rather than a calf. The *keruvim* (cherubs) were also golden statues, yet God actually commands us to place them right inside the *Mishkan* – in the Holy of the Holies, no less![15] Moreover, it was from the space between the two *keruvim* that God communicated directly with Moshe. The *keruvim* stood as guards at the portal between the physical and the spiritual worlds. There is no place more holy on Earth. And yet, like the *Egel*, they too were just statues. They too were just symbols. We are left wondering why the *Egel* that the Jews created on their own accord was so much worse than the *keruvim* that God commanded them to make.

The answer, of course, is just that: one was initiated by man and the other by God. When man makes an *Egel*, it is a sin of the highest magnitude, but when God makes one, He creates holiness in space. The distinction is anything but arbitrary. When man, in his limited understanding and insufficient imagination, attempts to create a representation of the transcendent revelation experience, he is doomed to fail. The ability to

---

14. *Shemot* 32:7–14.
15. See *Shemot* 25:18–20.

craft the appropriate symbol lies beyond his limited capacity. And when a symbol lacks accuracy of representation, it fails completely as an appropriate symbol. The object becomes at best a cartoonish caricature, and at worst an idol. God, however, completely comprehends the object to be represented, and thus knows how to fashion its symbol correctly. Only God can conceive of a symbol that captures the true essence of holiness.

INTENT VS. CONTENT

The explanation of the sin of the Golden Calf outlined above was originally put forward by the medieval Spanish philosopher and poet, Rabbi Yehuda ha-Levi, in his magnum opus, *The Kuzari*. True to its author's artistic spirit, *The Kuzari* presents an apologetic for the Jewish faith by way of a hypothetical conversation between two unlikely protagonists: a righteous non-Jewish king of the Khazar people and his friend, a Jewish sage.

The king had always been a very pious man in his own right; a man devoted single-mindedly to the service of God as he understood it within the framework of his native religion. But his curiosity about other faiths is piqued by a certain dream, oft repeated in his night time slumber, in which he is told, "Your intention is pleasing to the Creator, but not your manner of acting."[16]

This vision sends the king on a search for truth that engages him with thinking men of different faiths – Greek philosophy, Christianity, and Islam. Eventually, his search for the true path brings him into contact with a learned rabbi. During the course of their discussion, the sage leads the king with great competence through the world of Jewish philosophy, ultimately convincing him of Judaism's veracity. The king then converts to the faith of the Jews, together with his entire kingdom.

At the point where their conversation focuses on the *Chet ha-Egel*, the sage explains to the king the secret behind this sin. The problem, he tells him, arose in that the making of the *Egel* had not issued forth as a mandate by God. The people sinned by believing that they were able to grasp God and His relationship with humanity via the *Egel*. This, however, is idol worship. Only God knows which symbol is adequately capable of expressing this.[17]

---

16. *The Kuzari*, 1:1.
17. *The Kuzari*, 1:97.

To his credit, the astute king understands the implications of what the sage tells him. At this point he bursts forth in a sudden epiphany that captures the crux of the issue precisely:

> Behold, you have confirmed for me the opinion that I arrived at through meditation as well as that which I saw in my dream, and that is: the only way by which man may hope to reach the sublime is to be directed to it by the Sublime, through actions dictated by God.[18]

Like the Khazar king, the Jewish people failed to reach the Divine through their actions, despite their virtuous intentions. Man does not enjoy the freedom of choosing his own path to God. He must rather be guided upon that road by none other than God Himself.

The Jewish people meant well, but that did not suffice. Building the *Egel* on their own accord was wrong, no matter how noble the cause. The principle we learn from their mistake is that the noble intentions that motivate an action do not make it righteous. Only the divinely willed content of an action can give it real, positive, moral value.

DIVINE CONCESSION

In place of the *Egel*, God gives us the *Mishkan* – the true symbol of that which we sought to represent with the *Egel*. But He agrees to this compromise with a sense of regret, as it were. Service via *Mishkan* is not God's ideal manner of worship, but with the *Chet ha-Egel*, man proved himself incapable of relating to God in purely abstract, non-symbolic terms. Man demonstrated his weakness, conceding that he cannot live on an entirely elevated plane, constantly aware of God's presence. It has proven too difficult for him to realize that the entire universe is a single Temple. Ultimate reality must be watered down for him and translated into his own terms; he can only relate to it through the medium of a tangible symbol.

With the *Egel*, we mistakenly attempted to make our own symbolic representation. God therefore supplies us with the real one, namely the *Mishkan*. As conceived by Rashi and Seforno, then, the *Mishkan* represents a divine concession to man's spiritual weakness.

Listen to Rashi's explanation of *Mishkan ha-Edut*, the dwelling place of testimony: "Edut le-Yisrael she-viter la-hem ha-Kadosh Baruch Hu al

---

18. *The Kuzari*, 1:98.

ma'aseh ha-Egel" (It is testimony to Israel that God conceded to them regarding the incident of the Calf).[19]

With the *Egel* we showed that we needed to translate the revelation experience into our own terms. Henceforth, with the *Mishkan*, God provides us with just that. He gives us a specific and unique place in which to worship, a place where it will be possible to recreate the inspiration of Sinai; a place where we can palpably experience the presence of God. But as inspirational as that sounds, and as magnificent as it must have been, the Holy One never intended it as anything more than a compromise. In the realm of the ideal, the cosmos serves as God's *Mishkan*.

A HEALTHY DIET

Taking this insight into account, we can now begin to understand Seforno's answer to our original inquiry: why were the kashrut and purity laws introduced so late? Why, after all, do we only learn about them after the *Chet ha-Egel*, and not before? The answer, as we shall see, relates precisely to the incident of the Golden Calf.

> And God spoke to Moshe and to Aharon saying to them: Speak to the Children of Israel saying, "This is the type of animal that you may eat. . ."[20]

With this verse, the Torah presents us for the first time[21] with the Jewish dietary laws – which animals we may eat and which we may not. At this point, Seforno delivers his own remarkable and daring introduction to these laws:

> After the moment that Israel fell from the spiritual heights they had acquired at Sinai, a level upon which they were fitting for God to place His presence upon them without any medium or symbol . . . it became despicable to God to dwell amongst them at all. Until, that is, Moshe was able to achieve a degree of amelioration with his prayers, to the effect that now God would place His presence amongst them through the medium of the *Mishkan*. . . . And so too, God saw fit to

---

19. *Rashi* on *Shemot* 38:21.
20. *Vayikra* 11:1–2.
21. With the exception of meat and milk mixtures (*basar be-chalav*), which is mentioned earlier, in *Shemot* 23:19 and 34:16.

remedy their temperament so that it would be fitting for the light of eternal life, and this He accomplished through the regulation of diet and sexual relations.[22]

A most daring and remarkable thesis indeed! Just as the *Mishkan* had come as a concession to man's degraded spiritual status after the *Chet ha-Egel*, so too the laws of kashrut and family purity! In the same way that we lost the immediate impression of God's omnipresence, so too our entire ability to receive the influence of spirituality underwent a drastic transformation.

Before the *Chet ha-Egel*, the Jewish soul attained such a rarefied degree of perfection that it became insusceptible to the influence of impurity, whether dietary or sexual. These urges simply held no excessive power over our beings. But now, in this lower level of existence, the influence of impurity threatens to dilute our spiritual sensitivities.

To put it bluntly, the basic message Seforno wishes to impart is this: *when we are healthy we do not need a diet*; nor do we need to regulate our sexual activity quite so much. But when we fall ill, our defenses are down and we become susceptible to detrimental influences upon our spiritual health. It is then that we need to follow a stricter diet and to watch our bodily activity with greater care.

Perhaps, one may ask, why should such mundane activity affect the state of our lofty souls? But to pose such a question would be to ignore the integrated reality of our spiritual station after the Sin of the Golden Calf. Things have changed. The soul has now become susceptible to physical impurity. And hence, it must be treated appropriately. That is why God offers us an elixir in the form of dietary and sexual regulations.

These mitzvot do more than just help us ward off any further decline. As the reality of our spiritual standing after the *Chet ha-Egel* means that we have become susceptible to impurity, what these laws actually accomplish is to raise us beyond the limitations of our condition, to bring us back to the exalted level that we occupied before the Sin of the Golden Calf.

THE TIMELY TORAH

Following this logic will help to answer the other question that we raised. Why didn't the original Jews, our holy forefathers, receive the Torah? Why was it left only to their descendants in later generations?

---

22. *Seforno* on *Vayikra* 11:2.

The answer by now should appear quite obvious: the earlier generations simply did not need it. In their superior state of spiritual health, they could serve God without the mitzvot. As such, they lived on a level higher even than that of the Jews at Sinai. And while they certainly kept many of the mitzvot, they did so not out of duty, but as a natural expression of their closeness to God. Their service was a voluntary one issuing forth from the purity of their hearts, without the need of divine decree. They used the mitzvot to approach God, to come closer to Him, but they did not need them to combat a weak nature.

We need not rely on a mere extrapolation from the laws of kashrut, for indeed we find that this insight permeated Seforno's entire interpretation of biblical events. An example from his writings on the book of *Bereshit* should prove instructive:

The *parasha* (Torah portion) of *Vayetze* records the births of the children born to Ya'akov; twelve sons from four wives. As the competition to produce the *shevatim* (the tribes of Israel) ensues, we are awe-struck by the devotion of our matriarchs in their desire to forge the nascent nation. As Rachel so eloquently states in her naming of Naftali, she had to resort to "sacred schemes" in order to ensure her portion of the Jewish heritage.[23]

One problem that emerges from the story, however, is that it all takes place far too quickly. Even if there was some overlap in the pregnancies of Ya'akov's four wives (as Seforno suggests), at best we end up with nine births within seven years! In order to make sense of this scenario, we are forced to make a crucial assumption: that each conception took place immediately after the birth of the previous child.

But what happened to the laws of family purity? These laws require a period of restraint after the birth of a child. Leah, though, becomes pregnant over and over again far too quickly to allow for the observance of these laws. Therefore, concludes Seforno, it is possible that our forefathers simply did not keep the laws of family purity.[24]

SEFORNO AND HISTORICIZING THE MITZVOT

Our forefathers did not observe many of the laws we find in the Torah. We must realize of course, that this seeming lack of religiosity on their part is actually an expression of their incredibly high spiritual levels. They

---

23. *Bereshit* 30:8.
24. See *Seforno* on *Bereshit* 30:8.

were simply unaffected by certain elements of impurity that held sway over their lesser descendants. Only in later generations did the Jews come to need more laws to counter the flaws in their nature. Our ancestors, though, still gigantic in their spiritual stature, simply did not require all the mitzvot to serve God correctly. They could be entirely religious, even without so much religion.

This insight has dangerous implications. It seems to suggest that the binding nature of the mitzvot changes with the times. One might wish to conclude that if there was once a time when certain mitzvot were not mandatory, then perhaps such a time may well come around again. Or perhaps it has already come? There is indeed a view which states that in the messianic age some of the mitzvot will be abolished, but definitely not prior to this time.[25]

Of course, Seforno had no intention of historicizing the mitzvot (i.e., of weakening them by limiting their relevance to within a particular historical context). Just the opposite! To understand Seforno properly is to realize that our relationship to the mitzvot only strengthens with time. From his perspective, the argument for historicization runs straight in the opposite direction. Times certainly change, but only for the worse. As history progresses, we require more intense devotion to the Torah and mitzvot in order to relate properly to God.[26]

PROGRESSIVE REGRESSION

We usually think of progress in terms of scientific and technological advancement. Within such a framework, I admit, we may accurately describe the course of human development as a linear progression. As time marches on, our storehouse of knowledge grows exponentially, and so too do our technical capabilities. However, seen in such a light, the present takes primacy while the past finds itself relegated to "the trash heap of

---

25. See *Nidda* 61b; *Kiddushin* 72b regarding *mamzerim*; *Midrash Tehillim*, Buber ed., 146:4; *Ritva* on *Nidda* 61b; *Ramban* on *Devarim* 30:6; R. Avraham Shmuel Binyamin Sofer, *Ketav Sofer, Orach Chaim*, no. 4; R. Shlomo Kluger, *Avodat Avoda* on *Avoda Zara* 65a (Jerusalem: Machon le-Cheker Kitvei Yad Chochmat Shlomo, 1994), 560; R. Menachem Mendel Schneerson, "Halachot shel Torah she-Ba'al Peh she-Enan Betelin le-Olam," in *Sefer ha-Sichot 5752*, vol. 1 (NY: Kehot, 1993), 27–36. For an overview of this issue, see R. Yehudah Chayoun, *Otzrot Acharit ha-Yamim*, vol. 1 (Bnei Brak, 1993), chap. 12; R. Avrohom Yitzchak Baruch Gerlitzky, *Yemot ha-Mashiach be-Halacha* (NY: AYB Gerlitzky, 2005), 249–253, 318–329, 366–372; R. Michoel Peretz, *Ohalei Shem: Mashiach le-Ohr ha-Halacha* (Mexico, 2002), 106–109.

26. See, however, pp. 288–299 below for another view.

history." Man could never have been more advanced than he is at this very moment.

From such a perspective, though, the words of King Shlomo cry out emotively: "The superiority of man over beast is for naught."[27] It would seem as if the difference was one of mere quantity of knowledge, not quality of being. But the Torah maintains a very different calculus for evaluating man's worth. Unlike the popular notion of progress as set within scientific parameters, Judaism measures human development with the yardstick of the soul. And unlike science, by this standard our talents have only waned with the passing of time.

This idea is known in Judaism as the doctrine of *yeridat ha-dorot*, the decline of the generations: each generation falls lower in spiritual status than the generation that preceded it. The qualities of the soul, such as moral fortitude and spiritual purity, only become diluted as the generations pass. As we grow increasingly aware of our physical drives and desires, our sensitivity to ethical issues and matters of the soul becomes all the more obscured. We may progress in our technological aptitude, inventing new machines and better cures, but this kind of external advancement fails to portray an accurate picture of our intrinsic development as human beings. As for the unification of a body and a soul, man's progress can only be measured by the degree to which one's spirit holds sway over one's physical nature.

Man is much more than a maker of machines. What truly determines his worth is the degree of his moral perfection and closeness to God. As such, morality, purity, and spirituality provide the only genuine barometer of man's development. And by these criteria, history records our degeneration.

A MODICUM OF RESTRAINT

Seforno's extremely original approach applies the doctrine of *yeridat ha-dorot* to a global understanding of the mitzvot, with all that this implies. If previous generations stood on higher ground, then we can assume that their souls operated with less need for the mitzvot. Conversely, as we fall further with the passing of time, we become more in need of the mitzvot.

It must be stressed, however, that this is a highly daring assumption, especially for such a relatively recent Torah commentator as Seforno. It

---

27. *Kohelet* 3:19.

would all rest much more easily if we could find some backing for this thesis in the words of an earlier, perhaps even more classical text of Jewish thought.

Such support can indeed be found in one of the classic works of Jewish philosophy, the *Chovot ha-Levavot – Duties of the Heart* (Spain, 1040). Written by Rabbi Bachya ibn Pakuda, this powerful treatise provides both a fundamental introduction to Jewish thought and a comprehensive guide to character development. It is within these hallowed pages that we find a statement resonating with Seforno's wisdom.

Toward the end of the work, *Chovot ha-Levavot* discusses the character trait of restraint. Defining the term very generally as "a bridling of the inner lust," Rabbenu Bachya has this to say regarding its historical relevance:

> The difference between the earlier generations and us as concerns the trait of restraint is just this: men such as Chanoch, Noach, Avraham, Yitzchak, and Ya'akov . . . maintained a clear mind and yet a weak evil inclination, which therefore led them to follow after their intellects. As such, a minimum amount of mitzvot sufficed for them, together with the purity of their faith, to serve God fully and completely. . . . They had no need for asceticism, which departs from the Golden Mean that the Torah prescribes.
>
> But when their descendents went down to Egypt . . . their sensual lust strengthened and their desire increased until ultimately their evil inclination prevailed over their reason. Hence they stood in need of a mode of restraint to counter their desire and help them resist their evil inclination. God therefore gave them mitzvot that were to be obeyed by divine decree as a set minimum level of restraint, fitting not only to their capacity but even lower.[28]

In the generations preceding the Torah, the relationship of the body to the soul was such that essentially the soul retained the upper hand. The mind, as it were, held sway over the heart. In such a spiritual condition, man needed very little self-restraint to serve God correctly. Those elements within his psyche that distracted him from his divine service required nary an effort to overcome.

But as impurity slowly crept into the heart of man, it became necessary

---

28. *Chovot ha-Levavot, Sha'ar ha-Perishut*, chap. 7.

for him to muster more effort to control his own inclinations. Therefore, by the time the Jews left Egypt, they needed much more spiritual instruction to condition themselves to the service of God. While their ancestors found it possible to do so with only a few mitzvot, the Jews of the Exodus needed hundreds.

To this insight, Seforno would just add that after the Sin of the Golden Calf we needed yet a few more biblical laws. Having become more susceptible to impurity, the Jews required a further mode of restraint (in the form of kashrut and family purity laws), as food and sexual pleasure, while in themselves not negative at all, became major distractions from the true purpose of existence.[29]

---

29. There are several questions that Seforno does not address: Based on his thesis, would there not be a need for even more mitzvot in our days since the principle of *yeridat ha-dorot* applies today to an even greater extent? Maybe the 613 mitzvot of the Torah are insufficient? Or does Seforno hold that the 613 are sufficient even for generations that fall even lower? Does he believe that rabbinical law overcomes this problem? Moreover, since the prohibitions on Shabbat are derived from the work which was done to build the *Mishkan*, would this mean that Shabbat would have been observed differently were it not for the incident with the Golden Calf? Or is the deduction from the work to build the *Mishkan* only an *asmachta*, a "rabbinical leaning on," and not the real reason at all? See *Mishna Shabbat* 7:2 and associated commentaries.

Finally there is the question about the obligation to observe the mitzvot of the Torah in the messianic age. Is there still any need for this? Or will the mitzvot still apply on a higher and more perfect level? See Nathan Lopes Cardozo, *The Torah as God's Mind: A Kabbalistic Look into the Pentateuch* (NY: Bep Ron, 1988). See also n25 above.

See also Marc B. Shapiro, *The Limits of Orthodox Theology: Maimonides' Thirteen Principles Reappraised* (Oxford: Littman Library of Jewish Civilization, 2004), chap. 8.

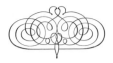

Chapter 19

Sacrifices: Progressive or Regressive Judaism?
Why Spinoza's Ethics Were Not Given at Sinai

Does Judaism really need animal sacrifices? Would it not be better off without them? After all, the sacrificial cult seems to compromise Judaism. What does a highly ethical religion have to do with the collection of blood in vessels and the burning of animal limbs on an altar?

No doubt Judaism should be sacrifice-free. Yet it is not.

So, is the offering of sacrifices Jewish, or not? The answer is an unequivocal yes. It is Jewish, but it doesn't really belong to Judaism.

If Judaism had had the chance, it would have dropped the entire institution of sacrifices in a second. Better yet, it would have had no part in it to begin with. How much more beautiful the Torah would be without sacrifices! How wonderful it would be if a good part of *Sefer Vayikra* were removed from the biblical text, or had never been there in the first place.

So what are these sacrifices doing there?

The answer is that the Torah doesn't really represent Judaism in its ideal form. Not in all its glory.

There are actually two kinds of Judaism. There is the Judaism of today and the Judaism of tomorrow. There is realistic Judaism and idyllic Judaism. What fills the gap between them is the world of Halacha. Halacha is the balancing act between the doable and the ideal; between approximate means and absolute ends; between what *is* and what *ought-to-be*. It is a great mediator, and a call for hope.

The Judaism of today is a concession to human weakness, but at the same time it is a statement of belief in the greatness and strength of man. It calls upon man to do whatever is in his power to climb as high as possible, but warns him not to overstep and fall into the abyss. Judaism asks man to be a magnificent being, but never an angel – because to be too much is to be less than.

But Judaism also believes that man may one day reach the point where what is impossible today may be possible tomorrow. What *ought-to-be* may someday *become* reality. It is that gap that Halacha tries to fill.

Many people believe that concessions to human weaknesses are incompatible with the Divine Will. The Divine Will should not be compromised by human shortcomings.

But Judaism thinks otherwise.

Judaism is amused by Baruch Spinoza's ideal world in which passions and human desires have no place, since they upset the philosopher's "good life" of *amor intellectualis Dei* (the intellectual love of God). Spinoza's philosophy is so elevated that, with perhaps a few exceptions, it is unworkable. He himself proved the shortcomings of his own philosophy when he became enraged at the political murders of the influential Dutch De Witt brothers in 1672. He told the great philosopher Gottfried Leibniz that he had planned to hang a large poster in the town square, reading *ultimi barbarorum* (extreme barbarians), but was prevented from doing so by his hostess who locked the door on him, as she feared that Spinoza himself would be murdered![1]

Perhaps Spinoza's *Ethics* is the ideal, but how immature to believe that it is attainable. How different the *Ethics* would have been if Spinoza had married, fathered children, and understood the limitations of daily life.

Halacha is pragmatic. It has no patience for Spinoza's *Ethics* and no illusions about man. Indeed, it expects man to extend himself to full capacity, but it acknowledges the long and difficult road between the *is* and the *ought-to-be*. And it understands all too well that the *ought-to-be* may never be reached in man's lifetime.

Judaism teaches that the Divine limits Itself out of respect for man. It was God Who created this imperfect man. Therefore He could not have given the *Ethics* of Spinoza at Sinai; instead He gave only divine, "imperfect" laws that deal with the here-and-now and offer just a taste of the *ought-to-be*. Judaism teaches that if the perfect is unattainable, one should at least try to reach the possible – the manageable – that which *can* be

---

1. K.O. Meinsma, *Spinoza En Zijn Kring: Historisch-kritische studiën over Hollandsche vrijgeesten* (Den Haag: Martinus Nijhoff, 1896), 358 n1 [Dutch].

achieved. If we can't have it all, let us attempt to make *some* improvement. If you must wage war, do it as ethically as possible. If universal vegetarianism is inconceivable, try to treat animals more humanely, and slaughter them painlessly. *That* is *doable* Judaism.

True, this is not the ideal – indeed, the Torah is sometimes an embarrassment – but it's all that God *could* command at Sinai. It is not the *ought-to-be* Judaism, but it is a *better-than-nothing* Judaism.

The great art is to make the *doable* Judaism, with all its problems, as ethical as possible; and instead of despairing about its shortcomings, to live it as joyfully as we can. As Spinoza has taught us, "Joy is man's passage from a lesser to a greater perfection."[2] Oh, Baruch, did you forget your own insights?

Sacrifices are not part of the *ought-to-be* Judaism. They are far removed from the Judaism that Spinoza dreamed of. But they are a realistic representation of the *doable* with an eye toward the *ought-to-be*.

In one of his most daring statements, Rambam maintains that sacrifices are a compromise to human weakness. The ancient world of idol worship was deeply committed to animal sacrifices. It was so ingrained in the way of life of the Jews' ancestors that it was "impossible to go suddenly from one extreme to the other," and "the nature of man will not allow him to suddenly discontinue everything to which he is accustomed."[3] Therefore, God permitted the Jews to continue the sacrificial cult, but only for "His service," and with many restrictions, the ultimate goal being that with time the Jews would be weaned from this trend of worship; from the *is* to the *ought-to-be*.

By making this and similar statements, Rambam no doubt laid the foundations for Spinoza's dream of an ultimate system of ethics, just as he planted the seeds of Spinoza's pantheism.[4] But Rambam realized that the time had not yet come; that it was still a long road from the reality to the dream.

In contradiction to his statements in *Moreh Nevuchim*, Rambam, in his

---

2. Benedictus de Spinoza, *Ethics*, part III, "Definitions of the Emotions."

3. *Moreh Nevuchim*, part 3, chap. 32.

4. See, for example, Joel L. Kramer, *Maimonides: The Life and World of One of Civilization's Greatest Minds* (NY: Doubleday, 2008), 326–329, 373–374; Moshe Idel, "Deus sive Natura – The Metamorphoses of a Dictum from Maimonides to Spinoza," in *Maimonides and the Sciences*, ed. Robert S. Cohen and Hillel Levine (Dordrecht: Kluwer Academic Publishers, 2000), 87–110; Carlos Fraenkel, "Maimonides' God and Spinoza's *Deus sive Natura*," *Journal of the History of Philosophy* 44, no. 2 (2006): 169–215.

Mishne Torah, speaks about the need for sacrifices even in the future Temple.[5] I believe he thus expresses his doubt that the *ought-to-be* Judaism will ever become a reality in this world.[6]

Rambam did not live in the Dutch town of Rijnsburg, in an ivory tower far removed from the real world, as did Spinoza. Rambam lived in a down-to-earth world full of human strife, problems, and pain. He was a renowned halachist, and he knew that the halachic system is one that instructs man to keep both feet on the ground while simultaneously striving for what is *realistically* possible.

Still, perhaps the institution of sacrifice is also grounded in deep symbolism, the meaning and urgency of which escapes our modern mentality. The fact that idol worshipers made use of it in their abominable rituals doesn't mean that it can't be of great spiritual value when practiced on a much higher plane, as something deeply ingrained in a part of the human psyche to which modern man no longer has access. And yet, it doesn't contradict the fact that it *ought to be* different, so that even the higher dimensions of sacrifices become irrelevant. When *ought-to-be* Judaism and Spinoza's *Ethics* will one day prevail, there will indeed be no need for sacrifices.

But what happened in the meantime? The Temple was destroyed and sacrificial service came to an end. Is this a step forward or backward? When religious Jews to this day pray for the reinstatement of sacrifices, are they asking to return to the road between the *is* and the *ought-to-be*, between the dream and its realization? Or are they praying to reinstate sacrifices as a middle stage, only to eventually get rid of them forever?

We need to ask ourselves a pertinent question: Is our aversion to sacrifices the result of our supreme spiritual sophistication, through which we left the world of sacrifices behind us? Or have we sunk so low that we aren't even able to reach the level of idol worshipers who, however primitive we believe them to have been, were of a higher spiritual level than some of us who call ourselves monotheists?

This question is of great urgency in a modern world that slaughtered six

---

5. *Mishne Torah, Hilchot Melachim* 11:1.
6. An alternative explanation is that in his *Moreh Nevuchim*, Rambam's discourse on sacrifices is governed by a theoretical-philosophical approach, whereas in his *Mishne Torah* he is governed by strict halachic-legal criteria.

million Jews and continues to slaughter millions of other people. Have we surpassed the state of *is* and are we on our way to the *ought-to-be* Judaism? Or are we on the brink of a lifestyle that is not even at the stage of *is*, but rather in a state of regression, while we convince ourselves that it is in a state of progression?[7] This is a haunting question – one that we cannot escape.

---

7. For a discussion about the various opinions on sacrifices, see R. Meir Simcha ha-Kohen of Dvinsk in his classic *Meshech Chochma*, introduction to *Vayikra*. Concerning the contradictions in Rambam's understanding of the sacrifices, see Nathan Lopes Cardozo, *Between Silence and Speech: Essays on Jewish Thought* (Northvale, NJ: Jason Aronson, 1995), chap. 1. See also R. Eliezer Ash-kenazi's explanation in his *Ma'aseh Hashem*, commentary on *Bereshit*, section 27 on the frequent expression that sacrifices must be brought "with a pleasant aroma to the Lord," which is quoted with my commentary in Nathan Lopes Cardozo, *Thoughts to Ponder: Daring Observations about the Jewish Tradition*, vol. 1 (Jerusalem: Urim, 2002), chap. 42.

Chapter 20

The Danger of Religion
Plato, Halacha, and Dreams

Being religious is fraught with danger. Man is often pulled in directions where he can easily break his neck. To be religious is to allow your *ne-shama* (soul) to surpass your body, taking it to places where it cannot dwell and may self-destruct.

In Plato's *Phaedo*, the metaphor used to describe the relationship of the soul to the body is that of a person locked in prison.[1] Platonic philosophy aims at liberating man from the prison of the body. Only in this way can man achieve self-perfection. For Aristotle, although ethics and politics are serious issues, the essence of man – that activity which is distinctly human – is intellectual contemplation of eternal truth. The highest human achievement lies in the privacy of his thoughts. Its content has no practical human benefit. The most exalted human being is the philosopher. He must be free of the body's demands, which interfere with contemplation.

In Judaism, this is not what life is all about. According to biblical thought, the body is not perceived as being in conflict with the soul. It is not an obstacle, but a most welcome companion. Otherwise, what is the purpose of the body? Just to be a nuisance that one would be better off without? Jewish thought holds that it can't be God's intention to create the human body simply to deliberately frustrate man. True, the body may sometimes pose challenges, but ultimately this is to allow the complete *human being*, not just the soul, to grow. The purpose of man is not to dwell in Heaven and contemplate, but to *act* with his body and bring Heaven down to the material world in order to transform the world into a better

1. Plato, *Phaedo*, 81e. See also the introduction in Plato's *Phaedo*, trans. Eva Brann, Peter Kalkavage, and Eric Salem (Newburyport, MA: Focus Publishing, 1998), 3.

place. The meaning in life is to be effectively realized by bringing about the interpenetration of the soul and the body.

The mind of man – the custodian of all spiritual and ethical values – is, on its own, incapable of action. On the other hand, all the forces and energy in the body are intrinsically indifferent to ethical or spiritual concepts. Only in a combined effort of mind and body can they build the world. All that man physically does must be able to permeate his thoughts, and all that man thinks must find a way into his body (Heschel). While this might very well lead to disaster, it can also bring man to an exalted state of life. This is the task and challenge for which he was created.

Knowledge alone is never a cause for action. Western civilization has mistakenly believed that it is possible to educate the body by reasoning with it. So it continued speaking to the mind, but never really reached the body. This has led to disastrous consequences. Many philosophers have delivered themselves into the hands of evil as a result.

The distinction between body and soul is similar to a difference in organic functioning; it does not reflect the radical dualism that is implicit in Plato's prison metaphor.

Perhaps the most acute case of a man nearly losing his body while being religious is that of Ya'akov falling asleep and dreaming of a ladder on which angels ascend and descend.[2] The top of the ladder reaches Heaven, and God stands over it. The great German Lutheran thinker, Rudolf Otto (1869–1937), called this experience "numinous," "a non-rational, non-sensory experience or feeling whose primary and immediate object is outside the self."[3] It consists of a *mysterium tremendum et fascinans* – an awe-inspiring and fascinating mystery; an altogether otherworldly experience of an objective presence that generates wonder, fear, and dependence, but also enormous spiritual vitality.

This, says Otto, is what Ya'akov experiences when he falls asleep and has his dream. There is no greater religious moment than this. It is an unprecedented encounter with God. But it is also extremely dangerous. The experience is so overwhelming that Ya'akov runs the risk of losing his body. The dream carries him to Heaven, a place where his body cannot dwell. It is paralyzed and nearly eliminated.

Just before his soul leaves his body, against all expectations and as if through a miracle, Ya'akov wakes up. His reaction is most telling: "Be-

---

2. *Bereshit* 28:11–12.

3. Rudolf Otto, *The Idea of the Holy*, trans. John W. Harvey (NY: Oxford University Press, 1958), 10–11.

hold, God is in this place and I did not know it."⁴ This is an instant of
ultimate crisis. It is tremendous to have a religious moment, but what
happens when it is impossible to handle? *What am I going to do in the real
world with this flash of intense unparalleled revelation?*

The biggest problem is not with the moment itself, but with how to
keep it alive and take it with me throughout the rest of my life, in a way
that is beneficial. And if I can't, what then is the purpose of this moment?
Not only will it fade into oblivion, but it will be a trauma that will haunt
me for the rest of my life! It can easily turn into madness. Ya'akov's religious experience leaves him without solid ground under his feet. Plato and
Aristotle would have been delighted, but Ya'akov is scared to death. *It is all
meaningless unless I can translate this into the mundane.*

While his mind and soul are still in Heaven, Ya'akov does the only right
thing to do: he looks to the ground and picks up a stone. He wants to find
the mundane, because it is there that life takes place. And unless he can
apply his experience in a practical way, all of these heavenly events will
have been in vain.

> And Ya'akov rose up early in the morning and took the stone that
> he had placed under his head and set it up as a memorial stone and
> poured oil on top of it. . . . Ya'akov made a vow. "If God will be with
> me," he said, "if He will protect me on the journey that I am taking
> . . . then I will dedicate myself totally to God. Let this stone, which
> I have set up as a memorial, become a house of God. Of all that You
> give me, I will set aside a tenth to You."⁵

Not only does Ya'akov root his heavenly experience in the mundane by
taking a stone to sanctify it with a physical substance, but more importantly, he links it to a mundane *financial* act. He translates it into *ma'aser*,
promising that he will tithe all his physical possessions. He "de-religion-
izes" his experience, understanding that being religious cannot mean
withdrawing from this world. It must mean *engaging* with this world and
giving it religious and heavenly meaning. He knows that his episode with
the ladder is a slippery slope on which one can easily break one's neck. To
redeem this experience, it must be established in a specific space – in a

---

4. *Bereshit* 28:16.
5. *Bereshit* 28:18–22.

physical act, in the ordinary – not by night, but only by day when human beings are awake.

What Ya'akov does is most remarkable. He introduces one of the great foundations of Halacha: To give a religious moment an ongoing effect, it must be translated into the tangible, the mundane. It must establish patterns of bodily reactions and conduct, which testify to an acute corporeal awareness of a reality beyond body. To achieve an authentic state of religiosity, there must be an element of everydayness, of the commonplace, which often includes what others may call trivialities. There must be a finite act through which one perceives the infinite (Heschel). Every trifle is infused with divinity.

Rather than ignore the body, Halacha draws a person's attention to its complexities. Halacha tells man not to fall victim to grandiose dreams. There are limits to human existence, and it is exactly this fact that makes life a challenge and a joy. The body places man firmly in a world where he cannot survive if he doesn't act. Man's view of the relationship between his body and soul reflects his attitude toward dependence on the outer world – is it embarrassing, or is it uplifting?

*

It is most telling that in the Torah, the world of dreams comes to an end with *Sefer Bereshit*, the book in which almost everybody experiences dreams: Avraham, Ya'akov, and Yosef dream, and even Avimelech, Lavan, and Pharaoh, too. But once the Torah is given, there are no more dreams. It is as if the Torah teaches us that mitzvot take the place of dreams. A dream is an expression of an illusory world. It represents dimensions of Heaven, where the impossible can happen – where time doesn't play a role, where man is passive and things happen *to* him that are beyond his actual capability. Dreams that take place as a religious experience transform man's world into a utopia for which there is no foundation, and those dreams have no chance of ever being actualized. They are unworldly and therefore dangerous. They are deaf and invulnerable to the cries of the real world.

But man needs to dream. Dreams allow him to be insane for a few moments. There's a need for it, but it cannot be the foundation of his life. We must dream in order to demand of ourselves the impossible, so that it becomes conceivable, even if only once. But it must have a link to reality. Once it is totally disconnected, it loses its purpose.

Dreams are also moments of anticipation – "I have a dream!" – and one way in which man can make his dream come true is by acting *as if* it is already taking place. *Halachic requirements are often frozen dreams*. They make man do things that he is not yet ready to do. They are still spiritually beyond him. An example of this is lighting the Chanuka menora for eight days. We are required to add another candle every night and light it. It is as if we are ascending in spirituality throughout those eight days, with the last night being the most intense and powerful one. In fact, though, it is the first night that excites most people. To the average person, the new is more exhilarating. So the Jew is asked to act as if in a dream: light the candles *as though* you are becoming more and more excited with each day, so that one day you may really feel that the last candle is the most electrifying one.

Man is not asked to dream the inconceivable. He is asked to dream what is actually achievable. It is the Halacha that rescues man from unrealistic dreams, substituting them with those that are viable. Mount Sinai and the giving of the law replaced impossible dreams with those that are within our grasp.

Chapter 21

Chanuka and Halacha
Hypocrisy or Authenticity?

One of the great problems any religious person must struggle with is whether or not it is actually possible to be religious. What, after all, is the essence of genuine religiosity? It is no doubt the cognizance that one lives in the presence of God and feels and acts accordingly. To do so, however, is nearly impossible. Abraham Joshua Heschel once made the profound observation: "Religion depends upon what man does with his ultimate embarrassment."[1]

While we may not agree with Heschel that embarrassment lies at the root of religion, we agree it is unpretentiousness combined with deep humility that moves genuine religion.

What lies at the root of all religion is the awareness that it is extremely difficult to live up to the awe of the moment. Our ultimate concern should be to grasp – emotionally and intellectually – that we are the contemporaries of God, and to experience this in the most elevated way. But, for the majority of us, it is an impossible mission. How can man ever encounter the divine otherness? It is the task of religion to guide us through this almost insurmountable situation. Paradoxically, admitting the impossibility of this undertaking and responding to it in a responsible way is what makes our humility a genuine religious experience.

How can one live in God's presence and not be humble? How can one live in the shadow of greatness and not sense it, be part of the great miracle of existence and ignore it? Yet, who among us is in fact spiritually uncomfortable? We have become so insensitive that we are not even embarrassed

---

1. Abraham Joshua Heschel, *Who is Man?* (Stanford, CA: Stanford University Press, 1965), 112.

by our lack of self-consciousness. This almost turns the religious lives of millions, including our own, into a farce.

We may sincerely convince ourselves that we are religious, while in fact we are guilty of self-deception. For religious Jews this may be an even greater problem than for those who follow other religions. Judaism's constant demand to follow Halacha may give the impression that the religion depends solely on the need to "observe" or carefully perform all of Halacha, with its nearly obsessive requirement to follow all rituals and laws down to the minutiae. How often do religious Jews believe that they are religious because they are observant? This is one of the major pitfalls of Jewish observant life. In truth, Halacha is not to be *observed*, but rather *experienced*, as a way to deal with one's lifelong existential awareness that one lives in the presence of God. It is a response to the problem of how to live with spiritual discomfort.

A remarkable feature of Halacha is that it often asks us to act *as if* we are deeply provoked by living in the presence of God, while in reality we aren't. This begs the question whether such an act can be authentic, as opposed to downright hypocritical. It is here that Judaism is not completely comfortable with its own demands. Should it ask the Jew to act *as if* he is moved and therefore do *as if* he is filled with the deepest religious feelings? Or, should it ask the Jew to act according to his *real* feelings and not pretend? Judaism is fully aware that whichever road it suggests, there will be a heavy price to pay. The Jew may feel hypocritical, or he may not even be aware that he lost his dream, since there is nothing that reminds him of it.

In a notable discussion between the great mishnaic schools of Bet Shammai and Bet Hillel, the question is posed whether it is better to light all eight candles of the menora on the first day of Chanuka, or on the last day. Bet Shammai suggests that one should begin with lighting all eight, subtracting a candle every subsequent day until only one is lit on the eighth day. Bet Hillel's opinion is that we should light only one candle on the first day and slowly build up to eight lights on the eighth day.[2] What is this conflict all about?

It has been suggested that the disagreement between these two schools of thought is rooted in the question of whether people should express their religious commitment through acts that honestly reflect where they stand *at that hour*, or through acts that express where they would like to

---

2. *Shabbat* 21b.

be in the future.[3] Is Judaism better served by making us act *as if* we are on a level of high spirituality, while in fact we are not, or does it prefer that we express our religious feelings "ba-asher hu sham" (where he is at that moment)[4] – reflecting our often middle-of-the-road religious condition?

Bet Shammai's suggestion that one should light all eight candles on the first night is, for the most part, an honest expression of our feelings. We are more excited on the first day than we are on the last. For most of us, the notion of novelty is felt at the start, instead of at the end. Hence, eight lights on the first day. But such excitement comes with a price. It does not endure. Like the sexual act that wears off after a moment when not accompanied by the binding of souls – *Post coitum omne animal triste est*[5] – so too all religious acts, when experienced solely as novelty and excitement, lose their impact as the exhilaration slowly dissipates. It is therefore logical that on the second day only seven lights be lit and on the last day only one. It is Bet Shammai's conviction that we should not put on a show and pretend that we are more than what we are.

Such an approach is thoroughly honest, but lacks a dream and vision of what *could* be. Bet Hillel therefore believes that if we do not inspire man with his potential and give him a taste of what *could* be, he will not even strive to achieve higher goals. As Robert Browning said, "Ah, but a man's reach should exceed his grasp, / Or what's a heaven for?"[6] According to Bet Hillel, we should start with only one light on the first day, since this reflects the condition of our soul at the beginning of Chanuka. We need to warm up and slowly strengthen our soul until it bursts with spiritual depth on the eighth day when we reach the fullness of the festival. The lighting of the menora should be a transformational act, and that can take place only when it is accompanied by an inner experience that touches the deepest dimensions of our souls, step by step. True, we may not feel this way, but we must awaken and educate ourselves toward this goal. The last day should be the greatest. We should act *as if*, so that one day we may reach this spiritual level. We taste the future in the present.

Novelty is often just a brand new form of mediocrity, while excellence is rooted in the old, but revitalized on a higher plane. It is not the honest mediocrity of today that we need, but an exalted dream of tomorrow.

---

3. Based on R. Eliyahu Eliezer Dessler, *Michtav me-Eliyahu* (Jerusalem: Kiryat Noar, 1963), 2:120–22.

4. *Bereshit* 21:17.

5. "Every animal is sad after intercourse."

6. Robert Browning, "Andrea del Sarto" in *Men and Women* (London, Chapman & Hall, 1855).

It is between these two positions that Judaism operates – a balancing act, as in the case of a tightrope walker. Most of the time, it requires a compromise. Sometimes Jewish Law will opt for a realistic understanding of the here and now; other times it will choose the dream. It is a difficult position to be in, and it is not always clear why Halacha will decide a certain way in one case and a different way on another occasion. The problem is that in the end it may not satisfy anyone. But it is the realistic understanding of "you can't have your cake and eat it too" that seems to move Judaism. Bet Shammai will sometimes have to agree that there is a need to reach for the dream, and Bet Hillel will on occasion have to go by the facts on the ground. Such differences are even found within the Torah itself, as well as among other sages and later authorities.[7] Judaism cannot survive by opting for only one of these ideals. That would be suicidal.

Most interesting is the fact that there is one opinion in the Talmud that says Bet Shammai continued to follow their own view, even after the Halacha was decided in accordance with Bet Hillel.[8] According to this opinion, it seems that Bet Shammai continued to light eight candles on the first day of Chanuka, although everyone else followed the opinion of Bet Hillel.[9] This makes us wonder. Although tradition tells us that Halacha will only follow Bet Shammai once the messianic era will have begun, there is no source for this in the Talmud.[10] Could it mean that for exceptional souls it would be possible to follow the views of Bet Shammai

---

7. See, for example, the Torah's toleration of Israelite slavery in *Shemot* 21:1–6 and the complete rejection of this institution as the ultimate dream to which it seems to aspire in *Vayikra* 25:55. See also *Eruvin* 65a concerning prayer, and *Shulchan Aruch, Orach Chaim* 98:2.

8. *Yevamot* 14a.

9. See also *Shabbat* 21b where the story is told that some people followed the custom of Bet Shammai on Chanuka. This was long after a divine voice instructed that the Halacha is in accordance with Bet Hillel (*Eruvin* 13b). *Biur Halacha* in *Mishna Berura, Orach Chaim*, 671:2, s.v. "ve-yesh omrim de-kol echad," makes an interesting observation that the Halacha is only in accordance with Bet Hillel when it lays down the *strict* Halacha, not in the case of *mehadrin min ha-mehadrin*, the beautification of the Halacha beyond its basic requirements (one light per day of Chanuka). *Biur Halacha* cautions that this should not be done in practice. This essay, however, argues that such practice may be a valid option.

10. This teaching is quoted in the name of the Arizal by the kabbalist R. Shalom Buzaglo, *Mikdash Melech* (Żółkiew: Shmuel Pinchas Stiller, 1864) on *Zohar Bereshit* 17a. See also R. Shneur Zalman of Lyady, *Likkutei Torah* (NY: Kehot, 2002), *Bamidbar*, p. 108; R. Moshe ben Menachem Graf of Prague, *Va-Yakhel Moshe*, (Dessau, 1699), 54a; Chida (R. Chaim Yosef David Azulay), *Petach Enayim* (Jerusalem: Ha-Techia, 1959), vol. 2, on *Pirke Avot* 5:17, p. 99b; Malbim, in his commentary *Torah Ohr* on *Bamidbar* 19:2 (Jerusalem: Pardes, 1957), 1308. For a detailed treatment of this issue, see R. Moshe Shverd, "Halacha ke-Bet Shammai le-Atid Lavo," *Ohr Yisrael* 42 (Nissan 5766): 216–228; R. Menachem Mendel Schneerson, *Sefer ha-Sichot 5752*, vol. 1 (NY: Kehot, 1993), 33–34; R. Avrohom Yitzchak Baruch Gerlitzky, *Yemot ha-Mashiach be-Halacha* (NY: AYB Gerlitzky, 2005), 280–284.

even today? No two souls are the same. It is this fact that makes religious life a far from easy task. Even if human beings know that religion is their response to their ultimate embarrassment, as Heschel would have it, they still will not know how to act. Shall they be honest so as not to pretend, or shall they pretend so that one day they will be honest to their dreams?

Seven

HALACHA, MORAL ISSUES,
AND ETHICAL DILEMMAS

Chapter 22

The Abuse of Halacha:
Keeping Halacha Under Control

The Purpose of *Sefer Bereshit*

Halacha is in trouble. More and more of the unacceptable is being done and said in its name. Besides causing infinite damage to Judaism's great message, it is a terrible desecration of God's name. And all of this is seen and heard by millions of Gentiles watching television, browsing websites, or listening to the radio. Many are repelled when they witness horrible scenes in which Jews attack each other in the name of Halacha. Media outlets around the world portray religious Jews in the most distressing ways. While it cannot be denied that anti-Semitism plays a role and tends to blow the picture out of proportion, the unfortunate fact is that much of it is based on truth. Non-Jews are dumbfounded when they read that leading rabbis make the most shocking comments about them, thereby demonstrating gross arrogance and discrimination. Even worse, many of them read about rabbinical decisions that seem to lack all moral integrity.

In 1995, Yigal Amir assassinated Prime Minister Yitzchak Rabin in the name of Halacha, claiming that the prime minister was a *rodef* (someone who is attempting or planning to murder) because he brought all of Israel's citizens into mortal danger by having participated in the 1993 Oslo accords. Amir believed that the prime minister therefore deserved the death penalty according to Jewish Law.

In 1994, Baruch Goldstein killed twenty-nine Arabs in the Cave of Machpela because he believed that Halacha obligated him to create havoc in order to stop Arab terror attacks, which had already killed thousands of Jews.[1]

---

1. Rabbi Aharon Lichtenstein, the late foremost leader of Modern Orthodoxy and *Rosh ha-Yeshiva* of Yeshivat Har Etzion, condemned this atrocity in the strongest terms: "A person, whatever his former merits may have been, departed this world while engaged in perpetrating an act of

Several years ago, the book *Torat ha-Melech* was published.[2] The authors, learned rabbis, argued that it was permissible to kill non-Jews, even without proper trial, if they became a serious potential threat to Jewish lives.

Minorities such as the LGBT community are being insulted by powerful rabbis who seem to be ignorant of the multifarious circumstances of fellow human beings.

A most important and brilliant ruling issued by the Tzfat Rabbinical Court in 2014 concerning a *get* by which a woman was freed of her *aguna* status was suddenly challenged by the Supreme Rabbinical Court of Israel who sought to nullify the *get*.[3] The latter completely ignored the fact that such a move is not only halachically intolerable,[4] but undermines the very institution of Jewish divorce itself. And so on.

How can it be that such things are carried out or even expressed in the name of Judaism and Jewish Law? Anyone who has the slightest knowledge of Judaism is fully aware that nothing within genuine Jewish Law would condone or even suggest such outlandish ideas and immoral acts as those mentioned above.

Why does this happen?

PAN-HALACHA

Throughout the years, several rabbinical authorities have made the major and dangerous mistake of reducing Judaism to a matter of law alone, a kind of Pan-Halacha (Heschel). They sincerely believe that Judaism consists

---

awful and terrible slaughter, *tevach ayom ve-nora*, and thereby, beyond the crime itself, desecrated the name of Heaven, trampled upon the honor of the Torah and *mitzvot*, soiled and sullied the image of *Kenesset Yisrael*, and endangered the future of [Jewish] settlement in Judea, Samaria, and Gaza. . ." See Rabbi Aharon Lichtenstein's letter in "A Rabbinic Exchange on Baruch Goldstein's Funeral," *Tradition* 28, no. 4 (1994): 59.

2. R. Yitzchak Shapiro and R. Yosef Elitzur, *Torat ha-Melech* (Yitzhar: Ha-Machon ha-Torani she-al yad Yeshivat Od Yosef Chai, 2010). For a response, see Ariel Finkelstain, *Derech Ha'Melech (The Path of the King): Racism and Discrimination of Gentiles In Halachah: A Halachik and Meta-Halachik Alternative to the book 'Torat Ha'Melech'* (Netivot: Yeshivat Hesder Ahavat Yisrael, 2010) [Hebrew].

3. The case involved a woman whose husband, injured in a motorcycle accident, had been in a persistent vegetative state for seven years. The Tzfat court decided to give her a *get ziku'i* – a divorce document issued on behalf of the husband. See "Heter Aguna she-Ba'ala Tzemach be-Emtza'ut Ziku'i Get," Bet ha-Din ha-Rabbani 861974/2. Documentation regarding this case can be accessed at: http://www.dintora.org/article/195/; http://www.daat.ac.il/daat/psk/psk.asp?id=1054; http://www.daat.ac.il/daat/psk/psk.asp?id=1069; http://www.daat.ac.il/daat/psk/psk.asp?id=1082. For a discussion of this case, see Michael J. Broyde, "Plonit v. Ploni: The Get from the Man in a Permanent Vegetative State," *Ḥakirah* 18 (Winter 2014): 59–90.

4. See *Mordechai, Hilchot Gittin*, section 455, quoting *Rabbenu Tam*.

only of rigid rules. In this way, they are paradoxically similar to Spinoza, who was also of this opinion and therefore rejected his faith. He referred to it as obsessive, a type of behaviorism, and an extreme form of legalism.[5] That Spinoza made this claim is one thing, but the fact that these learned rabbis now appear to agree with him is an unforgivable blunder. Nothing is further from the truth than to label Judaism as a legal religious system without spirit, poetry, and musical resonance. This is proven by the almost infinite amount of religious Jewish literature that deals with non-halachic matters.

The main reason for this terrible mistake is that these rabbis have failed to study the basic moral values of Judaism as they appear in the book of *Bereshit*. It is well known that, with a few exceptions, this book does not contain laws; it is mainly narrative. To appreciate this, one needs to consider the following.

In this first biblical book, we encounter Avraham, Yitzchak, and Ya'akov as the foremost players. They are considered the first Jews in history. But this makes little sense. How could they have been Jews if the Torah was given only hundreds of years later to Moshe at Mount Sinai? Although a Jew is a Jew even if they do not observe the laws of the Torah, it is still the Torah that defines them as such. How, then, could the *Avot* and *Imahot* (Patriarchs and Matriarchs) be full-fledged Jews when the Torah was denied to them? Would it not have been logical to have given the Torah to them long before Moshe? Only upon receiving the Torah could they have been real Jews! So why was it withheld from them?[6]

The answer is crucial. No law, including divine law, can function if it is not preceded by a narrative of the human moral condition and the introduction of basic ethical and religious values. These values cannot be *given*; they must develop *within*, through life experiences. No academic instruction, not even when given by God, would be of any benefit. Such ethics need to develop gradually, on an existential level, and be predicated on innate values that God grants to each person at the moment he or she is born; a kind of categorical imperative in the human soul.

More than that, laws become impersonal and therefore dangerous because they cannot deal with emotions and the enormous moral paradoxes

---

5. See, for example, Benedictus de Spinoza, *A Theologico-Political Treatise*, chaps. 3, 4, 13, in *The Chief Works of Benedict de Spinoza*, trans. R.H.M. Elwes (London: G. Bell and Sons, 1883), vol. 1.

6. See *Mishna Kiddushin* 4:14, where the sages state that Avraham observed the commandments. *Bereshit Rabba*, Vilna ed., 79:6 states that Ya'akov kept Shabbat; Ibid., 92:4 states that Yosef kept Shabbat. For a discussion on the topic of whether the *Avot* were considered Jews or Noachides, see *Talmudic Encyclopedia*, s.v. "Avot (ha-uma)," 1:36–37.

encountered by human beings. As a result, they run the risk of becoming inhuman and even cruel.

It is for that reason that God did not give the laws of the Torah to the *Avot*. First there was a need to learn through personal trials and tribulations. The *Avot* and *Imahot* had to see with their own eyes what happens when people are not governed by law. But most important, they had to become aware of basic moral values, such as the fact that all human beings are created in the image of God, that all are equal, that human life is holy, and that there is only one God Who is at the root of all morality. Only after people have been deeply affected by these ideas and values can law be introduced as a way to put it all into action.

It was only after the existential, moral turmoil in which Avraham, Yitzchak, and Ya'akov frequently found themselves, as well as their often problematic encounters with God, that a virtuous and religious awareness was born. This consciousness continued to work its way, with all its ups and downs, through the bondage in Egypt, the Exodus, and the splitting of the Reed Sea. Not until that point was there a chance that the law could be received and be beneficial when given at Sinai. And even then it was not very successful, as recorded in the many disturbing biblical stories about the Israelites failing to live up to the law in Moshe's days and long afterward.

But it is not just the fact that narrative, ethical values, and the encounter with the Divine are necessary to have before the law can be given. There is another important message: no law, including divine, can function without constantly and continually taking guidance from these preceding values. There is almost nothing worse than divine law operating on its own, without primary, innate moral values. It runs the risk of turning wild and causing great harm. It needs to be constrained.

This is the purpose of *Sefer Bereshit*.[7] It is a biting critique of the halachic system when the latter is applied without acknowledging that these prior moral values are needed in order to function. *The book of Bereshit, then, keeps Halacha under control.* It restricts and regulates it, and ensures that it will not wreak havoc.

Truly great *poskim* cannot lay down their decisions on the basis of Jewish Law alone. The *Shulchan Aruch* (Code of Jewish Law) of Rabbi Yosef Karo and the *Mishne Torah* of Rambam can become dangerous if applied

---

7. See R. Naftali Zvi Yehuda Berlin (Netziv), *Ha'emek Davar*, introduction to *Bereshit*.

in a vacuum. What *poskim* must realize is that they need to incorporate the great religious and moral values for which *Sefer Bereshit* stands.

CHOSENNESS

The foremost point of departure in any halachic decision must be that all people are created in the image of God and that all human life is holy. While different tasks, inclinations, and historical events should be recognized and considered when making distinctions between people, no discrimination can ever be tolerated. Halacha should surely acknowledge that the Jews are different from other nations, but only as long as it recognizes that other nations can make contributions that Jews cannot.[8]

For Jews to be the Chosen People, they need to recognize that this in no way can ever mean that they may look down on others. What it does mean is that they have an obligation to inspire the world, as a teacher inspires a student even while recognizing that the student may be more gifted than him or her.

It cannot be denied that throughout our long history this may have been forgotten and laws have appeared that have not always lived up to these standards. Even biblical laws seem to have violated this principle. On several occasions they demanded that Jews show no mercy for some Gentile nations that dwelled near and in the Land of Israel in biblical times.[9] But a closer look makes it clear that these laws were contrary to the original divine plan and reveal some kind of divine concession to highly unfortunate circumstances.[10] The laws in question were meant to deal with these nations' ongoing violence and immorality, which had to be dealt with so that Jews could survive and uphold moral standards for the good of all humanity.[11]

---

8. *Ohr ha-Chaim* on *Shemot* 18:21, toward the end. See also Nathan Lopes Cardozo, "Moshe's Fatigue and the Need for a Gentile's Advice" (Thoughts to Ponder 284), *David Cardozo Academy*, Feb. 9, 2012, https://www.cardozoacademy.org/thoughts-to-ponder/moshes-fatigue-and-the-need-for-a-gentiles-advice-ttp-284/.

9. *Devarim* 7:1–2.

10. See chap. 27, where I explain this concept at length.

11. Many rabbinical laws were instituted for similar reasons. They were mainly introduced as protective measures to ensure that Jews would not suffer at the hands of anti-Semites. At other times, laws were introduced to counter assimilation and undesirable non-Jewish influences. While these laws seem to discriminate against Gentiles, in truth they were meant to protest against those Gentiles who had low moral standards or were committed criminals and were nearly as evil as the Nazis in later days. These laws did not pertain to civilized non-Jews. See the many observations of the great talmudic commentator Menachem ha-Me'iri in *Bet ha-Bechira* – for example, his commentary on *Sanhedrin* 57a and *Avoda Zara* 2a. Surely these laws should be

ANTI-HALACHA AND AMALEK

Never should chosenness mean an aloofness or disinterest in the spiritual welfare of non-Jews. Never should it mean, as an imprudent but influential halachic authority did suggest, that Jews should not influence present-day Gentiles to observe the Seven Noachide laws, on the basis of the scandalous argument that encouraging Gentiles to keep these commandments generates "Gentile merit" and will only prolong their stability, thereby delaying our redemption (since, in his view, the total degeneration of the Gentile nations is a prerequisite for the redemption of the Jewish people).[12] Nor can it ever be permitted to encourage a Jewish doctor to apply euthanasia to a particular "primitive" Gentile,[13] or to forbid a blind man

---

abolished because they run contrary to the principle of divine equality as taught by the Torah. Perhaps any law that gives the impression that non-Jews are discriminated against, such as the law that non-Jews are allowed to do some work for Jews on Shabbat (the "Shabbos goy"), should be abolished, unless Jews will do certain work for Gentiles that they can't do on Sunday and their festivals. The fact that the State of Israel is still dependent on the "Shabbos goy" is highly problematic and inconsistent with the principle of national independence. Daring and innovative rabbinical decisions are far overdue. Violating Shabbat to save the lives of non-Jews is an absolute obligation, notwithstanding the fact that some authorities have questioned this. There is no doubt that Avraham, Yitzchak, and Ya'akov would have done so. See Netziv's introduction to *Bereshit* in his *Ha'emek Davar*. See also chap. 3.

12. See R. Moshe Sternbuch, *Teshuvot ve-Hanhagot*, vol. 3 (Jerusalem, 5757), no. 317.

Rabbi Sternbuch's arguments are perplexing, his proofs from the Talmud are flawed, and he misunderstands Christianity and the concept of the Trinity. It seems that Rabbi Sternbuch is motivated by his dislike of non-Jews. See the following works by Rabbi Menachem Mendel Schneerson, the Lubavitcher Rebbe, who refutes the very argument Rabbi Sternbuch is making and shows the importance of teaching non-Jews the Seven Noachide Laws: "Sheva Mitzvot Bnei Noach," *Ha-Pardes* 9 (Sivan 5745): 7–11; *Likkutei Sichot*, vol. 26 (NY: Kehot, 1988), 132–144; *Shulchan Menachem* (Jerusalem: Heichal Menachem, 2013), *Yoreh De'ah*, no. 23. In fact, the Lubavitcher Rebbe delivered an address on 19 Kislev, 5743 / December 5, 1982, and on countless other occasions, asking Jews to try to persuade the Gentiles to live by these laws. See the Rebbe's *Sichos in English: Excerpts of Sichos Delivered by Rabbi Menachem M. Schneerson; Kislev-Nissan, 5743*, vol. 16 (NY: Sichos in English, 1983), 22–31. He also asked President Ronald Reagan to publicly recognize these seven laws, which the president did on April 4, 1982, in celebration of the Rebbe's eightieth birthday. (See http://www.chabad.org/therebbe/article_cdo/aid/142535/je wish/The-Rebbe-and-President-Reagan-Reagan.htm/ and http://www.presidency.ucsb.edu/ws /index.php?pid=23514/.) See also Dovid Lichtenstein, *Headlines 2: Halachic Debates of Current Events* (NY: OU Press, 2017), 121–134.

On whether Christianity is regarded as *avoda zara*, much has been written about this issue. It is beyond the scope of the current essay to provide a comprehensive treatment. For some principal sources, see Rambam, *Mishne Torah, Hilchot Avoda Zara* 9:4 and *Hilchot Ma'achalot Asurot* 11:7; *Perush ha-Mishnayot, Avoda Zara* 1:3. While Rambam regarded Christianity as *avoda zara*, there are many dissenting views among the *Rishonim* and *Acharonim*. See, for example, the comments of Rema in the following places: *Darkei Moshe, Orach Chaim*, 156:2; *Shulchan Aruch, Orach Chaim* 156:1; *Shulchan Aruch, Yoreh De'ah* 151:1 and in the commentary of Shach 151:7. See also *Pitchei Teshuva* to *Yoreh De'ah* 147:2. For a study on this topic, see Eugene Korn, "Rethinking Christianity: Rabbinic Positions and Possibilities," in *Jewish Theology and World Religions*, ed. Alon Goshen-Gottstein and Eugene Korn (Oxford: Littman Library of Jewish Civilization, 2012), 189–215.

13. R. Moshe Sternbuch, *Teshuvot ve-Hanhagot*, vol. 3, no. 365. See also his *Ta'am ve-Da'at al*

to receive a corneal transplant from a Gentile, since the latter may have seen things that no Jew should ever see.[14]

All these rulings are as anti-halachic as they can be, violating the very cornerstones of Judaism and based on reckless ideas endorsed by those who invent them on their own and then promote them as Halacha without the backing of any authentic, traditional halachic source. They should be condemned and denounced using all means available to us.

Highly disturbing is the case concerning Israel's arch-enemy, the Amalekites, the Nazis of biblical times. Divine law required the Jews to wipe this nation off the face of the earth, including women and children. Such a law runs contrary to our innate moral intuition and the very values promulgated by *Sefer Bereshit*. Commentators have therefore gone overboard to explain this law in different ways, since they were unable to accept that such a commandment could ever have come from God Himself. Some even believed that God tested the Jews to see whether they would understand their calling and thus refuse to implement this genocide,[15] similar to the way that Avraham refused to listen to God in the case of Sedom and Amora when he uttered the famous words: "Shall the whole world's Judge not act justly?"[16] The commentators' attempt is not apologetic, but rather the outcome of their absolute conviction, based on *Sefer Bereshit*, that there could be no other explanation. At a later stage, they decided

---

ha-Torah (Jerusalem, 1987), vol. 1, pp. 127, 205, 210, 222; vol. 3, p. 3.

14. See R. Ovadia Hadaya, *Yaskil Avdi* (Jerusalem: 1982), vol. 6, *Yoreh De'ah*, no. 26, sections 6–9. See the strong objection to these rulings by R. Ovadia Yosef, *Yabia Omer*, vol. 8, *Choshen Mishpat*, no. 11. See a much more authentic view stated by R. Yisrael Lipschitz (1782–1860) in his commentary *Tiferet Yisrael* on *Avot* 3:14. Rabbi Lipschitz states that the following Gentiles were pious and will enjoy a share in the World to Come: (1) Edward Jenner (1749–1823), who discovered the vaccine against smallpox; (2) Sir Francis Drake (c. 1540–1596), who (according to Rabbi Lipschitz) brought the potato to Europe, thereby saving many people from starvation; (3) Johannes Gutenberg (c. 1398–1468), the inventor of the movable printing press; and (4) Johannes Reuchlin (1455–1522), who was a great friend of the Jews and put his life on the line in order to prevent the burning of the Talmud under the decree issued by the Viennese Emperor Maximilian in the year 1502. See Chaim Rapoport, *The Messiah Problem: Berger, the Angel, and the Scandal of Reckless Indiscrimination* (Ilford UK: Ilford Synagogue, 2002), 88. See also the beautiful observations about Gentiles by Chief Rabbi Avraham Yitzchak ha-Kohen Kook (1865–1935), the famous talmudist, halachic authority, and kabbalist, in *Igrot ha-Rayah* (Jerusalem: Mossad HaRav Kook, 2006), 142 (letter no. 112).

15. See *Yoma* 22b where King Shaul, who was commanded to kill the Amalekites (2 *Shmuel*, chap. 15), exclaimed: "If the adults have sinned, what is the sin of the children?" According to one problematic source (*Yoma* 22b), God responded that he should not be overly righteous. But in *Midrash Tanchuma*, Buber ed., *Tzav* 5, God "changed His mind" after Moshe showed Him the injustice of the commandment (*Devarim* 20:16–17) to wipe out the women and children of the seven nations.

16. *Bereshit* 18:25.

that the nation of Amalek no longer existed and that they could cancel the entire law.[17]

It is remarkable that the sages seem to have reacted similarly with several other biblical laws, such as the case of the *ir ha-nidachat*, in which the commandment is to annihilate the entire Jewish population in a city rampant with idolatry and immorality. The law was declared inoperative from the very start.[18] Another example is the case of the *ben sorer u-moreh*, the rebellious son who had to be executed. Here, too, the law was declared defective and only seen as a way to teach some important moral lessons.[19] In other instances, they seem to have been of the opinion that laws such as those regarding the *mamzer* (a child from an incestuous relationship) and *agunot*[20] should be severely limited to make them almost inoperative, and they often looked for loopholes to find a way out.[21] While it remains a question why they did not completely revoke these laws, it seems clear that in all of these cases it was the overriding moral principles of *Sefer Bereshit* that motivated them.[22]

The sages struggled, reinterpreted, and sometimes even abolished these laws because they fully understood that without the moral religious values developed in *Sefer Bereshit*, halachic chaos would reign and grave injustices would be done.

It is for this reason that some of the greatest tragedies of Judaism in modern times are caused by the fact that some halachic authorities, as well as people like Yigal Amir and Baruch Goldstein, forgot to study the first book of the Torah. They became so dedicated to the letter of the law and to misplaced religious fervor that they did the inconceivable and caused the degradation of Halacha.

It is time for the rabbinical community to make it abundantly clear that no halacha can ever be implemented without it resting firmly on the values of *Sefer Bereshit*. Only in that way will a healthy Halacha be guaranteed, and severe damage, evil, and the profanation of God's name prevented.

Throughout the thousands of years of our history, Israel's sages and religious leaders – unlike those of the Christians and Muslims – never called

---

17. *Mishna Yadayim* 4:4; *Berachot* 28a. There is even a tradition that the fulfillment of this commandment is deferred until the messianic age. See *Radbaz* on *Mishne Torah*, *Hilchot Melachim* 5:5.

18. *Devarim* 13: 13–19; *Sanhedrin* 71a. See pp. 288–299 below.

19. *Devarim* 21:18–21; *Sanhedrin* 71a. See pp. 288–299 below.

20. For a notable example of a rabbinical attempt to free the wives of missing soldiers from their *aguna* status, see R. Ovadia Yosef, *Yabia Omer*, vol. 6, *Even ha-Ezer*, no. 3.

21. See chap. 27.

22. For a discussion, see Eliezer Berkovits, *Ha-Halacha, Kocha ve-Tafkida* (Jerusalem: Mossad HaRav Kook, 1981).

on their fellow Jews to wage religious wars against the Gentile world. To them, this was a repulsive idea. At the most, they asked the Almighty to deal with their enemies. This matter stands out in all of Israel's history. Let us be proud of that and not change the rules of the game, unless it is a matter of unequivocal self-defense.

Chapter 23

There Is No Ideal Halacha
Halacha and the Prisoner Exchange 1

One of the most remarkable maxims in the Talmud is the concept of "Elu ve-elu divrei Elokim Chaim" (These and those are the words of the Living God).[1] This is a halachic-philosophical concept which states that, even when there are opposing views among the Sages of Israel concerning Jewish Law, all these views, being rooted in the Divine Word, are considered to be authentic and treated as if they come from God Himself. Just as light emanates from one source and separates into a spectrum of colors once it enters our space, so it is with the word of God.

This is the great secret behind the vitality of Halacha. *There are no finalized halachic conclusions*. Everything is open to debate. What was left for the Talmud and later authorities to do was to decide which of these views should be practically followed in day-to-day life. In that way, they prevented the Torah from fragmenting into many "Torot" and creating confusion in Jewish communities.[2]

Most of the time, such decisions were made on the basis of a majority opinion among the sages. This is not because the other opinions were considered to be invalid and untrue, but because one opinion was more acceptable to the majority of sages or the general public, or was more practical in day-to-day life, and often less demanding. Many times, it reflected a more broad approach to religious and moral issues and was less rigorous.

---

1. See *Eruvin* 13b.
2. See *Sanhedrin* 88b.

THE GREATEST GOOD

On a deeper level, however, this maxim is Judaism's pragmatic realization that there is no such thing as the "Greatest Good," in which everything can be accomplished to its full manifestation without resulting in less desirable consequences. It fully realizes that this ideal is not within the realm of possibility in this world. It acknowledges that certain values clash and cannot be reconciled or even combined, not just for purely practical reasons, but even conceptually.

Only in God Himself can this be possible, not within the world of human beings.

One cannot combine full liberty with complete equality. Justice and mercy, knowledge and happiness often collide. How much equality, how much liberty, how much kindness, how much truth?[3] The idea, then, of a perfect solution to human problems, moral dilemmas, and religious demands cannot be coherently conceived.

This is true also within the world of Halacha. Even God's pronouncements sometimes appear to clash, and all the more so their interpretations. *There is no such thing as an "ideal" halachic solution.* All that can be done is to find the best "trade-offs" in which less harm is done or more is achieved by following one opinion over another, but not because one is more valid than the other.

But even this is not always possible. Sometimes one is forced to choose between two supreme values which compete; one cannot decide which is better and which is worse. In that case, other criteria are used to establish the practical Halacha.

DECENCY

Most remarkable is the case where the Talmud discusses the famous disputes between Bet Hillel and Bet Shammai. The reason, says the Talmud, why the practical Halacha nearly always follows Bet Hillel and not Bet Shammai, is that the former were kind-hearted and modest and mentioned the opinion of Bet Shammai before their own! In other words, the Halacha was decided according to Bet Hillel not because of any supreme academic-halachic argument or majority vote, but because of modesty and

3. See Ramin Jahanbegloo, *Conversations with Isaiah Berlin* (London: Halban, 2007), 142–143.

decency![4] This is most telling and shows the profound virtuousness of Jewish Law. The sages also realized the truth of the well-known dictum of the American philosopher William James: not to make a decision is also a decision. They had the courage to make a decision, while knowing very well that there were equally good arguments on the other side.

What many people do not realize is that in cases of extreme moral dilemmas, it is almost impossible to find an ideal solution which settles everything in the most favorable way. Many believe that once a moral solution is found, all others are completely faulty and invalid, never to be considered. Reality, however, proves this to be far from the truth.

BLACKMAIL

In 2008, the State of Israel was confronted with one of the most difficult choices it has ever faced. Up against one of the worst forms of blackmail in all of the world's history, it had to decide whether or not to free an incarnate of evil, the arch-murderer Samir Kuntar, who killed a Jew in cold blood and crushed the skull of his four-year-old daughter, and who vowed to kill as many Jews as possible once he would be free. In exchange, Israel would receive two of its soldiers, alive or dead, from the terrorist organization Hezbollah, which is equally committed to killing the maximum number of Jews, and sees its objective as ensuring the destruction of the State of Israel.

The stakes were high. On the one hand, there were serious concerns that negotiating with terrorist organizations will only encourage them to kidnap more and more soldiers in the future. On the other hand, to fail to rescue any soldier who falls into enemy hands would shatter one of the most basic principles of the Jewish State: bringing every soldier home at all costs, preferably alive, but even dead, so that they would at least be brought to *kever Yisrael*, a Jewish burial. Failing to do so could also very well weaken the resolve of future generations to take up arms in Israel's defense. Again, other families would (and did!) object, maintaining that to free arch-terrorists would only encourage more violence and the kidnapping of more soldiers. These people threatened to disallow their children from serving in the Israeli army if the government would start freeing arch-terrorists!

This is a typical example of the talmudic principle "Elu ve-elu divrei

---

4. See *Eruvin* 13b.

Elokim Chaim" in the secular Israeli community. Both arguments are strong and sound. Neither one is necessarily more convincing than the other. It all depends upon which angle you view such an immense problem from.

Even if we totally disagree with the Israeli government's decision to free this arch-murderer so as to bring home two dead Jewish soldiers, nobody can condemn such a decision as totally wrong or evil. We can only respect it, if strongly objecting to it. Such an objection is completely legitimate and is, indeed, always acknowledged in Israeli society as fair.[5]

This is not to say that the Israeli government did not utterly fail in its dealing with the aftermath of this tragic exchange. It most certainly did, and once more proved its incompetence. Instead of turning its decision to bring its soldiers home into a major moral victory to be respected by all, it allowed its enemies, once more, to convince the world that Israel capitulated out of weakness and is on the brink of collapse. No greater mistake could have been made.

See the next chapter for a continuation.

---

5. I am fully aware of the mishna in *Gittin* 45a, which states that it is forbidden to redeem captives for exorbitant ransoms so as not to encourage further kidnappings. As several halachic authorities have stated, this ruling probably does not apply in the case of the Israeli army, since soldiers are sent to war with the explicit understanding and stipulation that they will unconditionally be brought back home, alive or dead. Moreover, the mishna does not discuss a scenario in which it is almost certain that the captives will be killed by the kidnappers. There are different halachic opinions about such a case.

Chapter 24

There Is No Ideal Halacha
Halacha and the Prisoner Exchange 2

I don't know whether or not the Israeli government made the right decision (in July 2008) when it agreed to receive the lifeless bodies of Eldad
Regev and Ehud Goldwasser in exchange for Samir Kuntar, the child
murderer who returned to Lebanon well fed and in good health. Such
choices are, after all, beyond man's moral judgment.

As I explained in the previous chapter, they are in the category of "Elu
ve-elu divrei Elokim Chaim." In moral dilemmas such as these, arguments
on both sides are compelling, and both embody strong Jewish moral fiber.
Even if we strongly object to this exchange, we still have to admit that the
government had a sound, moral reason to allow this deal: a commitment
to rescue at all costs any soldier who fell into enemy hands and, in case of
death, to bring him to *kever Yisrael*, a Jewish burial.

Still, the government utterly failed in the way it played its cards at the
time of the exchange. Instead of celebrating this decision to bring both
soldiers home (and granting them a Jewish burial), presenting it as a major
moral victory to be admired by all, it instead allowed its enemies and the
world to believe once more that Israel has become weak and vulnerable
and has been forced to give in to enemy demands.

It should have shown the world the difference between "us" and "them,"
between the values of Judaism and a bestial society which produces the
likes of Hassan Nasrallah, Samir Kuntar, and the whole Hezbollah gang.
We could have taken pride in our love for our soldiers and in our readiness

---

* This essay was written in 2008, when Israel's government showed great ambivalence and
weakness. The sentiments expressed here do not pertain to subsequent governments.

to risk bringing them home, even dead, fully aware that this may invite further kidnappings.

Compare this to the evil that knows no bounds in much of the Arab world. When Israeli soldiers are captured, they are strapped to their tanks and paraded through the Arab streets to the frenzied cheers of thousands of spectators. (This was the case with Zechariah Baumel in Damascus in 1982. What happened to him?)

Israel, on the other hand, treats even its arch-enemies with dignity. In civilized societies, child murderers are condemned and severely punished for their terrible deeds, living their lives as outcasts in their *own* societies. Samir Kuntar, however, not only emerged alive and well from his Israeli cell, but also received a hero's welcome from Hezbollah, as well as from all factions of the Lebanese government. There was not one word of condemnation by any of its leaders or, for that matter, within the whole of the Muslim world. The blowing up of innocent Jews, including small children, has become an act of religious and civil devotion to be proud of and admired within large sections of that society.

Israel holds many Arab prisoners, all of whom have been involved in terrorist attacks, and many of whom have blood on their hands. But unlike the immoral behavior of Nasrallah who deliberately kept the fate of both Israeli soldiers a secret even though he knew they were dead, with the deliberate intention of inflicting additional pain on their families, Israel makes no secret of where its Arab prisoners are, and whether they are alive or dead. Visits by the Red Cross and other international organizations are granted. The arch-murderer Samir Kuntar received and sent letters, and even enjoyed conjugal visits. While it may be unwise to grant such rights to imprisoned terrorists, once it's been decided to do so, it should at least be presented as a moral victory, not as a defeat.

While Hamas and other organizations intentionally create hysteria in the streets of Gaza by showing the bodies of every terrorist killed by the Israeli army, thereby assuring its appearance on international TV, Israel refuses to show images of the severed heads and legs of those killed in Arab suicide bombings so as to safeguard the sensibilities of their families. While Hamas constantly fabricates stories of Arab suffering so as to embarrass Israel, the Israeli army does everything to limit its military operations so as not to injure innocent people, and often pays a very heavy price for its compassion. In fact, if an Israeli soldier dares to injure an Arab terrorist without due cause, he is severely reprimanded and punished by the Israeli army.

Where, in all of Israel's history, has there ever been a case of an Arab terrorist being dragged through the streets to be jeered by crowds? Indeed, the examples of Israel's moral supremacy are endless.

Why, then, does our government, its ambassadors and spokesmen, only occasionally publicize Israel's moral grandeur, while for the most part ignore it? If it wants to contend with Arab terrorists, does it not realize that the imperative victory needs to be not only on the battlefield, but also in the court of public opinion? It should have created a massive campaign to show the world its great ethical code, its supreme commitment to higher Jewish standards. It could have pointed out what it means to be a Jewish State deeply rooted in Jewish Tradition, having a nearly "irresponsible" obsession with human dignity – even to the dead; even when it entails unprecedented risks for the future. Many Gentiles would have understood and admired us for this.

Or, does the government believe that the whole world is against us anyway, and that nobody cares about our decency and high moral values, so why even try to convince them of all this? If so, they could not be making a greater mistake. There are millions of Gentiles who admire us and Judaism's universal values, and there would be many more if only they would know who we are and what we stand for.

One wonders whether our government doesn't want to expose too much of its Jewish sensitivities that are rooted in Jewish Tradition. Perhaps it wants to hide the fact that we are indeed different and that we do have higher standards of conduct, expressed in our wish to give all our soldiers a Jewish burial, whatever the price.

Have our leaders lost their connection to their own Jewishness? Do they no longer understand the meaning of Jewish identity and are consequently unable to feel any Jewish pride – the pride to be different? Do they only pay lipservice to their Jewishness at funerals, *smachot*, and other events? Is it no longer in their "*kishkes*," in their inner being? Until now it was secular Zionism which gave them a feeling of purpose. Now, however, when it has become clear that this kind of Zionism no longer has a future, they seem lost, while being unaware of their own confusion. Do they no longer realize that the greatest thing that ever happened to them is that they were born Jews and are heirs to the most magnificent Tradition? Are they ashamed of their Jewish heritage?

Am I to conclude that our government's failure to make the world understand what it means to be a proud Jew speaks volumes about that government's spiritual condition? It has lost its pride in the Jewish State and is utterly confused about its moral justification. Over the years it has maneuvered itself into all sorts of political corners, so that by now it has become nearly impossible to extricate itself from the quicksand into which it has been sucked.

This is not so much a result of the undoubtedly crucial mistakes it has made, but rather because it has failed to explain itself in terms of strength, courage, and pride once it *did* make these mistakes. The words of despair uttered by Israeli leaders perhaps did more damage than the deeds and concessions themselves. When our leaders declare that the Israeli State will not survive unless we give in to Palestinian demands to statehood, or when they give up on neighborhoods in Yerushalayim because they are full of Arab terrorists, they are preaching a dangerous form of defeatism. Such declarations prove that our leaders no longer believe in our own cause and therefore have no claim to leadership.

What they should be saying is: The right to our homeland, including the so-called territories, is indisputable. This has been our home for nearly four thousand years. There is nothing to discuss. But, as Jews, we will do the Palestinians a favor and give them some of *our* land – only on *our* terms, not theirs. Though such decisions may turn out to be utterly wrong, at least they would be made out of a sense of pride, not defeat.

That our government did not take that road is most worrisome. Surely our leaders will tell us we are badly mistaken and they know better, but we should remind them that men are in the habit of raising a dust cloud and then convincing themselves they can still see.

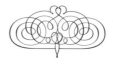

Chapter 25

Halacha Means Full Liberty
To Be Secular Would Be Hell: Everything Would Be Forbidden

I need space to breathe freely. I can't live in a cage where everything is forbidden and I am surrounded by prohibitions that will take all the joy out of my life and make it unbearable.

So, I can't be secular.

A few years ago I saw a cat hit by a car. It rolled over several times but escaped unhurt. Its face showed no sign of shock,[1] but its body language indicated clear signs of panic and disorientation. It ran to the side of the road, turned over several times more, as if in total confusion, and then calmed down. I waited a few seconds wondering what I could do to help, but a moment later the cat went on its way and then disappeared.

This unusual and painful sight triggered several thoughts that I have been contemplating for some time since.

How do we know that animals experience less pain than we do? How can we measure this? What is it that makes animals different from human beings and their lives of lesser value?

It has been argued that animals do not possess the sophisticated level of consciousness that humans have. Humans are aware of their very being, of their thinking. They are much more intelligent, far more creative. They can think in abstract terms. Animals are unable to do so, at least not on the same level as humans.[2]

---

1. I have been told that no animal has the ability to show its emotions in facial expressions. I wonder whether this is really true.

2. Actually, it is not at all clear how we can be certain of this. True, we don't see in animals any *manifestation* of self-awareness and cognitive thinking, but how can we know that it doesn't exist in some other form unbeknownst to us and which we ourselves do not possess? Clearly, some animals have senses that humans are unaware of.

Surely there is an ontological difference between animals and humans. Human beings live life on a level that animals do not share, but we don't even know what this consists of. We recognize that there is a "jump in level" from the animal to the human species, but we don't know what actually constitutes this jump.[3] We merely see the outer aspects of it. Physics and chemistry don't help; they can only describe it. To claim that they can explain it is like saying that Shakespeare's *Hamlet* is nothing but an aspect of a particular combination of letters. But in fact, the particular combination of letters is nothing but an aspect of Shakespeare's *Hamlet*. We cannot describe its *gestalt*. This ultimately remains mysterious. It seems that even the best life sciences can hardly explain *life as such*. It is simply elusive.

But even when we acknowledge that these differences are real, what criteria determine that the lives of animals are less valuable than those of human beings? How do we know that ontological inferiority also means a lesser claim to the sanctity of life? Who says that less *gestalt* means less significance and meaning?

What gives us the right to kill animals for our consumption, use them for scientific research, or force them to experience pain for the sake of human beings? Perhaps all forms of life, from the simple to the sophisticated, are of the same "life value" and none of them should have any claim on the other or be subordinate to the other.

What moral criterion, then, do we rely on when we kill animals for food? However careful we may be in sparing them pain while slaughtering, what gives us the right to kill them at all? This challenge does not stop here.

We must also ask what gives us the right to pluck a flower and stop its life flow, or to kill an insect, even if it is dangerous. How do we know that our blood is, as it were, redder than that of the insect? Perhaps human life must be sacrificed for the sake of an insect's life. The astonishing conclusion is that there *are* no objective criteria to follow.

Let us take this matter even further. What gives a husband the right to impregnate his wife, knowing she will no doubt undergo serious pain and discomfort when giving birth? Is this entirely dependent on his wife's consent? Who says we are allowed to put her in the slightest danger even if she has fully agreed? What gives us the right to have sexual relations

3. See E.F. Schumacher, *A Guide for the Perplexed* (London: Harper Colophon, 1977), chap. 2, especially p. 16.

with a human being but forbids us to do so with another creature? Once again, we lack absolute moral criteria.

It is for this reason that there are serious doubts as to whether "morality" could ever allow any of the above. If there are no absolute criteria by which we determine how to deal with these questions, a consistent approach may well lead us to conclude that the slaughtering of animals, the killing of insects, the plucking of a flower, and the impregnation of women should be strictly forbidden. In case of doubt, the rule should be: Forbidden!

Like it or not, we may be forced to conclude that much of what we assume to be permitted should in fact be prohibited. The list of forbidden acts would be nearly infinite.

This brings us to a most amazing conclusion: A strictly secular approach to major moral issues may have to be *much more restrictive* than that which any religion would ever demand. In fact, a secular moral attitude may make life extremely difficult and even impossible.

I therefore declare that I cannot be secular. It's too difficult. I'd have to live with so many constraints that I would collapse.

It is religion, and not a consistent secular attitude, that has the more liberal approach to moral issues. Religion, in fact, removes many restrictions that would otherwise be imposed by secular standards of morality. In the case of Judaism, Halacha rules that one is allowed to slaughter an animal, albeit under certain circumstances. It allows and even obligates us to kill a dangerous insect. And in the case of a married woman, it makes the radical claim that it is a mitzva for her husband to impregnate her and have children, even though childbirth is excruciatingly painful. It does so purely on the basis of its faith that the Creator not only permitted these acts but even demanded them. This, of course, cannot be proved, but if Halacha would reject these beliefs, it would have no option but to forbid all of the above, as would secular morality.

We may therefore have to admit that we have been wrong for hundreds, if not thousands, of years. It is not religion that restricts our lives – *it is secularism.*

True, we may not have seen secularism in this light and may have allowed ourselves many liberties in its name, but we should be aware that this approach may be entirely wrong. It should perhaps be the reverse: secularity makes life very difficult, not religion.

If so, we must argue that in the case of Judaism, the 613 commandments do not restrict us. On the contrary, they liberate us from hundreds, if not thousands of prohibitions that honest secularism would have imposed on us.

Professor E.S. Waterhouse was incorrect when he made the disturbing observation that just as a parasite is an independent organism but dependent on its host for survival, so is secular morality dependent on religious values for its restrictions.[4] I do not agree. The reverse is true: If secularism would stand on its own, it would be so restrictive as to make life extremely difficult, if not impossible. That it permits so much is due to the fact that it has adopted much from the "permissive" world of religion.

And therefore I can't be secular. It would be hell.

Rather an unusual observation prompted by a simple cat.

---

4. E.S. Waterhouse, "The Religious Basis of Morality," in *Essays in Honour of the Very Rev. Dr. J. H. Hertz: Chief Rabbi of the United Hebrew Congregations of the British Empire, on the Occasion of His Seventieth Birthday, September 25, 1942*, ed. I. Epstein, E. Levine and C. Roth (London: E. Goldston, 1942), 413–14.

Chapter 26

The Supreme Court of the United States, Same-Sex Marriage, and Other Prohibitions

In 2015, the Supreme Court of the United States legalized same-sex marriage. We need to ask ourselves why there has never been any discussion about other sexual relationships that are currently illegal, such as incest, and why a union as obvious as a heterosexual marriage is actually permitted. This question may sound very strange, even disturbing and shocking, but it is one of the most profound questions we must ask. Doing so will help us understand what is behind the fierce debate that is now taking place concerning the Supreme Court's decision. It raises many questions concerning marriage, sex, religious freedom, and the role religion plays in our society.

In *Mishna Chagiga*[1] we are confronted with several educational directives related to esoteric matters. The mishna instructs that some subjects, such as the secrets of *Ma'aseh Bereshit* (the Creation), should only be taught to one person at a time, while other metaphysical topics, such as *Ma'aseh Merkava* (the vision of the Divine Chariot mentioned in the book of Yechezkel), should only be taught to one pupil, and only if they are wise and have much knowledge of their own. The main reason given for these rulings is to prevent misunderstanding. When only one student at a time is present, there will be little chance of the mentor being misunderstood. The pupil will be forced to listen carefully to every word spoken by the teacher. There is no luxury of dozing off, hearing only half the lecture, and drawing the wrong conclusions.

At the opening of this mishna we are informed that matters of *arayot* (forbidden sexual relations) should not be taught to more than two stu-

---

1. *Mishna Chagiga* 2:1.

dents at a time. The standard explanation for this "lenient" rule (two students instead of only one) is that both students will make sure they hear all that is said about sexuality, since most human beings are preoccupied with the subject. Even when the teacher is speaking only to one of them, the other one will also listen. Three, however, is considered problematic, since the other two may start a discussion between themselves, draw the wrong conclusions, and permit what is forbidden, or vice versa.

Maharsha, Rabbi Shmuel Eliezer Eidels (1555–1631), however, gives a different interpretation regarding the nature of the rules related to sexuality.[2] According to him, these rules are not just based on the chance that the students may come to the wrong halachic conclusions, but because these matters of *arayot* are totally mysterious as well and belong in the same category as the esoteric *Ma'aseh Bereshit* and *Ma'aseh Merkava*. No explanation is available as to why certain sexual relationships are forbidden and others are permitted. They are also in the category of the "beyond." Maharsha asks, for example, why marrying one's sister is prohibited. He also questions why a man is prohibited from marrying his living wife's sister, but is allowed to marry the same sister after his wife has died.[3] (According to the Torah, one is allowed to marry more than one wife, but Rabbenu Gershom [c. 960–1028/40] forbade this around the year 1000.)[4]

To claim that any of the prohibited relationships are fundamentally "unethical" is untenable, for the obvious reason that the children of Adam and Chava clearly married their brothers and sisters. Nowhere is it written that this was forbidden. In fact, it was the only way God saw fit to propagate the human species. Similarly, we see that Ya'akov married two living sisters. The same is true about the parents of Moshe Rabbenu. According to Torah Law, Amram was not allowed to marry his aunt Yocheved.[5] Most remarkable is the fact that these marriages laid the foundation for the Jewish people and were therefore indispensable!

It is for this reason, says Maharsha, that one should teach these matters to only two pupils at a time so as to prevent any interpretations, since there are none. The laws of sexuality are so complex – in fact, completely incomprehensible – that two students might possibly start arguing between themselves while the mentor is concentrating on the third. The

---

2. See *Maharsha, Chiddushei Aggadot* on *Chagiga* 11b, s.v. "ba-arayot."
3. *Vayikra* 18:9, 18.
4. See *Shulchan Aruch, Even ha-Ezer* 1:9-10.
5. *Vayikra* 18:12-13.

students could advance all sorts of explanations, claiming that they found the *raison d'etre* of the subject and draw the wrong conclusions.

Maharsha's observation is therefore of primary importance. All discussions about why certain marriages or sexual relationships are forbidden are doomed to fail! No human reasoning can explain them in any consistent way.

Religious thinkers should therefore refrain from giving primary reasons for these prohibitions. It would be counterproductive and dangerous. There is no objective reason why homosexuality and incest are forbidden. From the religious point of view, these prohibitions are celestial, just like *Ma'aseh Bereshit* and *Ma'aseh Merkava*. They seem to touch on metaphysical criteria that are known only to God.

The same is true for the secular argument. On the basis of what rational principle should a homosexual relationship be permitted, but incest forbidden? Would it not be reasonable to allow the latter, on the condition that the couple ensure that there will be no children, so as to prevent any genetic defects?

On the other end of the spectrum, one could ask religious and secular thinkers why a heterosexual relationship is permitted and even encouraged? What, after all, are the moral grounds to permit such a relationship? Perhaps every kind of sexual activity should be forbidden and considered unethical, since, as Rambam approvingly quotes Aristotle, "the sense of touch is a disgrace to us."[6] This is what Danish philosopher and father of religious existentialism Søren Kierkegaard seems to claim when he argues against marriage.[7] The fact that this would ultimately result in the extinction of humankind in no way diminishes the ethical problem.

This problem is more pronounced when considering that heterosexual marriages result in women becoming pregnant, often suffering great pain and sometimes, mortal danger. Who says that this is ethically permitted? As a matter of fact, what gives us the right to even give birth to children when there is a serious chance that they will fall victim to diseases, war, and natural disasters? Is it not more responsible to avoid having children, since those who remain unborn would not suffer the slightest discomfort?

However unsavory our argument may sound, we are forced to ask, from a secular perspective, what could be wrong with incest and other relationships that are forbidden by secular law? As long as such relationships

---

6. *Moreh Nevuchim*, part 3, chap. 8.

7. See Julia Watkin, "The Logic of Søren Kierkegaard's Misogyny 1854-1855," *Kierkegaardiana* 15 (1991): 82–92.

are formed by mutual consent, and no one is physically or mentally hurt, there should be no reason for these relationships to be forbidden.

Arguments such as "the need for human dignity" are of little meaning, because it is unclear how one defines human dignity. And even if there was a clear definition, one could ask why it should be an absolute inviolable value.

We must therefore conclude that from the religious and secular perspectives, laws related to sexuality are arbitrary. In both societies these laws are rooted in a "will" that is outside of what we call "reason." For the religious, it is the Will of God that provides us with rules telling us what is permitted and what is prohibited. And for the secular, it is mutual consensus, the democratic vote, and often a kind of relativism that will decide what is permitted and what is prohibited. Secular law is probably rooted in the notion that certain sexual relationships are prohibited because they *feel* wrong, although we are unable to explain why. Paradoxically, we may call this a relative "categorical imperative," using Immanuel Kant's famous axiom. Some philosophers, however, would claim that this "imperative" is borrowed from religious principles as a result of a kind of Jungian archetype, although it is doubtful that Jung had this is mind or would have even agreed.

We are forced to conclude that any debate between the religious and secular communities on the permissibility or illicitness of certain sexual relationships is utterly meaningless. Both communities come from different foundational categories.

There is no way that either party can deliver an argument that is objectively sound. No ethical claim can be made to decide whether heterosexual, homosexual, and other relationships should be forbidden or permitted. Ultimately, it is an amoral issue which can be decided only on the acceptance or rejection of some will (such as God's), or of some type of cultural taboo grounded in a feeling of uneasiness with certain sexual activities.

Whether or not the homosexual act forbidden by the Torah is identical with same-sex marriage is a different question. Religious authorities and thinkers will have to put their minds to this weighty question. It will be one of the most daring decisions they will ever have to consider.

In the meantime, it is the task of both parties to make sure that people do not get hurt by these religious or secular principles and that their rights are ensured. Not only will it be necessary to protect the rights of same-sex couples, but it will be just as essential to protect the rights of synagogues, churches, and other religious groups to express and follow their religious convictions.

This will become a major headache for the United States Supreme Court, the lower courts, and all of us in the years to come. What will become clear is that the courts will be unable to come up with a consistent solution and will have to fall back on compromises and "legal trade-offs."

Perfect solutions to human problems cannot be coherently conceived.

Chapter 27

On the Law of the *Mamzer*

Between Fairness and Holiness in Halacha:
Possible Solutions and Rabbinical Courage
(The Theology of the Halachic Loophole
and the Meaning of Torah From Heaven)

INTRODUCTION

"A *mamzer* shall not enter into the congregation of the Lord."[1]

It is generally assumed that Jewish Law is morally sound. There is one law that, on the face of it, runs counter to this assumption.

The Halacha states that a *mamzer*[2] is prevented from marrying a fellow Jew or Jewess. Only fellow *mamzerim* or proselytes are potential candidates to be this person's partner in life.[3] According to rabbinic definition, a *mamzer* is a child born from a couple whose sexual relationship is forbidden according to the Torah and punishable by *karet*, or the death penalty.[4]

---

1. *Devarim* 23:3.

2. The definition of the word *mamzer* is complex. The only other reference to *mamzer* in Tanach is the verse in *Zecharia* 9:6, "And a mamzer shall dwell in Ashdod." Several suggestions have been made as to its meaning. *Ramban* on *Devarim* 23:3 quotes Rabbi Avahu's interpretation cited in JT *Kiddushin* 3:12, 64c, that *mamzer* is derived from the words *mum zar*, a strange blemish. This interpretation also appears anonymously in *Yevamot* 76b. *Radak* on *Zecharia* 9:6 suggests that the root word of *mamzer* is *zar*, a stranger. *Ibn Ezra* on *Devarim* 23:3 states that the term denotes a certain non-Jewish tribe. According to the Septuagint on *Devarim* 23:2, a *mamzer* is "[One born] of a harlot." Abraham Geiger suggests that the word *mamzer* is derived from *me-am zar*, from a foreign/strange nation. This would mean that a child of a mixed marriage is a *mamzer*. See David Novak, *Halakhah in a Theological Dimension*, Brown Judaic Studies 68 (Chico, CA: Scholars Press, 1985), 13–17. See also Abraham Geiger, *Urschrift und Übersetzungen der Bibel* (Breslau: Julius Hainauer, 1857), 52f. and A. Aptowitzer, "Spuren des Matriarchats im jüdischen Schrifttum (Schluss)," *Hebrew Union College Annual* 5 (1928): 271–272, where he also suggests a connection between the words *mamzer* and *me-im zona*, from a harlot. However, the rabbinical interpretation does not follow some of these suggestions.

3. *Kiddushin* 72b–73a; *Mishne Torah, Hilchot Isurei Biah* 15:7; *Shulchan Aruch, Even ha-Ezer* 4:22.

4. See *Mishna Yevamot* 4:13; *Yevamot* 44a–45b, 49a; *Kiddushin* 66b; *Mishne Torah, Hilchot Isurei Biah* 15:1; *Shulchan Aruch, Even ha-Ezer* 4:13. There are different opinions as to the exact nature of the punishment of *karet*. See *Sifra, Emor*, chap. 14:4 (Weiss ed. 102a); *Mo'ed Katan* 28a; *Yevamot*

Because of this, a marriage between them is void. Thus, for example, the child born of a union between brother and sister, or between a woman legitimately married to a man and having a child with another (Jewish) man, is a *mamzer*.[5] Even more problematic is the fact that all offspring of a *mamzer* are also *mamzerim* even if the *mamzer* marries a proselyte. This law applies *ad infinitum*.[6] Interesting enough is the fact that if there was an adulterous relationship with a non-Jew, the child is not a *mamzer*.[7] The law applies equally to both male and female, the latter referred to as a *mamzeret*.[8]

While recognizing the inherent wrong in these liaisons and the social damage caused thereby, one may be forgiven for wondering how the Torah could introduce a law so apparently unjustifiable and inhumane: that a child pay the price for the misdeeds of its parents. This would appear, in fact, to contradict another basic Torah principle, namely, that each person is responsible only for his or her own actions,[9] or for those of a fellow Jew when one is in a position to prevent a particular transgression. However, in this case the unborn child is already condemned for life, before he or she could do anything right or wrong!

Ethically, there seems to be no way to justify this biblical ruling, and therefore one might perhaps argue that it should be seen as purely theoretical. This, for example, is the case with the law concerning the *ben sorer*

55a; *Sanhedrin* 64b; JT *Bikkurim* 2:1, 64c. For an overview of this topic, see Yisroel Zichel, "Karet, Ariri u-Mita be-Yedei Shamayim: Gidrehem," *Magal* 11 (1995): 203–225; *Talmudic Encyclopedia*, s.v. "karet, mita be-yedei shamayim," 32:373–399.

5. There is a dispute in rabbinical sources regarding which kind of a child is considered a *mamzer*. See *Mishna Yevamot* 4:13. The Halacha, however, was decided in accordance with Rabbi Shimon of Teman who states that only those children who are born from an incestuous or adulterous relationship which is punishable by *karet* or the death penalty are deemed *mamzerim*.

6. *Yevamot* 78b; *Sifrei Devarim*, Finkelstein ed., section 248; *Mishne Torah, Hilchot Isurei Biah* 15:1; *Shulchan Aruch, Even ha-Ezer* 4:1.

7. *Yevamot* 45; *Mishne Torah, Hilchot Isurei Biah* 15:3; *Shulchan Aruch, Even ha-Ezer* 4:19. The fact that a child is not a *mamzer* when the father is a non-Jew is most remarkable and somehow disturbing. Why should this child not be a *mamzer* when adultery has taken place with a non-Jew? This obviously has to do with the fact that Jewish Law only recognizes a marriage between a Jew and a Jewess. It is only when such a relationship could have been legal had the woman not have been already married, that the law of a *mamzer* could be applied. This makes us wonder whether a mixed marriage (which is considered to be a very serious breakdown of the Jewish people's capacity to survive and to fulfill its mission) is not seen as severe as an adulterous relationship between two Jews, even in a case where there was an adulterous relationship between a Jew and a non-Jew, which could be seen as even worse!

8. See n6 above.

9. *Devarim* 24:16; 2 *Melachim* 14:6; 2 *Divrei ha-Yamim* 25:4. See, however, *Shemot* 20:5, 34:6; *Bamidbar* 14:18; *Devarim* 5:9. The sages have attempted to resolve this contradiction in several ways. See *Berachot* 7a; *Sanhedrin* 27b; *Midrash Aggada*, Buber ed., on *Shemot* 20:5.

u-moreh, the rebellious son.[10] The sages declared that the conditions for passing a death sentence in such a case were so stringent and far-fetched that they could never be met; rather, the case was only stated to increase the reward for those who study this verse as part of the mitzva of *Talmud Torah*, and to learn moral lessons from the philosophy behind this law.[11]

Why then do the rabbis, or for that matter the Oral Tradition, not declare the law of the *mamzer* to be similarly theoretical, as in the case of the *ben sorer u-moreh*? This might be the best solution; another approach would be impossible. To ignore the law or to see it as a moral error created by primitive men, as Spinoza and others would declare, is obviously not an option for the believing Jew, since Jewish Tradition sees every word of the Torah as being beyond reproach.[12] The law of the Torah is of divine origin and cannot be lightly cast aside.

We are thus confronted with an unusual situation, for we are forced to admit that this embarrassing and apparently unjustifiable law is part of our divine heritage! This is more than a paradox – it is shocking.

At this point, the reader may be wondering how the author dares to make such a controversial statement about a law found within the Torah. However, careful examination will show that in fact he has the full weight of Jewish Tradition behind him.

GOD VERSUS GOD

We read in *Kohelet* the following:

> So I returned and considered all the oppressions that are done under the sun, and behold the tears of such as were oppressed. And they had no comforter, and on the side of their oppressors there was power, but they had no comforter.[13]

The Midrash comments:

> "Behold the tears off the oppressed" – their fathers sinned, but what has this to do with these insulted ones? The father of this one went to a woman forbidden to him, but how did the child sin, and why does

---

10. *Devarim* 21:18–21.
11. *Sanhedrin* 68b–71a.
12. See, however, pp. 288–299 below.
13. *Kohelet* 4:1.

it concern him? "They have no comforter . . . but in the hands of the oppressors there is power" – these are the hands of the Great Sanhedrin,[14] which moved against them with the authority of the Torah and removed them from the community, because it is written: "A *mamzer* shall not enter in the congregation of the Eternal One." "And there is none to comfort them" – therefore says the Holy One, blessed be He: "It is upon Me to comfort them. . ." As Zecharia prophesied,[15] "Behold I see them all like pure gold."[16]

This midrash is one of the most remarkable and heartrending expressions of rabbinic humanity and concern for human pain in all of Jewish Tradition. It is perplexing that this above statement was made by Daniel Chayyata the tailor, who is apparently mentioned only one other time in rabbinical literature.[17]

It reflects an inherent paradox, which is symptomatic of traditional Jewish thought. It is a case of God versus God: God the Oppressor and God the Comforter. The same God who is the Author of "A *mamzer* shall not enter in the congregation of the Eternal One" is also the God who is the Great Comforter: "Behold I see them all like pure gold."

THE PROBLEM OF EVIL

The phenomenon of "God versus God" is most clearly expressed in the problem of good and evil: God is the Creator of both of them.

"Creating light, forming darkness, making peace and creating evil – I, the Lord, do all these things."[18]

Immediately, the age-old question comes to mind. Why does God, the merciful Creator of the world, need to create evil?

---

14. The Supreme High Court of ancient Israel.

15. *Zecharia* 4:2.

16. *Kohelet Rabba*, Vilna ed., 4:1, section 1.

17. See *Bereshit Rabba*, Vilna ed., 64:7. Apparently he was no halachist, had little influence on Judaism and was probably not even very learned. Still, the above midrash has had enormous influence on all rabbinical discussion regarding mamzerim and has become a cause célèbre for all those who are forced to deal with this and similar "harsh" laws in the Torah as a call for mercy by setting God up against His own law. On the identity of Daniel Chayyata, see "Daniel Ḥayyata," *Encyclopaedia Judaica*, ed. Michael Berenbaum and Fred Skolnik, 2nd ed. (Detroit: Macmillan Reference USA, 2007), 5:429; Louis Jacobs, *A Tree of Life: Diversity, Flexibility, and Creativity in Jewish Law* (London: Littman Library of Jewish Civilization, 2000), 247 n54.

18. *Yeshayahu* 45:7.

Could He not have created a world entirely without evil? Strangely enough, the answer is no!

The world, after all, has a purpose, a *raison d'être*.

John Hick, professor of philosophy at the University of Birmingham, calls the world "a soul-making place," a place where people can spiritually grow, overcome obstacles, and become more "soul-like." For our purposes, and more in line with Jewish thought, I would like to adapt Hick's phraseology and call the world a *tzaddik*-making place, namely, a place where righteous people can come into being. Since this world needs to be an arena for *tzaddik*-making, it must by definition consist of good and evil.

Here Hick introduces his "counterfactual hypothesis":

> Suppose that, contrary to fact, this world were a paradise from which all possibility of pain and suffering were excluded. The consequences would be very far-reaching. For example, no one could ever injure anyone else: the murderer's knife would turn to paper or the bullets to thin air; the bank safe, robbed of a million dollars, would miraculously become filled with another million dollars; fraud, deceit, conspiracy, and treason would somehow leave the fabric of society undamaged. No one would ever be injured by accident: the mountain climber, steeplejack, or a playing child falling from a height would float unharmed to the ground; the reckless driver would never meet with disaster . . . in a hedonistic paradise there would be no wrong actions – nor therefore any right actions in distinction from wrong. Courage and fortitude would have no point in an environment in which there is, by definition, no danger or difficulty. Generosity, kindness, the *agape* aspect of love, prudence, unselfishness, and other ethical notions that presuppose life in an objective environment could not even be formed. Consequently, such a world, however well it might promote pleasure, would be very ill adapted for the moral qualities of human personality. In relation to this purpose it might well be the worst of all possible worlds![19]

It all comes down to one principle: For man to reach ethical good, he will need to pay a price by learning to cope with evil.

---

19. John Hick, *Philosophy of Religion* (Englewood Cliffs, NJ: Prentice-Hall, 1983), 47. It is, however, very difficult to use Hick's argument in the case of the Holocaust and other extreme atrocities where people were not able to use these experiences to grow morally and spiritually. These kinds of evil belong to an altogether different category.

This is the divine dilemma: If God had created a *perfect* world from the outset, it would have been one of unmitigated evil. Since He wanted a world where evil would *no longer* exist, He was obliged to create one with evil! What this means in practice is that for the world to exist, certain fundamental conditions must be fulfilled. This is not an apology; it is a condition *sine qua non*.

To say that this world should be without evil is to say that the world should not exist.

Just as there can be no meaning in speaking about light without a concomitant darkness, neither can one speak about good without evil, sympathy without aversion, humility without arrogance, honesty without falsehood, *kedusha* (holiness) without *tum'ah* (impurity).

Now let us ask: Is evil fair? Is injustice, pain, war, and illness fair? From the human perspective, the answer must definitely be no! But if we ask the question: Are these necessary entities without which the world cannot exist? – the answer must be a resounding yes! They are the collateral we have to pay if we want to achieve and experience good health, peace, and justice.

KEDUSHA

All of this seems to be far removed from the law of *mamzerut*. Still, the same questions may be asked in this case as well. Is it fair? Most definitely not! It is as unfair as pain, war, and illness. This is exactly what the earlier quoted midrash says: a law stating that a child must pay the price for the transgressions of his or her parents cannot be anything else but unfair and, as such, unjustifiable.

What, then, is the divine imperative underlying the institution of *mamzerut*? Why indeed does it find a place in the Torah at all? The answer is the same as with the problem of good and evil. It is a necessary counterforce for the creation of a greater good, as explained by the counterfactual hypothesis. This time, however, it is not the creation of some sort of negative force to allow a positive one to come into realization (as in the case of good and evil), but the creation of a prohibition so as to achieve the highest level of biblical imperative: *kedusha*, holiness.

The Jewish people are called upon to become an *Am Kadosh* (Holy Nation) and a *Mamlechet Kohanim* (Kingdom of Priests).[20] They are asked

---

20. See *Shemot* 19:6, 22:30; *Vayikra* 11:44–45, 19:2, 20:7, 20:26, 21:6; *Bamidbar* 15:40; *Devarim*

to achieve a high level of *kedusha*, not for its own sake, but for the sake
of humankind: to be a light unto the nations. This, however, cannot be
achieved without a counterforce.

SEXUALITY

There is one litmus test by which a nation's *kedusha* can be measured. This
is the most basic element of the human personality and its expression:
sexuality.[21] Sexuality is one of the most powerful of human drives and, as
history has often shown, the breaking point of civilizations. Whole empires have fallen apart because of the idolization of sex; countless crimes
have been committed and even wars begun because of this most powerful
urge.

It is no coincidence that the *brit mila* (circumcision) is chosen as the
great sign of the Jewish Covenant with God. The attitude toward and
the handling of sexual passion is the ultimate test. It is the best yardstick
of man's commitment to *kedusha* and morality. This is perhaps the very
reason the Torah contains so many laws concerning sexuality. Judaism
shuns the abolition or the denial of the sexual urge. It abhors the extreme
idea that human sexuality is an aberration, a concession to sinful man. It
does not countenance the concept of absolute self-denial and suppression.
Rather, it calls for the careful handling and sublimation of this most important and God-given urge.

To make sure that the Jewish people achieve the greatest possible *kedusha* in the world, a counterforce had to be created. This is the underlying
purpose of the law of the *mamzer*. Nothing could make it more evident to
the Jew how careful he needs to be in dealing with matters of sexuality and
kedusha than this very law. By making the child pay for the transgression
of the most severe of all sexual prohibitions (adultery), the Torah created
a counterforce so far-reaching and so "unjustified" that it would, once and
for all, create the highest of all goodness: *kedusha*. To achieve that goal, the
Torah touched the Jew at his most sensitive nerve: his child. Many Jews
might perhaps be prepared to transgress the severest of prohibitions and
carry the consequences personally, but would not do so with the knowledge that their child will pay the price.

It is not just the *mamzer* law, or the individual involved, that is at the

---

7:6, 14:2, 14:21, 26:19.
21. See *Rashi* on *Vayikra* 19:2.

heart of the matter. Rather, the intention is that through this law the Jewish people would become aware of their highest goals, and know that human sexuality – the greatest of all drives – can and must be sanctified. Only then can one speak of a Holy Nation and of a Chosen People. Through this law, the existence of a proper family life, which is the foundation of the Jewish nation, becomes a reality. The *mamzer* law, then, hovers over the Jew's very being as a powerful force to guarantee the survival of the Jewish people and the fulfillment of their great mission toward the world community: to be a world-transforming people.

In this sense we may say that the *mamzer* law guaranteed the survival of the Jewish nation and gave it vitality, thus making it an inspiration for all other nations. Regretfully, to accomplish that goal casualties are unavoidable.

AKEDAT YITZCHAK

It was not without reason that the greatest of all Jews, Avraham, underwent the supreme test of giving up his child to show his total commitment to God and the Jewish mission. His faith and his endurance to pass that test became the paramount example and paradigm for the future of the Jewish people. Without that unprecedented experience, no Chosen People would have emerged and no Torah would have been given. It was God, however, who stopped Avraham from sacrificing his son, telling him that it was not the actual deed, but rather his willingness to carry it out that was the ultimate test. It was God versus God.[22]

But was *Akedat Yitzchak* (the Binding of Isaac) fair? Within the scope of the private life of Avraham, and even more so of Yitzchak, it was uncalled for! It was not even Yitzchak's trial. Similar, but not identical to the case of the *mamzer*, he was the victim of someone else's test! If, however, we ask whether this trial was a necessity in order to build the foundations for creating an *Am Kadosh* and a *Mamlechet Kohanim*, then the answer must be an unqualified yes.

Everything must be subsumed by the survival and the great task of the Jewish people. This is the purpose of Israel's ultimate sacrifice. This is the paradox of all Jewish religious thought.

---

22. See Nathan Lopes Cardozo, "The Religious Scandal of Akeidat Yitzchak and the Tragic God" (Thoughts to Ponder 463), *David Cardozo Academy*, Oct. 29, 2015, https://www.cardozo academy.org/thoughts-to-ponder/the-religious-scandal-of-akeidat-yitzchak-and-the-tragic-god -parashat-lech-lecha/.

FAIRNESS

What becomes clear is this: fairness is not the paramount criterion in Jewish Law or thought. It is not an ultimate standard. "Deracheha darchei no'am" (Your ways are ways of pleasantness)[23] expressed a rule much used by the Talmud to determine the more pleasant approach of Halacha toward otherwise unpleasant circumstances,[24] but this is *not* an overriding value. It can be overshadowed by an even higher imperative: *kedusha* and the survival and mission of the Jewish people. Fairness is only of value if it is not an obstacle to the achievement of *kedusha*.

And just as when trying to achieve peace we risk the lives of our soldiers, so the *mamzer* is offered for the sake of *kedusha*. It is not much different than the child whose father is jailed for a legitimate reason, and now, through no fault of his own, has to live life without a parent. In all of these cases, there is no fairness as far as the suffering of these blameless individuals is concerned.

In the great scheme of Jewish history, the law regarding *mamzerut* has been an *absolutely* essential and crucial element in the unfolding of God's purpose for humankind and the world. But God is also the Comforter. When the messianic era begins and Israel will have reached its ultimate goal, then the world will be transformed by the spiritual ideals of the Torah and the *mamzer* law will have no further purpose. This, then, is the meaning of the statement, "*Mamzerim* are to be purified in the messianic age."[25]

As long as these days have not arrived, the *mamzer* law functions as one of the most effective ways of achieving this very goal.

---

23. *Mishlei* 3:17.

24. *Sukka* 32b; *Yevamot* 15a, 87b; *Gittin* 59b; *Mishne Torah*, end of *Hilchot Megilla ve-Chanuka*. For a discussion on this topic, see Eliezer Berkovits, *Ha-Halacha, Kocha ve-Tafkida* (Jerusalem: Mossad HaRav Kook, 2006), 112–140. See pp. 288–299 below.

25. *Kiddushin* 72b and *Tosefta Kiddushin* 5:4 according to the opinion of R. Yose. Note that R. Meir disagrees with R. Yose. See the interesting difference of opinion between *Kiddushin* 72b and JT *Kiddushin* 3:13, 64d as to whether the Halacha is according to R. Meir that *mamzerim* will not be purified in the messianic era or according to R. Yose that *mamzerim* will be purified in the messianic era. It must be argued that even in the messianic age moral challenges will continue to exist in some form. Otherwise there is no longer any purpose to human existence, as Hick argues. See also *Mishne Torah, Hilchot Melachim*, 12:3.

THE CIVIL COURT

Still, this is not the whole story. After all, not all *mamzerim* are the result of indecent and immoral behavior by their parents. Some are the outcome of unintentional mistakes, such as where a woman divorced her husband in a civil court and was unaware that she needed a *get*, which is the only valid divorce according to Jewish Law. Or, where a woman thought that her husband had died, then married another man, only to discover that her first husband was still alive. In such cases, Jewish Law teaches that the first partner remained the legitimate husband, and *legally* the woman has committed adultery. *Morally*, however, she has not. There were no evil intentions, and the above-described purpose of the *mamzer* law clearly does not apply. What, then, is to be done?

SOLUTIONS TO THE *MAMZER* PROBLEM

Several suggestions have been made to solve such *mamzer* problems without declaring it officially obsolete.[26] In fact, it is specifically in such a case that the rabbis showed enormous courage and unprecedented creativity. Based on the principle mentioned above, that in the messianic age all *mamzerim* will be purified, they seemingly felt that the law was meant to apply temporarily, as opposed to those divine laws that should be seen as eternal. So there was reason to be lenient. Also, it appears that they were influenced by a talmudic observation that a *mamzer* who is not definitely known to be such would die within a month after his or her birth,[27] so that only in notorious cases is there a need to fear that they would marry into pure families. And if a *mamzer* may have indeed entered into a family, there was no reason to make an issue out of it, since "a family that has suffered an admixture has suffered an admixture."[28] In other words, the remedy was: Close your eyes![29] It even seems that the sages were aware that some *mamzerim* had bought their way into the best of families, and

---

26. For an overview, see Jacobs, *A Tree of Life*, 239–254.

27. See *Yevamot* 78b and JT *Kiddushin* 3:12, 64c. For a discussion of this topic, see R. Yehuda Herzl Henkin, "Ha-Yachas le-Mamzer," *Techumin* 22 (2002): 50–56.

28. *Kiddushin* 72a. See *Talmudic Encyclopedia*, s.v. "yuchasin," 22:290–297 for a discussion of this topic.

29. Rumors have it that Orthodox rabbis used to hint to *mamzerim* to move to another city where nobody knew they were *mamzerim*, and just marry a Jewish girl.

they just disregarded the issue, as if nothing happened.[30] No family was checked to see whether it may have *mamzerim* in its ancestry, and rumors of *mamzerut* were ignored.[31] Rabbi Moshe Isserles even states that if one knows of such a disqualification, they "are not permitted to disclose it, but it should be overlooked, since all families in which there has been an admixture will become pure in the future."[32]

Even when there was a very strong suspicion, the rabbis found ways around it. In a case where it was quite obvious that a woman had become pregnant from another man while her husband was overseas, they speculated that her husband may have somehow appeared in a highly improbable way, impregnated his wife, and returned to his place abroad![33] In a case where a woman had a child many years after her sick husband had left her without a *get*, the rabbis decided out of doubt that the father of the child may have been a non-Jew, and even if not, her sick husband may have died before she became pregnant.[34] For various reasons, the twentieth-century American halachic authority Rabbi Moshe Feinstein refused to believe a woman who declared that she never received a *get* from her first husband and that her son from her second marriage was a *mamzer*.[35] Similarly, the well-known authority Rabbi Aharon Walkin dismissed concerns of *mamzerut* in a case where indeed there was strong reason to suspect it.[36]

The custom of keeping registers of *mamzerim* so as to be able to trace them (after a war, for example), as was done in certain Western European countries, seems to run counter to the tradition of the earlier rabbis who were of the opinion that the absence of such registers was the best way to let *mamzerim* disappear among the people of Israel.

---

30. See *Kiddushin* 71a.

31. For a discussion of conflicting attitudes toward the *mamzer* and the competing interests of wanting to remove the stigma of the *mamzer* vs. the desire to maintain the purity of Jewish lineage and pedigree, see Novak, *Halakhah in a Theological Dimension*, chap. 2. For a striking example of a contemporary halachic authority who is concerned with maintaining the purity of the Jewish people in relation to the issue of *mamzerut*, see R. Menashe Klein, *Mishne Halachot*, vol. 17, nos. 6 and 8.

32. *Rema* on *Shulchan Aruch, Even ha-Ezer* 2:5. For a discussion, see Jacobs, *A Tree of Life*, 248–249.

33. See *Halachot Gedolot* on the halachot of *gittin*, section 39, comment on *Gittin* 89a; *Shulchan Aruch, Even ha-Ezer* 4:14 and the commentaries ad loc.

34. R. Moshe Sofer, *Chatam Sofer, Even ha-Ezer*, vol. 1, no. 10.

35. R. Moshe Feinstein, *Igrot Moshe, Even ha-Ezer*, vol. 3, no. 5.

36. R. Aharon Walkin, *Zekan Aharon* (NY: Sentry Press, 1958), vol. 1, *Even ha-Ezer*, no. 65.

THE CANAANITE SLAVE

The Mishna, in the name of Rabbi Tarfon, suggests a remedy to absolve the offspring of a *mamzer* from *mamzerut*. The *mamzer* is allowed to take a Canaanite slave-girl and have children with her. These children are not considered *mamzerim* since in most respects they are considered non-Jews. Once the owner of the slave-girl sets the children free, they are full-fledged, purified Jews.[37] To apply such a law today, when slavery is no longer an option, is obviously highly problematic, if not outright forbidden.[38]

The most obvious way to free a child conceived by a second marriage from *mamzerut* (when no *get* from the first marriage was delivered) is to prove that the first marriage was not valid. This can be done by arguing, for example, that the first husband was insane, and that he concealed this at the time of the marriage. Such a union is called a "mistaken marriage," since the wife would not have agreed to marry this man had she known of his insanity.[39] Another case is where the first marriage was performed only by civil law, which does not count in Jewish Law,[40] or where the first husband was not properly converted and is consequently not Jewish.[41] There are also ways to argue that the witnesses at the first marriage were invalid, or that the ring used did not belong to the husband, thereby voiding the

---

37. *Mishna Kiddushin* 3:13 according to the opinion of R. Tarfon. R. Eliezer disagrees, however, and maintains that these children are considered *mamzerim*.

38. For various views about the applicability of this law in contemporary times, see R. Zvi Ryzman, *Ratz ka-Tzvi: Asufat Ma'amarim, Pirke Mechkar ve-Iyun; Poriyut, Yuchasin, Ishut* (Los Angeles, 2016), no. 14 and Ryzman, "Taharat Mamzer be-Shifcha be-Zmanenu," *Olamot*, http://www.olamot.net//node/15598/.

39. See, for example, R. Moshe Feinstein, *Igrot Moshe, Even ha-Ezer*, vol. 1, no. 80.

40. There is much discussion among halachic authorities whether there is a need for a *get* when there was only a civil marriage. R. Moshe Feinstein argues in his responsum that although we should be stringent in the case of a civil marriage and require a *get*, still the children of the second marriage are not *mamzerim*! See *Igrot Moshe, Even ha-Ezer*, vol. 2, no. 19. Regarding civil marriages, see R. Ovadia Yosef, *Yabia Omer*, vol. 6, *Even ha-Ezer*, no. 1 and the illuminating correspondence between R. Shalom Mashash and R. Menashe Klein, "Nisuin Ezrachi'im u-Mamzerut," *Techumin* 24 (2004): 181–187. A similar discussion takes place concerning a Reform marriage. See R. Moshe Feinstein, *Igrot Moshe, Even ha-Ezer*, vol. 1, nos. 76, 77, and *Even ha-Ezer*, vol. 3, no. 25; R. Yitzchak Ya'akov Weiss, *Minchat Yitzchak*, vol. 2, no. 66.

41. See the fiercely debated decision by Chief Rabbi Shlomo Goren in the case of a brother and sister of the Langer family who were originally considered to be *mamzerim*. By proving that the first marriage of their mother was invalid since the father never sincerely converted, Rabbi Goren was able to free both children from *mamzerut*. See R. Shlomo Goren, *Psak ha-Din be'Inyan he-Ach ve-he-Achot* (Jerusalem: Chief Rabbinate of Israel, 1973); Mark E. Washofsky, "The Case of the Brother and the Sister: A Critical Analysis of the Decision of Rabbi Shelomo Goren in the Case of Hanokh and Miryam Langer" (rabbinical thesis, H.U.C.-J.I.R, 1980); and the summary provided by J. David Bleich, *Contemporary Halakhic Problems* (NY: Ktav, 1977), 1:167–197.

marriage and by extension the subsequent "infidelity" that would have caused the *mamzerut*.

ARTIFICIAL INSEMINATION

All these solutions are possible when a loophole can somehow be found. But what can be done when no such ambiguity is discovered and it is clear that the child is definitely a *mamzer*?

As was mentioned before, a *mamzer* is allowed to marry a *mamzeret* and have children. The problem, however, is that these children are also *mamzerim*. The same is true when a *mamzer(et)* marries a convert or when she or he marries a Jew(ess) in violation of Jewish Law. In all these cases, the children are *mamzerim* and also subject to all these troubling laws.

Rabbi Moshe Feinstein rendered a radical and much-debated decision that could solve this problem. In his responsa, he discussed the question of whether it is permitted to use artificial insemination if a couple is unable to conceive a child through intercourse;[42] for example, when the wife would still be a *nidda*[43] at the time that she is capable of conceiving naturally, or when the husband is infertile and the only way the couple could have children is by donor sperm. Rabbi Feinstein permits this, since no intercourse takes place and the prohibition of adultery does not apply.[44]

In light of the foregoing, Rabbi Baruch Finkelstein suggests that perhaps if a *mamzer* and a *mamzeret* make use of artificial insemination, the child born to them is not a *mamzer*.[45] While they are allowed to have in-

---

42. For R. Moshe Feinstein's views on artificial insemination, see *Igrot Moshe, Even ha-Ezer,* vol. 1, nos. 10, 71; Ibid., vol. 2, *Even ha-Ezer,* no. 11; Ibid., vol. 3, *Even ha-Ezer,* no. 11; *Dibrot Moshe* on *Ketubot* (NY: Mesorah Heritage Foundation, 1999), 233–247. For an in-depth overview of artificial insemination in Halacha, see Avraham Steinberg, *Encyclopedia Hilchatit Refu'it* (Jerusalem: Falk Schlesinger Institute, 2006), 2:545–594, translated into English as Avraham Steinberg, *Encyclopedia of Jewish Medical Ethics,* trans. Fred Rosner (Jerusalem: Feldheim, 2003), 58–73; See also the comprehensive bibliography by R. Ya'akov Weinberger and R. Meir Zichel, *Sefer Assia* 9 (2003): 387–403 [Hebrew].

43. *Nidda*: A woman who has not yet immersed in a *mikva* (ritual bath) after her monthly period and consequently is not allowed to have relations with her husband.

44. See n42 above.

45. R. Baruch Finkelstein, "Derech le-Tihuram shel Mamzerim," *Techumin* 28 (2008): 58–62. See also R. Mordechai Binyamin Ralbag, *Avnei Mishpat: Piskei Din u-Berurei Halacha be-Inyanei Even ha-Ezer ve-Choshen Mishpat* (Jerusalem: M. B. Ralbag, 2004), *Even ha-Ezer,* no. 2; R. Zvi Ryzman, *Ratz ka-Tzvi,* no. 13. See also R. Zev Litke, "Dino shel Mamzer she-Holid be-Hafraya Chutz Gufit," *Din,* May 22, 2012, http://tinyurl.com/ybvg8rzw/. Note that R. Moshe Feinstein, *Igrot Moshe, Even ha-Ezer,* vol. 3, no. 11, explicitly states that in a case where a female non-*mamzeret* is impregnated with the sperm of a male *mamzer* via artificial insemination, the offspring is not regarded as a *mamzer(et)*. However, he does not state explicitly that this applies in a case where the female is a *mamzeret*. Rabbi Finkelstein and others argue that the same law

tercourse, they should make sure that when they plan to conceive a child, it is done by artificial insemination.[46] In that case, the child is allowed to marry any Jew(ess), and all future generations will have been freed from the status of *mamzerut*.

While not all authorities agree with Rabbi Feinstein,[47] one could argue that his ruling should be relied upon in certain cases, especially where a woman was divorced in a secular court and subsequently remarried, but was unaware that she needed a *get* from her first husband. Here, there was no deliberate adulterous relationship, and no moral standards have been violated. True, their children would still be *mamzerim*, but those children could be happily married to other *mamzerim* while the grand-children would no longer be affected by this law. The same argument could be used in the tragic situation where a married woman was raped, impregnated, and bore a child. Although this child is a *mamzer*, he or she can have children by way of artificial insemination and the offspring will no longer be *mamzerim*. In these cases, it is even more critical to use Rabbi Feinstein's point of view, not only for the sake of the grandchildren but also so that Judaism does not get a bad name when no "wrong" has been done by the grandparents. It is not just the purely halachic arguments that should count. The opponents of Rabbi Feinstein's ruling (as applied by Rabbi Finkelstein) may have strong reasons to disagree with him, but they

---

should apply even when the female is a *mamzeret*, and that as long as the child was conceived via artificial insemination, it does not acquire the status of *mamzer(et)*.

An alternative suggestion has been raised to remedy the problem of *mamzerut* by having a non-*mamzeret* surrogate mother carry an embryo produced by *mamzerim* parents. See R. Oren Tzvik, "Tihur Mamzerim," *Me-Avnei ha-Makom* 15 (2003): 120–130; R. Zev Litke, "Hafraya Chutz Gufit shel Chayavei Kritot ve-Holada be-Pundaka'ut," *Din*, March 25, 2012, http://tinyu rl.com/yb8pjcv5/.

46. Different solutions have been suggested as to how the husband is allowed to secure the sperm with which his wife should be impregnated via artificial insemination. See Finkelstein, "Derech le-Tihuram shel Mamzerim," 61. In general, masturbation is forbidden since it is "wast-ing seed." (There is "no wasting of seed" when intercourse takes place but the woman is unable to conceive, since the purpose of intercourse in Halacha is not only seen as a means to beget children, but also as an act of love between husband and wife.) Several authorities believe that in this case masturbation is permitted since it not wasting seed, but in fact making it possible to conceive a child. See R. Chaim Ozer Grodzinski, *Achiezer*, vol. 3, no. 24. For a range of views, see Steinberg, *Encyclopedia Hilchatit Refu'it*, 2:560. Obviously, all this depends on the reliability of the couple that they indeed did not have intercourse but made use of artificial insemination when they conceived the child.

47. The most important authority who does not agree with Rabbi Moshe Feinstein and main-tains that artificial insemination does not alleviate *mamzer* status is Rabbi Shlomo Zalman Au-erbach of Yerushalayim. See the halachic journal *No'am* 1 (1958): 145–166, reprinted in *Minchat Shlomo, Tinyana*, no. 124. See also R. Menashe Klein, *Mishne Halachot* 4, no. 160. For a range of views, see Steinberg, *Encyclopedia Hilchatit Refu'it*, 2:576–579.

should be pleased nonetheless that a potential solution exists, and allow his opinion to prevail for humanitarian reasons.

THE "ALL JEWS ARE *MAMZERIM*" ARGUMENT

Rivka Lubitch, an advocate in the Israel Rabbinic Courts and a board member at the Center for Women's Justice, suggests an even more radical solution that once and for all would solve all *mamzer* problems. She suggests:

> . . . to declare in an all-inclusive way that the entire community is in the category of mamzerut. This declaration could be made after a simple calculation: according to the Halacha, if one parent is a mamzer, all the children are mamzers and it is passed to all their descendants forever. Without a doubt, throughout the generations, many mamzers have "passed" and assimilated into the general community, which was ignorant of their mamzerut. It is thus possible that the majority of the Jewish people, if not all, are indeed mamzers.[48]

In that case they are allowed to marry each other and, although their children would also be *mamzerim*, it wouldn't be a problem since everybody else would be *mamzerim* as well.

Mrs. Lubitch did not explain her position in any detail. We can add several arguments to back up her position. Based on the argument that if a majority is established, we presume everybody to belong to this majority,[49] we could then declare all Jews to be *mamzerim*. Thus her argument becomes even stronger. By doing so, the *mamzer* problem has been solved.

This argument, however radical, could also be justified on the basis that the rabbis opposed the investigation of families where possible *mamzerim*

---

48. Rivkah Lubitch, "It's Time to Destigmatize Mamzers. Here's How," *Forward*, June 8, 2014, https://tinyurl.com/lsj8bea/. See also the following articles by Lubitch: "Ha-Reshima ha-Shechora," https://tinyurl.com/mo6drwj/; "Za'akat ha-Mamzerim," https://tinyurl.com/kjfw r8m/; "Mamzerim Chasarei Tikva," https://tinyurl.com/lut8hfn/; "Batei ha-Din Nilchamim, ha-Yeled Yetzei Mamzer," https://tinyurl.com/lr5djce/; "Ot Kayin," https://tinyurl.com/k2ee7yl/; "Le-Vatel et ha-Reshima ha-Shechora," http://tinyurl.com/m6rdfcw/. See the following articles dealing with Lubitch's arguments: "Bi-Teguva le-Vatel et ha-Reshima ha-Shechora," http://tinyu rl.com/y8ko428t/; R. Avi Rosental, "Kulanu Mamzerim," http://tinyurl.com/y942zg59/. For an overview about the *mamzer* problem in the State of Israel, see Susan Weiss, "Women, Divorce, and 'Mamzer' Status in the State of Israel," in *Love, Marriage, and Jewish Families; Paradoxes of a Social Revolution*, ed. Sylvia Barack Fishman (Waltham, MA: Brandeis University Press, 2015), 256–284.

49. See *Talmudic Encyclopedia*, s.v. "chazaka," 13:680–684.

may have entered.[50] They ignored these likelihoods, and this surely must have increased the numbers of unknown *mamzerim* among the Jewish people.

There are serious problems, however, with Mrs. Lubitch's suggestion.

As mentioned previously, in certain instances the rabbis overlooked the taint of *mamzerut* by declaring, "A family that has suffered an admixture has suffered an admixture."[51] The apparent rationale behind this statement is that when individual *mamzerim* get lost in a crowd of non-*mamzerim*, thereby becoming indistinguishable from the multitudes, Halacha also regards them as such, and they lose their *mamzer* status (or at least we turn a blind eye and don't initiate an investigation in order to ferret out the *mamzer*). This would hold true in every case where there is an admixture of "kosher" Israelites and *mamzerim*, and as long as we cannot single out a definite *mamzer*, the whole group is considered non-*mamzerim*. To argue the reverse, namely that the existence of individual cases of *mamzerim* (however many) causes the multitudes to be collectively tainted with the stigma of *mamzerut*, contradicts this entire notion and seems highly problematic and untenable.[52]

There seems to be no other literature on her proposal, and future hala-

---

50. See nn28–29 above. However, see *Rema, Shulchan Aruch, Even ha-Ezer* 2:5. See also R. Moshe Feinstein, *Igrot Moshe, Even ha-Ezer*, vol. 4, no. 9; R. Asher Weiss, "Mishpacha she-Nit-ma'ah," *Din*, April 20, 2012, http://tinyurl.com/lkuclnx/.

51. See *Kiddushin* 72a.

52. Another point to consider: if we were to follow this argument to its logical conclusion, some people would argue it would have the mind boggling effect of profaning the sanctity of the Jewish people by declaring that *kehal Hashem* is a *kehal mamzerim*!

However, despite the strong emotional reaction and halachic arguments adduced here against implementing this suggestion, it does merit further consideration from a meta-halachic perspective. This proposition would effectively turn the original conception of *mamzerut* on its head. In other words, instead of distancing the *mamzerim* from the rest of Israel in order to maintain the sanctity of Israel, we would compromise the sanctity of Israel in order not to discriminate against the *mamzer*. David Novak in his *Halakhah in a Theological Dimension*, chap. 2, discusses this tension and the divergent attitudes of the rabbis toward this dilemma. Thus, from a meta-halachic perspective one can argue that the same way the rabbis have lifted the stigma in cases of incognito *mamzerim* in order to allow them to marry, so too, *theoretically speaking* the reverse strategy of considering all Jews as (definite or doubtful) *mamzerim* should be employed in order to achieve the same goal of allowing *mamzerim* to marry.

Indeed, such cases of subversion and inversion are not unknown in Halacha (e.g., R. Moshe Feinstein's invalidation of all Reform marriages as not halachically binding, thus effectively compromising the integrity of their marriages for the sake of avoiding cases of *mamzerut* on a large scale. See, for example, *Igrot Moshe, Even ha-Ezer*, vol. 3, no. 25 and the sources cited in n40 above, although it can be argued that the main value being upheld is the integrity of halachic marriages vs. non-halachic ones). See also later on in this chapter regarding the theology of the rabbinic loophole.

This raises the broader halachic and meta-halachic question regarding what to do when there is a conflict of values. Rabbis always need to ask themselves the question: what value do we need to uphold? In this case, for example, we are confronted with a clash of values between

chic authorities will have to contemplate her suggestion as it relates to several other issues as well. Firstly, according to this contention that all Jews are considered to be definite *mamzerim*, does that mean that the halachic category of "doubtful *mamzerim*" such as the *asufi* (an abandoned infant that doesn't know either of its parents), and the *shtuki* (the child who knows its mother, but not its father) has been abolished and that even they are considered to be definite *mamzerim*?[53] Secondly, if all Jews are considered *mamzerim*, are any of them still kosher *kohanim* (priests)? Thirdly, since *gerim* (converts) are surely not *mamzerim*, should they avoid marrying such people or only marry among themselves?

THE REMARKABLE SOLUTION OF MAHARSHAM

One of the most remarkable solutions for the *mamzer* problem was offered by Rabbi Shalom Mordechai Schvadron (1835–1911), of Brezen, Galicia, the author of *Teshuvot Maharsham*.[54] His solution became the topic of much dispute and is one of the most exceptional examples of rabbinic innovation. It is also an extreme example of how much the rabbis were willing to "bend the law" when they were confronted with human pain.

To understand his approach, we need to first study the mishna in *Gittin*.

---

kedushat Yisrael and pure pedigree (*yichus*) vs. the value of *ahavat Yisrael*, non-discrimination, and alleviating human suffering.

This dilemma is confronted in numerous other issues as well. A similar question arises, for example, when contemplating the annulment of marriages or the institution of conditional marriages in order to help alleviate the plight of the *aguna*. In such instances, we need to contemplate whether we are more concerned with the value of upholding the integrity of the general institution of marriage even if certain individuals will have to pay the price, or whether we alleviate the more acute suffering of the individual, even if the institution of marriage as a whole will be compromised. Does maintaining the sanctity of the institution of marriage outweigh the concrete consequences and acute suffering of individuals, or not? Similarly, with the issue of conversion, does the value of *kabbalat mitzvot* (acceptance of the commandments) outweigh the value of Jewish unity, or vice-versa?

While we have raised serious objections to this proposal which would effectively render all Jews as *mamzerim*, the deeper significance of this question from a meta-halachic perspective should not be ignored.

53. See *Mishna Kiddushin* 4:1–2; *Kiddushin* 73. See *Mishne Torah, Hilchot Isurei Biah* 15:12–13, 21–24; *Shulchan Aruch, Even ha-Ezer* 4:31–33. Note that this also has practical ramifications, as the laws of permissible marriage partners for *doubtful mamzerim* are different from the ones pertaining to *definite mamzerim*.

54. I am indebted to the following excellent overviews and discussions on this topic: Louis I. Rabinowitz, "The New Trend in Halakhah," *Tradition* 11, no. 4 (1971): 5-15; Yitzchak D. Gilat, "The Halakhah and Its Relationship to Social Reality." *Tradition* 13, no. 4 (1973): 71–79; Aaron Rakeffet-Rothkoff, "Annulment of Marriage within the Context of Cancellation of the Get," *Tradition* 15, no. 1 (1975): 173–185; J. David Bleich, *Contemporary Halakhic Problems* (NY: Ktav, 1977), 1:162–167.

It discusses the case of a man who sends an agent to his wife with a *get* to divorce her, and then cancels the *get*.

> If a man, after dispatching a *get* to his wife via a *shaliach* [messenger], meets the *shaliach*, or sends another messenger after him, and says, "The *get* I gave you [for my wife] is canceled," then it is canceled. If the husband meets his wife before the agent reaches her, or sends a second messenger (before the first got to her), and says, "The *get* that I sent you is canceled," then it is canceled. However, once the *get* has reached her hand (and she has accepted it) he is no longer allowed to cancel it.[55]

All of this seems obvious. However, the next mishna explains that there is a case where it is not obvious: when the husband canceled the *get* in front of a *bet din* (rabbinical court) while the agent is on his way to the wife:

> In former days, a man was allowed to set up a *bet din* and cancel a *get*, even if the agent was already on his way to the wife. But Rabban Gamliel the Elder [a formidable figure in Mishnaic Law] laid down a rule that this could no longer be done, *mipnei tikun ha-olam* – for the benefit of society, i.e., to prevent exploitation.[56]

There are two different explanations for this edict.[57] In the view of Rabbi Yochanan, Rabban Gamliel sought to prevent the birth of *mamzerim*. According to Rabbi Yochanan, the husband could potentially cancel the *get* in front of a *bet din* comprising of only two people. Therefore, the cancellation might not become public knowledge and the woman would be unaware of it. She would assume she was divorced and marry someone else. This would render her an "adulteress" and any child from her second marriage a *mamzer*. To prevent this, Rabban Gamliel forbade any husband to cancel a *get* via a *bet din* once it was on its way to his wife.

In the view of Resh Lakish, Rabban Gamliel sought to prevent the woman from becoming an *aguna*. According to Resh Lakish, the husband could cancel the *get* only in front of a *bet din* of three people, and not two. Therefore, the cancellation would become public knowledge, his wife

---

55. *Mishna Gittin* 4:1.
56. *Mishna Gittin* 4:2.
57. *Gittin* 33a.

would be aware of it and would be unable to remarry, thus leaving her in the chained state of an *aguna*.

In order to prevent either scenario, Rabban Gamliel forbade any husband to cancel a *get* via a *bet din* once it was on its way to his wife.

A major problem now arises: What happens when, in violation of Rabban Gamliel's decree, the husband *still* cancels the *get*? Is it canceled or not? It would seem obvious that a *get* cannot still be valid if by Torah Law it was canceled. Ostensibly, the cancellation of the *get* would be equivalent to it never having been written, and the woman would therefore still be married. The rabbis surely cannot then validate a *get* that is invalid under Biblical Law. This is of crucial importance.

The Talmud states that this scenario is subject to a rabbinic dispute.[58] According to Rabbi Yehuda ha-Nasi, the cancellation is valid and the woman is still married. According to Rabban Shimon ben Gamliel, the cancellation is invalid and the woman is divorced.

This, says the Talmud, is highly problematic.

How can the rabbis declare a *get* to be valid when the Torah considers it invalid? So the reason that Rabban Shimon ben Gamliel allows the woman to remarry can't be that the *get* is valid. There must be another reason.

It is here that the sages introduced a daring and unprecedented mechanism. They declared that when a man marries a woman, he does so subject to the will of, and under the conditions laid down by the rabbis.[59] And if at some point they believed that the marriage should no longer continue, they could declare it void (just as they had the power to declare it valid).[60]

This is why Rabban Shimon ben Gamliel would allow this woman to get married. *Not* because the *get* was valid, but because the sages have the right to undo a marriage when they see fit, and therefore they have the power to declare her first marriage null and void.[61]

But this highly surprising statement is not yet the full story. Instead

---

58. Ibid.

59. *Ketubot* 3a; *Gittin* 33a, 73a. For a discussion, see *Talmudic Encyclopedia*, s.v. "afke'inhu rabbanan le-kiddushin minei," 2:137–140.

60. One wonders why the rabbis did not make a similar declaration concerning a *get*: Whoever cancels a *get* does so only with the agreement of the rabbis. In that case the *get* would still be valid even when the husband cancels it. The answer is probably that since the Torah made clear that only a husband can give a *get*, the rabbis could not condition this.

61. However, *Mishne Torah, Hilchot Gerushin* 6:16 and *Shulchan Aruch, Even ha-Ezer* 141:60 rule like Rabbi Yehuda ha-Nasi that even if one contravenes the edict of Rabban Gamliel, the cancellation is valid and the marriage is not retroactively annulled. Nevertheless, *Tosafot* on *Gittin* 32b, s.v. "ve-Rav Nachman" argue that in a case where the husband cancels the *get* in front of only one person, the cancellation is ineffective and the marriage does indeed get retroactively annulled. See R. Yechezkel Landau, *Noda be-Yehuda, Mahadura Kamma, Orach Chaim*, no. 35.

of leaving it at that, the rabbis make a move that is even more radical. They declare that they can invalidate a former marriage *ab initio*, from its inception!

"And [in cases such as ours where the husband, against the decree of Rabban Gamliel still canceled the *get*] the rabbis retroactively abrogated his original betrothal."[62]

In other words, they did not just *stop* the marriage from still being valid; they retroactively denied that there ever was a marriage. By doing so, they even asserted that in a case where the husband betrothed his wife by cohabitation, it is rendered an illicit act![63]

It is for this reason that according to Rabban Shimon ben Gamliel, in a case where the husband acted against Rabban Gamliel's decree and canceled the *get*, he was penalized for this act. Rabban Gamliel's position was thus strengthened, since the rabbis had the power to overrule the institution of marriage, as it was contingent on their agreement. In our case, they no longer agreed to this marriage from its inception. So if the husband canceled the *get*, he was told that there was never a marriage, all his efforts were in vain, and his "wife" could marry someone else![64]

There is also another case where the rabbis annulled a marriage retroactively. This involves a situation where the husband granted a *get* on the condition that he will not perform a certain action. For example, he told his wife: I hereby grant you this document as a valid *get*, on condition that I do not come to a certain location by a certain date. What would happen, though, if the husband was *forcibly* prevented from going to that location? According to Torah Law, the divorce does not take effect, since

---

62. *Gittin* 33a.

63. The Talmud discusses two cases where the husband betrothed his wife. One with money and one by way of cohabitation. In both cases it argues that the marriage is retroactively canceled. And in the last case, this cohabitation was considered to be promiscuous in a legal sense. This, however, does not cover all the other cohabitations which took place later. Are all of them to be considered promiscuous? This would be hard to believe. It should be noted that Rambam, *Teshuvot ha-Rambam*, ed. Yehoshua Blau (Jerusalem: Chevrat Mekitzei Nirdamim, 1960), vol. 3, no. 356 and *Shita Mekubetzet* on *Ketubot* 3a argue that although the marriage is later canceled retroactively (and thus the act of cohabitation is henceforth legally rendered as promiscuous), this does not impugn the conduct of the couple, for during the actual time that the couple had relations, the act was permitted. Therefore, it is not regarded as sinful.

64. When I studied this page of Talmud in yeshiva, I always wondered why my teachers and fellow students were never astonished by this ruling. They seemed to have taken this for granted, as if nothing extraordinary is stated. Since they were so convinced of the truth of the Talmud, and they themselves were an integral part of its world, they were incapable of grasping the extraordinariness of all this and the enormous courage the rabbis showed to prevent human pain. To me, it was a ruling which made me realize that this was one of the most radical legal ideas I had ever encountered! It was shocking, highly problematic, and simultaneously incredibly impressive.

the condition was met by means of coercion, not voluntarily. The sages, however, decreed that the claim of coercion would be invalid. Thus, in order to produce the desired outcome – that the woman would no longer be married to her husband – they retroactively annulled the marriage.[65]

Few other rabbinical decrees have been as radical and surprising as this one. Indeed, who gave the rabbis the authority to declare a marriage retroactively invalid? Who says that the validity of a marriage depends on their agreement? The answer is they decided on their own that they had this authority, based on the fact that God left the Torah in their hands, and it was *they and not God* who could now decide how to apply it.[66] It is indeed an outstanding example of the rabbis' concern for a woman's well-being, and their determination to prevent the birth of *mamzerim*, even to the extent that they would defy the Biblical Tradition.

However, this decree is most dangerous and could easily lead to all sorts of promiscuous behavior. What would happen if a man had a sexual relationship with a married woman and impregnates her? The child would be a *mamzer*. To prevent that from happening, he could ask her original husband to send a *get* to his wife, and then – against the decree of Rabban Gamliel – cancel the *get*, after which the marriage would be retroactively void. This would result in the man not having committed adultery, since the woman was never married to her original husband. Therefore, the child would not be a *mamzer*.

This matter actually became a source of fierce debate. Rabbenu Tam declared that such deliberate misuse of this law runs contrary to the whole purpose of the law, and in this case we do not cancel the marriage: "The rabbis instituted the annulment to *strengthen* the law and not to enable Jewish daughters to indulge in wanton and unrestrained behavior."[67] However, others believed that as long as the law is observed, it is permitted even in this case because it will save a child from becoming a *mamzer*.[68]

Everyone realized that this was a slippery slope and, as so often happens, the strict and lenient opinions were in direct opposition to each other. What one was trying to repair, the other saw as a major violation of the ethical foundation of Jewish Law.

In the eighteenth century, this issue became relevant when Rabbi

---

65. *Ketubot* 2b–3a.

66. See the famous story in *Bava Metzia* 59b where the rabbis ignored God's interference in a law they were discussing based on the principle of *Torah lo ba-Shamayim hi*, the Torah is no longer in Heaven and now is in their own hands.

67. *Tosafot* on *Gittin* 33a, s.v. "ve-afkinan rabbanan."

68. See *Shita Mekubetzet* on *Ketubot* 3a.

Yechezkel Landau (1713–1793) was approached by a repentant adulterer.[69] The man had a sexual relationship with a married woman while he boarded at her home. Afterward he married her daughter and wondered, once he repented, whether he should tell his father-in-law that he had had a sexual relationship with the latter's wife. That would obligate the father-in-law to divorce his wife, as required by Jewish Law in such a case.[70]

As mentioned above, to solve this problem, the father-in-law could write a *get* to his wife and then cancel it while the agent was on his way to the wife, against Rabban Gamliel's ruling. The rabbis would then pronounce the marriage canceled *ab initio*, so that no adultery will have taken place. Rabbi Landau declined to do so, because he felt he had to follow Rabbenu Tam's view that this cannot be done since it was not for this reason that the rabbis had come up with such a ruling. It would increase the possibility of adultery by allowing people to get away with it.

However, this did not end the dispute. In the nineteenth century, Rabbi Avraham Yoel Abelson of Odessa asked the previously mentioned Rabbi Shalom Mordechai Schvadron about the following case: A woman had become the victim of a most unfortunate situation. Her husband, who was not of sound mind, had left her twelve years earlier and moved to the United States. Afterward, she was told by her husband's brother that her husband had died and never had children. This meant that she had to perform the procedure known as *chalitza*[71] with the brother who had actually come to her to do so. The rabbinical court believed the brother, and she even received a legal certificate from the American authorities stating that her husband had indeed died. *Chalitza* was carried out and the presumed widow was told by the rabbinical authorities that she was now permitted to remarry, which she did and subsequently became pregnant. To everyone's surprise, it soon became apparent that her first husband had in fact not died! He had lent his passport to another man and it was the latter who had died. She was now forced to get divorced from both husbands,[72] and her child from the second husband would be declared a

---

69. *Noda be-Yehuda, Mahadura Kamma, Orach Chaim,* no. 35.

70. See *Mishne Torah, Hilchot Gerushin* 11:14; *Shulchan Aruch, Even ha-Ezer,* 11:1 based on *Yevamot* 11b.

71. According to Jewish Law, a man is obligated to marry the widow of his deceased brother when the latter did not have any children (see *Devarim* 25:5–6). If he does not want to do so, the *chalitza* procedure is performed – a kind of semi-divorce – after which the widow is free to marry somebody else (see *Devarim* 25:7–9). Today, the rabbis are no longer in favor of the brother marrying her, and all such cases normally end with *chalitza*.

72. See *Mishna Yevamot* 10:1. The first husband was the "real" husband and is obligated by

mamzer. She did receive a *get* from her first husband, and the *get* from her second husband would soon follow.

In his response, Rabbi Schvadron stated that the child was indeed a *mamzer*, but then he threw in an observation that was highly unusual: "I will not conceal that had you consulted me before the woman obtained a *get* from the first husband, I would have suggested a resourceful solution, *le-halacha ve-lo le-ma'aseh* (theoretically, but not practically)."[73] He then explained that it would have been possible to retroactively cancel her marriage with the first husband, as detailed above. The child would then not have become a *mamzer* and all would have been well. No one would have had to worry about Rabbenu Tam's concern that it would encourage adultery, since this woman erroneously remarried, thinking that her husband had died. On top of this, she had received full permission from the *bet din* to remarry.

This makes perfect sense, except that Rabbi Schvadron had pointed out that all of this was theoretical and not to be used in actuality. It then becomes an issue why he had indeed made this stipulation. In this case it was too late to rescue the child from being a *mamzer*, because the first husband's *get* had already been given by the time Rabbi Schvadron was asked, so there was no longer a way to retroactively invalidate this marriage *ab initio*. But why not in other cases?

Indeed, in 1951 another case occurred, which turned Rabbi Schvadron's suggestion into a most practical one. Rabbi Reuven Katz, Chief Rabbi of Petach Tikva, was confronted with the case of a Yemenite girl who had been betrothed by her father when she was a minor.[74] The girl had immigrated from Yemen to Israel as part of Operation Magic Carpet in May 1949. She stayed with her grandmother and was not at all aware that her father had betrothed her while he was still in Yemen. She later married another young man according to Jewish Law and became pregnant. It seems that she was informed by her grandmother who was told by the girl's father that he had betrothed her, but the girl didn't take it seriously. She could not believe it possible that her father had betrothed her without her even knowing who the young man was.

Torah law to give her a *get*. The second husband is obligated by rabbinical law to give her a *get*, see *Yevamot* 88b. Afterward, she is allowed to get married to a third husband.

73. *Teshuvot Maharsham*, vol. 1, no. 9.

74. In previous times, a father had the right to betroth his minor daughter. This was often done to protect her and give her a secure future. This was still practiced in Yemen in recent times. For more information, see Chaim Z. Malinowitz, "*Kiddushei Ketana* – Betrothal of a Minor: A Halachic Discussion," *Journal of Halacha and Contemporary Society* 30 (1995): 5–24.

Rabbi Katz contacted Israel's Chief Rabbi Yitzchak Isaac ha-Levi Herzog, one of the greatest halachic authorities of his day, and asked him for his opinion.[75] Was she already married to the first man her father had betrothed her to? If yes, what had to be done regarding her current husband and the child that was to be born? Would it be a *mamzer*? Rabbi Katz explained to Rabbi Herzog that, firstly, it was customary in Yemen for a father to betroth his daughter without her having seen the young man. And secondly, it was customary not to specifically appoint two witnesses to verify the betrothal, but rather to rely on the witnesses, such as friends, who were already present at the betrothal/marriage. This was possible because, according to early commentaries, the bystanders would become part of the group of witnesses.[76] Rabbi Katz suggested that perhaps this could help to invalidate the first betrothal/marriage. Since it could be assumed that there were family members and other people present who were disqualified to be witnesses, consequently the entire group of witnesses could be disqualified, because "a company of witnesses that is partially voided is totally voided."[77] If so, the marriage never took place for lack of valid witnesses, and the child to be born will not be a *mamzer*. Rabbi Herzog was in doubt, believing that there were two problems. First of all, the observation that kosher witnesses were invalid once they mixed with non-kosher witnesses is a minority opinion, so they may not necessarily have been invalidated. Secondly, it's possible that there were two specially appointed kosher witnesses, since it was uncertain whether *all* Yemenites did not designate specific witnesses. It would then be irrelevant if non-kosher witnesses were also present.

It is not clear what Rabbi Herzog finally decided, but it seems that he had a conversation with Rabbi Katz about this matter. In an addendum to his responsum, Rabbi Herzog referred to the solution of Rabbi Schvadron and suggested that the first husband grant a *get* to his betrothed wife and then cancel it before it would reach her. The rabbis would then nullify the first marriage *ab initio*, and the child would not be a *mamzer*. While Rabbi Herzog admitted that Rabbi Schvadron had only suggested this theoretically, he felt that in this case it could be used since there was also a question concerning the validity of the witnesses.

According to Rabbi Rakeffet-Rothkoff's explanation,[78] this would create

---

75. See *Hechal Yitzchak, Even ha-Ezer*, vol. 2, nos. 17–19.
76. *Ritva* to *Kiddushin* 43a and to *Gittin* 18b, quoting *Rashba*.
77. See *Mishna Makkot* 1:8.
78. See n54 above.

a *sfek sfeka* (a double doubt) – first, regarding whether there were kosher witnesses or not; and secondly, that Rabbi Schvadron's solution would work even though Rabbenu Tam had objected to it, since others disagreed with Rabbenu Tam and felt it was permitted to use it *a priori*. That would be enough to allow this solution to work, because when there is a double doubt we are lenient, even with regard to a biblical prohibition. Rabbi Herzog added that the reason Rabbi Schvadron had said that this solution was purely theoretical may have been that he wanted other rabbis to agree with him before making it "practical," although he didn't mention this.

As we have seen thus far, some *poskim* have suggested implementing Maharsham's theoretical strategy in practice, and this would be another way to remove the stain of a *mamzer*.

This, I would suggest, should be especially relevant in situations where a woman and her second husband had no adulterous intentions but got married by secular law after she was legally divorced from her first husband, and out of sheer ignorance never asked him for a *get*. In such cases, we need not worry about Rabbenu Tam's argument of "wanton and unrestrained behavior," and we can permit the first husband to send his wife a *get* by way of an agent and then cancel it before it has reached his wife. We may even argue that this leniency, rooted in the Talmud, has become very important in modern times. It is as if the rabbis realized that the day may come when Jewish women of moral standing would no longer be aware that they needed a *get*, would suffer great anguish as a result, and would have children who are *mamzerim*.[79]

Most interesting is the essay by the former Chief Rabbi of South Africa, Rabbi Dr. Louis Rabinowitz, who believed that the application of Maharsham's suggestion is a *new trend* in Halacha. He quotes Rabbi Jacob Goldman, the editor of Rabbi Herzog's responsa: "In the Chief Rabbi's writings, the scholar and the student will be able to feel the scope of his encyclopedic knowledge, the breadth of his understanding, the nobility of piety which were of the essence of his personality."[80] Rabbi Rabinowitz

79. As mentioned, the approach of Rabbi Schvadron is subject to much debate. Rabbi Shlomo Zalman Auerbach raised many objections, some very technical, against the suggestions of Maharsham; see *Minchat Shlomo*, vol. 1, no. 76. Rabbi Auerbach states that he is very hesitant to use this approach. However, his study was not based on a real case but was purely theoretical, which in halachic literature is not binding. The approach of Maharsham was also discussed by the Israeli legal scholar and member of the Supreme Court of Israel, Professor Moshe Silberg, who wanted to use it in practice combined with some other enactments. His suggestion was contested by several rabbis and scholars. See *Panim el Panim*, nos. 705 (Jan. 12, 1973), 709 (Feb. 9, 1973), 710 (Feb. 16, 1973). See Bleich, *Contemporary Halakhic Problems*, 1:162–167.

80. *Hechal Yitzchak, Even ha-Ezer*, vol. 2, preface.

adds: "All these noble qualities are pressed into the service of searching for and exploring some form of relief particularly in such related cases which are the subject of discussion. They are eloquent evidence of the truth of the adage: 'He who says I have sought and not found, believe him not.'"[81]

Even more important are the words of Rabbi Rakeffet-Rothkoff:

> Even though the great rabbis of previous generations did not advocate this solution, nevertheless each new era is privileged to contribute to the function of Halacha. The Talmud declared: "Whenever a scholar reports a decision [however strange it may sound] he should not be rejected nor regarded as arrogant" (*Hulin* 7a). The Meiri elaborated upon this passage: A sage who institutes a new Halacha, whether he is more stringent or more lenient than the previous generation, is not to be considered arrogant. He is not acting improperly even though the earlier authorities did not advance such a viewpoint. As long as he indicates the reasons for his new decision he may be relied upon. The Torah has allowed every student a new area in which he may display his acumen.[82]

THE THEOLOGY OF THE HALACHIC LOOPHOLE

From the way the sages tried to solve the *mamzer* problem, it becomes clear that they sometimes used far-fetched, logic-bending, and even strange arguments; some so daring that one wonders whether they did not violate the integrity of the biblical text. One also wonders whether they themselves actually believed that their approach was genuine and legally acceptable.

To tell a husband to deliberately, and in violation of the law, send his wife a *get* with the intention to cancel it in order to invalidate the marriage *ab initio*, does not just seem to border on questionable practices, but appears to be a deliberate form of trickery.

What, then, motivated the rabbis to do so with a clean conscience?

It is my opinion that in order to answer this we need to deal with some fundamental questions about the divinity of the Torah and the moral notions contained therein.

---

81. Rabinowitz, "The New Trend in Halakhah," 8–9.
82. Rakeffet-Rothkoff, "Annulment of Marriage within the Context of Cancellation of the Get," 182–183.

I believe that the Torah is *min ha-Shamayim* (of divine origin) and that its every word is holy. But I do not believe that the Torah is (always) historically true (sometimes it seems like divine fiction), or that it is uninfluenced by external sources. Nor do I believe that all its laws are morally acceptable. They are not.

What I believe is that the Torah is often morally, deeply, and *deliberately* "flawed," and furthermore, that God Himself intentionally made it flawed.

It is the latter issue that I will discuss in the final portion of this chapter.[83]

My belief that the Torah is purposely morally flawed is closely related to the idea of the "halachic loophole," which Chazal (our Talmudic Sages) and later *poskim* frequently used to solve halachic problems.

FAR-FETCHED HALACHIC ARGUMENTS

Many of these loopholes are legal fictions the rabbis employed to deliberately ignore straightforward biblical *pesukim* (verses) or halachic standards.[84] In doing so, they often made use of far-fetched arguments and twists that violated the very intent of these verses or halachic norms.

They seem to have done so with no compunctions and without it becoming a major issue. To them, this method was seemingly a normal procedure whenever it was "convenient" to achieve their goals.

To us, however, some of these loopholes are not only far-fetched, but manifestations of trickery and, in fact, misleading.

A few examples may suffice: The sages declared that the case of the *ben sorer u-moreh* (the stubborn and rebellious son who had to be put to death) never was and never will be.[85] They said the same regarding the *ir ha-nidachat* (the subversive city, which had to be entirely destroyed because its inhabitants worshiped idolatry).[86] They decided that *lex talionis*, the principle of "an eye for an eye," meant financial compensation while the

---

83. The following was inspired by the writings of Rambam, *Moreh Nevuchim*; Maharal, *Tiferet Yisrael*; Eliezer Berkovits, *Jewish Women in Time and Torah* (Hoboken, NJ: Ktav, 1990); Tamar Ross, *Expanding the Palace of the Torah: Orthodoxy and Feminism* (Waltham, MA: Brandeis University Press, 2004); Nahum L. Rabinovitch, "The Way of Torah," *Edah Journal* 3, no. 1 (2003); Donniel Hartman, *Putting God Second: How to Save Religion from Itself* (Boston: Beacon Press, 2016); and many others. For the possible influence of Gentile wisdom on the Torah, see R. Tzadok ha-Kohen of Lublin, *Pri Tzaddik* on *Shemot, Parashat Yitro*.

84. For a general overview of the issue of rabbinic loopholes (*ha'arama*), see *Tamudic Encyclopedia*, s.v. "ha'arama," 9:697–713, and Elana Stein, "Rabbinic Legal Loopholes: Formalism, Equity and Subjectivity" (PhD dissertation, Columbia University, 2014), http://academiccommons.co lumbia.edu/catalog/ac%3A175659/.

85. *Devarim* 21:18–21; *Sanhedrin* 71a.

86. *Devarim* 13:13–19; *Sanhedrin* 71a.

text does not even hint at this.[87] As we have seen, to solve the problems of *mamzer* and *aguna* they found ways to circumvent these laws and violated normative halachic standards by inventing mechanisms that the Torah never mentioned.

There is a profound reason behind all this, which is not well understood by most religious Jews.

THE TORAH AS A DIVINE COMPROMISE

While the sages believed that the Torah is absolutely divine,[88] they did not believe that the text was indisputable or incontestable. *They did not see it as the final text.* They realized that the Torah text was a *stage* in God's plan at a particular moment in Jewish history.

The reason for this is that since revelation is a response to the human longing for a relationship with God, any revelation can be successful only to the extent that human beings can relate to it. So, the Divine Will is limited by what human beings are able to pragmatically and spiritually understand and accomplish.[89]

While the Divine Will may want to accomplish the ultimate, it is constrained by the limitations of human ability. In other words: The Torah is anthropocentric, while its aim is theocentric. The Torah, then, is really a divine compromise. It is filtered through the mindset and mores of its intended audience.[90] It is therefore flawed in the sense that it must sometimes allow or introduce laws that are far from ideal, but for now are the only possible option the Jewish people can cope with. This in no way contradicts the concept of *Torah Temima*, the idea that the Torah is perfect. In fact, it proves the point. The Torah is perfect because it accommodates itself to new and changing human conditions. In that way it will always stay applicable and relevant.

One famous example is given by Rambam, in his *Moreh Nevuchim*, regarding the sacrificial cult in the Tabernacle and later in the Temple. He suggests that the Torah carefully limited the already existing practice of

---

87. *Shemot* 21:24; *Vayikra* 24:20; *Devarim* 19:21; *Ketubot* 32b; *Bava Kamma* 83b.

88. See, however, Marc B. Shapiro, *The Limits of Orthodox Theology: Maimonides' Thirteen Principles Reappraised* (Oxford: Littman Library of Jewish Civilization, 2004), chap. 7; see also Yehuda Brandes, Tova Ganzel, and Chayuta Deutsch, *Be'einei Elohim Ve'Adam: Biblical Criticism and the Person of Faith* (Jerusalem: Bet Morasha, 2015) [Hebrew].

89. For a scholarly treatment of this topic, see Stephen D. Benin, *The Footprints of God, Divine Accommodation in Jewish and Christian Thought* (Albany, NY: SUNY Press, 1993), especially chaps. 5 and 6.

90. See Hartman, *Putting God Second*, chap. 5.

sacrifice and kept it for the sole purpose of weaning the Jewish people away from the primitive rituals of their idolatrous neighbors. Rambam believed that the sacrificial cult in Judaism was established as a *compromise to human weakness.*

> For a sudden transition from one opposite to another is impossible. And therefore man, according to his nature, is not capable of abandoning suddenly all to which he was accustomed. . . . Therefore He, may He be exalted, suffered the above-mentioned kinds of worship to remain, but transferred them from created or imaginary and unreal things to His own name . . . commanding us to practice them with regard to Him.[91]

But to give the sacrificial cult a more sophisticated, dignified, and monotheistic meaning, the Torah introduced many laws to refine this kind of worship. This would slowly move people toward being able to have it abolished altogether, which was the divine objective.

Still, the numerous and intricate sacrificial laws in the Torah, carefully detailed in the Oral Law, have tremendous symbolic and educational meaning far beyond the actual sacrificial deed. Many of them paradoxically make the worshiper sensitive to higher standards leading to genuine monotheism. This means that while one should really outgrow the actual sacrificial deed, the many spiritual *messages* behind these laws remain relevant even to this day.[92]

The same is true about slavery.[93] The fact that the Torah tolerates slavery only means that it was not yet possible to completely abandon it. Former societies would have been unable to sustain themselves economically had slavery come to a sudden end. So the Torah introduced laws to make slavery more ethical, by creating much better conditions for slaves, helping them to overcome their slave mentality, and giving them the opportunity to free themselves and start a new life.[94] Only at a later stage could slavery be eliminated altogether.

---

91. Maimonides, *The Guide of the Perplexed*, tr. Shlomo Pines, vol. 2 (Chicago: University of Chicago Press, 1974), part 3, chap. 32.

92. See the commentaries of Don Yitzchak Abarbanel and R. Samson Raphael Hirsch to *Sefer Vayikra*.

93. On this topic, see Gamliel Shmalo, "Orthodox Approaches to Biblical Slavery," *Torah U-Madda Journal* 16 (2012): 1–20.

94. See *Shemot* 21:1–11; *Kiddushin* 15a, 16b–17b; *Bava Metzia* 31b. These sources only pertain to a Hebrew slave. The case of a non-Jewish slave is different. In my opinion, this institution too was meant to be temporary and to be eventually abolished – as indeed it was.

In other words, these kinds of laws were a divine compromise, not meant to be eternal. In that sense, the biblical text does not express the *final* Divine Will but only God's provisional one at a *certain* moment in human history.

Morally and religiously speaking, the text is time bound and therefore "flawed." It does not inform us of the *ultimate* will of God.

We see then, that not only would the laws concerning sacrifices and slavery be totally abolished once the people outgrew the need for them, but they would actually not have appeared in the biblical text had it been revealed at a much later stage in history.[95]

UNDERSTANDING TORAH CORRECTLY

This has enormous consequences for a proper understanding of what Torah, in essence, is all about. Just as slavery and the cult of sacrifices would be abandoned, many other laws that may have been compromises to human weakness would not have appeared in the text had it been given at a later stage.[96]

But whether or not they would have appeared at a later stage would depend on the moral and religious sophistication of human beings, not on God. The more human beings purge themselves of earlier ideas and practices that still reflect primitive and amoral perceptions, the more the ideal divine law will be able to reveal itself. *So the text of the Torah is human in the sense that it is the human condition that will determine what will appear in the divine text and what will not.*

This, however, is not all. It is a person's obligation to aim for higher moral and religious standards. Because people are created in the image of God, they carry within themselves moral notions of the highest order,

---

95. Or, they would still appear, but in a different context in which only the moral lessons could be learned.

96. This refers only to moral laws, not to Shabbat and other rituals, since the latter topics touch on the relationship between God and man. For a discussion of a change in *all* of the laws, including laws such as Shabbat, see Nathan Lopes Cardozo, *The Torah as God's Mind: A Kabbalistic Look into the Pentateuch* (NY: Bep-Ron Publications, 1988) and Cardozo, *Between Silence and Speech: Essays on Jewish Thought* (Northvale, NJ: Jason Aronson, 1995), chap. 7. This has nothing to do with classical Christianity's total rejection of the commandments and Halacha. It believed that the commandments would only be an obstacle to the proper service of God. Such a notion is totally rejected by Judaism. For a range of studies on this topic, see E.P. Sanders, *Paul, the Law, and the Jewish People* (Philadelphia: Fortress Press, 1985); James D. G. Dunn ed., *Paul and the Mosaic Law* (Grand Rapids, MI: W.B. Eerdmans, 1996); Brian S. Rosner, *Paul and the Law: Keeping the Commandments of God* (Downers Grove, IL: InterVarsity Press, 2013); Chaim Saiman, "Jesus' Legal Theory – A Rabbinic Reading," *Journal of Law and Religion* 23, no. 1 (2007): 97–130.

which are very close to God's ultimate will. They may not be aware of them, since they were still subconscious at the early moments of Jewish history – such as at Mount Sinai – but at a later stage and throughout all of history, these moral notions slowly develop and come to the forefront.[97]

But this is possible only if the reader *morally disconnects* themselves from the biblical text when the text still represents lower moral standards. Would they constantly come back to the text, they would be unable to opt for higher moral and religious goals, since they would consider it to have the final word. The text would then become an obstacle, instead of a support system to achieve even higher levels of growth. *So, rather than the person following the text, the text should follow the person.*

What this really means is that would the Torah be given today, it would not be the same text that God gave at Sinai!

After all, over the many years people have developed a more sophisticated understanding of moral values. It is true that they have bitterly failed in living by those standards, but there is no doubt that humanity's understanding of what morality should be is far more advanced than it was in the days of the giving of the Torah.

It is interesting that the drive to reach for these higher levels is inspired by the Torah itself. By introducing such laws as "Love your neighbor as yourself,"[98] and laws that call for sexual restraint, the well-being of the stranger, respecting human dignity, and many others, the Torah gave people a taste of how things really *should* be. By doing so, it has greatly contributed to the ongoing development of many other values, some of which are not even mentioned in the Torah.

THE TORAH AS A PARADOX

As a result, the text carries a paradox. Sometimes it does reflect the highest standards, and sometimes it doesn't. Too much at once would probably have been impossible to accept by a society that was still rooted in conditions so at odds with those standards.

---

97. In truth, the very existence of the Jewish people is a compromise to human weakness. When looking into the stories of the Flood, the Tower of Bavel, and the birth of the Jewish people starting from Avraham's family, we clearly see that the ever-widening scope of corruption caused God, as it were, to no longer expect all of humanity to live by the highest moral standards. Instead, He charged Avraham and his family with the task of becoming an example from which others would learn. This ultimately led to the creation of the Jewish nation as a Chosen People. Had humankind behaved morally, there would have been no need for such a nation, and the Jewish people would never have emerged. See Cardozo, *Between Silence and Speech*, chap. 3.

98. *Vayikra* 19:18.

By sustaining this paradox, the text created a vision and aspiration in stages. It gave human beings a feeling of how things should *really* be, while not yet asking them to go all the way. It reveals an understanding, as Rambam teaches, that such changes need time to reach human beings, since a person cannot make a "sudden transition from one opposite to another."

It is here that one of the most far-reaching ideas in Judaism appears. Instead of God constantly upgrading the text to higher standards according to human capabilities, and giving the Torah over and over again, *He left it in the hands of the sages.*

After laying the foundations, God asks the sages to become partners in the creation of the Torah,[99] in the sense that humans would now be able to develop it to even higher levels. Just as in the Creation chapter, God provided the main ingredients and then asked Adam to fashion the world and improve it, so it had to happen with the Torah. *The text was meant as a point of departure, not as an arrival.*[100]

THE SAGES' RESPONSIBILITY TO "UPDATE" THE TEXT

It was the sages who were required to adapt the text. Not by changing the "underdeveloped," compromised, and "flawed" divine wording itself, but by their interpretation of the Torah text, or by advancing ideas and even laws that sometimes required drastic changes which violated the literal meaning of the verses.[101] That they were willing to do so is now obvious. They felt *obligated* to do so, since this was the very intention of the text. The divine but "flawed" text asked of humans to go beyond it and sometimes even ignore it. *The text demanded its own renovation.*

The Torah commands that a *ben sorer u-moreh*, a stubborn and rebellious son, must be put to death. The rabbis were of the opinion that this law could never have been enforced, since it completely violates the moral spirit of the Torah, even by its lower standard at Sinai. They therefore declared that such a law is only theoretical. "There never was a stubborn and rebellious son, and never will be."[102] Its message was purely educational. There are many important lessons to be learned from this so-called

---

99. See *Seder Eliyahu Zuta* 2, Friedmann ed., 2.

100. See Maharal, *Tiferet Yisrael*, chap. 69.

101. For a comprehensive treatment of this issue, see Moshe Halbertal, *Interpretive Revolutions in the Making* (Jerusalem: Magnes Press, 1999) [Hebrew]. For a different perspective, see David Weiss Halivni, "Can a Religious Law be Immoral?," in *Perspectives on Jews and Judaism: Essays in Honor of Wolfe Kelman*, ed. Arthur A. Chiel (NY: The Rabbinical Assembly, 1978), 165–170.

102. *Sanhedrin* 71a.

commandment, but that it should actually be implemented is not one of them.[103]

The second and perhaps more radical example of how far the rabbis were prepared to go, is the case of the *ir ha-nidachat*. Regarding this subversive city, the sages used a very far-fetched argument to abolish this biblical law for the sake of a higher morality. Here, too, they were convinced that "there never was a condemned city and never will be," and the law was meant only to convey some important lessons.[104]

It is most ingenious how the sages justified this ruling. They argued that it was impossible to destroy the entire city, since no doubt there must have been at least one *mezuza* in the entire city. (Alright, you can be a Jewish idol worshiper, but what Jew doesn't have a *mezuza* on their doorpost?) Since it is forbidden to destroy the name of God, which is found in the *mezuza*, and *everything* in the city had to be utterly destroyed, the law of *ir ha-nidachat* could not be enforced and was meant to be purely theoretical. That the *mezuza* could be removed before the city would be destroyed was something the sages did not want to contemplate! They must surely have been aware of this possibility. But since they believed that God could never have meant this law to be applied, they found an extremely far-fetched loophole and based their whole argument on a minor detail, which they could easily have solved and which they knew made little sense. It was deliberate trickery rooted in an unequalled moral awareness.[105]

Another case is *lex talionis*, the law of "an eye for an eye." This law was understood by the rabbis to be purely symbolic.[106] It was written as "an eye for an eye" to emphasize that ideally a person should suffer the same

---

103. It is interesting to note Rabbi Yonatan's statement (ibid.) that he sat on the grave of a rebellious son, indicating that the law *had* at some time been executed. This may reflect an earlier, more primitive understanding of the text in which people did not grasp its real meaning. It may have been as a result of laws that were practiced in other cultures, in which children were severely punished for not listening to their parents. It also seems to indicate that parents were actually willing to bring their children to court to have them killed, something the Talmud regards with extreme aversion. But in a society that in earlier days even practiced child sacrifices, anything could happen. Most interesting is the fact that it is inappropriate to sit on a grave, and that Rabbi Yonatan was a *kohen* - priest! See *Bava Metzia* 90b. In some editions of the Talmud, Rabbi Yochanan (not Rabbi Yonatan) is the sage who is mentioned. See *Daf al Daf* on *Sanhedrin* 71a.

104. *Sanhedrin* 71a.

105. See ibid. and *Sanhedrin* 113a. Here too, Rabbi Yonatan (*Sanhedrin* 71a) maintained that he sat on the ruins of such a city and the *mezuzot* must have been removed beforehand. His arguments in both of these cases seem to be far-fetched, since the sages must have known about such incidents. Either they were in denial about them or they wished to be in denial, so as not to undermine their viewpoint that these laws never did and never will apply!

106. See *Shemot* 21:24; *Vayikra* 24:20; *Bava Kamma* 83b–84a. For a discussion, see *Talmudic Encyclopedia*, s.v. "chovel," 12:693–695.

injury that he or she inflicted upon another, but in practice the offender only has to pay monetary compensation.[107] It is interesting to note that compared to the Hammurabi Code, even the literal meaning of this biblical commandment is an improvement. For example, that code requires that if a building collapses and kills the owner's child, the builder's child is to be put to death in retaliation.[108]

Still, the rabbis were reluctant to totally overturn a text if there was another way to get the same result.

It is here that the halachic loophole becomes even more vital.

In the case of the stubborn and rebellious son, they claimed that the moral problem with this law was so enormous that its implementation *had* to be argued away one way or the other. Instead of just ignoring the meaning of the verse, as in the case of *lex talionis*, they started reading the text extremely literally and used every means of deduction and legal hairsplitting available, so that it became totally impossible to enforce the law.[109]

THE *MAMZER* AND THE *AGUNA*

Two most striking cases, which show how far the sages were prepared to go in finding loopholes, are the *mamzer*, which is the subject of this chapter, and the *aguna*. Since the rabbis (according to our theory) considered both these laws flawed and perhaps relics of a primitive society which the Jews at the time were not yet able to dispense with, they argued that they were obliged to at least limit the damage until the day when these laws could be abolished altogether. This, after all, was exactly what God and

---

107. See *Mishne Torah, Hilchot Chovel u-Mazik* 1:3; the opinion of Rabbi Eliezer in *Bava Kamma* 84a; *Moreh Nevuchim* 3:41; *Seforno* on *Shemot* 21:24; Maharal, *Gur Aryeh* on *Vayikra* 24:20. For a discussion about the apparent discrepancy between the *peshat* of the verse and Chazal's reinterpretation, see R. Amnon Bazak, "Peshat and Midrash Halakha," shiur 10c, *The Israel Koschitzky Virtual Beit Midrash of Yeshivat Har Etzion*, http://etzion.org.il/en/shiur-10c-peshat-and-midrash-halakha/ and shiur 10d, http://etzion.org.il/en/shiur-10d-peshat-and-midrash-halakha/.

108. See *The Code of Hammurabi*, trans. Theophile J. Meek, in *Ancient Near Eastern Texts Relating to the Old Testament*, ed. James B. Pritchard, 3rd ed. with supplement (Princeton, NJ: Princeton University Press, 1969), 176, sections 229 and 230. See also Moshe Greenberg, "Some Postulates of Biblical Criminal Law," in *Yehezkel Kaufmann Jubilee Volume*, ed. Menahem Haran (Jerusalem: Magnes Press, 1960), 5–28; Barry L. Eichler, "Study of Bible in Light of Our Knowledge of the Ancient Near East," in *Modern Scholarship in the Study of Torah: Contributions and Limitations*, ed. Shalom Carmy (Northvale, NJ: Jason Aronson, 1996), 81–100.

109. *Sanhedrin* 71a. Since it says (*Devarim* 21:20) "He does not hearken to our voice," it must mean that both parents must have a similar voice; and from the fact that we require their voices to be similar, it follows that their appearance and height also must be similar, etc.

the Torah desired.[110] Ideally, the Torah does not want such laws to apply, since they violate its spirit, according to which no one may ever be punished for another's transgressions or become the victim of the law because of a malicious husband. Why punish children for the sexual misconduct of their parents? And why leave women in a situation where they can never remarry?

Still, the rabbis believed that for the meantime, these laws had meaning and were a very strong warning against sexual offenses. As such, the "flaws" did not yet have to be completely abolished, but had to be amended in such a way that they would *nearly* never apply, although it was clear that at a still later stage they would have to be altogether abolished.

There was no way, however, to reinterpret the text in order to accomplish this temporary goal, so another device had to be found.

As mentioned previously, the sages invented a mechanism that was so "out of the box," one can only stand in awe of their courage. They decided that the legality of a marriage was not contingent on any action taken by the husband and wife, or even by the rabbi who married them, but only on *their* (the sages') agreement to the marriage. If they no longer approved, they simply declared the marriage void.

The sages made use of this principle in several instances, especially in cases where there was concern that the woman would remain an *aguna* or would bear children that are *mamzerim*, as we explained before at length.[111]

To the outsider, this looks like trickery. How can one annul a sound marriage in order to legitimize an adulterous act?

Yet that is exactly the position that was taken by some *poskim* when the woman was innocently unaware that she was still married to her first husband.

They didn't see this as trickery, but as a way of achieving the higher objective of the Torah. They would argue that if the Torah were given in our day and age, it would say:

"And the Lord said to the Children of Israel: No woman who is innocent should ever be left in the hands of her recalcitrant husband. If he

110. Perhaps this has to be done in stages: first by stating, for example, that the law of the *mamzer* is only applicable to the child of such an adulterous marriage, but not to its offspring, unlike today's law that says all the offspring are forever *mamzerim*. See n6 above. Then, at a later stage, it would be abolished entirely. See the opinion of Rabbi Yose that in the days of the mashiach, all *mamzerim* will be purified and permitted to marry freely, a clear indication that they saw this law to be temporarily applicable (see *Kiddushin* 72b; *Tosefta Kiddushin* 5:4).

111. See n57 above.

refuses to give a *get*, you shall annul the marriage *ab initio* and let her go free, and the child shall not be a *mamzer*."

The sages believed that the Torah was completely divine but also "flawed." It was their task to refine it and bring it to the level that God had intended.

This, I believe, is the secret behind the halachic loophole and the divinity of the Torah.[112]

CONCLUSION

At the end of several tractates in the Talmud[113] the sages quote a verse: "And all your children (*banayich*) will be disciples of God, and your children's peace will be great."[114] Rabbi Chanina, using a play on words, states that the word *banayich*, your children, is of the same root as the word *bonayich*, your builders. He therefore understands this verse to mean that the Torah scholars are the builders who will bring peace to the world. The next verse in *Yeshayahu* states: "You shall be established through righteousness; you shall be far from oppression, and shall have no fear; and from terror, it shall not come near you."[115] This has been understood to mean that the sages will find ways to remove human pain, such as that of *mamzerim* and *agunot*.

They, the rabbis, will not be afraid to use any and all loopholes and arguments – even if they seem far-fetched – to solve these problems. They

---

112. In the case of the biblical commandment to destroy the nation of Amalek and the seven nations of ancient Canaan at the time that Joshua conquered the land, the sages also found ways to nullify this law and declared it inoperative by claiming that these nations no longer exist. (See *Mishna Yadayim*, 4:4; *Mishne Torah, Hilchot Melachim* 5:4 and *Minchat Chinuch* by R. Yosef Babad, mitzva 604.) However, the biblical text indicates that these nations once *did* exist and were partially destroyed – including women and children – by the Israelites. We have to wonder whether these stories really happened or whether they are purely figurative. Alternatively, perhaps only the males were killed. Most interesting is the observation in *Yoma* 22b where Rabbi Mani states that King Shaul argued with God about why the Amalekite children had to be killed for the sins of their fathers. King Shaul argued with God as Avraham did when God wanted to destroy Sedom and Amora (*Bereshit* 18:20–33). See chap. 22 n15. For a discussion of this topic, see Rabbi Dr. Norman Lamm, "Amalek and the Seven Nations: A Case of Law vs. Morality," in *War and Peace in the Jewish Tradition*, ed. Lawrence Schiffman and Joel B. Wolowelsky (NY: Yeshiva University Press, 2007), 201–238; Shalom Carmy, "The Origin of Nations and the Shadow of Violence: Theological Perspectives on Canaan and Amalek," in *War and Peace in the Jewish Tradition*, 163–199.

113. *Berachot* 64a; *Nazir* 66b; *Yevamot* 122b; *Kritot* 28b. Together they form an acronym of the Hebrew word **Banayich**. See below.

114. *Yeshayahu* 54:13.

115. *Yeshayahu* 54:14.

will bring "surprising arguments,"[116] even resorting "to strange things remote from nature."[117]

God will grant them the strength to do so, since He blesses His people with peace, and no peace prevails as long as these victims are not freed from their unfortunate status.[118]

Indeed, nowhere have the sages and the later rabbis shown so much courage in finding solutions to the most severe halachic problems as they did in the above cases. It is a supreme example of halachic invention and daring. May the rabbis of today have the same kind of courage!

116. *Maharsha, Chiddushei Aggadot* on *Yevamot* 122b.
117. R. Mordechai ha-Levi, *Darchei No'am* (Venice, 1697–1698), *Even ha-Ezer,* no. 43.
118. See Finkelstein, "Derech le-Tihuram shel Mamzerim," 62.

Eight

HALACHA AND THE MEANING
OF LIFE

Chapter 28

Halacha and Absurdity 1

Much has been written about the meaning and purpose of Halacha, based on philosophy, metaphysics, and psychology. Scholars have suggested that Halacha is the art of living in the presence of God. Others have posited that it requires the need to live a life dedicated to *kedusha*, while many argue that Halacha's purpose is to achieve a high level of ethical standards. There are those who maintain that its main purpose is to make man surrender to the Divine Will and teach him to ignore his subjective and often biased moral and philosophical insights, even when his moral intuition tells him that the Halacha's requirements are flawed. Proponents of this view are of the opinion that there is a higher morality, which man is unable to grasp. Still others believe that there is no purpose to Halacha other than to ensure that we observe the commandments, whether or not there is any moral meaning.

All these insights have merit and can be supported by a variety of Jewish traditional sources. What they fail to recognize, however, is that ultimately Halacha is an attempt to address the absurdity of human existence and give it meaning, despite and in contradiction to this absurdity.

There is a famous midrash that highlights the role played by Halacha in dealing with the absurdity of human existence. The midrash relates how Miriam, Moshe's sister, convinced her father, Amram, to have children with her mother, Yocheved, in the days when Pharaoh had decreed that all Israelite male children had to be killed at birth. Despite Amram's earlier insistence that he should not father any more children so as to avoid the killing of possible future sons, Miriam admonished him saying he was worse than Pharaoh because while the king of Egypt denied children the right to *continue* to live, Amram refused to give them any life at all.[1]

Miriam, in essence, is arguing that even if Amram is correct from a rational point of view (why have children if they will be immediately killed?), there is meaning beyond absurdity that transcends rational considerations. If one is commanded to have children, even genocide in progress is no reason to avoid fulfilling the obligation.[2] Her argument is straightforward: we cannot know why it is necessary for human beings to exist, or why a particular human being is meant to come into the world at a certain moment. We do not know why God decided to create life instead of leaving a void; nor, for that matter, do we know the ultimate purpose of anything. It follows, then, that we have no criteria by which to decide whether or not to have children, even if we know they will immediately die. After all, it may well be that life has infinite meaning even if it lasts no more than one second. But this is only known to God, the Creator.

Lacking any insight into God's motivations for creating man, we are forced to admit that our own observations about the ultimate purpose of human existence are by definition subjective and far from comprehensive.

When I consider whether there is righteousness in God's decision to create the world, I have to conclude that there can be no logical or moral justification for it, at least not in human terms. After all, the suffering a person endures outweighs any obvious benefits he or she gains from all of life. The reason for this is simple: non-existence precludes all suffering. From this point of view, earthquakes, tsunamis, and man's capability to wreak havoc and create holocausts are all unjustifiable – whether they are caused by God, or by man with his God-given free will to do evil. Either way, God is responsible for all suffering, directly or indirectly. How, then, can we argue that God was justified in creating humanity?

Moreover, there is nothing to justify human existence that includes even the slightest form of discomfort. The argument that pain and suffering are necessary for man to morally grow is untenable since we are unable to answer why man needs to *exist* in order to morally grow. Even if

---

1. *Sota* 12a, quoted in *Rashi* on *Shemot* 12:1.

2. While it is true that Miriam insisted that Amram should still father children even if they would immediately be killed, it cannot be denied that this is a moot point in Halacha, since in some cases Halacha permits abortion in the very early stages of pregnancy when the fetus is severely deformed and would not survive. Miriam may have argued that if it would be a daughter, the child would stay alive, or that Pharaoh's decree could possibly fail, as in the case of her brother Moshe (*Sota* 12a). However, the Talmud also states her argument that Amram would be denying these unborn souls a life in the hereafter. This may support our position if we replace the word "hereafter" with the phrase "ultimate purpose known only to God."

the world would exist in a way that man would experience only the most pleasurable and exalted moments, this would still not explain why it is necessary for man and the world to exist at all. In what way is existence more pleasurable than non-existence?[3] After all, non-existence would not include a human awareness that one is missing any pleasure or joy.

From the start we are faced with an enormous problem: our question as to why there is *any* existence is unanswerable. We have not the slightest hint why God chose to create the world, or human beings, or for that matter, Judaism. The Torah itself is completely unhelpful as far as this question is concerned. It never offers us any information about *why* God decided to create existence. It begins with the creation of the Earth, by which time God had already "made up His mind" to create a world with human beings. All the Torah does is tell us that once the world has come into existence, God demands of man to live a righteous life.

No doubt the Torah implies that there *is* a purpose, but it leaves us in complete darkness as to what that purpose is. Only God knows. Since man has no way of deciphering the ultimate purpose, from his perspective all existence is absurd. He is asked only to deal with this absurdity and be aware that there *is* purpose, which only makes sense to God. The fact that man is asked to do so is in itself completely absurd. It means that man deals with radical absurdity from the moment he is born until the day he dies. Whether his life is pleasant, or filled with constant hardship, it is absurdity he must deal with 24/7.

We cannot, then, escape the fact that Halacha is the art of dealing with existential absurdity. Its function, after all, is to guide man in how to live his life. And since life is absurd, Halacha, by definition, is absurd as well. In other words, its function is to help man deal with an absurdity in a way that gives meaning to this absurdity, although from the perspective of man, the meaning itself is ultimately absurd. Only to God, Who alone knows the ultimate purpose, does all this make sense.

Discovering the *nature* of Halacha therefore necessitates that we admit it is rooted in absurdity and that its response to that absurdity is itself motivated by absurdity. This is obvious since Halacha is part and parcel of this world.

All this is so vital that it is no exaggeration to say that any halachic response should really start with asking the question of why man, the Jew, and the Torah exist. While the ultimate answers to these questions

---

3. See the observation of John Hick on p. 267.

will never be known to us, it is most important that these questions be posed, so that the awareness of the absurdity of existence will become the foundation from which all halachic decisions flow forth and can be understood. Without this, Halacha can never be appreciated, and no answer can "make any sense."

To support our claim, we need only to mention the halachic demand to give up one's life rather than be forced to worship idols. Plainly, such worship does not hurt anybody, and while one could argue that it has some negative consequences, it should not be something one has to pay for with one's life. The same is true concerning certain incestuous relationships. What is wrong with a brother marrying his sister?[4] Why should they have to forfeit their lives rather than enter into such a relationship if they both consent to it?[5] The same can be argued concerning other prohibitions of incest, or those relating to bestiality. From the human being's perspective, the demand to give up one's life in this situation is absurd. Only when we admit that all of life is absurd while being very much the absolute and undeniable reality in which we live, can we fathom why there may be laws that make little sense – but still, unquestionably, have ultimate divine purpose. Without this awareness, no halacha could ever make sense or even be acceptable. Just as the existence of the world is a Godly decision, so too are these laws. Just as the ultimate purpose of the world's existence is totally unknown, so are the reasons for these laws. When asking why we need to live by these laws, we should simultaneously ask why there is a world, for essentially they are one and the same question.

Yet, I know of no *sheilot* or *teshuvot* (halachic responsa) that begin by asking why God created humanity. The truth, however, is that they really ought to! After all, how can one answer a halachic question without first acknowledging the absurdity of its being grounded in the absurdity of human existence?

Only when we establish the absurdity of life and the halachic question can we start trying to respond to the inquiry.

See the next chapter for a continuation.

---

4. See chap. 26.
5. See *Maharsha, Chiddushei Aggadot* on *Chagiga* 11b, s.v. "ba-arayot."

Chapter 29

Halacha and Absurdity 2

Once the human being has recognized that ultimately there is no way to know why God created the world and humankind, he can make his way back to reason and meaning. Once he leaves this "divine absurdity" behind as an unsolvable problem, his intelligence is able to guide him through the labyrinth of human existence.

It is our failure to understand the fundamental purpose of existence that forces us to become humble and know the limitations of our intelligence and reasoning. Only then does reason become a powerful instrument for us to understand the world and its subjective meaning. When we encounter inexplicable contradictions, or questions that are unanswerable, we realize that we have come to the end of the road of what is humanly possible to understand. We then have no choice but to resort to what *is* intellectually possible. Were we not to do so, cognitive chaos would ensue, all our reasoning would come to an end, and we would be completely paralyzed. *The art of reasoning is in direct proportion to the limitations of human understanding.* As such, one of the most important functions of reason is to recognize that there are an infinite number of realities that surpass it. This knowledge may not save us, but it can mitigate the absurdity of existence.

For the human being, therefore, life is absurd only as far as its ultimacy is concerned. Once he steps away from this, life could become extremely meaningful to him, and he may argue that this is what God had in mind as its purpose as far as human beings are concerned.

In other words, man can discover God's *secondary* purpose for human existence and find great satisfaction in this, as long as he recognizes that the *primary* reason is unknown to him. In fact, it is only *because* he recognizes this that he can find real significance in his life. It is the mystery behind his existence that gives him a feeling of ultimate meaning.

It cannot be denied that for the religious person this is a rather comfortable situation. At least he knows that there is purpose to his suffering and torment. This comfort is not available to the atheist who will have to deal with his suffering devoid of any such support. It may therefore be argued that for the atheist to continue to live and behave honorably is of greater moral value than for the believer to do so. The atheist places himself in a category of absolute unselfishness. For him there is *no* meaning beyond absurdity. Life and what is beyond (if anything) is *all* absurd. So when he acts morally it is not because he believes there is any ultimate meaning to his life, but because he believes it is the right thing to do. It is pure altruism.[1] We may postulate that God takes great satisfaction in this. On the other hand, it is much more painful for the believer to believe in a God Who needs to include suffering and cruelty as absolute essentials in His very creation. Here, the atheist is more comfortable. He does not have to deal with this problem.[2]

We must realize that the awareness of everything's ultimate absurdity does not mean that all is illogical. Logic or the lack of it only makes sense or non-sense once matters have been brought down to a level where absurdity is left behind and we enter the sphere where human intellect operates. To make "sense" of something means to limit the place within which the human being is able to conduct his life by way of his intelligence, and it is here that there is need for structure and a specific and orderly way of living combined with cognitive and rational thinking. But just as every form of rational thinking has its limits and must bend before that which can no longer be grasped – because it enters the space where unsolvable contradictions and enigmas have the upper hand – so life often reminds

---

1. Obviously, one cannot argue that since the atheist lives such an unselfish life, which the believer by definition is unable to reach, God does not exist. The level of unselfishness cannot be the parameter by which to decide whether God does or does not exist. But what it could mean is that this type of atheist is more loved by God than the believer will ever be. In that case, there could be great religious meaning to atheism. It may even be the reason why God created the possibility for it to exist. There may be greater *tzaddikim* among exceptional atheists than among the religious. This, however, is a broad topic!

2. One wonders how many people would be able to live on the level of the moral atheist. It has been argued that most atheists would probably live a life of "minimum" morality, unless they borrow subconsciously from the moral standards of religion or subscribe to the notion of "evolutionary ethics" in which the atheist is prepared to live a moral life because this is the only way he is able to survive. Still, while only few *tzaddikim* are found in atheist circles, it cannot be denied that there have been some outstanding exceptions such as Spinoza, perhaps. (Whether or not Spinoza was really an atheist is a separate discussion.)

the human being that he may be confronted with problems, including some moral ones, that are unsolvable.

Values often clash and cannot be reconciled, not only because of practical reasons, but even conceptually. One cannot combine full liberty with full equality. Full liberty for wolves cannot be reconciled with full liberty for sheep. Justice and mercy, knowledge and happiness may collide. A coherent and perfect solution cannot be conceived. All one can strive for is a trade-off: this amount of equality for that amount of liberty; this much justice for that much mercy.[3]

There are no perfect solutions to many of our moral problems. An aircraft carrying 120 passengers is hurtling out of control toward a densely populated area. There is no time to evacuate the area, and the impact of the plane is certain to kill thousands. The only possible move is to shoot down the plane. What should be done?

On a deeper level, philosophers have debated whether or not there are absolute moral criteria by which one could declare something evil. Some maintain that this is purely subjective and it is only our thinking that makes it so. Bertrand Russell's famous observation – "I cannot see how to refute the arguments for the subjectivity of ethical values, but I find myself incapable of believing that all that is wrong with wanton cruelty is that I don't like it"[4] – is well taken.

Matters like these constantly remind us that we cannot escape the absurdity behind these questions and situations. Still, we need to use our minds to deal with these problems on a practical level even if we cannot solve them on a conceptual one.

Halacha, too, is unable to solve these problems in an ideal way. All it can do is command a response without being able to prove it correct. In the case of the airplane that has gone out of control, Halacha cannot argue that it is *better* to shoot down the plane and have 120 people killed, just as it cannot argue that it is better *not* to shoot it down and have thousands of people killed. All it can do is claim that it has come to a conclusion on the basis of some subjective criteria, or that a Divine Will orders us to do such and such, although there is nothing "logical" about this Will. It really belongs to the category of the absurd, which is beyond our grasp and known only to God. Therefore, for the religious person to claim that Halacha is always morally right is missing the point. It is only right in the

---

3. See Ramin Jahanbegloo, *Conversations with Isaiah Berlin* (London: Halban, 2007), 142–143.
4. Bertrand Russell, "Notes on Philosophy, January 1960," *Philosophy* 35, no. 133 (April 1960): 146–147.

sense that it is God's Will, or deduced by some halachic argument that would break down once it touches the unknown and absurd.

But what is of utmost importance is to realize that Halacha could have decided differently, when bearing in mind other halachic opinions that could also be backed up by subjective arguments, as is often the case in the Talmud. A famous example is the difference of opinion between Rabbi Akiva and Ben Petura concerning two people who are walking in the desert and have only one bottle of water, which is not sufficient to keep them both alive if they share the bottle. What should the owner of the bottle do? Drink it all himself, surviving while his friend dies (Rabbi Akiva), or share it and have them both die (Ben Petura)?[5] Both have strong arguments, but ultimately, they clash conceptually because they use different value systems. This is the meaning of "Elu ve-elu divrei Elokim Chaim" (These and those are the words of the Living God).[6]

This dictum does not mean that each opinion is completely correct. Actually, the reverse is true. Each is forced to admit that its argument is problematic since it is impossible to come to a conclusive and absolutely correct decision. As such, each opinion has to make space for the other. Each is a trade-off, a compromise. All that is left for Halacha to decide is *which* tradeoff to follow. For that, it will need secondary reasons that may have little to do with the actual argument.

As is well known, the many different arguments between Bet Hillel and Bet Shammai are nearly always decided in favor of Bet Hillel. The reason given is most remarkable: Bet Hillel were easygoing and forbearing and would quote the opinion of Bet Shammai before stating their own opinion. In this way, Bet Hillel showed great *derech eretz* (respect) to Bet Shammai, something Bet Shammai did not reciprocate.[7] *This has nothing to do with the actual argument and therefore should be completely irrelevant.* Still, it is the reason why Halacha was decided in favor of Bet Hillel! Even more surprising is that the Talmud states that Bet Shammai were *mechadedei tfei* – sharper than Bet Hillel.[8] Yet this was still not a reason to decide the issues in accordance with Bet Shammai. The Talmud wants to convey that even though Bet Shammai are sharper and have better arguments, one can still not contend that their arguments are definitely right, since that is impossible. It remains a trade-off. The only thing required now is to

5. *Bava Metzia* 62a.
6. *Eruvin* 13b.
7. Ibid.
8. *Yevamot* 14a.

make a decision, *because a ruling needs to be made*. Without a decision, life cannot continue! On a pragmatic level, A and B cannot simultaneously be followed. Either we light the Chanuka candles from 1 to 8 (Bet Hillel) or from 8 to 1 (Bet Shammai),[9] but we cannot do both at the same time. One is reminded of William James' observation that not to make a decision is also a decision.

See the next chapter for a continuation.

---

9. See *Shabbat* 21b.

Chapter 30

Halacha and Absurdity 3

In the two previous essays we have seen that no objectivity is possible in Halacha. This enables us to understand not only why there are many opposing opinions in the Talmud, such as those of Bet Hillel and Bet Shammai, but also that the weltanschauung and ideologies of the halachic authorities play an enormous role in the way they decide halachic issues. In the case of Bet Hillel and Bet Shammai, we see how both schools differ on whether Halacha should reflect the realistic, here-and-now situation of man's religious status quo, or whether man's halachic lifestyle should be an expression of where he would like to be one day.[1] Is it mercy that should drive Halacha, or should it be uncompromising truth, however harsh, that stands at its foundation?[2] Is it better to have been born, or would it be better not to have been born so as not to transgress divine commandments?[3]

Similar ideological issues are often the motives behind other major differences of opinion. In modern times, Zionist halachic authorities will often rule on matters related to Israel and its security issues differently from those who do not share their views. Whether to give up land for the sake of peace with the Arab neighbors will depend to a great extent on whether or not one sees in the State of Israel the beginning of the messianic redemption and whether there is any intrinsic religious meaning to the State. The answer to the extremely sensitive question of whether yeshiva students should serve in the Israeli army will depend on whether one believes that learning Torah is *at least* as crucial (if not more) to the

---

1. See *Shabbat* 21b and R. Eliyahu Eliezer Dessler, *Michtav me-Eliyahu* (Jerusalem: Kiryat Noar, 1963), 2:120–22. For a detailed treatment of this topic, see chap. 21.
2. See *Ketubot* 16b–17a.
3. See *Eruvin* 13b.

survival of Israel as serving in the army. Another consideration would be the desire to ensure that young religious men not become spiritually tainted by the outside secular world.

Is it better to isolate religious communities in separate neighborhoods and keep secular influences out, protecting one's children from them? Or, perhaps one should ensure that religious Jews live in secular surroundings so that secular Israelis can understand what the other world has to offer, while simultaneously giving the religious Jews the opportunity to influence their secular neighbors to become more religiously inclined.

Should one ban the Internet and bar it from one's home because of the spiritual damage it may cause? Or, should one teach one's children how to deal with the Internet in a sensitive way and trust them to do so? Such issues cannot be dealt with in an isolated, mechanical, and solely halachic way. Attitudes to these matters are often rooted in the way people perceive the world and how they are prepared to face its challenges. They may even depend on whether people are more optimistic, or less so, in their general outlook on life. Halachic attitudes toward the non-Jewish world will frequently be determined by whether or not one lives in surroundings that are anti-Semitic, or how one feels about non-Jews in general.

It is often clear that halachic authorities will consult their consciences and rely on their intuition, thereby finding halachic arguments to support what their moral sense has already established, instead of allowing their halachic knowledge to decide on these matters without any other motives.[4] Here, psychology, philosophy, and even human emotions enter the domain of halachic decision-making. It is therefore a major mistake to believe that Halacha works like mathematics in which none of these factors have any real influence.[5]

Besides the classical interpretation of *Torah lo ba-Shamayim hi* (the Torah is not in Heaven), by which God leaves the final decision to a human majority vote,[6] this phrase also means that no person can ever be objective, and every rabbi is therefore authorized to decide Halacha as he sees fit, as long as he is able to find halachic sources to *support* his opinion, even if

4. See, for example, R. Mordechai Ya'akov Breish, *Chelkat Ya'akov*, vol. 3, *Even ha-Ezer* no. 29, concerning whether one is allowed to perform surgery on the prostate. See also chap. 27 for a full discussion.

5. Interestingly, there are mathematicians today, such as Reuben Hersh, who argue that even mathematics is not purely objective and is "influenced by politics and culture." See Edward Rothstein, "The Subjective Underbelly of Hardheaded Math," *New York Times*, Dec. 20, 1997.

6. *Bava Metzia* 59b.

they may not *prove* his point of view. Often these decisions are *a posteriori*, from effect to cause instead of the other way around.

It is remarkable that God leaves these decisions to man. In the wonderful yet astonishing story in the Talmud, God tries to interfere in the halachic process when He states that He agrees with one of the sages. God is then rebuked by the majority of sages because He had already established Himself in these matters as *persona non grata* when He declared in His Torah that halachic matters are to be decided by majority vote of the sages, and definitely not by God.[7]

Clearly, the Talmud alludes to the fact that God Himself cannot know the answer; answers are the product of the human mind. God has set up the world in a way that makes Him dependent on man, and He must await man's solution. Only subjective human beings can have answers to halachic questions. This paradoxical situation, in which God appears to be no longer omnipotent, but limited because He is *too* great and powerful, is one of the most daring ideas on which Halacha is founded. Once again, it is absurdity that enters the picture. How, after all, is God not able to answer questions? This time it is not just that Halacha has to deal with absurdity; it is the halachic process itself that reflects incomprehensible dimensions!

---

7. *Bava Metzia* 59b.

Nine

HALACHA: BETWEEN THE RIGID LETTER AND CREATIVE SPIRIT

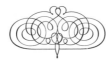

Chapter 31

Halacha: The Art to Complicate Life
The Microscopic Search for God

There is little doubt that Halacha greatly complicates life for the religious Jew. There is no other religion that requires so much dedication and includes so much emphasis on detail. There is hardly a nook or cranny of a Jew's life in which Halacha does not make its demands. Many halachic volumes and responsa have been written about minor issues, seemingly blowing them out of all proportion.

The exact amount of matza that must be eaten at the Pesach Seder is a case in point. The law requires the consumption of a *ke-zayit* (a unit of volume approximately equal to the size of an olive) to fulfill one's obligation. But what is the size of an olive? For hundreds of years, halachic scholars have debated this question, and have even deliberated over the exact weight of an olive. Is today's olive equal in size to the olive from the time of the Bible or of the Talmud? Many opinions have been suggested, and to this day a substantial number of religious Jews will adhere to one and reject others, believing that only a larger measurement will ensure that one has completely fulfilled one's obligation according to all opinions.

The same is true about the *lulav* and *etrog*.[1] How tall must a *lulav* be? How green do the leaves have to be so that they are not considered dry? What if the *etrog* is not completely spotless? Is it still halachically acceptable? What is the correct size? What happens when its *pitom*, which botanists call its stigma (a flowered blossom protruding at the top), has been partially damaged? Thousands of questions like these are found in the Talmud and in the writings of later authorities.

---

1. The *lulav* (palm branch) and *etrog* (citron) comprise two of the Four Species, or *Arba'at ha-Minim*, that are taken on Sukkot. See *Vayikra* 23:40.

To this day, the religious Jew takes delight in these debates, and in fact discusses them as if his life depends on it. To an outsider this looks altogether ludicrous, and the dismissal of it all as "hair-splitting" is well known. One wonders what people would say if they were told that their Christmas tree has to be of a certain measurement, with a particular number of leaves and ornaments. What if there were to be major differences of opinion among the authorities on whether the leaves must be fully green or may include some spots that are a bit yellow? And what if God forbid one ornament is missing or damaged?

What is behind this obsessive way in which Halacha deals with all these issues? What has this to do with religion? Isn't religion the realm of the soul, of deep emotions and beliefs?

In *Devarim*, we find a verse that directly deals with our problem:

> Safeguard the month of the early ripening [Nissan] and bring the Pesach offering unto the Lord your God, for in the month of the early ripening the Lord your God took you out of Egypt at night.[2]

According to Jewish Tradition, this verse instructs the people of Israel to ensure that Pesach, which commemorates one the most important events in Jewish history, will always be celebrated in the spring. Rabbi Ovadia Seforno, the great Italian commentator, comments on this verse in a most original way:

> Guard with constant care that Nissan will fall in the spring by means of the *ibbur*, the aligning of the lunar and solar months through calculations, so that the lunar and solar years are equal.

A careful reading of Seforno's comment seems to reveal a most daring thesis, which directly deals with our question. Since the lunar year has fewer days than the solar year, and since the Jewish year is, to a great extent, based on the lunar year, it is necessary after a few lunar years to add an extra month – Adar Sheni, around March – to make sure that Nissan (and therefore Pesach) will fall in the spring and not in the winter.

In that case, alludes Seforno, there is a most important question: Why does the Jewish calendar not simply follow the solar year? If, in any case, we must make sure that Pesach falls in the spring, what is the purpose of

---

2. *Devarim* 16:1.

consistently following lunar years when eventually one has to align these with the solar years?

His answer is most telling: *so as to complicate life*. In order to make sure that the month of Nissan and the festival of Pesach will always fall in the spring, one has to make difficult astronomical calculations. The Torah deliberately complicated the Jewish year by modeling it on the lunar year, so that Nissan would *not* automatically fall in the spring, and so that the sages would have to make complicated calculations. Sure, it would have been much easier to follow the solar year. But that would have come with a serious religious setback. "A smooth sea never made a skillful mariner," says the English proverb.

Judaism wants to make the sages and the Jewish community constantly aware that they live in the presence of God, and to accomplish that goal life must be complicated and an ongoing challenge! Only through constant preoccupation with the divine commandments and their minutiae, and only by confronting the obstacles to implementing these commandments, can one be cognizant of God's presence.

Religion's main task is to disturb. It should ensure, on a very pragmatic level, that we do not take anything for granted in our day-to-day lives. It is through challenges and complications that we are constantly surprised. These give birth to wonder, which then reminds us of God's presence. It is not philosophical contemplation that brings man closer to God. God is not an intellectual issue, but the ultimate reality of life. Only in the deed, in the down-to-earth and heart-rending existence of daily life, which asks for sweat and blood, does one escape superficiality and enter awareness and attentiveness. By studying astronomy, encountering major complexities, and using scientific instruments for the purpose of ensuring that Pesach falls in the spring, the sages were forced to find solutions, which then made them aware of the sheer uniqueness of this world. Their total commitment to a biblical commandment, including the need to investigate, discuss, and implement it, gave them a sense of the mystery of life. Through the constant wonder that accompanied them in their search and ultimate resolution, they became aware of the Living God.

This idea runs contrary to our way of thinking. If anything, Western civilization looks for ways to make life *less* complicated. Many of our scientific inventions are founded on this premise. And no doubt this is of great importance. Man's life *should* be less complicated. It would grant him more time to enjoy life, to investigate elements of spirituality, and to search for deep, sacred beauty. But in these matters it is ongoing effort that is re-

quired. Were that not to be the case, one would fall into devastating boredom, which, after all, is the result of no longer noticing the uniqueness of
our lives. This has disastrous consequences for the human spirit. It will
slowly die. To live means to stay alert, to take notice. When it comes to the
spirit, man should never live an effortless and uncomplicated life.

Scientific research has often revealed parts of our universe that can stir
the heart of man in ways that were not possible in earlier times. Scientists
dedicate their lives to the minutest properties of our physical world. They
are fascinated with and often get carried away by the behavior of cells, the
habits of insects, and the peculiarities of the DNA code (Heschel). As the
saying goes, God is in the details.

So too, halachic authorities look for the smallest details so as to make
man sensitive to every fine point of life. By making us careful about how
much matza to eat, what size *lulav* to use, and to what extent our *etrog*
should be spotless, they create a subconscious awareness in us of every
dimension of life. Everything is put under a microscope in order to ensure
that we never take anything as a given. *Halacha is an anti-boredom device*. It
is the microscopic search for God.

Indeed, Judaism's main purpose is to complicate life so as to create a psychological environment that makes the Jew constantly aware they are living
in the presence of God and enjoying it to the fullest. This is in no way an
eccentric observation; it is consistent with the very purpose of religious life.

Religion is a protest against taking life for granted. There are no insignificant phenomena or deeds in this world, and it is through Judaism's
demands and far-reaching interference in our daily life that we are made
aware of God as our steadfast Companion.

This is clearly the meaning of the famous talmudic statement by Rabbi
Chanania ben Akashia when he said: "The Holy One, blessed be He, desired to make Israel worthy, therefore He gave them Torah and mitzvot
in abundance, as it is said:[3] 'God desires for the sake of His righteousness
that the Torah be expanded and strengthened.'"[4]

But all this comes at a heavy price: One of the great challenges confronting Judaism today is the problem of behaviorism. The habitual
performance of Halacha is the result of getting used to the way Judaism
wants man to respond to life; all aspects of life *should* be nothing less than
extraordinary, but for many of us, this is no longer the case.

---

3. *Yeshayahu* 42:21.
4. *Makkot* 23b.

The observance of Halacha for the sake of observance can easily lead to "hair splitting," when man becomes robotic, is obsessed with detail, and can no longer see the forest for the trees. This, in turn, drives him to fanatical behavior.

Halachic living has become self-defeating for many of us. It actually encourages what it wishes to prevent: observing Halacha by rote, and failing to see the extraordinary. New ways must be found to prevent this phenomenon. We must teach Halacha as a musical symphony in which all students see opportunities to discover their inner selves. Halacha teachers must stand in front of their classes as a conductor stands before the orchestra and draw the Halacha out of its confinement, moving it beyond itself. They must show their students how to pull the ineffable out of the dry law and turn it into an encounter with God, the Source of all mystery, thereby transforming the world into a place of utter amazement where one lives in a constant state of awe and surprise. This will be possible only when we take a fresh look at ourselves and ask *who* we are and *why* we live. But as long as man hides behind his own superficiality, no halacha will accomplish its goal. We live on the fringes of this world and have lost contact with our inner selves. Halacha then becomes an external entity, cut off from its living roots.

No halacha can be taught in a vacuum. It can be transmitted only when the entirety of life is present. We must ensure that we can see all of life reflected in one detail of the Halacha, that it is infused with all the colors life offers us. This is impossible when the codes of Jewish Law are taught as self-contained works. They are just the outer shells of the music behind the notes. Just as musical notes are useless unless you play and pace your *own* music with these notes, so studying the codes is a meaningless undertaking unless with these notes we hear and play the music that cries out from our inner selves.

In a play on Nietzsche's observation that "anyone who has looked deeply into the world may guess how much wisdom lies in the superficiality of men,"[5] I would suggest that one of the great tragedies of today's halachic man is his obliviousness to how much profundity his halachic superficiality hides.

To paraphrase Abraham Joshua Heschel: *Halacha is of no importance unless it is of supreme importance.*

---

5. Friedrich Nietzsche, *Beyond Good and Evil: Prelude to a Philosophy of the Future*, trans. Walter Kaufmann (NY: Vintage Books, 1966), 71.

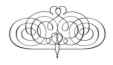

Chapter 32

Halacha: The Greatest Chess Game on Earth

There is probably no game as difficult and as captivating as chess. Millions of people spend years learning its ins and outs and break their heads over strategies to win. It holds them captive as nothing else does. They dream about it and discuss the move of one single pawn as if their lives depended on it. They will follow the most important chess tournaments and discuss every move of a world champion for days and even years. These chess aficionados replay classic games of the past and try to improve on them, often getting into heated arguments about a brilliant or foolish move that took place half a century ago. Thousands of books and tens of thousands of essays have been published on how to improve at playing the game. The rules are set up in the World Chess Federation's *FIDE Handbook*. Strategies are developed and tactics suggested; countless combinations have been tried to the point that some typical patterns have their own names, such as "Boden's Mate" and "Lasker's Combination." Mikhail Botvinnik (1911–1995) revolutionized the opening theory, which was considered nothing less than a Copernican breakthrough. Famous chess studies, such as the one published by Richard Reti in 1921, are revelations of tremendous depth. (He depicted a situation in which it seems impossible for the white king to catch the advanced black pawn while the white pawn can be easily stopped by the black king.)

The rules are ruthless. There are no compromises, no flexibility. Zero *rachmanut* (mercy). It is all about *midat ha-din* (harsh rendering). The terrifying rigid rules can make players mad to the point of possibly considering suicide.

The rules seem easy until you start playing. The entire game takes place on a chessboard smaller than the size of a side table, but the game is larger than life. Each player has sixteen pieces, which are played on sixty-four squares, but they become so enormous in one's psyche that they dazzle the eyes of the spectator. Some of the pieces can move in any direction; others can move any number of squares along any rank or file, but may not leap over other pieces. There are those that can only move diagonally and others that are allowed to move two squares horizontally and one square vertically, or two squares vertically and one square horizontally, thus making the complete move look like the letter "L."

It may sound very easy, but what any player soon realizes is that these basic rules allow for thousands of combinations, maneuvers, and sub-rules, depending on the position of a pawn, a rook, or a knight. These rules can become so complicated and require such intense thought that one may prefer to take on higher mathematics, which looks easy in comparison. (It is not!) There is good reason why the most famous chess players are considered not only brilliant people, but geniuses with advanced mathematical minds.

But is chess rigid? Does it constrain? Is it "fundamentalist," or perhaps "dogmatic"? Does it deny the player his freedom of thought or action? In one sense, it does. The player cannot move the pieces in any way he would like to. There are rules that make the game incredibly difficult. But that fact is exactly what makes this game so exciting. It leads to an unprecedented outburst of creativity. "In der Beschränkung zeigt sich erst der Meister, / Und das Gesetz nur kann uns Freiheit geben," said Goethe.[1]

The chessboard becomes the world; the pieces are the phenomena of the universe; the rules of the game are the laws of nature; and man roams freely on this board once he applies the rules in a way that will deepen their impact to such an extent that a whole new world is revealed.

But let us never forget that he who knows all the rules is not necessarily a great player. What makes him a formidable opponent is his ability to use these rules to unleash an outburst of creativity, which resides deep within him and emerges only because of the "unbearable" limitations. He then strikes! One small move forces a major shift, creating total upheaval and causing the opponent to panic as never before. And all this without ever violating one chess rule. It's mental torture.

But it's the height of beauty as well. A well-executed move is like poetry,

---

1. "It is in limitation that the master really proves himself, and it is [only] the law which can provide us with freedom." Johann Wolfgang von Goethe's sonnet "Natur und Kunst, sie scheinen sich zu fliehen" (Nature and Art, they go their separate ways) in *Was wir bringen* (Tübingen: J. C. Cotta, 1802).

as melody is to music. It is like a gentle brushstroke from Rembrandt that changes the complexion of the entire canvas, or like the genius musician playing her Stradivarius, recreating the whole of Mozart's Violin Concerto no. 5. It transports the chess player to heaven. His body must be in top form, because his playing ability deteriorates when his body does. They are inseparable. An entire world of feelings, images, ideas, emotions, and passions come to the forefront.

There are hundreds of opening moves and end games. And all of them are authentic.

And that is why so many talmudic scholars, religious Jews, and secular Jews love this game and are often very good at it.[2] Chess reminds them, consciously or subconsciously, of the world of talmudic halachic debate with all its intrigues, its restrictions, and its seemingly deliberate tendency to make life more difficult and sometimes nearly impossible. The truly religious Jew loves it because it is these challenges that make life exciting and even irresistible. For the true *posek*, the tension, challenge, and delight involved in discovering an unprecedented, mindboggling solution is the ultimate *simcha* (joy). Skipping through a maze of obstacles, circumventing what seems impossible in the eyes of his halachic opponents, and backing them into a corner like a pawn on the chessboard, thereby solving a serious halachic problem: this is the peak of divine satisfaction that a halachic authority can experience.

Chess reminds one of the talmudic concept of "elu ve-elu divrei Elokim Chaim." There are *Rishonim* (early authorities) and *Acharonim* (later authorities). There are commentaries, sub-commentaries, major differences of opinion, fiery clashes, and even mistakes that carry dimensions of truth.

Halachic discussion is like chess. It is a clash of minds. Sometimes, "the free passed pawn is a criminal, who should be kept under lock and key. Mild measures, such as police surveillance, are not sufficient."[3] Its position is *treif* (non-kosher) by all standards. Other times, maneuvers are possible in the opinions of some, while still others have their doubts. But above

---

2. Jews make up 0.2 percent of the world population, but 54 percent of the world chess champions. (David Brooks, "The Tel Aviv Cluster," *New York Times*, Jan. 11, 2010.) The Israeli city Be'er Sheva has the most chess grand masters per capita in the world. (Gavin Rabinowitz, "Beersheba Masters Kings, Knights, Pawns," *LA Times*, Jan. 30, 2005.) A typical example of a great Jewish chess player is David Ben-Gurion, first prime minister of Israel, who used to secretly play chess behind the Knesset plenum when he was bored with the superfluous debates in the Israeli government!

3. See Aron Nimzowitsch, *My System*, ed. Lou Hays (Dallas, TX: Hays Publishing, 1991), 33–34. Note that the wording there is slightly different.

all, "chess is so inspiring that I do not believe a good player is capable of having an evil thought during the game."[4]

And so it is with Halacha. Who would have a bad thought while studying the *Avnei Milu'im*[5] and *Ketzot ha-Choshen*,[6] two of the most sophisticated halachic works ever to appear on earth?

Halacha is like the greatest chess game on earth. It is the Jewish "game" par excellence. For the person who wants to live a life of great meaning and depth, nothing is more demanding and torturous while simultaneously uplifting and mind-broadening. He or she loves the rules because they are the way to freedom. *All the real chess player wants is to play chess.*

They recognize that others may wish to play dominoes or Rummikub. And that's fine. But the chess player smiles, for those games can't hold a candle to chess. They are child's play. The serious chess player embraces this greatest game of all because the impossible rules give him the thrill of life as nothing else does. They make him divinely insane. On top of that, he has to choose from among many options of genius chess players to follow, which reminds us of the varied halachic positions of Rambam (Maimonides, 1135–1204), Ra'avad (Rabbi Avraham ben David, 1125–1198), Maran Rabbi Yosef Karo (1488–1575), author of the *Shulchan Aruch*, and the unparalleled Rogatchover Gaon (Rabbi Yosef Rozin, 1858–1936).

Certainly chess is just a game, while Halacha, if properly understood and lived, deals with real life, deep religiosity, moral dilemmas, emotions, and intuitions far more significant than a chess game. One who plays chess in real life will realize that if he "plays" well he's on the right track to drawing closer and closer to the King, until he is checkmated and, unlike in a chess game, falls into the arms of the King.

---

4. This quote is attributed to Austrian and later American chess Master player Wilhelm Steinitz, the first undisputed world chess champion from 1886 to 1894.

5. A halachic work by R. Aryeh Leib ha-Kohen Heller (1745–1812), which explains difficult passages in *Shulchan Aruch, Even ha-Ezer*, which deals mainly with marital issues.

6. A halachic work by Rabbi Heller, which explains difficult passages in *Shulchan Aruch, Choshen Mishpat*, which deals mainly with business and financial laws.

Chapter 33

Halacha, Legal Hairsplitting,
and the Great Compliment

Few matters are as misunderstood as Judaism's "obsession" with Halacha. Not a moment goes by in the life of a religious Jew that he is not reminded of his many obligations, both religious and moral, as codified in the various works of Jewish Law. While there is a great need to reconsider many of these laws in light of global modernization and new developments, it cannot be denied that its relentless demands appear to be out of all proportion and sometimes bordering on the absurd. Halacha often deals with seemingly hairsplitting trivialities, such as how to tie one's shoe, or how many grams of matza one must eat on the first night of Pesach.

This stands in opposition to Judaism's principles of faith, where we find nearly endless freedom of thought. Beliefs were never finalized in a dogmatic system such as we find in the Church. Not even all of Rambam's Thirteen Principles of Faith were accepted as final. In fact, they were strongly criticized and even rejected. Throughout the centuries, and to this very day, there has been an ongoing debate about what the Jew is "obligated" to believe.[1]

Halacha, on the other hand, is far more normative and standardized. Moses Mendelssohn's observation, "The spirit of Judaism is freedom in doctrine and conformity in action,"[2] is most illuminating. Judaism is basically a religion without (an authorized) theology, in which the correct deed is much more valued than any of its beliefs.

Since the earliest days, Judaism has often been attacked, even ridiculed,

---

1. See Marc B. Shapiro, *The Limits of Orthodox Theology: Maimonides' Thirteen Principles Reappraised* (Oxford: Littman Library of Jewish Civilization, 2004).
2. Moses Mendelssohn, *Jerusalem*, chap. 2, quoted in Abraham Joshua Heschel, *God in Search of Man: A Philosophy of Judaism* (NY: Farrar, Straus and Cudahy, 1955), 322.

by Christian thinkers as well as by some of the most sophisticated philosophers in modern times. Baruch Spinoza, Immanuel Kant, and many others have accused Judaism of dangerous behaviorism in which man loses his freedom and becomes imprisoned in a web of laws that make his life miserable and devoid of spiritual joy. How, after all, could such a system be conducive to the kind of life we all long to live? Where is its spirituality?

Even more surprising is the fact that Jews throw a party every time another member of their community is literally coerced to comply with all these laws. The bat mitzva girl and the bar mitzva boy are both forced into this covenant of the law when they respectively turn twelve and thirteen years old. While up to that moment they are not obligated by any of these laws (except for educational reasons) and are therefore able to still enjoy their freedom, all of this changes overnight when they reach the age of twelve or thirteen.

Instead of a party, one would expect a solemn gathering of heavy-hearted friends and relatives, where these children can mourn and are offered consolation, similar to people who have just lost a dear one. After all, losing one's freedom is not much different from losing life itself.

Yet, religious Jews have an inborn love for the law. Anyone who has ever studied in a yeshiva cannot forget the joy that permeates the study hall when a student manages to "discover" a new explanation or "invent" one when no explanation was known to exist. While Orthodox Jews sometimes seem to be more in love with the law than with God, demonstrating that they do not see the forest for the trees, one cannot help but be flabbergasted by the fact that they would nearly give up their lives for one little law that seems, in the eyes of others, to be of no importance and even ridiculous.

What is the secret behind this devotion?

Religious Jews seem to know something that few people have understood. For them, freedom can be earned only by great discipline. One needs to conquer it and work hard to maintain it every moment of one's life. *Freedom is the will to be responsible*. It is a mental state, not just a physical condition. Its primary requirement is to live for something that is worth dying for. A life without a mission is not worth being born into. It is only through dignity that one becomes free, and "the dignity of a person stands in proportion to his/her obligations."[3]

There is no greater injustice than bringing a child into the world without

3. Heschel, *God in Search of Man*, 216.

giving her or him a mission to live for. While most people today believe that one should not burden children with obligations and rather allow them to make their own choices, Judaism teaches that giving children the feeling that they have a great task to fulfill is giving them the option to experience immense joy. *Joy is what human beings experience once they feel they are growing in their moral and spiritual responsibilities.*

Most people will complain when asked by their employer to take on a difficult task and will try to free themselves of the assignment. What they don't realize is that by doing so they miss out on exactly what they are looking for – a compliment. A wise boss will know the art of judging his employee properly. By giving him a difficult task, he sends a strong message: "I believe in you." Every challenge presented is, in fact, a vote of confidence: "I know you can do it."

It is for these reasons that religious Jews revel in their many obligations. They do not see them as a yoke, but rather as tributes and praise for their greatness and unlimited potential. For them, they are not just 613 *commandments*,[4] but 613 *compliments*. To them, the question is not why they have so *many obligations*; the question is why so *few compliments*. Only 613? It is this that prompts them to look for many more, and they will sometimes use the most far-fetched arguments to derive yet another custom or law. They will debate, arguing backward and forward, just to discover one more "compliment," as if searching for a diamond. Nothing motivates them more than the potential joy of receiving another such vote of confidence.

When Jewish religious children reach the age of twelve or thirteen, their parents are elated at the prospect that they too will now enter into "the covenant [of compliments]." To celebrate this, they will throw a party, however exorbitant the cost. It is a moment of great joy. And even when the non-religious Jew or Israeli no longer understands this truth, but still insists that his daughter will celebrate her bat mitzva or that his son will celebrate his bar mitzva, that insistence indicates that deep down he still knows what it really means to be Jewish.

Still, this can't be the whole story. It cannot be denied that Halacha sometimes seems to go overboard. It turns a triviality into a major issue, as if life depended on it. Is there any meaning to a law that requires one to

---

4. This is traditionally accepted to be the number of commandments mentioned in the Torah. Obviously, not all these commandments apply to the average Jew. See *Makkot* 23b–24a. For a discussion, see R. Yerucham Fishel Perlow in his commentary to *Sefer ha-Mitzvot* of Sa'adia Gaon (Jerusalem: Keset, 1973), 1:5–7.

tie the left shoe before the right one? What is the purpose of rabbinical arguments over the size of a *Kiddush* cup, or the length of a *lulav*, or whether the middle leaf at the very top of the *lulav* can be slightly split or not? Yet, these are part of halachic discussion, and many pages in the Talmud are devoted to such issues. Indeed, this seems to justify the claim that much of Halacha is absurd legal hairsplitting. It appears as though Halacha is the art of making a problem out of every solution.

What, then, is the purpose of all this?

Upon taking a closer look, we discover a most remarkable idea: Halacha apparently tries to turn everything, including the mundane and the trivial, into a moment of eternity. It searches for the infinite by looking carefully at the finite. It wants to mesh the earthly with the holy. It seems to reveal God's concern with man by calling on him to leave the world of mediocrity and turn a simple deed into a divine moment. Halacha is convinced that no action can be trivial, not even tying a shoe, since it takes place in God's presence and must therefore be significant.

Scientists dedicate their lives to the minutest details of animal life. They are fascinated by the properties of a cell, the habits of an insect, and the peculiarities of the DNA code. It is the minutiae that captivate them, not the generalities. In a similar way, the great halachic authorities tremble over the smallest particulars of human life (Heschel). They look for the specifics of every human move and try to discover the divine breath in the tiniest detail. Nothing is too small to escape their attention.

How is the scientist able to sit for months behind a microscope watching a cell move? Is this not torture? Not at all. For the scientist, it is most meaningful and a moment of tremendous excitement. It is deeply moving. Here is life in its grandeur! Similarly, the religious Jew will look into the microscope of his soul and wonder which blessing is the appropriate one for a certain food. After all, each edible item, with its unique taste and color, represents something wondrous that should really command our full attention. One of the great privileges offered to humankind is the opportunity to unravel a minor matter and respond to it appropriately, thereby turning the ordinary into a great encounter with the Infinite. Only when man takes advantage of this gift can he claim that he really lives.

But all of this makes sense only as long as one is constantly mindful. Once the blessing on food becomes automatic and commonplace, much of its purpose is lost. No doubt most of us suffer from this problem. We are no longer sensitive to the world as were the sages who looked for the microscopic peculiarities and spiritual DNA of our lives. This has become one of the greatest tragedies of modern Jewish religious life.

The last thing to do, however, would be to stop saying a *beracha*, or to drop some other halachic requirement. After all, we can't wait for a great moment of religious fervor, which often eludes us for long periods of time. It may never come. Our souls would remain utterly silent if not for the fact that Halacha creates a routine of wake-up calls. But we must *know* that such halachic requirements *are* wake-up calls, and treat them accordingly. Once we forget this, the observance of Halacha becomes almost hypocritical.

Just as musicians practice daily in the hope that one day they will "get it" and play Bach's Piano Concerto no. 1 in E Major in all its enormous vitality, so must the religious Jew practice Halacha in the hope that perhaps, even if only once in his life, he will "get it" in religious terms. Once he lets go of such aspirations, he has lost the very essence of living a halachic life.

To realize this goal, religious education will have to wake up from its slumber and make a drastic turnabout. It will first have to introduce its students to the magnificent music behind the commonplace and the trivial.

To encounter the Infinite while standing with one's feet on the ground is the great privilege of humankind. Judaism's claim that human beings can achieve this is one of the highest compliments it has bestowed on them. Even when they tie their shoes!

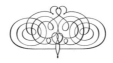

Chapter 34

Pesach, the Paradox of Freedom, and Hefty Halachic Restrictions

Nothing is more dangerous to the wellbeing of the human species than the mistaken understanding of the notion of freedom. Today, freedom is defined as the ability to do whatever one wants. Entire generations have been thrown into a life of meaninglessness, passivity, and boredom in the name of this artificial freedom. It wreaks havoc on many fine souls who no longer have a sense of what they are living for. After all, a life with no mission and commitment is not worth living.

Even in the religious community we find many youngsters who observe the commandments by rote because of social pressure or out of fear of punishment. They dream of freedom, of liberating themselves from their many obligations. Yet, they are unaware that these very obligations are the manifestations of genuine freedom, and a life with no boundaries is a life of confinement.

It is remarkable that Pesach, the Jewish festival of freedom par excellence, is associated with so many restrictions and obligations. All forms of *chametz*, leaven, are forbidden to be in one's possession, and even a crumb can become an issue. The precise rituals to be followed on the Seder night, when Jews celebrate their freedom, are painstaking and even grueling for the modern, carefree soul. What kind of freedom are Jews celebrating on the very evening of their forefathers' departure from Egypt? A life of even more restrictions?

When speaking of obligation, people say, "My duty calls me." The metaphor is clear: a duty *calls*. It is far removed and needs to call so that one shall hear. For human beings to hear, they must come closer. But they may decide to keep their distance, living their lives free of duty.

This is not the case in the Hebrew language, which expresses the concept of obligation very differently. In its worldview, duty has arms that embrace human beings and will not let them go. The Mishna often uses an illuminating expression. When describing someone who has not yet done his duty, it states: "Lo yatza yedei chovato" (This [mitzva] has not yet left the hands of his obligation). In Judaism, one's duties are not long distance calls. Rather, they hold human beings in their grasp, and only when one has lived up to one's duty can the human being claim to be free. *It is the refusal to do one's duty that casts one into confinement.*

Judaism is the art of making a problem out of every solution. It correctly believes that what is taken for granted is boring; it does not get our attention and therefore has no significance. Only when we see something as a challenge and give it thought do we come alive. A sense of duty reflects awareness that the trivial is critical. There is no growth except in the fulfillment of one's duty. Without it, man does not live fully; he merely exists, but does not experience the seasons in his soul.

Surely man must hear the music of his obligation and realize the privilege of being charged with a sense of duty. He must simultaneously be aware that by containing himself he proves to be not the victim of his own desires but the master who rises above his limitations. He needs to know what he is free from, to experience this freedom daily, and, above all, to know how to use it.

"In der Beschränkung zeigt sich erst der Meister, / Und das Gesetz nur kann uns Freiheit geben,"[1] said Johann Wolfgang von Goethe, expressing a fundamental Jewish concept: A man is never more free than when he is involved in a life of Torah.[2]

---

1. "It is in limitation that the master really proves himself, and it is [only] the law which can provide us with freedom." Johann Wolfgang von Goethe's sonnet "Natur und Kunst, sie scheinen sich zu fliehen" (Nature and Art, they go their separate ways) in *Was wir bringen* (Tübingen: J. C. Cotta, 1802).
2. *Pirke Avot* 6:2.

Ten

HALACHA, SECULAR SOCIETY, AND THE STATE OF ISRAEL

Chapter 35

The Menora: Left- and Right-Wingers
Theocracy, Democracy, and Halacha

The Chanuka menora, sometimes called the *chanukiah*, has its roots in the menora-candelabra of the Temple. While there are many halachot regarding the appearance and structure of the biblical menora, Rashi, the great French commentator, points to a most remarkable halachic feature that commands our attention. Regarding the Torah's instruction to arrange the lamps in a way that they will shine "toward the menora,"[1] Rashi explains this to mean that all the flames in the lamps should point toward the middle light.

The Italian sage and physician Rabbi Ovadia Seforno, in his masterful commentary on the Torah, elaborates on Rashi's comments and explains that the extremists on both ends of the spectrum need to focus on the middle road, which is symbolized by the central light of the menora. While both groups are completely dedicated to Torah and its tradition, the right-wingers need to know that without those who occupy themselves with the affairs of the mundane world, Judaism will not succeed. At the same time, the left-wingers must understand that without those who occupy themselves with the study and implementation of Torah, their worldly occupations would lack the opportunity for sanctification.

Only in a combined effort, symbolized by the middle light, will there be the degree of balance required by the Torah and Judaism. This is based on the talmudic principle: "If not for the leaves, the grapes could not exist."[2]

Rabbi Samson Raphael Hirsch (1808–1888), known for his philosophy

---

1. *Bamidbar* 8:2.
2. *Chullin* 92a.

of *Torah im Derech Eretz* (the study of Torah combined with worldly occupation), comments on Ya'akov's final blessings to his children:

> The nation that will descend from you is to be *one single unit outwardly oriented*, and *a multiplicity of elements united into one – inwardly oriented*. Each tribe is to represent a special national quality; is to be, as it were, a nation in miniature.
>
> The people of Ya'akov is to become "Yisrael," is to reveal to the nations God's power, which controls and masters all earthly human affairs, shaping everything in accordance with His Will. Hence, this people should not present a one-sided image. As a model nation, it should reflect diverse national characteristics. Through its tribes, it should represent the warrior nation, the merchant nation, the agricultural nation, the nation of scholars, and so forth. In this manner it will become clear to all that the sanctification of human life in the Divine covenant of the Torah does not depend on a particular way of life or national characteristic. Rather, all of mankind, with all its diversity, is called upon to accept the uniform spirit of the God of Israel. From the diversity of human and national characteristics will emerge one united kingdom of God.[3]

Rabbi Moshe Schreiber, the Chatam Sofer (1762–1839), offers a slightly different explanation for the halachic requirement as to which direction the lights should face. He warns his readers not to deviate from the middle road. As long as Jewish Law is fully observed, one should not be too much of a right-winger or too much of a left-winger.[4] In other words, the call is not for the extremists to find a *modus vivendi*, but rather for each individual to live a life in which both extremes are avoided. The ways of God testify to religious balance. This is not to suggest a mediocre attitude toward observance or the maintaining of a religious status quo in which people no longer strive for higher spiritual dimensions. On the contrary, it advises one to understand that the ultimate goal is not to become religiously obese, but to become spiritually elevated. To become extreme is to grow plump, with the result that one topples over; to become elevated is to keep growing in smooth and continuous stages.

---

3. R. Samson Raphael Hirsch, *The Hirsch Chumash*, trans. Daniel Haberman, vol. 1 (Jerusalem: Feldheim, 2002), 693 [*Bereshit* 35:11–12].

4. R. Moshe Sofer, *Torat Moshe* on *Bamidbar* 8:2.

To walk the middle path is an art, and is much more difficult than adopting an extreme position. Those who live by extremes often do so because it is more convenient. Things are black or white, clearly identifiable. Those who love the middle road have learned to perform the balancing act, which is much closer to the truth, but a great deal more challenging. Extremism reflects a simple diagnosis of the world's problems and the conviction that everybody who disagrees is either an ignoramus or a dangerous villain.

Since the establishment of the State of Israel, the question whether the State should be governed by Jewish or by democratic values remains at the center of our national debate. Both values seem almost irreconcilable. Judaism represents a theocentric worldview in which God is placed at the center. *He* is the focus and absolute authority, while the democratic worldview places the people at the center.

In some of the most remarkable discourses by Rabbi Nissim of Gerona (14th century Spain), also called Ran, this great talmudist and thinker launched a theory in which he argued that Judaism does not subscribe to the idea of a full-fledged theocracy, but in fact favors a halachic democracy.[5] He framed a daring and highly intriguing political theory that created a separation between the law of the Torah and "the law of the king," societal law. Since Ran, like English philosopher Thomas Hobbes (1588–1679), saw the major problem of any society to be the destructive nature of man, he believed it necessary for the state to establish laws that deal with the reality of day-to-day life, which often does not live up to the spiritual requirements of the Torah. This theory, claims Ran, follows from the fact that the Torah demands, or at least allows, for the appointment of a king. The judges of the Sanhedrin, the rabbinical High Court of Israel, judge the people by the law of the Torah only. The king or the political establishment, however, is permitted – and even required – to judge citizens by different criteria in accordance with the needs of the time, and sometimes even against the standard ruling of the Torah.

According to this model, Halacha seeks to create a certain duality within the Jewish polity and allows space for a democratic model in which *man* decides the law, not only God. This is with the full permission, nay, on the initiative of God Himself as reflected in the Torah. In other words, the Torah itself gives its imprimatur to state law: "Appoint yourselves *shoftim*

---

5. *Derashot ha-Ran*, nos. 8 and 11.

[judges sitting in the Sanhedrin] and *shotrim* [magistrates who judge according to 'the law of the king,' civil law]."[6]

Likewise, the Torah writes: "Tzedek tzedek tirdof" (Pursue perfect justice).[7] The repetition of the word *tzedek* (justice) can be understood as referring to justice according to Torah Law as well as justice according to "the law of the king."

We see here a fascinating balance between divine law and democracy. Both are represented and together allow society to function, while the law of the Torah is seen as the ultimate spiritual and moral objective.[8]

Rabbi Avraham Yitzchak ha-Kohen Kook (1865–1935), Chief Rabbi of Palestine before the State of Israel was established, takes this even further and points out that although we can no longer appoint a king in Israel – since only a prophet may anoint him – we see that there were Jewish kings during the Hasmonean period of the Second Commonwealth when prophecy had already ceased. Therefore, he claims, it is possible for a secular Jewish government to be appointed, like a king, once the electorate, by means of a democratic election, decides to give it authority.[9]

This, I believe, is yet another aspect of what the menora's design with the focus upon the middle light signifies.

---

6. *Devarim* 16:18.

7. *Devarim* 16:20.

8. See *Derashot ha-Ran* nos. 8 and 11. This differs from the view of Rambam and some other important halachists. See, for example, *Mishne Torah, Hilchot Melachim*, 4:10. For other opinions, see Don Yitzchak Abarbanel (1437–1508), commentary on *Devarim* 16:18 and on 1 *Shmuel* 8:4–6. R. Yosef Hayyun (15th century), commentary on *Pirke Avot, Mili de-Avot* 3:2; R. Yeshaya Horowitz (c. 1565–1630 – the Shelah ha-Kadosh), *Shnei Luchot ha-Brit*, part 2, *Torah Ohr* on *Parashat Shoftim*. For a thorough study and additional sources on this topic, see Aviezer Ravitzky, *Religion and State in Jewish Philosophy: Models of Unity, Division, Collision and Subordination*, trans. Rachel Yarden (Jerusalem: Israel Democracy Institute, 2002).

Also related to this issue is the fascinating disagreement between Rabbi Chaim Ozer Grodzinski (1863–1940), leading member of the Council of Sages of Agudat Yisrael prior to the Holocaust, and Rabbi Yitzchak Isaac ha-Levi Herzog (1888–1959), former Chief Rabbi of Israel, concerning the question of whether or not to establish a halachic state in modern Israel. Rabbi Grodzinski, who was not a Zionist, was of the opinion that the State of Israel should adopt the approach of Ran and allow for a secular government and legal system, while Rabbi Herzog, a fervent Zionist, wanted to implement a fully halachic state, not based on Ran's position, but on Rambam's legal theory! Remarkable is the fact that Rabbi Grodzinski was one of the greatest halachic authorities and had minimum interaction with secular studies, yet he was prepared to give secular law much power in the Jewish State, while Rabbi Herzog, who was as halachically brilliant as Rabbi Grodzinski and held several advanced degrees including a PhD, would not hear of it! Rabbi Chaim Ozer Grodzinski's letter was published in Rabbi Yitzchak Isaac ha-Levi Herzog, *Techuka le-Yisrael al pi ha-Torah*, ed. I. Warhaftig (Jerusalem: Mossad HaRav Kook, 1989), 2:75. For more information about this debate, see ibid. 65–89; Ravitzky, *Religion and State in Jewish Philosophy*, 11–14.

9. *Mishpat Kohen*, no. 144, section 14.

Chapter 36

Halacha and Secular Law
Duties or Rights?

There has never been a period in Jewish history during which Halacha has been so challenged as it is in our days in Israel. For nearly two thousand years, Jews were living under foreign rule and as such were able to play the role of what I call "comfortable spectators," as far as governance was concerned. They stood on the sidelines while the nations under whose rule they lived – monarchies, democracies, and everything in between – struggled with their legal and moral problems. These nations often looked for new ways to improve their legal systems. They often changed their minds about standards of morality and kept on searching for more successful political systems.

On a few occasions Jews secretly smiled when they saw how these nations miserably failed to succeed. As such, the Jew saw himself as the good old wise brother who knew it all. We convinced ourselves that if only these nations would listen to *us*, things would work out better. While it is true that Jewish individuals were sitting in many a Gentile government, as a *nation* the Jews never participated in these governments. Under such circumstances it was relatively easy to criticize and to convince oneself of one's supreme wisdom. We were sure we would do it much more successfully. We did not have to prove ourselves. After all, we did not have a country in which to do so. And so we were able to hold on to our convictions without being challenged. This was indeed one of the very few luxuries we were granted in exile. We could easily criticize and feel smug while the Gentile world was struggling. We were, and stayed, spectators.

Since our return to our homeland, however, everything changed. We were no longer the onlookers. We became full actors. Suddenly we were asked to create a legal system for our new Israeli state. Suddenly we had to do it ourselves and now it was up to others to feel smug.

To run a secular but Jewish country is an almost impossible task. It is nearly a contradiction in terms. This is due to many factors, but one of them is no doubt the fact that the purpose of secular law is different from the purpose of Jewish Law.

Two great Jewish thinkers, living in two totally different worlds, made this point in an almost identical way. One was Rabbi Eliyahu Eliezer Dessler (1892–1953), who was the *Mashgiach Ruchani*, spiritual leader, of the Ponevezh Yeshiva in Bnei Brak, and the other was Professor Moshe Silberg (1900–1975), deputy member of the Supreme Court of Israel.

Both made the following point:

Secular law is *rights* orientated, while Jewish Law is *duty* orientated. While the main point in secular law is to defend and to uphold the rights of citizens, Halacha is a system which constantly emphasizes the moral and religious duties of all men. This is borne out by the fact that the Torah never expresses itself in terms of human rights, but always in the form of human obligations: "Thou shalt . . . and thou shalt not. . ."[1]

This automatically creates tension between modern society and the Jewish ideal. Modern society sees its success in terms of making sure that its citizens are content, living comfortably and with great physical satisfaction. It is in this that man must find his liberty. Not so in Judaism. Judaism sees man's liberty in terms of duty; not what man would like to do, but what he ought to do.

We could say this a little differently. Secular law's major task is to guarantee and uphold the concept of civilization, i.e., to make sure that man behaves in a civilized way. After all, this will lead to the greatest form of comfort and physical welfare.

This is not the purpose of Halacha, Jewish Law. Judaism is not interested in the civilized man per se. Judaism is the art of surpassing civilization (Heschel). Judaism is interested in the creation of *tzaddikim*, righteous people. Its most central word is *kedusha*, holiness. It is the task of man to be holy, not just to be civilized.

I believe that this lies at the root of the great conflict between the religious ideal of the Jewish State and the secular one. Is it at all possible to create equilibrium between these two value systems or ideologies, or

---

1. See Moshe Silberg, *Kach Darko shel Talmud [Principia Talmudica]* (Jerusalem: Magnus Press, 1998); R. Eliyahu Eliezer Dessler, *Michtav me-Eliyahu* (Kiryat Noar, 1963), vol. 1, *Kuntras ha-Chesed*.

are they mutually exclusive? Right/Duty; *Kedusha*/Profaneness; God centered/man centered.

There is, however, a second question: Does the Halacha incorporate a system in which it is able to function in a secular system which does not buy in to its ideology? And even more important is the question of whether the Halacha knows of a way in which it is capable of inspiring the secular system to slowly but surely incorporate more and more of its duty and *kedusha*-orientated ideology.

And above all: is Halacha capable of initiating a step-by-step healing process so as to bring its original ideology of *kedusha* back into the center of Jewish life? Are there halachic limitations on Halacha for allowing this to happen? The answer to these questions is a resounding yes. See the previous chapter.

The Halachic Toleration of Heresy
A Command to Cancel the Commandments

Halacha deals with human life on two levels: the intellectual and the emotional. Life is the constant interaction between the two. To deny one of them is to deny life itself. Halachic demands must therefore function in a dialectical setting. Sometimes they must respond to cold intellectual human calculation, and other times they must provide guidance during emotional upheavals in life. Mostly, they attempt to bring some purpose into the emotional condition of man so as to return him to the ways of reason and religious thinking.

Only in *one* case does Halacha allow man's emotions to have the upper hand with hardly any restraint demanded, or even suggested.

"One whose dead relative lies in front of him is exempt from the recital of the *Shema* and from prayer and from *tefillin* and from all positive precepts laid down in the Torah."[1]

This is a remarkable and revolutionary ruling which runs contrary to conventional halachic thinking. Why would a person whose relative just died and is not yet buried be exempt from all precepts? Were the mitzvot not given to be observed at *all* times? Since when is one permitted to cancel commandments?

Moreover, would the fulfillment of mitzvot at this hour not be of tremendous religious and therapeutic meaning? Would it not be Judaism's obligation to step in and offer consolation by demanding religious commitment and asking the surviving relatives to be even more particular in their devotion to God? Perhaps in this way people could better deal with

---

1. *Berachot* 17b.

their loss. Why relieve them of their religious obligations at the very time when it is most needed?

Even more astonishing is the fact that Halacha's leniency does not merely *allow* the person to discontinue the mitzvot but *insists* that the person does so. It *forbids* the Jew from observing the precepts.[2]

By reflecting more deeply, one cannot but marvel at Halacha's profound insight into human nature. By recognizing the full emotional implications of having lost a relative, Halacha allows, and even demands, a most unusual condition: momentary heresy.

During the time period between the death and burial of a close relative, i.e., "when the dead is [literally] still in front of us," there is no way that a human being can be fully religious. At this hour, doubt in the justice of God often sets in, accompanied with questions about the very existence of God. How could God have done this to me? Why did He cause my loved one to die? Why should I continue to believe in Him? The mourner's fright and confusion at this moment are too overwhelming for him to accept any rational argument that, after all, God does exist and knows what He is doing. Halacha tolerates these torturous thoughts and does not try to repress them. By doing so, it reflects great compassion for the suffering human being. "It permitted the mourner to have his way for a while and has ruled that the latter is relieved from all *mitzvot*."[3] Although Halacha is convinced of the eternal existence of the human soul as well as God's absolute justice, it fully recognizes man's emotional devastation at this hour and allows such a person to have heretical views, and even a temporary exemption from positive mitzvot and the yoke of Heaven.[4]

It may well be that Halacha alludes to something even deeper: By insisting that man *stops* observing the commandments, it warns him not to fall victim to *constant* religious certainty. It is impossible for even the most religious person not to have strong doubts about God's justice, or even His existence, when confronted with death and suffering. Not having these doubts renders authentic religiosity impossible. When one has

---

2. See *Shulchan Aruch, Orach Chaim* 71:1 and *Yoreh De'ah* 341:1. For a discussion, see R. Yitzchak Yosef, *Yalkut Yosef, Hilchot Bikur Cholim ve-Avelut*, siman 7:11 n11.

3. These observations were made by Rabbi Joseph B. Soloveitchik in his eulogy for the Talner Rebbe, Rabbi M. Z. Twersky. See Joseph B. Soloveitchik, *Shiurei Harav: A Conspectus of the Public Lectures of Rabbi Joseph B. Soloveitchik*, ed. Joseph Epstein (Hoboken, NJ: Ktav, 1974), 66–70. While the thoughts expressed in this essay are inspired by R. Soloveitchik's observations, I depart from his interpretation of this idea and offer a different approach.

4. See *Tosafot*'s remarkable observation on *Berachot* 17b, s.v. "patur me-kriat Shema" in the name of the Jerusalem Talmud that one can only observe mitzvot when one is busy with life and not with death.

no doubts, one can neither have genuine certitude. *Doubt proves that one is serious about faith.* The quest for certainty surely blocks the search for meaning. So how can one ask the mourner to say a *beracha* or a *tefilla* when it is impossible for him to back up any of these words? Hypocrisy ensues in those who convince themselves always to be sure and never to doubt.[5]

Only after burial, when the dead is no longer before the mourner, can the spiritual healing process begin. From that moment on, the mourner is again fully obligated to observe all the precepts. Certainly, doubts are still there. But at this stage, by demanding full participation in all the commandments once again, Halacha applies its golden rule of "Na'aseh ve-Nishma" (*we shall do* preceding *we shall hear,* as uttered by the Israelites at Sinai).[6] There is a need to re-enter life.

Judaism's recognition of God is not the triumphant outcome of philosophical deduction. It results from the performance of mitzvot. Through the observance of the commandments we perceive the Commander. In *doing,* one *perceives.* In carrying out the word of the Torah, man is ushered back into the everlasting covenant and into the certainty of God's presence. The divine sings in the mitzvot. After burial, once the shock of what happened has lost some of its impact, Halacha asks the Jew again to make use of his or her religious nature. It appeals to their *neshama* and reminds them that by definition they belong to the category of *homo religiosus* and therefore have no escape from God and His Will.[7] The healing process will surely take a long time, but it is set in motion the moment the dead has been buried. There is then a need to go back to life and recognize that one lives in the presence of God.

---

5. The conventional reason for the dispensation from precepts at this hour is the halachic ruling "Osek be-mitzva patur min ha-mitzva." See *Sukka* 25a, 26a. When one is fully occupied with a mitzva, in our case the preparations for the burial, one is exempt from all other mitzvot since one cannot perform two mitzvot at the same time. This, however, does not explain why, according to most authorities, other relatives who are not fully occupied with the burial are also forbidden to pray, etc. Our interpretation fully explains why this is so.

6. *Shemot* 24:7.

7. It should be noted that the mourner is only forbidden to observe the *positive* precepts. The prohibitions continue to apply at all times since dispensation from them would wreak havoc in the person and destroy the fabric of society. One may also argue that observance of the prohibitions are not so much to fill the need to recognize God, but more to prevent negative conditions which make this recognition much harder. Obviously, the mourners, who are already shaken in their beliefs, should not have their doubts reinforced.

Eleven

PRACTICAL ISSUES IN HALACHA

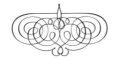

Chapter 38

Take the Bike or Tram, Get a Free Coffee, and Observe Shabbat!

The religious and traditional Israeli Jewish population is on the rise, while the secular population is shrinking. Over the last few years, studies have shown that the number of Israelis who do not observe religious traditions has decreased, comprising only one-fifth of the total Israeli population. This is in contrast to earlier times (in 1974) when 41 percent of Israelis declared themselves secular. Approximately one-third of the general Israeli population considers itself fully observant and the number of (partially observant) traditional Israelis has risen from 38 percent to about 50 percent.[1]

This should make us think. While it is true that the increased observance among Israelis is not always for genuine and healthy reasons, and often goes hand in hand with extreme political views, it cannot be denied that within the next fifty years Israel will probably see an enormous growth in Jewish pride and religious commitment.

As a matter of fact, it is well known that a greater number of secular Israelis would like to become more observant. However, for various practical reasons or due to social pressures, they are unable to make this switch.

One of the great challenges to observance, if not the greatest, is Shabbat – the only official day of rest in Israeli society when people enjoy visiting their family and friends who may live far away or who may be in

---

1. See Asher Arian and Ayala Keissar-Sugarmen, *A Portrait of Israeli Jews: Beliefs, Observance, and Values of Israeli Jews, 2009* (Jerusalem: Israel Democracy Institute Publications, 2012). The book is based on a survey conducted by IDI's Guttman Center for Surveys for the AVI CHAI Foundation. See also the report by Matthew Wagner, "Drastic Decline in Israelis Who Define Themselves as Secular," *Jerusalem Post*, Nov. 23, 2007.

hospital. Many would love, on Shabbat, to go to a restaurant and enjoy an afternoon ride through neighborhoods in Yerushalayim or other cities. But none of this is possible without the use of cars or taxis and with no open kosher restaurants.

SHABBAT BICYCLES

Here are some suggestions to overcome these obstacles:

According to one of the greatest halachic Sephardic authorities, Rabbi Yosef Chaim of Baghdad (c. 1834–1909), also known as the Ben Ish Chai, there is no prohibition against riding a bicycle on Shabbat; that is, where carrying is halachically permitted, through the use of an *eruv* (a symbolic wall around a city or part of a city), which is found in almost every city in Israel. In his opinion, all objections to riding a bicycle on Shabbat are highly questionable. The three most quoted reasons for forbidding it are: (1) *shema yetaken mana* – if the bicycle breaks down there is concern that the rider may repair it; (2) it is considered one of the *uvdin de-chol* – weekday activities, which are not in the spirit of Shabbat; and (3) *mar'it ayin* – an act that is permitted, but might be confused with something else that is definitely forbidden.

According to the Ben Ish Chai, these objections have no halachic foundation. Firstly, he says, "There are numerous items vulnerable to breakage that we would have to prohibit" and "we should not issue new decrees that weren't made by the Rabbis of the Talmud." Secondly, riding a bicycle is not considered a weekday activity (surely not in Israel!). And thirdly, the *mar'it ayin* argument does not apply, since no one can confuse riding a bike with riding other vehicles such as cars or even horses and wagons, which are inherently different.[2]

This is why members of the Syrian Orthodox community in Brooklyn, NY, ride bicycles on Shabbat to the synagogue, to visit their parents, or just to get around the neighborhood.[3]

---

2. R. Yosef Chaim of Baghdad (Ben Ish Chai), *Rav Pe'alim, Orach Chaim*, vol. 1, no. 25.

3. With many thanks to my dear friend and great halachic authority, Rabbi Moshe Shamah, rabbi of the Sephardic Institute in the Syrian community of Brooklyn, who brought these sources to my attention. Not all authorities agree with the Ben Ish Chai. R. Ovadia Yosef initially seems to agree with his opinion, but out of deference to the many halachic authorities who ruled stringently on this matter, he ruled that it is appropriate to be stringent and refrain from riding a bicycle on Shabbat. See the following works by R. Ovadia Yosef: *Livi'at Chen* on *Hilchot Shabbat* (Jerusalem, 1986), 181–184; *Halichot Olam* (Jerusalem: Machon Me'or Yisrael, 2002) 4:241–245; *Yabia Omer*, vol. 7, *Orach Chaim*, no. 37; Ibid., vol. 9, *Orach Chaim*, no. 108; Ibid., vol. 10, *Orach Chaim*, nos. 27, 54, 58; *Yechaveh Da'at*, vol. 2, nos. 48, 52. See also R. Ya'akov Chaim Sofer, *Kaf*

In Israel, permitting the use of bicycles on Shabbat would greatly increase Shabbat observance among those who now drive cars to visit their parents and friends. Once they know that they could take a bike, some would be delighted to become *shomrei Shabbat*. Perhaps specific paths for bike riders could be designated for Shabbat so as to prevent accidents. Special Shabbat bikes should be available, which can't go faster than a certain speed, are decorated with beautiful colors, and have a halachically permitted Shabbat light to indicate that this is not an ordinary bike. Ultra-religious neighborhoods could decide not to permit this in their own localities.

There is little doubt that this would result in fewer cars on the road and a wonderful atmosphere of nationwide tranquility, something that Israelis only encounter on Yom Kippur. It would also allow people to walk in the middle of the road on Shabbat, which would become a national joy. Our psychologists, environmentalists, and physicians will surely encourage such a novelty, even though they may lose some business!

SHABBAT TRAM

Now that Yerushalayim has introduced the light rail, and many other cities may follow suit, it might be a good idea to consider a "Shabbat tram," which would have a special service to visit the various hospitals.[4] This will no doubt require considerable technical, innovative, and halachic thinking to ensure that Shabbat is not violated, but in an age of unprecedented major scientific breakthroughs, it should not be so difficult to overcome all the obstacles. We can leave it to the great inventors at the Zomet Institute in Alon Shvut, Gush Etzion.

Obviously, these trams should run infrequently in order not to spoil the Shabbat atmosphere in the streets. They should be colorfully decorated with flowers and Shabbat themes, have comfortable seats, and drinks available. They should travel more slowly than on weekdays and be free of charge. We should not ask non-Jews to operate these trams – it is time to stop the "Shabbos goy" phenomenon in modern Israel! We must make sure that we can run it ourselves, making use of several halachic leniencies and innovations.

---

ha-Chaim, Orach Chaim, 403:8. For a general overview, see D. Super, "Bicycle Riding on Shabbat and Yom Tov," *Or Hadorom, The Australian Journal of Torah Thought* 6 (Summer 1989): 5–15. For a comprehensive survey of the various opinions, see R. Yitzchak Yosef, *Yalkut Yosef, Orach Chaim*, 337:3 n3 ("Din Davar she-Eno Mitkaven").

4. See also J. Simcha Cohen, *Shabbat, The Right Way: Resolving Halachic Dilemmas* (Jerusalem: Urim, 2009), 181–202.

RESTAURANTS

Finally, I wonder whether it would be possible to open some kosher restaurants on Shabbat, especially in the less religious neighborhoods.[5] Such restaurants would be fully Shabbat observant, where people could get a drink and a piece of cake free of charge and have the opportunity to meet their friends. Bnei Akiva and other youth organizations should take an active role in running such cafés. They could become a place for communal singing, lectures, debates, and other religious-cultural activities on Shabbat. Perhaps relaxing Jewish music could be played in the background by setting an MP3 player on a Shabbat clock.

Large American and Israeli companies should finance such initiatives, and people could pop in during the week to donate some money to the restaurant they visited, or they could pay in advance if they so desired.

SPIRITUAL SHABBAT

It is, however, especially important that we do not lose sight of the *spiritual* aspect of Shabbat, which is a day that protests against the bustling commerce and the mundanity of our lives. It must save us from our weekday agitation and the almost insatiable appetite for acquisitiveness that threatens to betray our spiritual needs.

Israel greatly needs traditional Shabbat observance before it falls victim even more to the idolization of ourselves and our physical needs. We must therefore make sure that all the above suggestions go hand in hand with a call for more spirituality and authentic religiosity. These suggestions should not be seen as an attempt to seek leniencies for the sake of leniencies. The goal must be more genuine Shabbat observance and more people tasting the immense joy and serenity of the day.

It was the great Jewish American psychologist Erich Fromm who wrote: "One might ask if it is not time to re-establish the [traditional] Shabbat as a universal day of harmony and peace, as the human day that anticipates the human future."[6]

We should therefore look for ways that will allow the less observant to experience the wonders of Shabbat by making it easier for them to participate in its holiness.

---

5. Lately several organizations have taken up this idea. Unfortunately, it has been opposed by the official rabbinate.

6. Erich Fromm, *To Have or To Be* (London: Abacus, 1979), 58.

Chapter 39

Let Us Violate Shabbat so as to Sanctify It
The Holy Day and the Tel Aviv Railway

He who wants to enter the holiness of the [Sabbath] day must first lay down the profanity of clattering commerce, of being yoked to toil. He must go away from the screech of dissonant days, from the nervousness and fury of acquisitiveness and the betrayal in embezzling his own life. He must say farewell to manual work and learn to understand that the world has already been created and will survive without the help of man. Six days a week we wrestle with the world, wringing profit from the earth; on the Sabbath we especially care for the seed of eternity planted in the soul. The world has our hands, but our soul belongs to Someone Else. . . .

The seventh day is the exodus from tension, the liberation of man from his own muddiness, the installation of man as a sovereign in the world of time. . . .

The Sabbaths are our great cathedrals; and our Holy of Holies is a shrine that neither the Romans nor the Germans were able to burn. . .[1]

Shabbat is serious business, not only because of its halachic requirements, but also because of its magnificent and majestic message. To violate it is not just a transgression, but a tragedy. Its desecration undermines what it means to be human and to be a real Jew. It deprives humankind of its own sublimity.

It is not the renouncement of technical progress that Shabbat requires,

---

1. Abraham Joshua Heschel, *The Sabbath: Its Meaning for Modern Man* (NY: Farrar, Straus and Giroux, 1951), 13, 29, 8.

but rather the attainment of a degree of independence from the never-ending race that is our physical existence – the everyday struggle that denies us the ability to embrace the presence of an eternal moment.

There is only one sanctity that is even greater than Shabbat and that is the holiness of the human being. When we have to choose between these two sanctities, Jewish Law is clear: The human being takes precedence.[2]

If it is true[3] that the Tel Aviv Light Rail and the high-speed train connecting Tel Aviv and Yerushalayim will indeed save countless human lives by having people switch from car to rail, Halacha will, without doubt, demand of us to work on Shabbat to complete construction as soon as possible. Any postponement would be a terrible violation of Halacha itself.

But as Jews, let us make it into a celebration. We can observe Shabbat while working on this holy day. Instead of asking non-Jews to take our place, let us gather as many religious Jews as possible to join in this undertaking and do this work in the spirit of Shabbat and Halacha. Here are some suggestions:

We can organize shacks at the work sites where some people will make *Kiddush* (sanctification of Shabbat with a blessing over wine) and where a special Shabbat atmosphere will be created, and tasteful Shabbat meals, kept warm according to the laws of Shabbat, will be served. There will be alternate *minyanim* (sing. *minyan* – quorum of ten required for public prayer) where the workers can hear the reading of the *parasha* (weekly Torah portion) and say their Shabbat prayers in shifts. Participants can sing Shabbat songs and someone could give over a *devar Torah* informing everyone of the great mitzva they are performing by working on the holy Shabbat so as to save lives.

Let us give all the workers specially designed Shabbat helmets and ask all others involved to wear special *kippot*.

There can be flags and ribbons flying and large posters displayed at the work sites proclaiming: "The people of Israel shall keep the Shabbat, observing the Shabbat throughout the ages as a covenant for eternity."[4] "And one shall live by them [My laws] . . ."[5] "and not die because of them."[6]

Let us make a Jewish celebration out of this. We can show our fellow

---

2. *Yoma* 85b; *Mishne Torah, Hilchot Shabbat* 2:3.

3. For a broad discussion about the concept of *pikuach nefesh* (preservation of life) and its halachic ramifications, see R. Isser Yehuda Unterman, *Shevet me-Yehuda: Mahadura Kamma u-Batra* (Jerusalem: Mossad HaRav Kook, 1983), *Sha'ar Rishon*, "Pikuach Nefesh," 3–103.

4. *Shemot* 31:16.

5. *Vayikra* 18:5.

6. *Sanhedrin* 74a.

Israelis and the world that we love Shabbat, but that it will not stand in the way of the sanctity of human life. It will actually advance our spirit and commitment to Judaism.

We can reveal that Halacha can deal with the requirements of a modern democratic Jewish state in an unprecedented way.

This is a once-in-a-lifetime opportunity. Let us not fail to live up to the challenge of making us all proud to be committed Jews.

After all, is it not Shabbat that made us Jews and that now gives meaning to the State of Israel? Why, in fact, be Jewish if not for this great institution called Shabbat?

Sure, some of my readers will say that these suggestions are insane. But remember what philosopher and writer George Santayana once said: "Sanity is a madness put to good uses."[7]

---

7. George Santayana, *Interpretations of Poetry and Religion* (NY: C. Scribner's Sons, 1900), 261.

Twelve

CONVERSION
AND WHO IS A JEW?

The following essays on conversion are paradoxical.
The author's goal is to suggest different sides to this serious
issue, and these essays should be read in this spirit.

Chapter 40

Soul Jews and Halachic Jews
Ideal and Reality

What makes one a Jew? Being born to a Jewish mother? Converting to Judaism? Not really. It is living by the *spiritual order* of Judaism that makes one a Jew; living *through* the Jews of the past and *with* the Jews of the present and future. We are Jews when we choose to be so; when we have discovered Jewishness on our own, through our search for the sacred; when we engage in the never-ending spiritual struggle to find God, realize that the world needs a moral conscience, and carry that exalted burden so as to save the world and provide it with a mission.

One becomes a bit more Jewish when one realizes that there cannot be nature without spirit and there is no neutrality in matters of moral conscience. But all this is not enough. We have a long way to go before we grow into full-fledged Jews. We must recognize the noble in the commonplace; endow the world with majestic beauty; acknowledge that humankind has not been the same since God overwhelmed us at Sinai;[1] and accept that humankind without Sinai is not viable.

To create in ourselves Jewish vibrations we need to see the world *sub specie aeternitatis* (from the perspective of eternity). We must be able to step out of the box of our small lives and hold the cosmic view, while at the same time not losing the ground under our feet. We achieve this not by escaping our trivial day-to-day endeavors through denial or by declaring them of no importance, but rather by dealing with them and using them as great opportunities to grow. In this way they become sanctified. As one painstakingly discovers this, one slowly becomes a Jew.

---

1. Abraham Joshua Heschel, *Moral Grandeur and Spiritual Audacity: Essays*, ed. Susannah Heschel (NY: Farrar, Straus and Giroux, 1996), 185.

Some of us have to struggle to attain this – others seem to be born with it. They possess a mysterious Jewish soul that nobody can identify, but everyone recognizes. It has something to do with destiny, certain feelings that no one can verbalize. What is at work is the internalization of the covenant between God, Avraham, and later, Sinai. It is in one's blood even when one is not religious. It murmurs from the waves beyond the shore of our souls and overtakes our very being, expanding our Jewishness wherever we go.

Most Jews "have it," but so do some non-Jews. They *know* they have it. It is thoroughly authentic. They are touched by it as every part of one's body is touched by water when swimming, its molecules penetrating every fiber of one's being. Nothing can deny it.

These are the authentic Jews, but not all of them belong to the people of Israel. Some are Gentiles with Gentile parents; others are children of mixed marriages. If they should wish to join the Jewish people they would have to convert in accordance with Halacha, although they have been "soul Jews" since birth.

But why are they not already full-fledged Jews, without a requirement to convert? All the ingredients are present! Why the need for the biological component of a Jewish mother, or the physical act of immersing in a *mikva* (ritual bath)?

The reason must be that Halacha is not just about religious authenticity and make-up of the soul. It is also about the down-to-earth reality of life. It asks a most important question: How shall we recognize who is Jewish and who is not? Can we read someone's soul? How can one know for sure whether one is really Jewish? Can one read one's own soul and perceive it? How do we know that our Jewish authenticity is genuine?

The world is a complex mixture of the ideal and the practical, where genuineness can easily and unknowingly be confused with pretentiousness. To live one's life means to live in a manner where the physical constitution and the inner spirit of man interact, but also clash. There is total pandemonium when only the ideal reigns while the realistic and the workable are ignored.

Tension, even contradiction, between the ideal and the workable is the great challenge to Halacha. It therefore needs to make tradeoffs: how much authenticity and how much down-to-earth realism? How much should it function according to the dream and the spirit, and how much in deference to the needs of our physical world?

As much as Halacha would like to grant full dominion to the ideal, it must compromise by deferring to indispensable rules that allow the world to function. Just as it must come to terms with authenticity versus conformity, so it must deal with authentic Jewishness and the necessity to set external and even biological parameters for defining Jewish identity. And here too, there will be victims and unpleasant consequences.

Some "soul Jews" will pay the price and be identified as non-Jews, despite the fact that "ideal" Halacha would have liked to include them. However unfortunate, Halacha must sometimes compromise the "Jewish soul" quality of an individual, who, because of these rules, cannot be recognized as Jewish. Were we not to apply these imperatives, chaos would reign.

But there is more to it than that. There needs to be a *nation* of Israel, a *physical* entity able to carry the message of Judaism to the world. All members of this nation must have a common historical experience that has affected its spiritual and emotional makeup. There need to be "root experiences," as Emil Fackenheim calls them,[2] such as the Exodus from Egypt, the crossing of the Reed Sea, and the revelation at Sinai. The impact of these events crafted this people into a most unusual nation, ready to take on the world and transform it. For Jews to send their message to the world they need to have a historical experience – as a family and later on as a nation – in which people *inherit* a commitment to a specific way of living even when some of its members object to it.

The fact that Judaism allows outsiders to join, though they were not part of this experience, is not only a wondrous thing, but is also based on the fact that not all souls need these root experiences to become Jewish. They have other qualities that are as powerful and transforming, and that allow them to convert as long as they are absorbed into a strong core group whose very identity is embedded in these root experiences.

In terms of a pure and uncompromised religious ideal, this means that some Jews should not be Jews and some non-Jews should be Jews. Authenticity, after all, cannot be inherited; it can only be nurtured. Ideally, only those who consciously take on the Jewish mission, and live accordingly, should be considered Jews. If not for the need for a Jewish people, it would have been better to have a Jewish *faith community* where people can come and go depending on their willingness to commit to the Jewish

---

2. See Emil Fackenheim, *God's Presence in History: Jewish Affirmations and Philosophical Reflections* (NY: Harper Torchbooks, 1970), 8–14.

religious way and its mission – similar to how other religions conduct themselves.

So, the demands of Halacha create victims when some "soul Jews" are left out of the fold, as is the case with children of mixed marriages who have non-Jewish mothers, or children of Jewish grandparents but non-Jewish parents. Similarly, there may be Gentiles who have Jewish souls but no Jewish forefathers at all. All of these are casualties.

This is the price to be paid for the tension between the ideal and the need for compliance; for the paradox between the spirit and the law. That Halacha even allows any non-Jew to become Jewish through proper conversion is a most powerful expression of its humanity. In fact, it is a miracle.

There are probably billions of people who are full-fledged "soul Jews" but don't know it, and very likely never will. Perhaps it is *these* Jews whom God had in mind when He blessed Avraham and told him that he would be the father of all nations and that his descendants would be as numerous as the stars in the sky and the grains of sand on the seashore.[3]

---

3. *Bereshit* 22:17.

Chapter 41

Conversion Is Not About Halacha

Is conversion at all possible? This may sound like a rhetorical question since the answer is in the affirmative. Yet, this question goes to the very core of the institution of conversion, and as long as we do not deal with it, all deliberations concerning this matter are more or less meaningless. The reason for this is obvious: *Logically speaking, conversion to Judaism should not be possible.*

Just as it is impossible for a Jew whose father is not a *kohen* (priest) to become a *kohen*, similarly, it should be out of the question for a Gentile to become a Jew. Either one is born into a family of *kohanim*, or one is not. Presumably, then, either one is born a Jew, or one is not. God chose the *Avot* and their descendants as His people, and it is only *they* who can claim to be Jews. It would follow, then, that one is either part of this nation, or one is not.

Yet, conversion to Judaism is possible! How? It is the philosopher, Michael Wyschogrod (1928–2015) who, in his book *The Body of Faith*, gives an authoritative answer to this question: *By means of a miracle.*[1] A Gentile who converts to Judaism miraculously becomes part of the people of Israel. Unlike with Christianity, this does not just mean that the Gentile now shares the beliefs of Judaism, but rather that he or she *literally* becomes the seed of the *Avot* and *Imahot*. For this to happen, a quasi-biological miracle is required. The Gentile needs to be reborn as a direct descendant of Avraham and Sara. This is accomplished by immersion in a *mikva*, clearly symbolizing the mother's womb through which

---

1. See Michael Wyschogrod, *The Body of Faith: God in the People Israel* (Northvale, NJ: Jason Aronson, 1996), xvi–xxi.

one is born. The proof for this far-reaching conclusion is the fact that, according to the Torah, a convert is technically allowed to marry his or her own mother, father, brother, or sister. This may sound immoral, but for the profound, reflective thinker it is most telling and meaningful. The Torah views a convert as a completely new human being, recently (re)born with no biological attachments except to Avraham and Sara. This speaks volumes. It is true that the rabbis forbade converts to marry their close relatives, fearing that people might claim the Gentile gave up a stricter religion for one with more lenient rules of morality.[2] But the fact that such marriages are rabbinically forbidden does not change the fact that they are biblically permitted.

This is radically different from baptism in Christianity. After baptism, the prohibition of incest is not waived. The biological relationship between parents and the baptized person continues as before. Not so in Judaism. What is required is the *total* rebirth of a person, as if new. While Jewish Law requires full respect for one's biological, non-Jewish parents, it simultaneously makes it clear that conversion is an extreme step with radical consequences. That Judaism is prepared to make this step, against all logic, so as to allow a non-Jew to become, literally, a child of Avraham and Sara, shows it to be one of the most daring and open-minded religions. No non-Jew should be denied the possibility to join our nation when there is a sincere desire to do so, even when this very idea makes no sense.

For this reason, it is completely impossible to argue that mere immersion in a *mikva* is sufficient. It is crucial that the potential convert *desire* to become a different person and undergo a deeply spiritual transformation. Human beings are not just a mass of plasma, complicated robots, or tool-making animals who can change their fundamental selves simply by immersing in a well of water. They are souls, with deep emotions, who experience spiritual and moral struggles in which religious beliefs play a critical role. Therefore, conversion should be a well-thought-out decision, with an awareness of its implications, and rooted in the deepest recesses of the human soul. While this clearly includes the desire to become a part of the Jewish people, it is not enough. There is much more at stake.

---

2. See *Yevamot* 22a. This seems to oppose the rule (*Kiddushin* 78a and *Mishne Torah, Hilchot Isurei Biah* 18:3) that a *kohen* cannot marry a convert since she may have had sexual relations before she converted or because she comes from a (potentially) promiscuous background. It may be that this ruling came from a different talmudic tradition, or that the rabbis just felt that a woman from a (potentially) promiscuous background is not suitable to marry a priest. Halachic authorities need to examine this strange paradox more carefully and find a solution.

The convert must become a follower of Avraham's and Sara's great legacy. This includes the acceptance of the Oneness of God, the need to be righteous, and the desire to inspire the world with the great moral foundations which were later solidified at Sinai. He or she must somehow embrace the great institutions of Judaism such as Shabbat, kashrut, and sexual dignity. Striving for *kedusha*/holiness and *tahara*/spiritual purity is of primary importance.

Whether or not the convert must *a priori* take on *all* the commandments, or only some, is a matter of great debate among the authorities.[3] There are some who maintain that only a full *kabbalat mitzvot* (acceptance of the commandments) is sufficient. Anything less will not do. Others maintain

---

3. There is a vast literature dealing with the requirement of *kabbalat mitzvot* and the debate surrounding its application in contemporary times. Note the talmudic statement that "a convert who accepts the entire Torah except for one thing, we do not accept him. R. Yose ben Yehuda says, this applies even to a minor precept of the rabbis." (*Tosefta Demai*, Lieberman ed., 2:5; *Bechorot* 30b.) Indeed, based on this statement, some halachic authorities maintain that without a complete acceptance of all biblical and rabbinic laws, the conversion is null and void. See, for example, R. Yitzchak Schmelkes, *Bet Yitzchak, Yoreh De'ah*, vol. 2, no. 100. There are other authorities who take a more lenient stance. See, for example, R. Chaim Ozer Grodzinski, *Achiezer*, vol. 3, no. 26. Note also the story in *Shabbat* 31a where Hillel accepted a prospective convert although he initially refused to accept the authority of the Oral Law. For more views regarding the requirement of *kabbalat mitzvot*, and whether the lack thereof can invalidate the conversion, see R. Moshe Feinstein, *Igrot Moshe, Yoreh De'ah*, vol. 1, no. 157; Ibid., *Yoreh De'ah*, vol. 3, no. 108; Ibid., *Yoreh De'ah*, vol. 5, no. 40; Ibid., *Even ha-Ezer*, vol 2, no. 4; R. Menashe Klein, *Mishne Halachot*, vol. 10, no. 181 and *Divrei Yatziv, Even ha-Ezer*, no. 102; R. Ovadia Yosef, "Ba'ayot ha-Giyur be-Zmanenu," *Torah she-Ba'al Peh* 13 (1971): 21–32; R. Shiloh Raphael, "Giyur le-lo Torah u-Mitzvot," ibid., 127–132; R. David Bass and R. Yisrael Rozen, "Tokfo shel Giyur be-Di'avad im ha-Ger Eno Shomer Kol ha-Mitzvot," *Techumin* 23 (2003): 186–202; R. Avraham Weinrot, "Shlavei ha-Giyur u-Markivav," *Sinai* 106 (1990): 115–137, 265–280; R. Avraham Avidan, "Be-Inyan Gerut," *Torah she-Ba'al Peh* 32 (1991): 77–96; R. Asher Weiss, "Be-Inyanei Gerut," *Moriah* 18, nos. 11–12 (1993): 79–85; R. Zvi Lipshitz, "Bitul Giyur ke-she-Kabbalat ha-Mitzvot Hayta Peguma," *Techumin* 19 (1999): 115–138; R. Yitzchak Ralbag, "Kabbalat Mitzvot be-Gerut," *Seridim* 17 (1997): 42–49; R. Yisrael Rozen, *Ve-Ohev Ger: Ohr al ha-Giyur be-Yisrael* (Alon Shvut: Zomet Institute, 2010); R. Yitzchak Brand, *Briti Yitzchak: Kuntres be-Dinei Gerut* (Bnei Brak, 1982); R. Shmuel Eliezer Stern, *Sefer Gerut ke-Hilchata* (Israel, 2004); R. Mordechai Alter, *Ka-Ger ka-Ezrach* (Jerusalem: M. Alter, 2013); R. Shmuel Zajac, *Kachem ka-Ger: Knisa la-Brit be-Kabbalat ha-Mitzvot* (NY: S. Zajac, 2013); R. Zev Weitman, "Nusach Kabbalat Mitzvot la-Bet Din la-Giyur," *Tzohar* 37 (2015): 169–186; R. Chaim Amsellem, *Zera Yisrael: Chikrei Halacha be-Inyanei Gerut ve-Giyur* (Jerusalem: Mekabetz Nidchei Yisrael, 2010) and his numerous other works on this topic. See also the list of sources compiled by Itai Gitler, "Kabbalat Ol Mitzvot ba-Giyur be-Yamenu," Oct. 2013, http://rotter.net/User_files/forum/560106e825f51569.pdf.

For academic studies on the requirement of *kabbalat mitzvot*, see *The Jewish Responsa: Conversion in Jewish History*, ed. Yedidia Stern (Tel Aviv: Yediot Aharonot, 2008), 51–149, 349–360 [Hebrew]; Menachem Finkelstein, *Conversion: Halakhah and Practice* (Ramat-Gan: Bar Ilan University Press, 2006), 48–55, 161–221, 545–648; Avi Sagi and Zvi Zohar, *Transforming Identity: The Ritual Transition from Gentile to Jew – Structure and Meaning* (London: Continuum, 2007), especially chaps. 13 and 14; David Ellenson and Daniel Gordis, *Pledges of Jewish Allegiance: Conversion, Law, and Policymaking in Nineteenth- and Twentieth-Century Orthodox Responsa* (Stanford, CA: Stanford University Press, 2012), especially chaps. 4 and 5.

that a sincere desire to be a part of the Jewish people is sufficient, though not ideal.[4]

Why this difference of opinion about such a crucial and far-reaching issue?

Judaism and the Jewish people are intertwined and interact in ways which nobody can fully grasp. Are we a religion, or a nation? If we are a religion, how can it be that somebody who does not believe in God or refuses to observe even one commandment still remains Jewish as long as he or she is born to a Jewish mother? And if we are a nation, how does religion come in, telling us who belongs to the nation and who does not? Any attempt to find a solution to this problem will always fail, as it has in the past. There is no way to nail down these definitions. They elude us, and we must admit that we are confronted with one of the greatest mysteries of Jewish identity. We become aware of the existence of something we cannot penetrate.

It is for this reason that our authorities have different views on the question of conversion. Is one converting mainly into a religion, or mostly joining a nation? They realize that there is no completely satisfactory answer and have therefore been wise enough to somehow leave the question open.

Still, we must remember that without a strong religious component, conversion is a farce, just as it would be completely ridiculous to claim, conversely, that even though somebody is totally committed to all the mitzvot of the Torah and lives in its spirit, he or she would not be considered part of the Jewish people. He or she *is*, but we do not really know why or how. We need both components, religion and nationhood, but we cannot figure out how they relate to each other.

While caught in this strange mystery, however, we should neither make the mistake of thinking that only living by the laws of the Torah and Halacha and being part of the Jewish people is what is ideally required. Much more emphasis must be given to the great experience of *being* Jewish. There is something called a Jewish *neshama* (soul). Again, were we to try and define that, we may find ourselves accused of racial discrimination. Still, we all know the *neshama* is there. There is some built-in Jewish substance within us. Judaism is not only about nationhood and observance, but about living in a spiritual, emotional order which cannot be narrowed down to doctrines, dogmas, or commandments. It is important and nec-

---

4. See the conflicting statements in *Bechorot* 30b and *Yevamot* 47. See chap. 43 n5.

essary to emphasize this to someone who wants to convert. Halacha and beliefs are not enough. Somehow, he or she must inherit the great spirit of Avraham and Sara, which is more than the sum of all of the above parts, but also different from all the above. What it really is, we do not know. But it is! And how it transpires? Again, we do not know. But it happens. Again, it is a miracle wrought by God.

We can only ask that the convert accept all of this and initiate the climb up the "ladder of observance,"[5] slowly but surely, combining nationhood with spiritual nobility.

Sounds paradoxical? Well, it is! Let it be, let it be. It has served us well through thousands of years and has made us into an eternal and indestructible nation. Let us not take this lightly.

---

5. A phrase coined by Abraham Joshua Heschel, *The Insecurity of Freedom: Essays on Human Existence* (NY: Farrar, Straus and Giroux, 1966), 206.

Chapter 42

Conversion and Annie Fischer's Interpretation of Schumann's Klavierkonzert in A Minor

In the previous chapters, I suggested that we take much more notice of the Jewish people's spiritual uniqueness and of the power of Judaism so as to deeply inspire possible candidates for conversion, especially those who are living in Israel and are of Jewish descent, though not halachically Jewish.

Too little attention has been given to this matter, and most conversion programs have implemented nothing even close to what we have suggested. They pay lip service only.

It is as if the heads of these programs no longer believe in the power of Judaism, or have not understood the sweeping ideological dimensions of Jewish religiosity. So they offer a lukewarm introduction to Judaism's thought.

There is absolutely no point in teaching the intricate laws of Shabbat unless the candidate has a deep understanding of the ideological basis of Shabbat and is shown how these laws emerge from this ideology. This is true regarding every other aspect of Judaism as well.

It cannot be done in a few standard classes, quoting several authorities and thinkers. It requires in-depth treatment in which candidates can state their own opinions and are encouraged to argue with the teacher. The last thing that should happen is for the teacher to spoon-feed the students. One cannot inherit Judaism; one can only discover it on one's own with a little help from a great teacher.

This problem is widespread not only in conversion classes. It is a tragic malady afflicting a large part of mainstream Orthodoxy. We teach our children Talmud and Halacha, but little time, if any, is given to the great musical symphony behind the talmudic texts or behind the halachic codes such as the *Mishna Berura*. What is the point in teaching them these texts when they have little or no idea of what they are actually studying?

Mainstream (Orthodox) Judaism has lost its belief that Judaism is something unique and is actually the greatest idea that was ever launched in world history.

We see this decline in the fact that by now many rabbis are rewriting Judaism in ways that make it dogmatic, small-minded, and ultimately just like another mediocre religion that is completely disconnected from reality. It no longer has much to do with what Judaism actually stands for.

It is no surprise, then, that this kind of Judaism is losing many of its young people.

To argue that most people have no interest in Judaism is a fundamental mistake. Most human beings long for meaning in their lives, but are unable to find it on their own. Some don't even recognize their deep desire for it.

Just as a human being who has never had an encounter with classical music won't know what he's missing until he is introduced to Mozart, Beethoven, or Bach, so it is with Judaism. *But it all depends on who is playing the music.* Performing music is more than just playing musical notes. It is liberating them from their confinement while not transgressing them. The notes are only the departure, not the arrival.

Who will not be deeply touched and feel their souls bursting out of their bodies when they hear the late pianist Annie Fischer (1914–1995) play Schumann's Klavierkonzert in A minor?[1] Heaven descends on every sensitive human soul that hears these sounds as the intimate reverberations burst out of the instrument, which is more than just a piano.

Suddenly, the listener feels his soul being touched and taken on an incredible journey, which he has never before known. A whole new world opens up and man becomes transformed. Just as a symphony is a mission in which all the emotions of the composer, the conductor, and the musician come together, so it is with Judaism. Judaism is a mission, and it is one that most people in the world long for. *Every human being carries the potential to look at a pile of stones and imagine a cathedral.*

Most people want to be part of a mission, but since it was never offered to them, they aren't even aware of what it is they are seeking.

Somehow, many rabbis and teachers seem to have lost their own search.

---

1. Watch and listen: https://www.youtube.com/watch?v=wkMQ1q4V4Vs/.

If you have not been to paradise, you cannot lead another through this heavenly experience. French philosopher Michel de Montaigne (1533–1592) said that "the great and glorious masterpiece of man is to know how to live to purpose."[2]

Still, one cannot expect that all candidates for conversion are alike, and surely it will take time before they can grasp the uniqueness of Judaism and hear its music. Some will never be able to grow into it; others will need a long time, and for some the commitment will be too much. All this needs our serious attention.

See the next chapter for a continuation.

---

2. Michel de Montaigne, "Of Experience," in *The complete works of Michael de Montaigne*, ed. William Hazlitt, new ed. (NY: Worthington co., 1889), 561.

Chapter 43

Courage, Rabbis, Courage!
The Need for Mass Conversion

Renowned British Philosopher Sir Isaiah Berlin (1909–1997), a proud secular Jew, warns us that our need for ideal solutions is often beyond our reach and in fact dangerous.

> I believe . . . that some of the ultimate values by which men live cannot be reconciled or combined, not just for practical reasons, but in principle, conceptually. . . . You cannot combine full liberty with full equality – full liberty for the wolves cannot be combined with full liberty for the sheep. Justice and mercy, knowledge and happiness can collide . . . the idea of a perfect solution of human problems – of how to live – cannot be coherently conceived . . . there is no avoiding compromises; they are bound to be made: the very worst can be averted by trade-offs. So much for this, so much for that. . . . How much justice, how much mercy? How much kindness, how much truth? The idea of some ultimate solution of all our problems is incoherent. . . . All fanatical belief in the possibility of a final solution, reached no matter how, cannot but lead to suffering, misery, blood, terrible oppression.[1]

Powerful Orthodox rabbis who deal with the crisis of conversion in the State of Israel had better take these words to heart.

If we do not act quickly, growing assimilation will not only overwhelm the Jewish character of the State of Israel, but actually undermine its very existence and security. Nearly 400,000 Russian legal residents of Jewish descent, but who are halachically not Jewish, could unwittingly bring an

---

1. Ramin Jahanbegloo, *Conversations with Isaiah Berlin* (London: Halban, 2007), 142–143.

end to the Jewish State within the next fifty to a hundred years, once their non-Jewish children marry into Jewish families. While it is true that if their sons marry Jewish women their children will be Jewish, this is far from a healthy option. The conversion issue is not just a halachic problem, but also a sociological one. It is highly undesirable for so many people of Jewish descent to ultimately remain non-Jews, especially in Israel. It will create serious social difficulties, including discrimination and feelings of rejection, which can easily undermine a society that is already dealing with enough problems.

Unresolved issues accumulate and inevitably create catastrophes. Many people see them coming, but like sleepers in the midst of a nightmare, they do nothing because the nightmare paralyzes them.

While much more must be done to inspire people to become Jewish and observe Halacha – through a welcoming atmosphere, exciting and convincing seminars, invitations to our homes, and other means, as I pointed out in the previous chapters – demanding of people to observe all of the commandments is too much for many of them.

Here is where we need to take notice of Sir Isaiah Berlin's warning. There are no perfect solutions. A far-reaching compromise and an ideological trade-off will be necessary. We must choose between *a priori* halachic standards – only converting people who are prepared to live according to Halacha, consequently causing a flood of assimilation in the State of Israel and endangering its existence as well as the security of millions of Jews – or using every lenient halachic view to prevent that.

It will be necessary to establish a halachic ruling and to admit that the survival of the State of Israel overrules the need for such a halachic commitment on an individual level. However painful, we are not permitted to apply the conventional standards of conversion as stated in our traditional sources, since these sources never imagined a modern Jewish State that would absorb nearly 400,000 non-Jews of Jewish descent. It would be a colossal mistake to apply the strict halachic ruling, constituting a transgression of the very Halacha to which we are committed. The halachic need to convert these people, no matter what, is not the lenient ruling, but in fact the stricter one.

Instead of waiting until the candidates are ready to take on Jewish Law and only then converting them, we should *first* convert them, make them feel comfortable, invite them to our homes and synagogues, and slowly introduce them to Jewish religious values and Halacha. This should be done by way of gentle persuasion and love, with no coercion whatsoever.

We must give them the option of making their own choices, introducing them to a "ladder of observance" that they can climb at their own pace and within their own abilities. This will be much more effective than making all sorts of preconditions, which for the most part are counterproductive.

Let's tell them that it would be great if they would start observing some biblical laws and that there's no need for them to observe all rabbinical laws.[2] Let it be optional. We can inform them about the many minority opinions in the Talmud that may be more applicable to them and will speak more to their hearts. When they are ready for it, they may introduce alternative laws and practices and decide how to observe Shabbat while making use of tradition. Let us suggest that saying *Shema Yisrael* in the morning and evening is a major accomplishment; putting on *tefillin* once in a while is a most meaningful undertaking; and wearing a *kippa* all the time is not even a halacha, but can be a beautiful and pious act.[3] Let them make their own *berachot* if they want, or just say "Wow" before they eat and "Thanks" after they are satisfied.[4] Let them use their creative imagination and feel that they are gradually building their own Judaism and seeing its wonders. Slowly, some of them will discern the wisdom of the sages and introduce more of rabbinical law into their lives. They will do it willingly, out of a sincere desire to be part of this great tradition.

It is high time the rabbis realize that the very standing of Halacha is at stake. If it cannot find a realistic solution to the conversion problem, it will become less and less significant in the eyes of Jews the world over. In fact, it will prove that contemporary Halacha has run its course. Ultimately, it will lose its influence on our young people. *It is not only the survival of Jews that is at stake, but also the survival of Halacha itself.*

Most important to remember is that *kabbalat mitzvot* is not the only issue as far as conversion is concerned. Judaism is much more than just Halacha. The first convert and Jew, Avraham, was only asked to observe a few of the commandments, such as circumcision. An incubation period was required to allow for an embryonic form of Judaism which was to develop slowly and be solidified at Sinai with the giving of the Torah. In this time frame, the great moral-religious foundations of Judaism and the conditions for creating the Jewish nation were shaped. Only afterward was it possible to introduce the world of mitzvot and Halacha. We should allow potential converts this option to slowly work their way up to Sinai.

---

2. For a more elaborate treatment of this issue, see chap. 47.
3. *Biur ha-Gra* on *Shulchan Aruch, Orach Chaim* 8:2. See chap. 14.
4. See the minority opinion in *Berachot* 40b.

And if they will not arrive at this destination, we should be pleased that they have cast their fate with our people. Every mitzva the convert does is done as a Jew, and that in itself is a great accomplishment.[5] We can then hope that the convert's child will observe many more commandments.

At the same time we should not forget that strict adherence to the law only can actually do great harm. Every legal system works in categories of right and wrong, lawful and unlawful. But life itself is much more than any law can ever sustain or cover – even divine law. There is a narrative that slips through the net of the law and rises above it. *A nation with a mission must be constantly aware that sometimes it has to break the law so as to allow the spirit of the law and its ultimate goal to have the upper hand.*

While far from ideal from a religious or conventional halachic point of view, it may be necessary to introduce mass conversion as the only option to overcome the impending danger of countless mixed marriages in Israel, which will otherwise break the backbone of the Jewish State. Inclusiveness is now the order of the day.[6]

We must remind ourselves that since the State of Israel was established, our future is in our own hands. Never have we had such freedom to do whatever we wanted when it comes to our own destiny. No one can stop us from doing what needs to be done. This is unprecedented in the last two thousand years of Jewish history. *All that is required is courage.*

This is true about Halacha as well. It is up to the leading Orthodox rabbis to realize this and show us the way. Whether they like it or not, ultimately they will be forced to take drastic steps and change their attitude toward the issue of conversion in the State of Israel. The only question is how many casualties will there be before they come around. They should be most careful not to extend their imprimatur after the fact.

"The paradox of courage is that a man must be a little careless of his life even in order to keep it," said English author G.K. Chesterton.[7]

---

5. Chacham Ben-Zion Uziel, *Mishpatei Uziel, Yoreh De'ah* 2:58.
6. See R. Yoel Bin-Nun, "Tzarich le-Vatze'ah Giyur Hamoni," *Eretz Acheret* 17 (July–August 2003): 68–69.
7. G.K. Chesterton, "The Methuselahite," in *All Things Considered: A Collection of Essays* (CreateSpace Independent Publishing, 2016), 76.

Chapter 44

Why Did Ruth Convert Against All Odds?

When carefully reading the story of Ruth, the question of why Ruth decided to convert to Judaism is of crucial and far-reaching importance. What motivated this young woman who was educated in a most adulterous and idolatrous society to make such a radical step and commit herself to a lifestyle which, like no other, makes great moral and ritual demands on its followers? What is there in Judaism which is able to defeat the lusts of sensuality, materialism, prestige, and easy lifestyle which was represented by the nation of Moav?

This question is most intriguing and of great importance. Once we can discover the answer, we may be able to find a solution to a problem which has the State of Israel in a quandary and which may very well become its most taxing problem in the near future. With a population of hundreds of thousands of inhabitants who are, although of Jewish descent, halachically not Jewish, there is a need to find a way to motivate many of them to make the conversion step. Not to do so will otherwise lead to a great amount of mixed marriages which, in years to come, will undermine the Jewishness of the Jewish State.

In the case of Ruth, this question is even more complex since Ruth never did live in a Jewish environment. It is in Moav, not Israel, where she meets the highly assimilated Jewish family of Naomi, her future mother-in-law. Elimelech, the husband of Naomi, is a selfish personality who had run away from his own people because he was not prepared to help its poor at the time of a severe famine. His commitment to Judaism must have been a watered-down version with little inspiration. It seems that Elimelech was more interested in the lifestyle of Moav than in the possibility of convincing anybody to become Jewish. His two sons Machlon and Kilyon seem to have lost the Jewish connection altogether when they decided to marry non-Jewish Moabite girls. There was no Jewish trace to be found in these girls, no Jewish connection whatsoever.

The only person who seems to have been intensely Jewish was Naomi, and it would not be an exaggeration to claim that there must have been a great amount of tension in the home of Elimelech and Naomi due to all the contradictions in the make-up of the family. Not a place in which to become inspired by Judaism!

It must have been Naomi and nobody else who had such an extraordinary influence on Ruth. It kept her spellbound and made it almost impossible for Ruth to make any other decision but to become Jewish. Something about Naomi must have been so persuasive that Ruth could not resist converting. It must have been so powerful that it transformed Ruth into another person.

What Naomi shows Ruth is the existence of a completely different mindset of how to see the world, its challenges, its ups and downs. When Naomi is left on her own after losing her husband and sons and is confronted with extreme poverty, she turns fate into destiny and shows a new side of what the human being can be; something that was totally unknown to Ruth.

In her time of need, Naomi showed Ruth that one can only live life as if it is either superfluous or indispensable. It is either tragic or holy. There can be no neutrality. Either we are the ministers of the sacred or the slaves of evil and tragedy. There is no escape. Either one lives in blasphemy and eternal scandal or in the presence of God and eternal holiness.[1]

Just as at Sinai, when God lifted the mountain over the Israelites and declared: "Either you accept the Torah or be crushed beneath the mountain,"[2] so too every human being must make this decision in his or her own lifetime. This is what the American philosopher William James called the forced option: There can be no compromise when it comes to the very meaning of human existence and living accordingly. Better to live in a physical wilderness than to be abandoned to profound existential meaninglessness.

What Naomi showed Ruth is that if man is not more than human, then he is less than human.[3] To really live is to surpass being average. There

---

1. See Abraham Joshua Heschel, *God in Search of Man: A Philosophy of Judaism* (NY: Farrar, Straus and Cudahy, 1955), 420–421.

2. *Shabbat* 88a.

3. Abraham Joshua Heschel, *Who Is Man?* (Stanford, CA: Stanford University Press, 1965), 103.

is no place for commonplace in a life of meaning. It was in spiritual but lonely nobility that Naomi lived all her years, absorbing this into her personality. As such, she had transformed herself into a powerhouse of deep religiosity and uncompromising commitment to the existential meaning of life. While other civilizations build physical monuments, Ruth realized that Naomi built spiritual monuments to life. She realized that in such a life God does not enslave, but sets free.

What became clear was that Naomi lived a life of spiritual protest. A protest against the neutrality in which one divides one's time between some religious rituals and secularity – in which religious life is another extra layer added to human existence instead of a radical transformation of all that one is. How we live and what we live for are the most fateful decisions we ever make.

This component of human existence did not exist in the weltanschauung of Ruth until she met Naomi. The idol worship of Moav, like all other forms of idol worship, is the worship of the common. Likewise, adultery is the outcome of existential boredom in which man, for a lack of a higher meaning, turns to his body as his redeemer to find satisfaction. It is not *having*, but *being*, which is the key to a real meaningful life.

Ruth saw that Naomi lived in a spiritual world in which all so-called trivialities take place in holiness and thereby become transformed in moments of tremendous significance. It is a world in which nothing is trivial and everything is of radical existential importance – to the point that even the tying of a shoelace is a holy act, since it takes place in the presence of God and therefore has noble meaning.

It is a life of grandeur in which nothing is taken for granted and in which all matters become profound opportunities to be amazed by. It is not a life which is compatible with the ordinary, but one to marvel at.

What Naomi teaches Ruth is that it is not worth being born into a life without commitment. The dignity of man stands in proportion to his obligations, and it is not human rights which are ultimately important but human duties.[4]

No doubt Ruth must have been a sensitive soul, but what she proved against all odds is that all human beings have sensitive souls, which when properly approached can be transformed into a flame of deep meaning. With her Moabite background, nobody would have believed that she would be even minimally open to Jewish values and living. Still, not only

---

4. See Heschel, *God in Search of Man*, 216.

did she become genuinely Jewish, but she became the mother of the royal house of David, which one day will give birth to the mashiach. Ruth's story decisively puts an end to the argument that some people are beyond hope and cannot transform. And it was only one person, Naomi, living in an un-Jewish family, in an anti-Jewish environment, opposed by her husband and children, who was able to convey this to Ruth using nothing but her example and commitment.

When the State of Israel wants to convince its non-Jewish inhabitants to become Jewish, it will first have to learn how to create a grand picture of life and its meaning. *There is no point in starting to teach the Jewish religion, customs, and laws, or how to observe Shabbat and kashrut if one has not shown that all these observances are a response to the ultimate questions of human existence.* One first needs to convince people that the question of the meaning of life is addressed and that it demands an answer of grandeur which uplifts its members to a place in which all other matters which are not part of this picture are of no importance. But at the same time it needs to show that *all* matters, when correctly approached, take place in holiness and become significant. In this way one does not lose by becoming Jewish, but wins access to new worlds of tremendous delight.

As long as Judaism is taught as a luxury to be added to life, it is misrepresented and will be of limited appeal in the eyes of those who are asked to become Jewish. But when we teach it as being indispensable, it will become life itself and will make waves in the souls of all those we approach.

Chapter 45

Solving the Conversion Crisis
The Birth of Non-Jewish Jewish Communities:
Another Approach

Conversion is a serious matter. It signals a transformation and involves a tremendous amount of soul-searching. Human beings are more than just accumulations of plasma, complex robots, or tool-making creatures that can change and adapt at the drop of a hat. Human beings have souls and profound emotions. They experience spiritual and moral struggles in which religion plays a major part.

Conversion is a far-reaching decision: it culminates in immersion in a *mikva*, a ritual bath that symbolizes the mother's womb. "A non-Jew who converts is like a newborn baby," says the Talmud.[1] Conversion also implies a deep commitment to Jewish Tradition. It requires a pledge to follow a particular lifestyle, the observance of the commandments, and a deep emotional connection with the Jewish people. It means becoming part of this mysterious "Jewish soul," which remains unexplainable but is as real as it can be.

So, what should we do with all those people who are unable to take that drastic, far-reaching step, but still want to be part of the Jewish people? Today, Israel has many thousands of immigrants who are of Jewish descent, yet not halachically Jewish. Should we convert them even though we know that they will not live a fully committed Jewish life? Or should we abandon them, basically ignoring and excluding them as we do now? Should we suggest that they lie to the rabbinical courts and tell the rabbis that they intend to live a halachic life, although we know that they will *not*, forcing them to violate a central principle of Judaism which is to speak the truth? Should we make them guilty of ignoring countless other com-

---

1. *Yevamot* 22a.

mandments after their conversion, a situation which would be avoided if they did not convert?

Or should we convert them anyway, because of our obsession with Jewish unity and our fear that the State of Israel would otherwise be unable to survive? Yet, notwithstanding this concern, have we forgotten that the Jews exist to keep the great mission of Judaism alive? It is not the function of Judaism to keep the Jewish people alive. After all, what is the point of even having a Jewish people if Judaism is compromised and its great ethical and deeply religious message for all humankind, based firmly on Halacha, *becomes a joke?*

The answer, I suggest, is the "two brotherly people solution": *Jewish Jews and non-Jewish Jews.* This would involve creating communities of "non-Jewish Jews" in which those who are not prepared to go the whole way could develop their own brand of Judaism. They could have their own synagogues in which to practice aspects of Jewish Tradition that they wish to keep. They could decide for themselves to what extent to observe Shabbat or keep kosher. Their wedding ceremonies could make use of many Jewish rituals, and they could have their own "Jewish" cemeteries where they could adopt as many Jewish religious practices as possible rather than be forced to bury their dead in totally secular or non-Jewish burial grounds. We could set up outreach programs for them, enabling them to study Judaism and choose whichever aspects they wish to adopt. We could even create yeshivot and seminaries for this specific purpose.

In this way they would feel part of the wider Jewish community and would not feel coerced into complying with Halacha, while the Halacha would itself remain uncompromised.

To ensure that they feel at home in the Jewish State, we could offer them various privileges and advantages. We could provide a benign sort of *protekzia*, so that they would feel comfortable as loyal citizens of the State of Israel. We should help them succeed in their endeavors, so that they would want to continue living in this great country. After all, they are our brothers and sisters. *They are not goyim.* We share a sense of Jewishness with them and they are part of the family, though slightly removed.

True, this would not solve all our problems. There would be "mixed marriages" between the two communities, the non-Jewish Jews and the Jewish Jews. Yet it would be reasonable to expect that the more familiar they become with Jewish Tradition on their own terms, the more likely it would be that they would take that final step and convert properly and honestly according to Halacha. In this way they and the Halacha would both be protected against dishonesty.

The benefits of this approach would be many. And not just for the non-Jewish Jews. There can be little doubt that many halachically recognized (but distant) Jews would join the educational programs and attend the non-Jewish synagogues. It would allow many to rediscover what it means to be a Jew and give them an opportunity to become more observant without being coerced.

Halachic authorities, educators, and the government should consider this option seriously, rather than bury their heads in the sand, pretending nothing can be done. For those who suggest that we should convert our immigrants without asking them to commit to Halacha, this is surely a convincing alternative to their convoluted attempts to justify the unjustifiable. Halachic Judaism offers tremendous scope for flexibility and creativity on a level that many of our leaders have never really considered. It is time they did.

Chapter 46

Solving the Conversion Crisis
and Global Judaism

You see things; and you say "Why?"
But I dream things that never were; and I say "Why not?"
GEORGE BERNARD SHAW – *Back to Methuselah*

*In the previous chapter concerning conversion, I suggested, in contradiction
to chapter 43, another approach to deal with the crisis: the creation of Jewish
Non-Jewish communities. I propose this as a concession to those who, for sincere
reasons, could not agree with the idea of mass conversion. In this chapter I will
defend and explain their position.*

WHY, FOR THE TIME BEING, MASS CONVERSIONS ARE NOT
APPROPRIATE

Israel has been confronted with the plight of *hundreds of thousands* of
people who made aliyah, mostly from Russia, who are children of mixed
marriages or who have other Jewish ancestry, such as Jewish grandparents. Most of them are not halachically Jewish, since their mothers are
not Jewish. Yet many of them would like to become Jewish. The problem,
however, is that the majority do not want to commit themselves to a halachic way of life. (I am obviously not speaking about those immigrants who
came for purely financial or other reasons and have no interest in joining
the Jewish people. I consider it to be a major mistake on the part of the
Israeli government to allow them to immigrate without proper conditions
in place.)

The government and some other organizations want to convert many
of these people, even if it means they will not be observing Shabbat, eating

kosher, etc. By encouraging them to convert, they believe that it is solving the problem of a massive number of mixed marriages in Israel between halachic Jews and those with a Jewish background, but who are halachically not Jewish. In this way, the government seeks to prevent a major split within the Jewish people and Israel. Indeed this is a most serious issue which should be prevented wherever possible.

Although important thinkers and halachists such as Rabbi Eliezer Berkovits (1908–1992)[1] and Chacham Ben-Zion Uziel (1880–1953)[2] would (reluctantly) support such an approach, it could be argued that this is highly problematic for two reasons. Conversion is not just a commitment to become part of the Jewish people, but also to the spirit and practice of Judaism. Asking people to become Jews when there is either no or little commitment to Jewish spirit and practice is most troublesome. In religious terms it means that we are encouraging them to violate Jewish Law. While there are many opinions as to *what extent* Jewish Law requires a commitment to Halacha by the potential convert,[3] it is fundamentally

---

1. See the following works by Eliezer Berkovits: *Crisis and Faith* (NY: Sanhedrin Press, 1976), chap. 8; "Conversion and the Decline of the Oral Law," in *Eliezer Berkovits: Essential Essays on Judaism*, ed. David Hazony (Jerusalem: Shalem Press, 2002), chap. 3; *Not in Heaven: The Nature and Function of Halacha* (NY: Ktav, 1983), 106–112; "Berurim be-Dinei Gerut," *Sinai* 77 (1975): 28–36; "A Suggested Platform of Unity on Conversion According to Halakha," (Unpublished manuscript, 1974).
   For an analysis of Eliezer Berkovits' approach, see Rahel Berkovits, "The Philosophy of Rabbi Professor Eliezer Berkovits z"l Part 3: Conversion and the Unity of Am Yisrael," *Elmad*, March 20, 2016, http://elmad.pardes.org/2016/03/the-philosophy-of-rabbi-professor-eliezer-berkovits -zl-part-3-conversion-and-the-unity-of-am-yisrael/; David Ellenson, "Rabbi Eliezer Berkovits on Conversion: An Inclusive Orthodox Approach," in *Jewish Meaning in a World of Choice* (Philadelphia: Jewish Publication Society, 2014), 301–318.
   2. Chacham Ben-Zion Uziel, *Piskei Uziel be-Sheilot ha-Zman*, no. 65 and *Mishpatei Uziel*, vol. 2, *Yoreh De'ah*, no. 58. Chacham Uziel was the Sephardic Chief Rabbi of Mandatory Palestine and then Israel from 1939 to 1954, and was one of the most courageous halachists of our times. For general primary sources on Chacham Uziel's views on issues of intermarriage and conversion, see *Piskei Uziel be-Sheilot ha-Zman*, nos. 59–67; *Mishpatei Uziel*, vol. 2, *Yoreh De'ah*, nos. 53, 58. For an analysis of Chacham Uziel's views on conversion, see Zvi Zohar, "Caring for an Intermarried Jew by Converting His Partner: Rabbi Uzziel's Earliest Responsum on Giyur (Salonica, c. 1922)," in *Between Jewish Tradition and Modernity: Rethinking an Old Opposition*, ed. Michael A. Meyer and David N. Myers (Detroit: Wayne State University Press, 2014), 17–34; Zohar, *Conversion (Giyyur) in Our Times: A Study in the Halakhic Responsa of Rabbi Uzziel* (Jerusalem: Ha-Va'ad le-Hotza'at Kitvei ha-Rav Uziel, 2012) [Hebrew]; David Ellenson and Daniel Gordis, *Pledges of Jewish Allegiance: Conversion, Law, and Policymaking in Nineteenth- and Twentieth-Century Orthodox Responsa* (Stanford, CA: Stanford University Press, 2012), 126–133; Avi Sagi and Zvi Zohar, *Transforming Identity: The Ritual Transition from Gentile to Jew – Structure and Meaning* (London: Continuum, 2007), 52–53, 60–63, 229. For a study on Chacham Uziel, see Marc D. Angel, *Loving Truth and Peace: The Grand Religious Worldview of Rabbi Benzion Uziel* (Northvale, NJ: Jason Aronson, 1999).
   3. What this practically entails is a major question of which I wrote in the preceding chapters. All these matters require careful study. I believe that it is possible to make the conditions for conversion more attractive and spiritually uplifting by using altogether different criteria than those used by the standard rabbinical courts of today. See also chap. 1.

wrong to convert people when it is clear that the *basics* of Shabbat observance, kashrut, the laws of family purity, *chesed*, and Jewish ethical behavior are not going to be observed. Not only do most halachic authorities not agree with such a conversion, it is also important to emphasize that it is not in the *spirit* of Judaism either. What, after all, is the meaning of being Jewish if not for living Judaism? So when the practice and weltanschauung are not (yet) Jewish (enough), we do not do anyone any favors by signing people up as Jews.

As I have made clear in the earlier chapters, I also question the correctness of converting people when the candidates are not asked to identify with the great spiritual, moral, and religious mission of the Jewish people *even* if they do commit to live according to Halacha. Religiosity, mission, and spirit are not (solely) halachic issues, but they are part of the great Jewish spiritual narrative. Jews are there to serve humankind, to inspire it and to be a moral example. There is much more to Judaism than just halachic living. This, I believe, is a problem with many of the Orthodox conversions. *There is too much emphasis on Halacha and too little on the spirit.*

ANOTHER OPTION INSTEAD OF MASS CONVERSION

On the other hand, there is a concept in halachic thinking which states that children of mixed marriages (and similar cases) are from *zera Yisrael*, from Jewish seed,[4] and consequently cannot be viewed as complete Gentiles. Still, they are not halachically Jewish. They are somehow part of the family, but not fully.

As such, we have a moral religious duty to help these people, especially those who are living in Israel today. A lot of them mean well and would sincerely like to join us. Somehow they are part of us, but are not (yet) prepared to go the whole way and convert properly. We need to realize that all these people are living in great emotional pain and confusion. Many came on aliyah thinking they were Jewish only to discover that they are not. This is an enormous tragedy.

---

4. This idea is based on the verse in *Yechezkel* 44:22 and the exegesis in *Kiddushin* 78a. For the halachic ramifications of this concept in relation to the issues of intermarriage and conversion, see the responsum of R. Zvi Hirsch Kalischer (1795–1874), published in *Shu"t R. Azriel Hildesheimer*, vol. 1, *Yoreh De'ah*, no. 229; Chacham Ben-Zion Uziel, *Piskei Uziel be-Sheilot ha-Zman*, nos. 61, 62, 64, 65 and *Mishpatei Uziel*, vol. 2, *Yoreh De'ah*, no. 58. For a discussion on this topic, see Sagi and Zohar, *Transforming Identity*, 53–65; R. Chaim Amsellem, *Zera Yisrael: Chikrei Halacha be-Inyanei Gerut ve-Giyur* (Jerusalem: Mekabetz Nidchei Yisrael, 2010).

WHAT COULD BE DONE AND WHAT SHOULD NOT BE DONE

For this reason, I propose that we create communities, outreach programs, religious services, "Tents of Abraham"[5] *in the spirit* of Judaism – where they can choose their own style or degree of Judaism and adopt whatever they want without having to convert (yet).[6] This is different from Israeli institutions for conversion which have, as their sole goal, proper conversion, and often in a short amount of time.

---

5. See Nathan Lopes Cardozo, "The Beth Midrash of Avraham Avinu: Tentative Thoughts Towards a Jewish Religious Renaissance," in *The Tent of Avraham: Gleanings from the David Cardozo Academy*, ed. Nathan Lopes Cardozo (Jerusalem: Urim, 2012), chap. 1.

6. Note that several halachic issues pose a challenge to this suggestion, such as the talmudic prohibition against Gentiles studying Torah (*Sanhedrin* 58b), which Rambam extends to include a prohibition against non-Jews innovating religious rites of their own (*Mishne Torah, Hilchot Melachim* 10:9). There is much discussion in halachic literature about the exact parameters of these prohibitions and whether they apply to a prospective convert, a *ger toshav* (resident alien), or to a non-Jew who voluntarily wishes to accept additional commandments. For a general overview, see *Talmudic Encyclopedia*, s.v. "ben Noach," 3:357–359.

Regarding the prohibition against non-Jews keeping Shabbat, see Elchanan Adler, "The Sabbath Observing Gentile: Halakhic, Hashkafic and Liturgical Perspectives," *Tradition* 36, no. 3 (2002): 14–45; R. Ya'akov Moshe Charlap, "Ha-Shabbat ve-Umot ha-Olam," *Shma'atin* 129–130 (1997): 51–71.

Regarding the prohibition against non-Jews studying Torah, see R. Moshe Feinstein, *Igrot Moshe, Yoreh De'ah*, vol. 2, no. 132; Ibid., *Yoreh De'ah*, vol. 3, no. 89; R. Ovadia Yosef, *Yabia Omer, Yoreh De'ah*, vol. 2, no. 17; R. Yechiel Ya'akov Weinberg, *Seridei Esh*, vol. 2, no. 56; R. Yitzchak Isaac ha-Levi Herzog, "Talmud Torah le-Nochrim," in *Techuka le-Yisrael al pi ha-Torah*, ed. I. Warhaftig (Jerusalem: Mossad HaRav Kook, 1989), 1:31–38; R. Yehuda Herzl Henkin, "Limud Torah le-Nochrim be-Universita," *Seridim* 14 (1994): 58–63; Isaac H. Mann, "The Prohibition of Teaching Non-Jews Torah: Its Historical Development," *Gesher* 8 (1981): 122–173; J. David Bleich, "Survey of Recent Halakhic Periodical Literature: Teaching Torah to non-Jews," *Tradition* 18, no. 2 (1980): 192–211.

Regarding the prohibition against non-Jews performing the mitzvot, see *Igrot Moshe, Yoreh De'ah*, vol. 2, no. 7; R. Menashe Klein, *Mishne Halachot*, vol. 17, no. 91.

Regarding the special status of a prospective convert during various stages of conversion vis-à-vis the aforementioned prohibitions, see *Igrot Moshe, Yoreh De'ah*, vol. 3, no. 90; J. David Bleich, "Observance of Shabbat by a Prospective Proselyte and by a *Ger she-Mal ve-Lo Taval*," in *Contemporary Halakhic Problems*, vol. 4 (NY: Ktav, 1995), chap. 7; R. Mordechai A. Brali, "Va-Teira ki Mitametzet Hi: Ma'amad ha-Mitgayer Terem Siyum Giyuro," *Ha-Ma'ayan* 44, no. 4 (2004): 22–32; R. Yisrael Rozen, "Heter Shemirat Shabbat le-Mitlamdei Giyur," in *Ve-Ohev Ger: Ohr al ha-Giyur be-Yisrael* (Alon Shvut: Zomet Institute, 2010), 189–199 and "Ma'amado ha-Hilchati shel Mi she-Nimtza be-Tahalich Giyur", ibid., 200–212.

For more inclusive approaches regarding the keeping of mitzvot and the performance of other religious rites by non-Jews, see David E. Sklare, "Are the Gentiles Obligated to Observe the Torah? The Discussion Concerning the Universality of the Torah in the East in the Tenth and Eleventh Centuries," in *Be'erot Yitzhak: Studies in Memory of Isadore Twersky*, ed. Jay M. Harris (Cambridge, MA: Harvard University Press, 2005), 311–346; Gerald Blidstein, "Maimonides and Me'iri on the Legitimacy of Non-Judaic Religion," in *Scholars and Scholarship: The Interaction Between Judaism and Other Cultures*, ed. Leo Landman (NY: M. Scharf Publication Trust of the Yeshiva University Press, 1990), 28–33; Menachem Hirshman, *Torah le-Chol Ba'ei Olam: Zerem Universali be-Sifrut ha-Tana'im ve-Yachaso le-Chochmat he-Amim* (Tel Aviv: Ha-Kibbutz ha-Me'uhad, 1999).

This proposal has nothing to do with Reform Judaism which wants to be an authentic option for *halachic Jews* and would like to convert Gentiles or people of Jewish descent according to Reform standards which are not in accordance with Halacha and definitely unacceptable to the Orthodox.

I am proposing to create something *before* or *instead* of conversion with which the Orthodox can also agree. My suggestion will solve a major problem without violating the stricter interpretation of halachic criteria and the basic requirements of conversion. At the same time, it will prevent thousands of well-meaning converts from violating basic Halacha, which is seen by many as a tragedy.

I believe that when all those who are of Jewish ancestry (but who are not halachically Jewish) will start to taste the beauty of Judaism and grow closer to it on their own terms and at their own pace, they will in turn feel part of the Jewish people to a much greater degree, even though they may never make the final step of conversion. Additionally, many of them may then wish to convert *properly* at a later date whenever they feel ready.[7]

Other solutions avoiding any middle ground – rejecting them as if they are complete Gentiles or converting them without commitment – will lead to great problems. On the one hand, rejecting them could create great animosity against Jews and Judaism which could undermine the State of Israel. (These feelings are already coming to the surface.) After all, to be considered a Gentile when in fact one has a Jewish background and perhaps (strong) Jewish feelings, is an intolerable situation which could easily lead to a great amount of resentment.

On the other hand, trivializing Judaism makes Judaism cheap in the eyes of so many well-meaning people. Judaism requires the strong commitment of its followers. As I mentioned before, on the *minimum* level this means a minimal observance of Shabbat, kashrut, family purity, and ethical behavior. To ask anybody to convert without such a commitment

---

7. It is important to remember that this suggestion has *nothing* to do with halachic Jews, who stay complete Jews even when they violate Jewish Law. Just as American law will not allow a foreigner to become an American if it is known that he will violate American law or has made it clear that he has no intention of living according to American law, so it is with Halacha.

Still, we know that many native-born Americans violate American law. Nobody claims that they are no longer allowed to be Americans and that they should be forced to leave the country. On the contrary, they are Americans who violate American law, but they stay Americans. This, however, does not apply to non-Americans who want to "join"; they have to commit to American law. It is the same with Halacha.

I have dealt with the intriguing question of why Judaism continues to identify an apostate Jew as a full-fledged Jew even when he denies his Jewishness or converts to another religion. See Nathan Lopes Cardozo, *Between Silence and Speech: Essays on Jewish Thought* (Northvale, NJ: Jason Aronson, 1995), chap. 3.

could mean that many born Jews would not wish to marry them and they will ultimately feel betrayed. Even worse is the fact that many Jews will no longer take authentic Judaism seriously, thinking that nearly anything goes. It would also seriously undermine an important part of our tradition, i.e., the call to each one of us to keep striving for more and better observance, religiosity, and ethical behavior.

LET'S FACE IT

No doubt my suggestion will meet with opposition and is far from ideal, but in the course of time, people will realize that it may be the only option. To let the problem stay unresolved is much too dangerous. We will see a growing community of Israelis who feel more and more hostile toward Judaism and the Jewish people. (Closely related is obviously the controversy between movements such as the Orthodox, Conservative, Reform, and secular society.) Problems like these have wreaked havoc throughout Jewish history. One only needs to think of the previous era of Jewish autonomy within the Land of Israel. The Roman destruction of Jerusalem began with a war of Jew against Jew. The parallels between the fractionalization of Jewish life at the time of both the Maccabean revolt of 166–164 BCE and the revolt against Rome of 66–70 CE, and the divisions now evident in the Jewish world, are uncomfortably close.

Few people may see this danger at present, but it is clearly looming and growing stronger and may explode within fifty years. If, instead of this, we make Judaism available to all those who have a keen interest in the Jewish people and Israel and love to be connected on some level with Judaism, we may then see the growth of dynamic communities which can be of great help and an asset to our people and the State of Israel.

Most important to remember is that for this to have any chance of succeeding, changes can only take place by a slow process and not through any sudden transformation. These kinds of concepts need to be nurtured until they slowly become acceptable and even desirable. By starting with one or two communities of this sort, we may pave the way for a much larger undertaking at a later date. As often is the case, once a small group of people enthusiastically opt for this alternative, many may follow. In the event of more problems being created than solved, at least we will have tried.

Again, my proposal is not without risk, but a wise man will turn a risk into good fortune. (And an idea is made clearer and better by good opponents!) Those who seem to lose today may win tomorrow. There is no stronger enemy than an idea whose time has come, but people have not yet realized it. Many great ideas have a dangerous side to them, yet they may save us in the end.

The question is ultimately this: Is it better for people to live in this country and be recognized as either strictly Gentiles or strictly Jews, when in fact they are neither – or to be recognized as "brothers and sisters once-removed"?

In the previous chapter I suggested calling them non-Jewish Jews, but many of my friends felt that this is too confusing and perhaps dangerous. This may be true. It only means that we have to look for other possibilities. (The fact that we cannot immediately find the right terminology should never mean that we should drop an idea!) Here are several suggestions that I received from different people: Jewish non-Jews (instead of Non-Jewish Jews), Jewish Noachides, Jewish Gentiles, Israelites, Hebrews, or Abrahamists.

All of them are problematic and it will, in all likelihood, be impossible to find the terminology which is completely satisfactory. It may quite well be for the best, in the meantime, not to give these communities any name. This, however, should not prevent us from looking for ways to help those people feel part of the Jewish nation without asking them to convert and thereby prevent a much larger and more dangerous situation in the days to come. By doing so, we do not only serve those who do not want to convert and yet want to be part of our nation, but we also help the Jewish people and the Jewish State at large.

Ultimately we have to ask ourselves what is preferable. We can create an opportunity for them to connect with Judaism on their own terms. Alternatively, we have the prospect of thousands of people converting without a basic commitment to Shabbat, kashrut, etc., or conversely treating them as complete non-Jews and thereby causing a lot of injustice and animosity.

There is a need to seize the chance to solve a major problem, even if it takes courage, given that we cannot be sure of all that will be required ahead of time. This is much preferred to taking a clearly wrong turn or doing nothing, both of which will surely foster a disaster. There is a time for everything, said Shlomo ha-Melech,[8] and the time to plant and build is now.

---

8. *Kohelet* 3:1.

WORLD JUDAISM IN THE MAKING

Beyond all this, and on another plane altogether, we have to realize that the direction of humankind is slowly but radically changing. What is becoming more and more evident to those who are carefully following world history and looking beyond the here and now, is that another world is emerging in which Judaism is on the way to becoming a global movement.

After a nearly two-thousand-year-long Christian fiasco to build a better world, the increasing dangers of Islamic fundamentalism, and the failure of secularism to give man any existential meaning, humankind is looking toward Judaism more and more for moral and spiritual support and meaning. While it is not explicitly there yet, it is happening on a global scale in the minds of many fine and influential Gentiles who will shape the world of tomorrow. There will be an unquenchable thirst for the study of Judaism and an increasing number of Gentiles will start to adopt Jewish rituals and ethics. *We will see the opening of "Gentile synagogues" throughout the entire world community, taking the place of churches and mosques.* Classical Shabbat observance on Sundays will become common in many countries, as will adoption of some kind of dietary law focusing more on the human soul instead of only on the body, and it will be accompanied by a revolution on matters related to sexuality, in which Jewish marital laws will start to play an important role.

No, there will be no need to convert, and Jews will stay Jews and Gentiles will remain Gentiles. But this small, unique people will increasingly become the focus of world attention, this time as a well from which the Gentile world will drink for the acquisition of its wisdom.

The leadership of the State of Israel, together with the religious establishment, will be dumbfounded and will not know what to do when the Gentiles call for guidance. Only new creative voices within authentic Judaism, of which we are in desperate need, will show the way.

Conventional rabbis, not having the foresight to see all this, will have great trouble coping with these new winds blowing and will lose all their influence and become irrelevant. Just like email has become unstoppable today (forgive the comparison!) so too will this new spiritual trend toward World Judaism. There will be no escape. It is in the air and we are already able to smell its fragrance.

May the Holy One, blessed be He, give us wisdom.

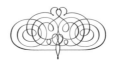

Chapter 47

Solving the Conversion Crisis
New Halachic and Spiritual Criteria for Conversion

When suggesting new ways to approach religious and halachic problems in Judaism, one must be conscious of the great responsibilities that such suggestions carry. One should never forget that one enters holy territory and touches on issues which could shake the foundations of Judaism and Jewish existence. Still, one cannot escape one's religious responsibilities by denying that there may be ways to help Judaism find solutions to serious problems, even though they may be controversial in the eyes of many greater than oneself.

It is for this reason that I reluctantly suggest new criteria for conversion. They must be seen as a response to the need of the hour in which our people finds itself. This is especially true for the State of Israel, to which tens of thousands of people of Jewish descent have made aliyah, primarily from Russia, yet who are not halachically Jewish.

JUDAISM FOR NON-CONVERTS

In the preceding chapters I suggested that we should not propose conversion to our fellow (Russian) Israelis if this clearly means that they would violate the most basic rules of Shabbat observance, kashrut, and *taharat ha-mishpacha* (family purity). (In fact some of them do not wish to convert, knowing that it would be contrary to the spirit of Judaism; nor do they want to be hypocrites by deceiving the rabbinical courts.) Instead, I suggested that we should encourage them to become involved in the values and some rituals of Judaism according to their own pace and desire. This could be done through the creation of special outreach programs and even special "synagogues," thereby creating a love in their hearts for Judaism without violating the basics of normative Halacha for conversion. As such, they could somehow be part of "the family" without being fully Jewish.

As mentioned before, the creation of such an option would have to be a process which could slowly but surely become increasingly acceptable to all those to whom it applies, and may even be an inspiration to the Jewish people in general.

"MINIMUM" CONVERSIONS

I also mentioned in the previous chapters that, in those cases where we *do* speak of conversion for those immigrants, *minimum* standards of Jewish observance should be required, but with great doses of inspiration. Obviously such conversions are not ideal since we would like to see a *full* commitment to Jewish law and spirit. Still, there are reasons why we should perhaps permit such "minimum" conversions as an alternative to conversions without any halachic commitment, as reluctantly suggested by Chacham Uziel, Rabbi Eliezer Berkovits, and others.[1] This is especially urgent because of the precarious situation of those (Russian) Israelis who would like to become Jewish, but for whom it is too much to commit to *all* of Jewish Law at once. No less important is the fact that my suggestion incorporates a greater opportunity for converts to slowly grow into Judaism and make it into a much greater spiritual experience. Let me now try to explain what I mean by minimum standards and spirituality.

RABBINICAL LAWS IN THE TALMUD

Over the past two thousand years, Judaism has become a complex way of living. The reason for this is that many adjustments had to be made to deal with changing circumstances, whether internally or externally induced. Rabbinical laws had to be added,[2] including *gezerot* (decrees) and *takanot* (enactments)[3] in response to these new circumstances. In order to accommodate the enormous challenges Jews would have to face, especially in *galut* (exile), the sages created a labyrinth of additional laws and customs. In general this was a most successful undertaking. For nearly two thousand years, Judaism was not only able to stay alive, but even managed

---

1. See chap. 46 nn1–2.
2. See *Talmudic Encyclopedia*, s.v. "divrei soferim," 7:91–106.
3. See Nathan Lopes Cardozo, *The Written and Oral Torah: A Comprehensive Introduction* (Northvale, NJ: Jason Aronson, 1989), 114–118.

to continue to develop into a very rich tradition that would inspire many generations to come.

The greater part of the Talmud deals with these rabbinical ordinances and only a small part deals with the biblical laws themselves. As is well known, the latter include not only the biblical laws as found in the *text* of the Torah itself, but also the oral interpretations of these laws which, as the Jewish Tradition claims, were simultaneously given by God to Moshe at Sinai. Therefore these oral laws are also biblical in nature and need to be treated as such.

One of the most famous examples is the 39 types of work which are forbidden on Shabbat. Although these are not mentioned in the biblical text, since they were given orally at Sinai together with the biblical text prohibiting "work" in general, they are in fact considered biblical and of divine origin.[4] They are *not* rabbinical laws. The Talmud calls them *mi-de-Oraita* (from the Pentateuch).

DISPUTES IN THE TALMUD

In post-biblical times, especially when the Jews were forced to live outside the Land of Israel, the general commitment to these biblical laws started to waver. Once it became apparent that many Jews were increasingly violating these laws, the sages started to build fences around them so that the biblical laws *themselves* would not be violated. (An example is the rabbinical institution of the law of *muktza* which forbids the moving of any item which could lead to the violation of the biblical laws of Shabbat, for example a pencil that one might inadvertently write with.) Such laws are to be found throughout the Talmud and they deal with almost all the biblical laws. However, they are also the cause of most of the disputes in the Mishna and both Babylonian and Jerusalem Talmuds. Many hundreds of pages have been written discussing these sub-laws and arguing about the best ways to accomplish their goals.

Some sages had a more lenient attitude while others were stricter. Some considered certain suggested laws to be too extreme while others thought they were too lax. But without any doubt it is *these* laws which have made Jewish religious life both complicated *and* beautiful. They gave a unique flavor to Jewish life in the Diaspora and created a Jewish culture

---

4. See *Shabbat* 49b.

full of customs and halachic details as well as a special way of conduct and thinking.

Following the days of the Talmud and in subsequent centuries, several great authorities, such as Rambam (1135–1204), continued to discuss and codify these laws, culminating in the "finalization" of them in the most famous and influential code of Jewish Law, the *Shulchan Aruch*. It was authored by Rabbi Yosef Karo (1488–1575), a sage of tremendous learning (with glosses by Rema, Rabbi Moshe Isserles [1525–1572]), and became the standard work of Jewish Law until this very day.

Here one can find *all* the biblical and rabbinical laws (that are still applicable in exile), yet one can no longer differentiate between them since they are all treated as equal in status. To distinguish which are biblical and which are rabbinical, one has to go back to the Talmud itself, and even there it is not always clear.

ONLY BIBLICAL LAWS

Instead of insisting that every convert commits him/herself to all these rulings (as required by the major rabbinical courts today) or conversely, as suggested by Chacham Ben-Zion Uziel and Rabbi Eliezer Berkovits[5] to (reluctantly) allow conversion without even a minimal commitment, perhaps there could be a third option: i.e., to demand from all converts that they fully observe all the *biblical* laws (as understood by the Oral Tradition), but *not* make the same requirements as far as rabbinical law is concerned.[6] While it is true that this might not always be possible or appropriate,[7] it could be suggested in many instances.

---

5. See chap. 46 nn1–2. It is important to realize that the requirement of *kabbalat mitzvot* as the most important and crucial requisite for conversion is not accepted as such by all authorities, although it is by the vast majority. There is a minority view which states that what counts is the willingness to join the Jewish people. It is not entirely clear what the underpinnings of this opinion are in theological terms since it may lead to the violation of the commandments, as I already mentioned. It is, however, this opinion on which Chacham Uziel and Rabbi Berkovits seem to rely. My argument here is that this opinion is not only not accepted, but is in fact utterly rejected by nearly all rabbinical courts and the rabbinical establishment and does not seem to have a chance of ever being accepted. It is for this reason that I suggest another approach. No doubt my suggestion could also be rejected, but as long as it has not yet been properly discussed, it is our duty to bring it to the attention of our rabbinical authorities. Moreover, my suggestion is more conservative than those of Chacham Uziel and Rabbi Berkovits (although others may argue it is also more radical). For an outstanding study about conversion, see R. Yaaqov Medan, *Tikva me-Ma'amakim: Iyun be-Megillat Rut* (Alon Shvut: Tevunot, 2007), chap. 2.

6. See chap. 41 n3.

7. There are instances where rabbinical laws make the applications of biblical laws easier by combining several biblical rules which are very complicated, such as in the case of the laws relat-

PRAYER, SHABBAT, BICYCLES, AND MUSIC

Here are just a few *simple* suggestions: Does there need to be a requirement that male converts *must* pray three times a day? (According to some
authorities, only the recitation of *Shema Yisrael* in the morning and evening is biblical, and even according to Rambam who writes that there is
a requirement to pray every day, the requirement to pray the designated
prayers three times a day is a rabbinic obligation.)[8] Is it necessary to go to
the synagogue on weekdays and Shabbat? Or to insist that one is not to
ride a bicycle on Shabbat?[9] Not play music on Shabbat?[10] Do men need
to go with their head covered at all times?[11] Put on *tefillin every* weekday?
Must married women cover their hair?[12] Is it necessary for the convert to
know *all* the different kinds of *berachot* when the blessing of *she-hakol nihya
bi-devaro* (by Whose word everything came to be) would be sufficient for
most food products? What would be if the convert does not say any *bera-*

---

ing to sexuality, purity, and impurity (*nidda*). On other occasions, the removal of rabbinical laws
could create too serious a danger of violation of the biblical laws.

8. For a comprehensive survey of the various opinions, see R. Yitzchak Yosef, *Yalkut Yosef,
Orach Chaim,* "Hakdama le-Hilchot Tefilla," 1 n1.

9. Till this day, many Orthodox members of the Syrian Jewish communities bicycle to the
synagogue on Shabbat (when there is an *eruv* permitting carrying objects in the street). This was
allowed by one of the greatest Sephardic halachic authorities, Rabbi Yosef Chaim of Baghdad,
the Ben Ish Chai, in *Rav Pe'alim, Orach Chaim* 1:25. See chap. 38 for a more comprehensive
treatment of this issue.

10. The prohibition of playing musical instruments on Shabbat and festivals is rabbinic. In the
First and Second Temples, singing and musical instruments accompanied the sacrifices that were
offered, including on Shabbat and festivals (see *Mishna Arachin* 2:3; *Sukka* 50b; *Mishne Torah,
Hilchot Klei ha-Mikdash,* chap. 3). However, playing musical instruments on Shabbat and festivals
in a non-temple setting was prohibited, lest one come to fix a musical instrument (see *Betza* 36b),
or because of excessive noisemaking, which disturbs the Shabbat rest (see *Shabbat* 18a and *Eruvin*
104a). *Mishne Torah, Hilchot Shabbat* 23:4 and *Shulchan Aruch, Orach Chaim* 338:1 rule accordingly. *Tosafot* on *Betza* 30a, s.v. "tnan en metapchin ve-en merakdin," however, maintain that this
only applied when people were skilled to fix musical instruments. R. Menachem ha-Me'iri wrote
that the students of Ramban played instruments on Shabbat. See *Magen Avot, Teshuvot Rabbenu
ha-Me'iri* (Jerusalem: Ma'ayan ha-Chochma, 1958), 60–61. For a detailed discussion, see R. Ovadia Yosef, *Yechaveh Da'at,* vol. 3, no. 49. Interesting is the fact that according to some opinions
all music is forbidden – even on a weekday – since the days of the destruction of the Temple (see
Gittin 7a). For a detailed discussion, see Aharon Kahn, "Music in Halakhic Perspective," *Journal
of Jewish Music and Liturgy* 9 (1986–1987): 55–72. The article continues in *Journal of Jewish Music
and Liturgy* 10 (1987–1988): 32–49 and in *Journal of Jewish Music and Liturgy* 11 (1988–1989):
65–75.

11. Many members of the Orthodox Syrian communities never walk with their heads covered
unless they are praying, learning Torah, or eating. In earlier rabbinic sources, walking with a head
covering was considered a pious deed, but not a halachic demand. For an excellent overview of
this issue, see Dan Rabinowitz, "Yarmulke: A Historic Cover-Up?," *Ḥakirah* 4 (Winter 2007):
221–238. See also chap. 14.

12. Some opinions state that this law is biblical, whereas others say that it is rabbinical. See,
for example, *Ketubot* 72.

cha at all, or formulates his or her own one?[13] We can suggest many more examples, but this would be beyond the scope of this essay.

Many of these are rabbinical in nature[14] and some are even of lesser status. Some originally started as customs and became, over the years, standardized as law.

LET THE CONVERTS DECIDE

Would it not be better that they, the converts themselves, decide in an autonomous way which rabbinical laws they will adopt and which not? Why not just suggest these beautiful laws and customs, but not actually *insist* on them? As long as the biblical laws are being observed, both the positive and the negative ones, we should perhaps allow such conversions.

MINORITY OPINIONS?

Another most serious question to consider is whether it would be permissible to suggest minority opinions in the Talmuds as halachic options for the convert, even though they are not accepted by mainstream Judaism. After all, these rejected alternative opinions are recorded because they are considered to be of great value, especially in emergency situations where they are often relied upon. And is that not exactly what we are talking about?[15]

MAKING JUDAISM MORE ATTRACTIVE

The motivation behind our suggestions is not just to make it easier on the potential convert. To make Judaism just "comfortable" is, in my humble opinion, entirely the wrong strategy. What is at stake here is to make it more attractive and meaningful. My suggestion allows the convert to grow into Judaism, step by step, and to discover it in an autonomous way, which may lead to a much deeper commitment than when he or she is forced to commit to everything at once in a short span of time.[16] A gradual

---

13. See chap. 2 n31.

14. As mentioned, it should be noted that there are disputes in the Talmud as to whether certain laws are biblical or rabbinical.

15. See chaps. 2 and 46.

16. This may be behind the Talmud's statement in *Yevamot* 47a, that the *bet din* needs to inform the potential convert of *some* of the mitzvot, but seemingly not *all*. "Once he/she accepts them, we immediately accept him/her." This is codified in *Shulchan Aruch, Yoreh De'ah* 268:2. See the

acceptance of more and more of the Halacha makes it possible to internalize more deeply the new way of life with desire and integrity, instead of a
quick and superficial adherence through demand and compliance.

At the same time, it could solve the most urgent problem of mixed
marriages between halachic and non-halachic "Jews," which is critical for
the State of Israel and the future of the Jewish people.[17] After all, both
would be halachic Jews.

THE NEED FOR SPIRITUAL CONVERSIONS

This brings us to my second suggestion: The need to emphasize much
more spirituality when dealing with conversion. This is not to be seen,
as Paul[18] suggested, *instead* of Halacha, but as a *result* of halachic living.
Judaism is a response to the mystery of life and what to do about it. The
ultimate question is how to live in the presence of God, which is by far the
most difficult task a human being can ever be confronted with. Halacha is
the way to sanctify even the most trivial aspect of a human being's life. It is
not there to be "observed," but to be experienced in the deepest chambers
of one's soul. It is the way to perceive the infinite through the finite. Or,
as Abraham Joshua Heschel so beautifully states, "A Jew is asked to do
more than he understands in order to understand more than he does."[19]
Halacha is also there to live with the right kind of deeds so as to pave the
way to correct thinking, feelings, and emotions.

The meaning of Judaism is to live with a mission for the sake of the
betterment of all humankind and to introduce it to God and His ethical

---

whole section which shows a very balanced way in which the potential convert is approached by
the rabbinical court.

17. It can obviously be argued that this suggestion could also apply to all Jews and not just to
converts. One might suggest that they should also be able to decide which rabbinical laws they
would like to keep and which ones not. Indeed, this would be a possibility for all those Jews
who are not fully committed. Better that they keep the biblical laws than no laws at all. Still, it
would be too dangerous to make this the *official* policy for all religious Jews. It would undermine
the unity of the religious community in ways that would compromise the survival of Judaism.
Rabbinical laws are an *inherent* part of Judaism, not to be discarded lightly. The Torah itself
emphasizes the need to listen to the sages' directives and considers them crucial. See *Devarim*
17:11. See also Nathan Lopes Cardozo, *The Written and Oral Torah: A Comprehensive Introduction*
(Northvale, NJ: Jason Aronson, 1989), 74–78. As such, one needs to deal with the question of
whether this directive should also apply in the case of conversion, since, as mentioned above, the
Talmud demands from the rabbinical court that it informs the converts of *some* of the commandments, but not of *all*. See n16 above.

18. Since Paul, the rejection of Halacha became a major foundation of Christianity. See chap. 7.

19. Abraham Joshua Heschel, *God in Search of Man: A Philosophy of Judaism* (NY: Farrar, Straus
and Cudahy, 1955), 283.

guidance. Jews are asked to be a holy people and are told that it is not enough to be civilized, but to try to surpass civilization.

To be a Jew is to refuse to surrender to mediocrity, normalcy, and even to the laws of conventional history. It is a covenant which the first Jew, Avraham, agreed on with God, to build a world on the basis of ethical monotheism and to bring humankind to the messianic age.

Judaism is a protest movement against all that hinders this goal. These points are undoubtedly insufficiently emphasized when people convert. Often they are totally neglected, and the minutiae of the Halacha are *all* that counts. This is a great tragedy. It ignores much of the very essence of why these minutiae are of such vital spiritual importance and what Judaism is all about.

ACCEPTABLE TO THE REFORM AND CONSERVATIVE MOVEMENTS?

Finally, I wonder whether Reform and Conservative Judaism have a place in this approach. Would they be prepared to tell their potential converts that they *must* observe all the applicable *biblical* laws, as we mentioned above, as their requirements for conversion? If they would, all conversions could be done under the auspices of such an Orthodox *bet din*.

BELIEF AND HALACHIC OBSERVANCE

Of course, there are major differences of opinion between these denominations concerning the fundamental beliefs of Judaism. While Orthodox Judaism believes in the absolute divinity of the Torah text, the Conservative movement is not completely committed to this belief, and the Reform movement even less so. But the halachic question is whether one needs to fully believe in this "principle of faith," or whether it is sufficient to *treat* the text *as if* it is entirely divine and live accordingly, even when one has doubts about it.[20] This is a matter of dispute, and there are definitely

---

20. There is also a difference between those who doubt and those who definitely do not believe. See Rabbi Dr. Norman Lamm's brilliant article in his book *Faith and Doubt: Studies in Traditional Jewish Thought* (NY: Ktav, 1971), chap. 1. It is most important to realize that nearly all thinking religious people have moments of doubt, just like secular people have doubts concerning their secular ideologies. After all, one does not have complete control over one's thoughts. The beauty of Judaism is that it considers somebody to be fully religious when he or she *lives* according to Halacha and its spirit even when one has doubts. One is reminded of William James' famous remark that no decision is also a decision. One must act even when one is in doubt. This is the reason why Rambam's insistence that one must fully believe in his Thirteen Principles of

halachic opinions which seem to state that it is not absolutely required.[21]
If so, could this not be the basis for my suggestions above?

THE RESPONSIBILITY OF HALACHIC AUTHORITIES

As mentioned earlier, all of this needs careful consideration and study by
the great halachic authorities of our days. But it must be made clear that
they can only do so if they are open to this approach and seriously prepared to consider it. But to just reject it out of hand is unacceptable. Too
much is at stake.

Most important is to see the issue in a much larger framework than the
conventional one of conversion *only*. The matter must be considered in
the light of the precarious condition of the Jewish people today, the State
of Israel, the philosophy and religious purpose of Halacha, and the need
for authentic religiosity and the spiritual needs of Jews around the world.

This may require the halachic authorities to seek advice from those
experts who deal with the above issues so that they can see the full picture.
This is similar to the many halachic cases where they consult scientists
and medical experts. Only *then* is a halachic decision possible.

Faith has been rejected by many halachic authorities. For a discussion, see Marc B. Shapiro, *The
Limits of Orthodox Theology: Maimonides' Thirteen Principles Reappraised* (Oxford: Littman Library
of Jewish Civilization, 2004), chap. 1.

21. See, for example, R. Chaim Hirschensohn, *Malki ba-Kodesh* (Hoboken, NJ: Moinester
Printing, 1921), 2:243–245; Chief Rabbi Avraham Yitzchak ha-Kohen Kook in *Igrot ha-Rayah*
(Jerusalem: Mossad HaRav Kook, 1985) 1:20–21. See also the sources cited in Shapiro, *The Lim-
its of Orthodox Theology*, chap. 1.

Thirteen

ADDITIONAL THOUGHTS

Chapter 48

Rabbinical Courage and the Frozen Text

The Talmud discusses the identity of a *Gavra Rabba*, an exceptionally great person or Torah sage. It quotes a most remarkable observation made by the well-known sage Rava, who states: "How foolish are some people who stand up [out of respect] for a Sefer Torah, but do not stand up for a *Gavra Rabba*."[1]

When asked what is so exceptionally great about these men, Rava ignores their astonishingly vast knowledge of Torah, and even their outstanding ethical and religious qualities. Instead, he notes their power and courage to *change* the obvious and literal meaning of a commandment as mentioned in the Torah. This, to say the least, is most remarkable!

The example that Rava gives is very telling:

While the Torah commands the *bet din* to administer 40 lashes for certain offenses,[2] the sages reduced them to 39. The courage, says Rava, to change the literal meaning of the text is what made them into extraordinarily great people. They recognized the power and authority vested in them to interpret the biblical text in accordance with the spirit of the Oral Torah. This authority gave them the right, even the obligation, to change the literal meaning of certain biblical texts if it became clear that a deeper reading of these texts called for such a move. In our case, they concluded that the number 40 could not be taken literally and should therefore be reduced to 39 – or even less, in case of need.[3]

---

1. *Makkot* 22b.

2. *Devarim* 25: 2–3.

3. In earlier days, Jewish Law would sometimes demand physical lashes under very specific circumstances, but only if offenders would be able to endure them without risk to their lives. It therefore could have happened that the court would administer only a few lashes, since more

For this reason, Rava maintains that these sages should be respected even more than the actual Sefer Torah, the biblical text. After all, the text is only the frozen aspect or outer garment of the living organism, the essential Torah. It is only in the Oral Torah as explained by the sages that the real meaning of the text becomes apparent.

Still, this cannot be the full meaning of Rava's statement. If the power of the sages is revealed in their willingness to change the meaning of a text (such as in the case of the number 39 instead of 40), one should ask the following: Why didn't Rava quote the *first* case ever mentioned in the Torah where the sages changed the specific biblical number to a lesser number, and use *that* to prove that they are great people?

It is well known that on an earlier occasion the sages changed the number 50 to 49. This was in the case of the Omer counting, when the Torah requires counting a full 50 days between the first day of Pesach and the festival of Shavuot, which would then fall on the 51st day.[4]

After carefully studying the text, the sages reduced the number of these days to 49 and stated that the 50th day, not the 51st, should be Shavuot. It is remarkable that in this case Rava does *not* state that their willingness and courage to reduce the number of days made them exceptionally great men. This is especially surprising since it is the Talmud's custom to always bring proof for a specific teaching from the *earliest* biblical source possible, never a later one.

In our case, the proof of the sages' courage is learned from a verse mentioned in *Devarim*, at the very end of the Torah! This is perplexing. Why didn't Rava use the earlier verse in *Vayikra*?

The answer is crystal clear. Changing the meaning of the biblical text, or reducing a number, is not enough for a sage to warrant the title of *Gavra Rabba*.

One is a Gavra Rabba when one reduces the pain of fellow human beings!

When a sage finds ways, through biblical interpretation, to mitigate the legal punishment of another human being, only then can we speak of a *Gavra Rabba*, an extraordinarily great person.

In our case of 40 lashes prescribed by the Torah when certain offenses have been committed, it is an act of mercy to find ways to reduce the offender's sentence and administer only 39, or even less. Such initiative and courage shows absolute moral greatness.

---

would have created life-threatening conditions. See *Shulchan Aruch, Choshen Mishpat* 420:1 and *Shulchan Aruch ha-Rav*, "Hilchot Nizkei Guf ve-Nefesh ve-Dinehem."

4. *Vayikra* 23:15–16; *Torat Kohanim*, ad loc.

But in the case of reducing 50 days to 49 so as to make Shavuot fall one day earlier, there is no evident alleviation of human pain, so Rava does not characterize the sage in question as a *Gavra Rabba*, however brilliant he may be.[5]

This insight is crucial. The virtue and stature of the sages are not measured by their great learning *but by their courage.* Especially when dealing with human pain. Throughout Jewish history the great sages were prepared to look for ways to change the meaning of the divine text because they believed that this is what God expected of them when dealing with human suffering. *Apparently, they believed that the text was deliberately testing them to see how they would respond and find a good argument or loophole to reduce the devastating effect of a commandment.*

Sometimes they nullified a commandment, as in the case of the *ben sorer u-moreh*, the rebellious son.[6] They also abolished the death penalty, although the text required it.[7] This approach explains many extraordinary cases where the sages even used far-fetched arguments to avoid the sometimes harsh pronouncements of the divine text, as when they were able to free a woman from the status of *aguna*,[8] or a child from the status of *mamzer*.[9]

No one understood better than the sages the danger of an inflexible, immovable text – even one that is divine. They saw it as their task to unfreeze the frozen text of God, because that is what brings the text to life and makes it humanly livable.

Today, few things are as relevant as this principle. When dealing with so many new halachic problems that touch people's lives, we are in great need of talmudic scholars who will once again apply this remarkable approach of our sages. Those sages were proud when they found solutions to human suffering because they were convinced that this was God's will.

Rabbinical courage – nothing less.

---

5. This idea is based on an oral teaching that was transmitted to me in the name of one of the pre-Holocaust Chassidic leaders whom I was unable to identify.

6. *Devarim* 21:18-21; *Mishna Sanhedrin* 8:4; *Sanhedrin* 71a. See chap. 27.

7. *Mishna Makkot* 1:10.

8. *Gittin* 3a; *Yevamot* 122b.

9. *Kiddushin* 71a, 72b. See also the remarkable observation in *Kohelet Rabba*, Vilna ed., 4:1. See chap. 27.

Chapter 49

Are You Really Eating Kosher?
On Camouflage, Hypocrisy, and Hiding Behind the Kashrut Laws

With devotion's visage
And pious action
We do sugar o'er
The devil himself

S H A K E S P E A R E – *Hamlet*

Kosher animals, as is well known, can be identified by two *simanim* (physical signs). They must chew their cud, and their hooves must be entirely cloven.[1] In order to be kosher, the animal must possess both *simanim*. The Torah goes out of its way to emphasize the fact that an animal which displays only *one* sign cannot be considered kosher at all.

> The camel, because it chews the cud but does not part the hoof, it is unclean to you. And the rock-badger, because it chews the cud but does not part the hoof, it is unclean to you. And the hare, because it chews the cud but does not part the hoof, it is unclean to you. And the swine, because it parts the hoof and is cloven-footed, but does not chew the cud, it is unclean to you.[2]

A careful reading of this text makes us wonder. Why did the Torah need to state that these non-kosher animals chew their cud or have cloven hooves? After all, *that's* not what makes them spiritually "unclean." On the contrary, having one positive sign seems to suggest that *perhaps* they could be

---

1. *Vayikra* 11:2-3; *Devarim* 14:6–8.
2. *Vayikra* 11:4–7.

kosher! If the Torah would just mention the negative indicators in these animals that clearly identify them as non-kosher, we would have known enough: Not kosher!

Moreover, why are the kosher signs mentioned *before* the non-kosher signs? Would the reverse order not be more accurate? Surely their non-kosher signs bear more relevance in a discussion of why these animals are not kosher! In what way, then, do the kosher *simanim* make the animal *more* non-kosher than the non-kosher signs themselves?

Rabbi Ephraim Shlomo ben Chaim of Luntshitz, known as the Kli Yakar (1550–1619), gives us a most illuminating explanation for why the Torah specifically chose this wording and no other. In his opinion, we might have thought that indeed the non-kosher aspects of these animals make them impure, but the kosher signs somehow moderate that impurity. Instead, the Torah comes to tell us that the kosher signs of non-kosher animals make them *all the more* unclean.

Why? Because animals with only one kosher sign represent a negative character trait – namely, hypocrisy. The camel, the rock-badger, the hare, and the swine all give the *appearance* of being kosher. The first three can demonstrate their "kashrut" by emphasizing that they do, after all, chew their cud. The swine, too, can show its cloven hooves in order to "prove" its virtue. They all, therefore, have the ability to hide their true natures behind a façade of purity. Only upon close inspection do we realize that these animals are unclean.[3]

They are waving a kosher flag, but hiding unclean cargo.

This is indeed much worse than possessing both non-kosher *simanim*. Animals with both non-kosher *simanim* don't try to "deceive" us about their impurity, but rather openly and honestly declare where they stand. With them, there is no hypocrisy and there are no misleading impressions. For this reason, the Torah first mentions the kosher signs of these animals, because it is these deceptive signs that make them even *more* unclean.

When reading the story about the coat of many colors, Ya'akov's gift to Yosef, the Torah states, "and his [Yosef's] brothers saw that their father [Ya'akov] loved him more than all his brothers, so they hated him and could not speak with him peacefully."[4] Rashi comments on this verse: "From their faults we learn their virtues, for they did not speak one way

3. See *Kli Yakar* on *Vayikra* 11:4.
4. *Bereshit* 37:4.

with their mouths and think differently in their hearts."[5] Even as they erred we see their honesty.

The issue of hypocrisy and religious integrity presents a most severe problem. For what is ghastly about evil is not so much its apparent power, but its uncanny ability to camouflage itself.

In our days, when every human deed and thought is the object of suspicion, man begins to wonder whether it is at all possible to live a life of integrity. Is piety ever detached from expediency?[6] Is there not a vicious motive behind every action? Are we not smooth-tongued and deceitful even when we appear to be honest?

Judaism fully recognizes this problem. It is difficult, if not impossible to know whether one acts out of self-interest or out of absolute integrity. But as long as the question hounds us and we admit to possibly being the victim of our own camouflage, we can try to extricate ourselves from this malaise and we will have done what is humanly possible. Our greatest problem is when we are no longer disturbed by our ability to hide behind our own camouflage. Once hypocrisy begins to be a state of mind, it becomes real evil. "The true hypocrite is the one who ceases to perceive his deception, the one who lies with sincerity."[7]

This is also true on a very practical level. There is little doubt that one of the functions of the kashrut laws is to protect the animal from pain even during the slaughtering. This is accomplished by the many strict laws of *shechita* in accordance with Halacha. Attacks on this method, by several European countries or political parties, are nothing but expressions of anti-Semitism camouflaged by so-called animal rights arguments. In fact, we see constant and severe violations of these rights in their own abattoirs, where animals are horribly mistreated and sometimes mercilessly killed. In short, this is flagrant hypocrisy.

Still, we cannot deny that in our own slaughterhouses, where proper *shechita* is done, there have been serious violations of another law – *tza'ar ba'alei chaim* (the Torah's prohibition against inflicting unnecessary pain on animals).[8] How are these animals handled just before the *shechita* takes place? Are they treated with mercy when they are put on their backs so as to make the *shechita* easier? (This can easily be accomplished with the

---

5. *Rashi*, ad loc.
6. See Abraham Joshua Heschel, *God in Search of Man: A Philosophy of Judaism* (NY: Farrar, Straus and Cudahy, 1955), 390.
7. André Gide, *The Counterfeiters*, trans. Dorothy Bussy (NY: Vintage Books, 1973), 427.
8. *Bava Metzia* 32b. For a discussion, see Immanuel Jakobovits, *Jewish Medical Ethics* (NY: Bloch Publishing Company, 1967), 102–103, 297–298 nn30–37.

Weinberg Pen, or by other methods.) What if chickens or other fowl are kept under the most unacceptable conditions, such as in overcrowded containers? Are these animals still kosher, even if the *shechita* was 100 percent accurate?

Since when is the actual *shechita* more important than the laws of *tza'ar ba'alei chaim*? It seems self-righteous and duplicitous on the part of very religious Jews to insist on *glatt kosher shechita*, with all its stringencies, when the animals are badly treated prior to *shechita*, in defiance of Halacha's requirements. Are they not as *treif* (non-kosher) as any other animal that is not slaughtered according to Halacha? Can we hide behind the laws of *shechita* and then look the other way when the laws of *tza'ar ba'alei chaim* are violated? Is that any less hypocritical?

Since the massive growth of the meat industry in which thousands and thousands of animals are slaughtered daily, it has become more and more difficult, if not impossible, to treat animals humanely, as Jewish Law requires.

The laws of *shechita* and *tza'ar ba'alei chaim* were meant for Jewish communities who would eat meat occasionally, not for the huge industry we have today where these laws can no longer be properly applied. That being the case, wouldn't it be appropriate and advisable for religious Jews to become vegetarians?

In all honesty: How many of our *glatt kosher* kitchens, including my own, are still truthfully kosher? A haunting question, from which we cannot hide!

Chapter 50

The Prohibition to Carry on Shabbat
Walking Mountains and the Buddha

It is well known that the institution of Shabbat is one of the best inventions God ever came up with. It no doubt qualifies Him to receive the Nobel Prize for innovative thinking, and the venerable judges in Sweden should sincerely consider bestowing this honor on the Lord of the Universe. Now that most of the world has adopted the concept of a weekly day of rest, the time has come to act. The idea is nearly six thousand years old; a Nobel Prize is long overdue.

That we all need a weekly rest is common knowledge. What is much less known is that the Jewish Tradition believes such rest should not only consist of refraining from strenuous labor, but also from any kind of work that presents human beings as having dominion over the world. One day a week we are asked to return the world and all its potential to God and, instead of being creators, acknowledge that we are also creatures in God's eyes – not much different from a flower, a leaf, or a small bird. By refraining from cooking, writing, creating electricity, driving cars, flying airplanes, and other such activities, we learn that the world has already been created and will no doubt survive without us. As Abraham Joshua Heschel pointed out: "The world has our hands, but our soul belongs to Someone Else."[1]

Shabbat is a day when we stop worshiping technology, money, and power. Instead, we focus on our internal lives and our families – learning Torah, singing songs, and creating an inner palace of tranquility. Shabbat is holiness in time, when we allow for personal conversations with friends,

---

1. Abraham Joshua Heschel, *The Sabbath: Its Meaning for Modern Man* (Farrar, Straus and Giroux, July 2005), 13.

reading a book, playing games with our children, and ungluing ourselves from the cell phone, iPod, and computer. Shabbat means living in full liberty, which is paradoxically achieved by heeding prohibitions. We free ourselves from all sorts of activities that often disturb our internal balance. What can be greater than abandoning the cell phone and suddenly discovering that we have a spouse and children? We find an island of stillness in a turbulent sea of worldliness.

Yet there is one law that, while rarely applicable in Israel and large Jewish communities around the world, really sums up the whole message of this remarkable day: the prohibition against carrying any object in the public domain, besides our clothing and jewelry. Today, many cities are surrounded by an *eruv*,[2] so as to permit people to carry things they need for Shabbat for reasons of convenience. But it is really this prohibition against carrying that captures the essence of the Shabbat rest, and it is a pity that its message has been nearly forgotten. What is the secret behind this law?

The great Zen Buddhist monk Master Furong Daokai (12th century, China) really hit the nail on the head when he made the following remarkable observation: "The green mountains are always walking . . . If you doubt mountains' walking, you do not know your own walking."[3]

What did they mean?

There are two reasons for walking – one is to reach a destination, and the other is for the sake of strolling (*le-tayel* in Hebrew; *spazieren* in German). When someone walks *to* something, their goal is outside themselves: they have to be at a business meeting or need to bring a package to a specific place. But when people take a stroll, the walking *itself* is the goal. It is not a means, but *das ding an sich*, the thing itself. Every step is its purpose. At

---

2. The Talmud (*Shabbat* 14b; *Eruvin* 21b) attributes the institution of the *eruv* to King Shlomo. There are different types of *eruvin*. The *eruv* under discussion here is the setting up of a symbolic enclosure which turns a semi-public area into a private domain by surrounding it. The *eruv* has been adopted in cities all over the world, including parts of London, Amsterdam, New York, and, of course, Yerushalayim, as well as most other cities in Israel. It allows people to carry things that they need, as well as alleviating situations when not being able to carry on Shabbat would result in undesirable circumstances – for example, by preventing young couples from attending synagogue because their children are too young to walk. For a history of the *eruv*, see Adam Mintz, "Halakhah in America: The History of City Eruvin, 1894–1962" (PhD dissertation, New York University, 2011), accessible online at http://www.rabbimintz.com/wp-content/uploads/Mintz-Dissertation-Final. The *eruv* is a typical example of how the Halacha has to work with two opposing spiritual values. As in secular law, it suggests what legal philosopher Sir Isaiah Berlin calls a trade-off for the sake of the realities of life.

3. See *Sutra on the Establishment of Mindfulness*, or *Satipatthana Sutta*. I thank Prof. Yehuda Gellman of Yerushalayim for bringing this text to my attention.

such a moment, people are connected with their very being. They are walking with themselves in peace and in complete harmony. They carry only themselves.

Green mountains walk in the sense that they, in an existential way, stroll with themselves. They need not do anything but be mountains. Nothing outside themselves disturbs them in being mountains. They need not go anywhere; therefore they just stroll.

People must know how to carry themselves. They should know that their inner being is the goal of their life. It is their *internal* life that needs to spiritually and morally grow. Their happiness depends not on outside circumstances, but on their *attitude* toward those conditions. The rare and simple pleasure of being themselves will compensate for all their misery. If they meet their family or friends, they will not want to *own* them as objects but rather relate to them in a mode in which they stroll with them, accompanying them while spiritually growing. They realize that being is *becoming*.

No longer is the goal of life about obtaining things, or being some-where for the sake of proving oneself, achieving external goals, or making money. They refuse to be the slaves of their own inventions, whether it is their car, computer, or cell phone. What one acquires on Shabbat is a way of life that brings the joy of tranquility or, as Spinoza calls it – *sub specie aeternitatis* – a perspective of eternity.

When we are told not to carry in the public domain on Shabbat, we are essentially being asked *not* to see our life goals in the public sphere, where life is about getting somewhere. While for livelihood one no doubt needs to travel, that activity remains a weekday endeavor; a *means* to something, but never *das ding an sich*.

On Shabbat, we turn our *outer* mode into a *being* mode, and for one day a week we become people who by just carrying ourselves and nothing else, are able to deal with a world that has little knowledge of the soul's needs. On Shabbat, we stroll even when we go to synagogue. Only then will we realize how great we are and that nobody can make us inferior without our own consent.

In a world where we refuse to take notice of what is beyond our sight, where we turn mysteries into dogmas and facts, ideas into a multitude of words and routine, we Jews are asked to surpass ourselves by being ourselves; we are summoned to discover another world.

Refraining from carrying is an act of protest against the shallowness of our world. And while today we are permitted to carry outside our homes if an *eruv* is in place, we should never forget the great symbolic meaning inherent in the prohibition against carrying on Shabbat, which can advance us – both spiritually and morally – further than anything else.

Our society stands on the precipice, and one false step can plunge us into the abyss. We have, for the most part, become a civilization of notoriously unhappy people – lonely, anxious, depressed, destructive, and dependent – people who are glad to kill the time that they are trying so hard to save.

Shabbat is a day of truce in the midst of the human battle with the world. It teaches us that even pulling out a blade of grass is a breach of harmony, as is lighting a match. And while we need to carry objects on weekdays so as to physically survive, one day in the week we are taught that what really counts is our ability to carry our own selves. Shabbat teaches us that the survival of the human race depends on a radical change of the human heart.

The time has come for all of humankind to observe Shabbat – whether on Friday, Saturday, or Sunday. The Lord of the Universe has told us to do so, and we Jews owe it to our fellow human beings.

Perhaps the rabbis should suggest that even when there is an *eruv*, people should once a month abstain from carrying so as not to lose the important message of this prohibition.

Fourteen

RABBI JOSEPH BER SOLOVEITCHIK – A CORRESPONDENCE

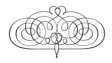

Chapter 51

The Genius and Limitations
of Rabbi Joseph Ber Soloveitchik

Based on an introduction to a discussion between Professor William Kolbrener and Professor Elliott Malamet[1] honoring the publication of Professor William Kolbrener's new book The Last Rabbi.[2]

YAD HARAV NISSIM, YERUSHALAYIM, FEB. 1, 2017

Dear Friends,

I never had the privilege of meeting Rav Soloveitchik or learning under him. But I believe I have read most, if not all, of his books on Jewish philosophy and Halacha, and many of his talmudic novellae and halachic decisions. I have also spoken with many of his students.

Here are my impressions.

No doubt Rav Soloveitchik was a *Gadol ha-Dor* (a great sage of his generation). He was a supreme talmudist and certainly one of the greatest religious thinkers of our time.

His literary output was astounding.

Still, I believe that he was not a *mechadesh* – a man whose novel ideas really moved the Jewish Tradition forward, especially regarding Halacha. He did not solve major halachic problems.

This may sound strange, because almost no one has written as many

---

1. A video of this event can be viewed at: https://www.youtube.com/watch?v=86vvnPFgCRU/.

2. William Kolbrener, *The Last Rabbi: Joseph Soloveitchik and Talmudic Tradition* (Bloomington: Indiana University Press, 2016). While there have been many books and articles on Rav Soloveitchik's life and thought, Professor Kolbrener's book is groundbreaking and entirely novel. It offers a much richer and more complicated reading of his life and thoughts. It can be purchased at https://www.amazon.com/Last-Rabbi-Soloveitchik-Tradition-Philosophy/dp/025302224X/.

novel ideas about Halacha as Rav Soloveitchik.[3] His masterpiece, *Halakhic Man*, is perhaps the prime example.

Before Rav Soloveitchik appeared on the scene, nobody – surely not in mainstream Orthodoxy – had seriously dealt with the ideology and philosophy of Halacha.[4]

In fact, the reverse is true. While many were writing about Jewish philosophy, the Bible, the prophets, and universalism, no one touched the topic of Halacha and its weltanschauung.

Halacha was ignored as an ideology, and the impression is that most Orthodox scholars were embarrassed by the strange and incomprehensible world of halachic thought and argument, and chose to disregard it. Its highly unusual way of thinking, its emphasis on the most subtle details – often comprised of farfetched arguments, hairsplitting dialectics, and casuistry – made it something that no one wanted to approach, and the subject was consequently a non-starter.

I once argued that Halacha is the art of making a problem out of every solution.[5] Its obsessive need to create obstacles where no difficulties exist is well known to all talmudists. Its constant fixation with creating life-and-death situations out of the grossest trivialities is typical.

Rav Soloveitchik, however, saw the need to deal with this problem head-on and undertook this extremely difficult task. For him, Halacha was the supreme will of God, and behind its strange disposition lay a fascinating and highly original world that needed to be revealed in a society that increasingly tried to undo it. As far as he was concerned, there was nothing to be embarrassed about. In fact, there was no greater and more sophisticated ideology than the world of Halacha.

Single-handedly, he turned the tide and made Halacha the center of philosophical discussion. Not even Rambam, the greatest of all halachists, had done anything like that.

Rav Soloveitchik's classic work, *Halakhic Man*, is highly sophisticated and full of deep insights using general philosophy, psychology, and epistemology, which place the philosophy and theology of Halacha not only on the map but at the center of all discussion concerning Judaism. No

---

3. See, however, n12 below.

4. See David Singer and Moshe Sokol, "Joseph Soloveitchik: Lonely Man of Faith," in *Modern Judaism* 2, no. 3 (1982): 227–272. For an introduction to *Halakhic Man*, see David Shatz, "A Framework for Reading Ish ha-Halakhah," in *Turim: Studies in Jewish History and Literature: Presented to Dr. Bernard Lander*, ed. Michael A. Shmidman, vol. 2 (NY: Touro College Press, 2008), 171–231.

5. See chaps. 32, 33, and 34.

doubt it took time before this essay had any impact. It was first published in Hebrew in 1944, as *Ish ha-Halakhah*, in the journal *Talpiot*.[6] When it appeared in English in 1983, as Lawrence Kaplan's translation *Halakhic Man*,[7] it slowly became the object of serious debate and contemplation.

It may be argued that *Halakhic Man* forced the Conservative, Reform, and even Reconstructionist movements to give much more attention to Halacha, which grew to be the norm to the extent that general Jewish philosophy almost became of secondary importance.[8] For Rav Soloveitchik, Jewish theology had to be an outgrowth and expression of the normative halachic system. A great example of this would be his *teshuva drashot* (sermons) where the laws of *teshuva* (repentence) and the *lamdanut* (talmudic analytic learning) of *tzvei dinim*[9] were explored as concepts in Jewish philosophy.

*

And here is where we encounter one of the greatest and most tragic paradoxes in Rav Soloveitchik's legacy.

In complete contradiction to his philosophy of Halacha, Rav Soloveitchik did not move Halacha forward in areas that most urgently needed it. He did not innovate a new, *practical* halachic approach to major problems confronting the larger Jewish community. While brilliantly explaining what Halacha essentially is, he made no practical breakthroughs.[10]

---

6. R. Yosef Dov ha-Levi Soloveitchik, "Ish ha-Halakhah," *Talpiot* 1, nos. 3–4 (1944): 651–735.

7. R. Joseph B. Soloveitchik, *Halakhic Man*, trans. Lawrence Kaplan (Philadelphia: Jewish Publication Society of America, 1983).

8. It is interesting to note that one of the first academic studies of Rav Soloveitchik's thought was written by the Reform theologian Eugene B. Borowitz. See Borowitz, "The Typological Theology of Rabbi J.B. Soloveitchik," *Judaism* 15, no. 2 (1966): 203–210. See also Borowitz, "Abraham Joshua Heschel and Joseph B. Soloveitchik: The New Orthodoxy," in *A New Jewish Theology in the Making* (Philadelphia: Westminster Press, 1968), 161–173; Borowitz, "Orthodoxy: Rabbi Joseph B. Soloveitchik," in *Choices in Modern Jewish Thought: A Partisan Guide* (NY: Behrman House, 1983), 218–242.

9. "*Tzvei* [two] *dinim*" is a term that is widespread in the lexicon of the yeshiva world. It refers to a method of talmudic analysis whereby a talmudic law or concept is divided into two constituent elements. One common example is the distinction between *gavra* and *cheftza* (subject and object). This method is the hallmark of the Brisker approach to talmudic study, championed by Rabbi Chaim Soloveitchik (1853–1918) of Brisk (Brest-Litovsk, Belarus), the grandfather of Rabbi Joseph B. Soloveitchik. For an analysis of the Brisker method, see Norman Solomon, *The Analytic Movement: Hayyim Soloveitchik and His Circle* (Atlanta, GA: Scholars Press, 1993); Yosef Blau, ed., *Lomdus: The Conceptual Approach to Jewish Learning*, The Orthodox Forum Series (Newark, NJ: Ktav, 2006); Chaim Saiman, "Legal Theology: The Turn to Conceptualism in Nineteenth-Century Jewish Law," *Journal of Law and Religion* 21, no. 1 (2005–2006): 39–100; Jeffrey Saks, "Rabbi Joseph B. Soloveitchik on the Brisker Method," *Tradition* 33, no. 2 (1999): 50–60.

10. Although Rav Soloveitchik did not author books of responsa like classical *poskim*, he did

This is true about issues such as the status of women in Jewish Law (with the exception of women learning Talmud);[11] the *aguna*; the *mamzer*

---

deal extensively with halachic issues, mostly on an abstract level in his numerous lectures and shiurim on talmudic and halachic concepts. He also issued rulings in practical Halacha (*Halacha le-ma'aseh*). For a recent study, see Avraham Munitz, "A Study of Rabbi J.B. Soloveitchik's Halakhic Responsa," *Netuim* 20 (2016): 233–271. See also Isaac Boaz Gottlieb, "On Rabbi Joseph B. Soloveitchik's Halachic Approach," *Shana be-Shana* (1994): 186–197 [Hebrew].

Rav Soloveitchik also served as the chairman of the Halacha Commission of the Rabbinical Council of America from 1953 until his retirement from public life. In this capacity he issued many halachic rulings and public policy decisions. Some of these responsa and halachic rulings appear in R. Joseph B. Soloveitchik, *Community, Covenant and Commitment: Selected Letters and Communications*, ed. Nethaniel Helfgot (Jersey City, NJ: Ktav, 2005). For more details about Rav Soloveitchik's involvement with the RCA, see Louis Bernstein, *Challenge and Mission: The Emergence of the English Speaking Orthodox Rabbinate* (NY: Shenghold, 1982) and Bernard Rosensweig, "The Rav as Communal Leader," *Tradition* 30, no. 4 (1996): 210–218, republished in *Memories of a Giant: Reflections on Rabbi Dr. Joseph B. Soloveitchik zt"l*, ed. Michael A. Bierman (Urim and Maimonides School, 2003/2013), 271–280.

For an evaluation (perhaps one-sided) of Rav Soloveitchik as a *posek*, see Walter S. Wurzburger, "Rav Joseph B. Soloveitchik as Posek of Post-Modern Orthodoxy," *Tradition* 29, no. 1 (1994): 5–20, republished in Wurzburger, *Covenantal Imperatives: Essays by Walter Wurzburger on Jewish Law, Thought and Community*, ed. Eliezer L. Jacobs and Shalom Carmy (Jerusalem: Urim, 2008), 133–149, and the response by Moshe Sokol, "'Ger Ve-Toshav Anokhi': Modernity and Traditionalism in the Life and Thought of Rabbi Joseph B. Soloveitchik," *Tradition* 29, no. 1 (1994): 32–47, republished in Sokol, *Judaism Examined: Essays in Jewish Philosophy and Ethics* (NY: Touro College Press, 2013), 434–450. We see a similar phenomenon in the writings of R. Avraham Yitzchak ha-Kohen Kook, where he suggests the most novel ideas about Halacha, but refuses to use them in his responsa.

Much of Rav Soloveitchik's treatment of talmudic and halachic issues appear in Hebrew in the numerous books and articles devoted to his talmudic novellae, including *Shiurim le-Zecher Abba Mari*, 2 volumes (Jerusalem: Mossad HaRav Kook, 2002); *Reshimot Shiurim*, 6 volumes, ed. H. Reichman; *Harerei Kedem*, 3 volumes, ed. Michel Zalman Surkin (Jerusalem, 2000–2013); *Shiurei ha-Rav*, 6 volumes; *Shiurei ha-Grid*, 3 volumes, ed. Yair Kahn (Jerusalem: Mossad HaRav Kook, 2004–2013); and the numerous articles that appear in Torah periodicals such as *Ohr Hamizrach*, *Beit Yitzchak*, and *Mesorah*, etc. Rabbi Hershel Schachter has recorded many of Rav Soloveitchik's halachic rulings and practices in his books *Nefesh ha-Rav* (NY: Flatbush Beth Hamedrosh, 1994); *Mi-Peninei ha-Rav* (NY: Flatbush Beth Hamedrosh, 2001); *Divrei ha-Rav* (NY: OU Press, 2010). There is also a seven volume series in English by Rabbi Aharon Ziegler, *Halakhic Positions of Rabbi Joseph B. Soloveitchik* (published between 2004 and 2017). For a comprehensive bibliography of Rav Soloveitchik's writings, see Eli Turkel, *Mekorot Ha-Rav: An index by location and topic to the works of Rabbi Joseph B. Soloveitchik and his students* (Jerusalem: Rubin Mass, 2001) [Hebrew].

11. For Rav Soloveitchik's views on women studying Torah and feminist issues, see R. Joseph B. Soloveitchik, *Community, Covenant and Commitment*, xxi, 81–83; Aaron Rakeffet-Rothkoff, *The Rav: The World of Rabbi Joseph B. Soloveitchik*, ed. Joseph Epstein, vol. 2 (Hoboken, NJ: Ktav, 1999), section 13.12, "Women Saying Kaddish," 36; Moshe Meiselman, "The Rav, Feminism and Public Policy: An Insider's Overview," *Tradition* 33, no. 1 (1998): 5–30; Mayer Twersky, "Halakhic Values and Halakhic Decisions: Rav Soloveitchik's Pesak Regarding Women's Prayer Groups," *Tradition* 32, no. 3 (1998): 5–18; Simcha Krauss, "The Rav: On Zionism, Universalism and Feminism," *Tradition* 34, no. 2 (2000): 24–39; Seth Farber, "Rabbi Joseph B. Soloveitchik and Co-Educational Jewish Education," *Conversations* 7 (2010): 103–112; Rachel Adler, "Between a Rock and a Hard Place: Rav J. B. Soloveitchik's Perspective on Gender," in Michael A. Meyer and David N. Myers ed. *Between Jewish Tradition and Modernity: Rethinking an Old Opposition. Essays in Honor of David Ellenson* (Detroit: Wayne State University Press, 2014), 209–220; Tomer Persico, "Acharei ha-Rav Soloveitchik," *Lula'at ha-El* (blog), Sept. 26, 2011, https://tomerpersico.com/20 11/09/26/hartman_lichtenstein_books/.

problem; the application of Halacha in the State of Israel; and similar crucial halachic issues.

In that sense he was not at all a *mechadesh*, but rather a conservative halachist.

He *did*, however, stand out as a highly gifted exponent of the ideology of Judaism and Halacha. He had no equal – perhaps with the exception of the renowned Rabbi Abraham Joshua Heschel. In his work *God in Search of Man*, Rabbi Heschel laid out a theology of Judaism and Halacha, which, while dramatically different from Rav Soloveitchik's, was also a tour de force explaining what Halacha is really all about.[12]

*

When it came to talmudic learning, Rav Soloveitchik was an old-fashioned *Rosh Yeshiva* (in Yeshiva University), whose brilliance was no different than that of my own *Roshei Yeshiva* in Gateshead, England, and later in Yerushalayim's Mirrer Yeshiva. He was the proponent of the Brisker method of talmudic learning, which is widespread in many of today's yeshivot, and from which I personally have greatly benefited, although I doubt its real value.

*

Rabbi David Hartman, in his book *The God Who Hates Lies*, rightly criticizes Rav Soloveitchik for his refusal to find a way to allow a *kohen* to marry a *giyoret* (convert).[13] While Rabbi Hartman uses purely ethical reasons to oppose the negative response of Rav Soloveitchik, it was Rabbi Moshe Feinstein, the most important halachic authority in America in those days, who often found halachically permissible ways to allow these people to marry.[14] This no doubt must have been known to Rav Soloveitchik,

---

12. Abraham Joshua Heschel, *God in Search of Man: A Philosophy of Judaism* (NY: Farrar, Straus and Cudahy, 1955), chaps. 22–33. The other rabbi who proposed a philosophy of Halacha was Rabbi Eliezer Berkovits in *God, Man, and History: A Jewish Interpretation* (Middle Village, NY: Jonathan David, 1959), part 2.

13. David Hartman with Charlie Buckholtz, "Where Did Modern Orthodoxy Go Wrong? The Mistaken Halakhic Presumptions of Rabbi Soloveitchik," in *The God Who Hates Lies: Confronting & Rethinking Jewish Tradition* (Woodstock, VT: Jewish Lights Publishing, 2011), 131–157. See also David Hartman, *Love and Terror in the God Encounter: The Theological Legacy of Rabbi Joseph B. Soloveitchik*, vol. 1 (Woodstock, VT: Jewish Lights Publishing, 2011). The incident with the *giyoret* was mentioned by Rav Soloveitchik in his address to the RCA, published in Rakeffet-Rothkoff, *The Rav*, vol. 2, section 13.11, "Surrender to Halakha," 35–36; see also vol. 1, 123–125. See also n16 below.

14. Rabbi Feinstein was of the opinion that if a family of *kohanim* was no longer observant and was assimilated, their claim to be *kohanim* could not be relied upon. I received this information by

and I am utterly astonished that he did not discuss it with or take advice from Rabbi Feinstein. It's even more mind-boggling when one takes into account that Rav Soloveitchik did not see himself as a *posek* but only as a *melamed* (teacher).

*

Rav Soloveitchik's famous argument with Rabbi Emanuel Rackman – renowned talmudic scholar and thinker, later to become dean of Bar-Ilan University – is another example of the former's sometimes extreme halachic conservatism. In several places, the Talmud introduces a rule that states: "Tav le-metav tan du mi-le-metav armelu" (It is better to live as two than to live alone),[15] which refers to the fact that a woman would prefer to marry almost any man rather than remain alone. Rav Soloveitchik sees this as a "permanent ontological principle," which is beyond historical conditions, and that even in our day needs to be applied and cannot be changed. This principle operates under the assumption that even today's women prefer to stay in a marriage, no matter how unfortunate the circumstances may be. To be alone is worse. This means that a woman cannot claim that had she known what kind of person her husband is, she never would have married him. If she *could* make this claim, her marriage would be a "mistaken marriage," which would not even require a *get*, since the marriage took place on a false premise and the woman would never have agreed to it had she known. In that case, she was never considered lawfully married and could leave her partner without receiving a *get*. Since this obviously has enormous repercussions for today's society, it could help thousands of women.[16] Rav Soloveitchik was not prepared to

---

personal correspondence from one of his students. See his *Igrot Moshe, Even ha-Ezer*, vol. 4, nos. 12, 39. See also R. Mordechai Tendler (grandson of Rabbi Feinstein), *Masoret Moshe: Hanhagot ha-Gaon ha-Rav Moshe Feinstein* (Jerusalem, 5773), 396.

15. See, for example, *Ketubot* 75a; *Yevamot* 118b; *Kiddushin* 7a, 41a; *Bava Kamma* 111a.

16. For Rav Soloveitchik's view on this matter, see the transcript of his talk delivered at the RCA convention in 1975, published as "Surrendering to the Almighty," in *Light*, no. 116 (17 Kislev 5736), 13–14. A full transcript of this lecture, "Talmud Torah and Kabalas Ol Malchus Shamayim," is accessible online at http://arikahn.blogspot.co.il/2013/03/rabbi-soloveitchik-talmud-torah-and.html. See also Abraham R. Besdin, "Surrendering our Minds to G-d," in *Reflections of the Rav* (Jerusalem: World Zionist Organization, 1979), 99–106. Remarkable is the fact that some assumptions of the Talmud were definitely lifted in later times. See, for example, the assumption that a woman would not be so bold as to declare in front of her husband that he had divorced her unless it was in fact true. But Rabbi Moshe Isserles, quoting others, states that nowadays this is no longer the case, and (depending on the circumstances) she can't be relied upon (*Rema, Even ha-Ezer* 17:2). See Natan Slifkin, "The Rav and the Immutability of Halacha," *Rationalist Judaism* (blog), July 11, 2011, http://www.rationalistjudaism.com/2011/07/rav-and-immutability-of-halachah.html.

take that approach and thus blocked the possibility for many of them to leave their partners without a *get*.

Rabbi Rackman, who had the greatest respect for Rav Soloveitchik, strongly disagreed and claimed that a talmudic presumption such as this depends on historical circumstances, as in the days of the Talmud when women had no option to live a normal life if they were not married. They were often abused and would suffer extreme poverty and other misfortunes. Understandably, women in those days would prefer to remain married; but none of this is true in modern times when women have great freedom and are able to take care of themselves, both financially and physically. If so, there would be good reason for a woman to claim that had she known her husband's true nature, she would never have married him, and she would then be able to leave her husband without the need for a *get*.[17]

There is little doubt that Rabbi Rackman was right in this matter. Interestingly, he noted that Rav Soloveitchik told him: "Rackman, you may be right and I may be wrong. You view the Halacha historically and I like to view it meta-historically."[18] I have heard statements from other students

---

For a comprehensive analysis of this complicated issue, see Aliza Bazak, "The 'Tav Lemeitav' Presumption in Modern Halakhic Discourse," (unpublished doctoral dissertation, Bar-Ilan University, 2012); Moshe Be'eri, "Is the Presumption of 'Tav le-Meitav Tan Du' Subject to Change?," *Techumin* 28 (2008): 63–68 [Hebrew]; Aviad Hacohen, *The Tears of the Oppressed – An Examination of the Agunah Problem: Background and Halakhic Sources* (Jersey City, NJ: Ktav, 2004), chaps. 6–8; Ruth Halperin-Kaddari, 'Tav Lemeitav Tan Du Mi-Lemeitav Armalu': An Analysis of the Presumption," *Edah Journal* 4, no. 1 (2004): 1–24; Susan Aranoff, "Two Views of Marriage – Two Views of Women: Reconsidering 'Tav Lemetav Tan du Milemetav Armelu,'" *Nashim* 3 (Spring/Summer 2000): 199–227; J. David Bleich, "'Kiddushei Ta'ut': Annulment as a Solution to the Agunah Problem," *Tradition* 33, no. 1 (1998): 102–108. Many more articles in Hebrew have been written on this topic.

17. Emanuel Rackman, *Modern Halakhah for Our Time* (Hoboken, NJ: Ktav, 1995), 71–73; Rackman, "From Status to Contract to Status: Historical and Meta-Historical Approaches," in *Marriage, Liberty and Equality: Shall the Three Walk Together*, ed. Tova Cohen (Ramat Gan: Bar-Ilan University, 2000), 97–100 [Hebrew]; Rackman, "The Problems of the Jewish Woman in this Generation and the Ways to Solve Them," in *Ha-Penina - Sefer Zikaron le-Penina Refel*, ed. Dov Refel (Jerusalem: Bnei Chemed, 1989), 187–188 [Hebrew]. For a comprehensive treatment of Rabbi Rackman's disagreement with Rav Soloveitchik, see David Singer, "Emanuel Rackman: Gadfly of Modern Orthodoxy," *Modern Judaism* 28, no. 2 (2008): 134–148; Lawrence Kaplan, "From Cooperation to Conflict: Rabbi Professor Emanuel Rackman, Rav Joseph B. Soloveitchik, and the Evolution of American Modern Orthodoxy," *Modern Judaism* 30, no. 1 (2010): 46–68. See also the following illuminating exchange: Emanuel Rackman, "Rackman on 'Borowitz on Soloveitchik,'" *Sh'ma* 15, no. 298 (1985): 137–139; Eugene Borowitz, "Borowitz on Rackman on Feminism," ibid., 139–140; Susan A. Handelman, "Inscribe Me in Your Book," ibid., 140–143; Rackman, "Clarifying Soloveitchik's Halachic Ideal," *Sh'ma* 16, no. 302 (1985): 12–16.

18. Emanuel Rackman, "Soloveitchik: On Differing with My Rebbe," *Sh'ma* 15, no. 289 (1985): 65. See also the letter that Rav Soloveitchik wrote to Rabbi Rackman on the nature of Halacha in R. Joseph B. Soloveitchik, *Community, Covenant and Commitment*, 273–277. Although the recipient of the letter is unidentified in the English version of the book, he is identified as Rabbi Rackman in the Hebrew version of the book, titled *Ish al ha-Edah* (Tel Aviv: Yediot Aharonot, 2011), 289.

that Rav Soloveitchik admitted this. Even stranger is the fact that, like all his predecessors, Rav Soloveitchik considered Rambam the ultimate halachic authority and defended him whenever possible. Professor Menachem Kellner points out that Rambam viewed Halacha in a historical context and clearly not in an ontological one![19] So one wonders why Rav Soloveitchik didn't follow in Rambam's footsteps and agree ab initio with Rabbi Rackman; unless one argues that Rav Soloveitchik didn't follow Rambam's *philosophical* approach to Halacha.

Indeed, this observation is astonishing. If Rav Soloveitchik was not even sure himself, and all evidence was against him, he could have single-handedly liberated many women. No doubt he must have been worried that such a ruling might be misused. But this is an extremely weak justification for his conservatism, considering the immense suffering of so many women whose husbands refused to grant them a *get*. He could have made a major contribution in this field had he accepted Rabbi Rackman's compelling argument.[20]

*

It is even more perplexing when we compare Rav Soloveitchik's highly conservative stand with those of other great halachists of his day, such as Rabbi Eliezer Berkovits, the preeminent student of Rabbi Yechiel Ya'akov Weinberg, author of the responsa *Seridei Esh* and one of the greatest halachic luminaries of the post-Holocaust era. Rabbi Berkovits was of the opinion that with the establishment of the State of Israel and the radical changes that had taken place among modern-day Jewry, there was a need to liberate Halacha from its exile status. According to Rabbi Berkovits, the unfortunate conditions under which the Jews had lived for nearly two thousand years created a "defensive halacha," which now had to be liberated. It had been in "waiting mode" and now had to return to its natural habitat. In his important work *Ha-Halacha, Kocha ve-Tafkida*, Rabbi Berkovits shows how we can solve many serious problems related to the status of women, *agunot*, *mamzerim*, conversion, and even the *shemitta* year with its enormous burden on modern Israeli society and its often inconsistent and paradoxical application.[21]

---

19. Menachem Kellner, "Contemporary Resistance to the Maimonidean Reform," in *Maimonides' Confrontation with Mysticism* (Portland, OR: Littman Library of Jewish Civilization, 2007), 286–296.

20. See also Emanuel Rackman, *One Man's Judaism* (Jerusalem: Gefen, 2000) and Rackman, *Modern Halakhah for Our Time*.

21. Eliezer Berkovits, *Ha-Halacha, Kocha ve-Tafkida* (Jerusalem: Mossad HaRav Kook, 1981).

In many ways he reminds us of Rabbi Chaim Hirschensohn (1857–1935) who, as a first-class halachist, also realized these new conditions and, in his responsa *Malki ba-Kodesh*, suggested new approaches that would solve many problems.[22]

It was especially in the Sephardic world that two outstanding halachic luminaries – Chacham Ben-Zion Uziel (1880–1953), Sephardic Chief Rabbi of Mandate Palestine from 1939 to 1948, and of Israel from 1948 to 1953; and Rabbi Yosef Mashash (1892–1974), rabbi of the city of Tlemcen in Algeria and later Chief Rabbi of Haifa – demonstrated ways to overcome halachic problems. Their courage is mind-boggling and proves what can be done when one has an approach to Orthodox Halacha that in so many ways is completely at odds with that of Rav Soloveitchik and other traditional Ashkenazic halachists.[23]

*

Most remarkable are the observations of Rabbi Abraham Joshua Heschel when he was asked to give his opinion about Rav Soloveitchik's book *Halakhic Man*. According to his student, Samuel H. Dresner, he said the following:

> *Ish Ha-Halakha* [Halakhic Man]? *Lo hayah velo nivra ela mashal hayah* [There never was such a Jew]! Soloveitchik's study, though brilliant, is based on the false notion that Judaism is a cold, logical affair with no room for piety. After all, the Torah *does* say, 'Love the Lord thy God with all thy heart and soul and might.' No, there never was such a typology in Judaism as the halakhic man. There was – and is – an *Ish*

For a discussion about the difference between Rabbis Soloveitchik and Berkovits' philosophical approaches, see Jonathan Cohen, "Incompatible Parallels: Soloveitchik and Berkovits on Religious Experience, Commandment and the Dimension of History," *Modern Judaism* 28, no. 2 (2008): 173–203; Ira Bedzow, *Halakhic Man, Authentic Jew: Modern Expressions of Orthodox Thought from Rabbi Joseph B. Soloveitchik and Rabbi Eliezer Berkovits* (Jerusalem: Urim, 2009).

22. R. Chaim Hirschensohn, *Malki ba-Kodesh*, new edition of first two volumes (Ramat Gan: Bar Ilan University, 2006 / Jerusalem: Shalom Hartman Institute, 2012). See also David Zohar, "Rabbi Hayyim Hirschensohn – The Forgotten Sage Who Was Rediscovered," *Conversations* 1 (2008): 56–62; Ari Ackerman, "Judging the Sinner Favorably: R. Hayyim Hirschensohn on the Need for Leniency in Halakhic Decision-Making," *Modern Judaism* 22, no. 3 (2002): 261–280; Marc B. Shapiro, review of *Jewish Commitment in a Modern World: Rabbi Hayyim Hirschensohn and His Attitude to Modernity*, by David Zohar, *Edah Journal* 5, no. 1 (2005).

23. On Chacham Ben-Zion Uziel, see Marc D. Angel, *Loving Truth and Peace: The Grand Religious Worldview of Rabbi Benzion Uziel* (Northvale, NJ: Jason Aronson, 1999). On Rabbi Yosef Mashash, see Marc B. Shapiro, "Rabbi Joseph Messas," *Conversations* 7 (Spring 2010): 95–102.

Torah [a Torah man], who combines Halakhah and Aggadah, but that is another matter altogether.[24]

While I wonder if these are the exact words of Rabbi Heschel – since there are, after all, some emotional and not only logical dimensions to *Halakhic Man* – it cannot be denied that this work depicts an image of an ideal halachic human being who in many ways lives a mathematical and almost stony life, although various parts of the book paint different if not contradictory images. The book is also definitely poetic.

It is interesting to note Rav Soloveitchik's observations concerning Heschel's famous book *The Sabbath*.[25] After praising it, he said: "What does he [Heschel] call Shabbat? – A sanctuary in time. This is an idea of a poet. It's a lovely idea. But what is Shabbat? Shabbat is *lamed tet melachot*, it is the thirty-nine categories of work and their *toladot*, and it is out of that Halacha, and not of poetry, that you have to construct a theory of Shabbat."[26] These are remarkable words, because Rav Soloveitchik was constantly trying to lift the "harsh" Halacha out of its own confines and give it a poetic, perhaps even romantic dimension.

*

The earlier-mentioned *poskim* thought out of the box when it came to Halacha, and introduced creative and new halachic approaches to major problems. With few exceptions, we see little of that in Rav Soloveitchik's methodology for practical application.

It seems that he did not realize, or did not want to accept, that Halacha had become defensive and was waiting to be liberated from its exile and confinement.

---

24. For all of Rabbi Heschel's observations, see Samuel H. Dresner, ed., *Heschel, Hasidism, and Halakha* (NY: Fordham University Press, 2002), 102–104.

25. Abraham Joshua Heschel, *The Sabbath: Its Meaning for Modern Man* (NY: Farrar, Straus and Giroux, 1951).

26. See Jonathan Sacks, "A Hesped in Honor of Rav Yosef Soloveitchik," in *Memories of a Giant*, ed. Michael A. Bierman (Jerusalem: Urim, 2003), 286–287.

Note, however, the following illuminating and candid statement by Rav Soloveitchik: "In my youth I occasionally harbored critical feelings against my father and even against my grandfather. Most everyone has at some time gone through this rebellious state against parental authority. Sometimes the obstinate son asks whether we must always mold our lives in accordance with the halacha, which appears to him as pedantic and insensitive. Should not Judaism place more emphasis on compassion and mercy? Why not stress refinement and aesthetic values? Can the Sabbath only be observed under the exacting demands of Halacha as expressed in the various chapters of the Talmudic tractate of Shabbat?" – R. Yosef Dov Soloveitchik, *Yemei Zikaron*, ed. M. Krona (Jerusalem: Elinor Library, 1986), 104; English translation in Rakeffet-Rothkoff, *The Rav*, vol. 1, section 5.12, "Appreciating Parents," 201–202.

In many ways, this is an extraordinary tragedy. With his exceptional standing in the Modern Orthodox halachic community, Rav Soloveitchik could have made breakthroughs that would have given Orthodoxy – especially Modern Orthodoxy – much more exposure and influence in the Jewish world and would probably have been a major force against the growth of Reform and Conservative Judaism, of which he was so afraid. In many ways, Modern Orthodoxy was unable to develop naturally, because it had become too dependent on Rav Soloveitchik's conservative halachic approach.[27]

Exactly at the point where Rav Soloveitchik put Halacha on the map, in all its grandeur (without denying its possible shortcomings), and transformed it into the most dominant topic of discussion on Judaism, *there* is where he seems to have been afraid of his own thoughts and withdrew behind its conventional walls. Had he taken the road of Rabbis Berkovits, Hirschensohn, Uziel, Mashash, and others, Orthodoxy would have become a driving force in contemporary Judaism, able to show the way and lead all other denominations.

It seems to me that the above-mentioned rabbis were *talmidei chachamim* no less than Rav Soloveitchik was. Their disadvantages were that they didn't occupy a central role in Modern Orthodox and Yeshiva University circles, and above all they didn't belong to renowned Ashkenazic rabbinical families. Had they been called Soloveitchik, their Torah may have received far more attention and would probably have been more effective.

*

Finally, I am deeply disturbed by the almost unhealthy obsession with Rav Soloveitchik within Modern Orthodox circles. It borders on *avoda zara* and has almost transformed into a cult, something he would not have liked. In all my years in the Charedi Gateshead and Mirrer Yeshivot, I never saw such exaggerated admiration for our great *Roshei Yeshiva*.

There is, however, a very good reason for this. Modern Orthodoxy has always been insecure with its own philosophy and halachic approach. Over the years, it has looked over its shoulder to see what the Charedi

27. See also Irving (Yitz) Greenberg, "Two Doors Rabbi Soloveitchik Opened and Did Not Walk Through: The Future of Modern Orthodoxy," available at http://rabbiirvinggreenberg .com/wp-content/uploads/2014/06/Two-Doors-reduced.pdf. Originally published in Hebrew as "Shtei Dlatot Patach ha-Rav Soloveitchik – ve-Lo Avar ba-Hem: Al Atida shel ha-Ortodoxia ha-Moderni," in *Rav ba-Olam ha-Chadash: Iyunim be-Hashpa'ato shel ha-Rav Yosef Dov Soloveitchik al Tarbut, al Chinuch ve-al Machshava Yehudit*, ed. Avinoam Rosenak and Naftali Rotenberg (Jerusalem: Magnes Press, 2010), 245–277.

community had to say. As a result, it hid behind Rav Soloveitchik, the only figure who equaled the Charedi talmudists in their level of talmudic learning; and only he could protect them against the onslaught of the Charedi community.

What Modern Orthodoxy did not realize is that Rav Soloveitchik himself was a Charedi, who combined that ideology with religious Zionism and tried very hard to give it a place in the world of philosophy and modernity. He therefore wavered and showed signs of a troubled man who was unable to overcome the enormous tension between these two worlds, and turned into a "lonely man of faith" with no disciples but with many students, each one of whom claimed their own Rav Soloveitchik. The truth is that the real Rav Soloveitchik was more than the sum total of all of them – a man of supreme greatness who was a tragic figure. May his memory be a blessing.

Chapter 52

Response by Tanya White

Dear Rabbi Cardozo,

  For many years, I have read your articles and publications with interest.
I greatly admire the way in which you present the complexity of religion
and existence and do not shy away from the burning issues of the moment,
sometimes at the expense of long held dogmas that need reappraisal. I
would, however, like to comment on the recent article you penned about
Rav Soloveitchik. As you rightly said, Rav Soloveitchik was perhaps one of
the greatest thinkers and halachic authorities in the last century. It is for
this reason he became known by his students as simply "The Rav." The
gist of your article, if I can brusquely summarize it, suggests that despite
his standing, he was not a *mechadesh* in the important areas of Halacha and
seems to implicitly suggest that even his philosophical thinking provided
little by the way of novelty. I cannot claim to have studied Rav Soloveitchik's halachic responsa in depth, neither can I claim to have read every
single one of his writings. However, I can say that over the years I have
been fortunate to have dissected elements of his thinking which has, on
a personal level, profoundly affected the way I approach my faith, my
life and my existential struggles. I have read many Jewish thinkers from
Levinas to Cohen, Buber to Borowitz, Heschel to Greenberg. They have
all added much to my weltanschauung, but I think the book that both
affected me the most and defined for so many the inner drama of a religious human being, must be Rav Soloveitchik's *The Lonely Man of Faith*.
Furthermore, one could argue that some of the greatest thinkers and
halachic innovators today stand basking in the light of the Rav's thought.
Surely Rabbi Eliezer Berkovits' book *Not in Heaven* was influenced by

the Rav's *Halakhic Man* and *Halakhic Mind*. By their own admissions, Rabbi David Hartman, Rabbi Yitz Greenberg and Rav Lichtenstein, to name just a few, were influenced and shaped by the innovative theological framework of their teacher and colleague. It is true, as you state, that there is a fight for his legacy, which has, as you claim, transformed him into a kind of cult leader. I would suggest that it is the very tension you explicate between the novelty in the philosophical realm and the conservatism in the halachic realm that has created the multifaceted interpretations of the Rav's positions. Furthermore, I would disagree that he has become, so to speak, idolized, but rather emulating his view of creative and autonomous thought, many of his greatest students are also his greatest critics, which is not something one finds in the Charedi world.

Your article focused on one essay and one aspect of the Rav's corpus of thinking and life works. Its narrow focus meant that it also lost the complexity in the development of his thought. *Halakhic Man* was penned in 1944. Whilst writing the book, the very legacy to which the Rav owed his knowledge and foundations were being gassed to oblivion. The Rav felt an obligation to retain the Brisker tradition which as you describe "depicts an image of an ideal halachic human being who in many ways lives a mathematical and almost stony life." The dialectical struggle that we see at the start of the book between cognitive man, who is as you describe, a cold, calculated individual almost bereft of any emotional attachment to reality, and *homo religiosus* who is a more traditional religious mystic interested in the transcendent elements of the religious experience, seems to quickly lose ground. By the end of the book, there is no real dialectical swing between the two. *Homo religiosus* has no place in *Halakhic Man's* persona. This is in contrary to *The Lonely Man of Faith*, which, if we compare and contrast to *Halakhic Man*, retains throughout a deep dialectical tension between Adam 1 and Adam 2 typologies. Adam 1 the scientist can be compared to cognitive man, and Adam 2 the philosopher or religious man, can be compared to *homo religiosus*. What has changed? Why in *Halakhic Man* is the ideal persona a Mitnagged Brisker, almost neo-Kantian personality who views the world only through the lens of halachic data, and in *The Lonely Man of Faith*, the ideal religious personality oscillates between the two? The answer is the years in-between, and here I get to what I think you miss in your analysis of the Rav.

Halakhic Man is written in 1944, *The Lonely Man of Faith* is written in 1965. There is no doubt that twenty years in the life of such a deep and reflective individual will change their weltanschauung. In their now infamous article, Singer and Sokol[1] make a claim about the Rav that I think is pertinent to your analysis. They claim that the differences between the two essays lie in the chasm of the twenty years in between the two writings. In 1944, the Rav must remain loyal to his roots; the rabbinic academy of Brisk, from where the origin of his *yahadut* emerged, is being destroyed as he writes, and thus as they claim, "he is loyal to the tradition of his father and grandfather, which emphasized study, pure emotional detachment and stoic indifference."[2] However, twenty years later he feels at greater ease to throw off the yoke of the Brisker tradition and immerse himself in a more Hassidic existential aura that celebrates defeat, retreat and humility. He is able to accede to the conflictual and multi-dimensional aspects of a religious personality.

Halakhic Man has all the trappings of a neo-Kantian outlook. Absent are any existential allusions. *The Lonely Man of Faith*, written after the death of his wife and deep into the life of an individual who has lived and seen life through the lens of loss, loneliness and struggle, presents a far more complex face of the religious experience. Halacha is not seen solely as a monolithic system or normative framework, rather as the very tool used to create the constant tension and oscillation within the persona of every individual who lives an authentically religious life. This change is reflected not only in these two essays but can be seen as a developing trend throughout his lifetime, in essays such as "Majesty and Humility," "Al Ahavat Ha-Torah u-Geulat Nefesh Hador," "Kol Dodi Dofek," to name a few. This dialectic is seen most poignantly in 1977 through a eulogy the Rav delivers for his son-in-law's mother, the Rebbetzin of Talne, where he describes the difference between the approach to Judaism of his mother and his father. He writes:

> The laws of Shabbat, for instance were passed on to me by my father; they are part of *musar avikha*. The Shabbat as a living entity, as a queen, was revealed to me by my mother; it is part of *torat imekha*. The father *knew* much about Shabbat, the mothers *lived* the Shabbat, experienced her presence, and perceived her beauty and splendour. . . . most of all I learned that Judaism expresses itself not in formal compliance of the law but also a living experience . . . I learnt from her [his mother] the

---

1. David Singer and Moshe Sokol, "Joseph Soloveitchik: Lonely Man of Faith," *Modern Judaism* 2, no. 3 (1982): 227–272.
2. David Hartman, *Love and Terror in the God Encounter: The Theological Legacy of Rabbi Joseph B. Soloveitchik*, vol. 1 (Woodstock, VT: Jewish Lights Publishing, 2001), 98.

most important things in life is to feel the presence of the Almighty and the gentle pressure of His hand resting on my frail shoulder.[3]

In your article, you use Rabbi Heschel to critique Soloveitchik, but there is no doubt that here in this extract we hear echoes of Heschel's *The Sabbath*. Perhaps only in his later years, having gained the insight of a life lived to the full, does Rav Soloveitchik allow himself to let go of the neo-Kantian epistemology of *Halakhic Man* and move towards the more existential, empiricist feel of *The Lonely Man of Faith*.

Though your criticism may be justified, one must not underestimate the impact his thought had on so many. His seamless interweaving of Western philosophy with Jewish tradition spoke and continues to speak to so many who are struggling between the two worlds. His elevation of classic concepts such as inner defeat, self-negation and self-sacrifice, from antiquated destructive values to the highest form of freedom, was antipathetic to the societal norms of autonomy, freedom, self-aggrandizement in the 1960s, yet this was his accomplishment whose impact is still being felt today.

The Lonely Man of Faith has been an inspiration for so many spanning a plethora of cultural and religious divides. (Just yesterday I finished a book by American journalist David Brooks on the state of American society today. He uses the framework of Adam 1 and Adam 2 to build his innovative theory of individual and societal character building. Even the fact that your own autobiography is called *Lonely but Not Alone* is reminiscent of Rav Soloveitchik's *Lonely Man of Faith*.)

How does this address the critique you levy at him in your article for his lack of innovation in the halachic realm? The answer, I believe, is that for many reasons[4] the Rav was halachically straitjacketed, and his unwillingness, or inability to take a controversial and novel stance on important halachic issues is one that is both disappointing and surprising, considering his innovation in the philosophical realm. However, just as we see in *Halakhic Man*, the Rav felt a strong obligation to the tradition of his fathers. Perhaps he felt it was too early to depart from or radically reinterpret thousands of years of halachic stringencies and inertia. However, he laid the path for those after him to do the work. His insistence on women's learning, especially of Gemara, was an opening of doors for the developments we see today. As I have argued in an article to be printed in

---

3. R. Joseph B. Soloveitchik, "A Tribute to the Rebbitzen of Talne," *Tradition* 17, no. 2 (1978): 77.
4. It is beyond the scope of this letter to go into all the political constraints of his position, mainly during his days at Yeshiva University.

an upcoming book on Rabbi Greenberg, the Rav's essay "Confrontation" was theologically ambiguous and thus paved the way for interpretation that could ultimately lead to interfaith dialogue.

Rav Soloveitchik, like any great individual, was human. He was working within the confines of political, religious and personal constraints. However, perhaps if we focus on the development of his thought, if we see the movement from a neo-Kantian, strictly mitnagged outlook to a more existentially religious experience, we might argue that his thought as opposed to his halachic rulings define the man and his legacy. Rabbi Yitz Greenberg titles one of his essays "Two Doors Rabbi Soloveitchik Opened but Did Not Walk Through," which points to the fact that it may be that his greatness lay in positioning the groundwork for doors his students and future generations would walk through.

Finally, I hope you do not mind me mentioning something that has bothered me over the years and that is particularly relevant in light of this essay. As I mentioned at the start, I greatly admire your thinking, and I believe you raise issues that deserve much attention and debate. Like Rav Soloveitchik, you are a bold and innovative thinker. However, your call for halachic innovation and change is seldom followed by any action. I understand that unlike the Rav, you are not a *posek* in the same fashion, though you could by anyone's standards be a respected rabbinical authority. Surely the only way to create change, as you correctly preach and advocate, would be to take the action in the halachic realm that is needed. Thus my question is, are you so far removed from the critique you levy against the Rav? In your thought, you are bold, innovative and assertive, but in practical halachic terms, unless I am misinformed, I have not seen any great steps. You argue quite correctly that Halacha has become stagnant where it should be innovative and dynamic, but the flourishing of Halacha *is* happening again, perhaps more at the grassroots than at the helm, but for it to be truly successful we need people like yourself to take the wheel and steer in the right direction. We live in a time of great change, I pray our great great grandchildren will look back on this period and proclaim we were the engineers of a new and bold religious reality, which, as I have argued, may have begun with the Rav. However, it will require not just the ideas but the practical halachic guidance and courageous decisions to allow it to happen, and the question is who will be brave enough to actually walk through that door?

With best wishes,
Tanya White
www.contemplatingtorah.wordpress.com

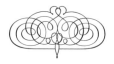

Chapter 53

Rabbi Joseph Ber Soloveitchik
and his Paradoxical Influence

An Answer to Tanya White

Dear Mrs. White,

Shalom u-vracha.

Thank you for your very balanced reaction to my essay on Rav Soloveitchik. I apologize for responding only now.

To begin with, it seems that you agree with most of what I wrote. However, I admit that perhaps I didn't give enough attention to some remarkable works, such as *The Lonely Man of Faith*. They are no doubt major breakthroughs in the world of religious philosophy, and that is no small accomplishment.

However, this only underscores my critique on Rav Soloveitchik's *Ish ha-Halakhah* (in English, *Halakhic Man*) and some of his *piskei din*. In fact, it makes it more complicated.

People reading *Ish ha-Halakhah* can sometimes get the impression that they are reading Immanuel Kant in a Jewish religious framework. I agree that there are major differences, especially with regard to the great Kantian thinker Hermann Cohen who was the subject of the Rav's PhD dissertation;[1] and without denying that writing *Ish ha-Halakhah* is itself a major accomplishment, I still doubt the originality of this work. Genius, yes; original, I'm not sure!

More important, though, is the fact that, as you and many others claim, it was in his later years that the Rav moved away from this almost stony

---

1. Rav Soloveitchik's doctoral thesis was "Das reine Denken und die Seinskonstituierung bei Hermann Cohen" (PhD dissertation, Friedrich-Wilhelms-Universität zu Berlin, 1932); in English, "Pure Thought as the Constitution of Being in Hermann Cohen's Philosophy." See also R. Joseph B. Soloveitchik, *Community, Covenant and Commitment: Selected Letters and Communications*, ed. Nathaniel Helfgot (Jersey City, NJ: Ktav, 2005), 272.

life as expressed in *Ish ha-Halakhah*. This begs the question: Why didn't the Rav take the time to write another work on Halacha, stating that his original one no longer reflects his ideas on the subject, and giving us a new perspective and interpretation? This was never done, and that's why *Halakhic Man* is still seen as *the* authoritative interpretation of Halacha by the Rav. It could be argued that the essay "U-Bikashtem mi-Sham"[2] was an attempt to soften the earlier harsh approach, but it still did not take the place of *Halakhic Man*. Doesn't this mean that the Rav did not change his mind, at least as far as the major premise of this work is concerned? While I, as well as other Orthodox thinkers, still greatly admire this work – even with all its problems – *Halakhic Man* has done much harm outside the Orthodox community and has pushed many people away from Halacha. I know this from my personal interactions with non-Orthodox and even Orthodox readers.

A man of the Rav's caliber could easily have written another major book on Halacha – warmer and reflecting his new ideas, which he so beautifully expressed in his *hesped* (eulogy) for the Talner Rebbetzin, when he also spoke about his mother's Shabbat.[3] While the Rav did bring some emotional dimension in *Halakhic Man*, it is minor compared to the stony "Brisker approach." And I'm not even sure whether it's fair to hold Brisk responsible for all of this.

When another of his essays, *The Halakhic Mind* – even more complex than *Ish ha-Halakhah* and originally written in 1944 – was republished in 1986, it was not even updated, and clearly gave the impression that the Rav had not changed his mind. I say this with full recognition that it contains beautiful new insights!

*

Concerning Rabbi Eliezer Berkovits' approach to Halacha, I don't see any evidence that it was influenced by Rav Soloveitchik's writings. In fact, I believe the opposite is true. These two great men fundamentally clashed and disagreed on the nature and workings of Halacha.

---

2. "U-Bikashtem mi-Sham" was first published in *Hadarom* 47 (1978): 1–83, reprinted in *Ish ha-Halakha: Galuy ve-Nistar* (Jerusalem: Elinor Library, 1979), 115–235. An English translation was published years later; Rabbi Joseph B. Soloveitchik, *And from There You Shall Seek*, trans. Naomi Goldblum (NJ: Ktav, 2009). See also Rav Soloveitchik's letter in *Community, Covenant and Commitment*, 321–323, where he explicitly states that the essay that was later published as "U-Bikashtem mi-Sham" is a continuation of *Halakhic Man*.

3. R. Joseph B. Soloveitchik, "A Tribute to the Rebbitzen of Talne," *Tradition* 17, no. 2 (1978): 76–77. See also his "Torah and Shekhinah," in *Family Redeemed: Essays on Family Relationships*, ed. David Shatz and Joel B. Wolowelsky (Hoboken, NJ: Ktav, 2000), 158–180.

*

You are right about Rabbi Aharon Lichtenstein, Rabbi David Hartman, and Rabbi Yitz Greenberg. They are indeed deeply influenced by him. But the latter two moved away from the Rav in striking ways. It is true that these giants did not idolize the Rav, but the vast majority of Modern Orthodox leaders were and are under the spell of Rav Soloveitchik in ways that I believe are unhealthy and that he would have strongly opposed. Rabbi Greenberg wrote me that this idolization began in his later years, but my impression is that during these later years the idolization only increased, for reasons I have explained in my original essay.

Your claim that the Rav's halachic conservatism, caused by his Brisker background, paved the way for his students to go beyond him and find new ways that he encouraged, sounds untrue. Here is Rabbi Greenberg's response to my essay: "You are right about his halachic conservatism. This was compounded by his own lack in encouraging students to go beyond him. He cut them down (as he did Rackman when Rackman went beyond him)."[4] Where, then, did he pave the way for those after him? The reverse is true. He blocked such developments.

*

You state that "perhaps he felt it was too early to depart from or radically reinterpret . . . halachic stringencies and inertia." I wonder when, in your opinion, would the time have been ripe to do so, if not in the days of the Rav? He lived during a time of radical shifts in the Jewish world and a growing crisis in religious belief and halachic commitment. There was no better time than those very days to make these changes, and there was no greater man than he to embark on these departures. Do not forget that he was seen as the *leader*, *symbol*, and *figurehead* of Modern Orthodoxy, and not just as another *posek* or talmudist. As such, there were high expectations of him to move Halacha forward.

*

While I agree that the Rav's encouragement for women to begin learning Talmud was a breakthrough,[5] I can't see it as a major accomplishment in the way that you do. (I wonder how much of a say his wife, Mrs. Tonya

---

4. R. Yitz Greenberg, email message to author, Feb. 9, 2017.
5. See chap. 51 n11.

Soloveitchik – a strong personality with a PhD – had in this matter.) Yes, by doing so he may have revolutionized Jewish learning for women; but feminism was on the rise, and it would have come anyway. The Jewish world was ripe for it and, as has often been the case, it would have been halachically justified after the fact. Women were already learning Talmud before the Rav's days. More important, they could decide this on their own. No one could stop them from doing so in their private lives; nobody needed to know.

But in cases such as the *aguna*, the *mamzer*, and the *kohen/giyoret*, there was no way to decide these matters on their own. They were, and still are, completely dependent on the *poskim*, if they wish to remain within the Orthodox community.

*

I can't see any justification for the Rav openly rejecting Rabbi Rackman's argument, which claims that there is historical contextualization in the world of Halacha. Acceptance of that fact could have helped many Jewish women in his days and today. To this day, women still pay the price for this rejection. Yes, some may argue that these matters are very complex and far beyond the scope of an essay like mine, but a total dismissal is unjustified. True, the Rav was concerned that halachic tradition not be undermined, but he could have achieved that without completely rejecting approaches such as that of Rabbi Rackman. It would not have been seen as surrendering to nontraditional forces, but rather as a victory of halachic strength.

Even more astonishing is the fact that, as I mentioned in my original essay, the Rav admitted to Rabbi Rackman that he may have been right. Surely the Rav knew that historical contextualization had often been applied throughout halachic history.[6] Again, I wonder whether the Rav ever discussed this with his beloved wife, who must have had her own ideas about this, especially when it came to women's issues.

*

As some of his students told me, and as is my impression as well, the Rav felt isolated because his own world of the old-fashioned yeshivot had rejected him once he took a different stand on some matters, such as Zionism, secular studies, and trying to establish a joint *bet din* together with

---

6. See Louis Jacobs, *A Tree of Life: Diversity, Flexibility, and Creativity in Jewish Law* (London: Littman Library of Jewish Civilization, 2000).

the famous Rabbi Saul Lieberman of the Conservative Jewish Theological Seminary to deal with all matters related to marriage and divorce – an attempt that unfortunately never succeeded.[7]

We must no doubt admire him for this, but he was never able to overcome his fear of isolation, and remained stuck. Compare this to Rabbi Eliezer Berkovits, who was much more radical and much more isolated, but never gave in to this situation, and he didn't have a major rabbinical institution like Yeshiva University behind him. He simply moved on and fought a lonely, difficult battle that must have been extremely painful.

*

One more observation: While I greatly admire Rabbi Soloveitchik's writings, such as *The Lonely Man of Faith*, I wonder why he never dealt with some extremely important issues that keep many people away from Orthodoxy. Two examples suffice: (1) The issue of *Torah min ha-Shamayim* and biblical criticism; and (2) the matter of belief in God (especially after the Holocaust) and the conflict between science and faith. It may be true – as Rabbi Walter Wurzburger suggests[8] – that the Rav avoided the issue of biblical criticism out of principle. But if it *is* true, then the Rav was out of touch with reality. At the time, biblical criticism was a major topic of discussion, as it still is. This subject is of utmost importance, and if anyone could have dealt with it head-on, it was the Rav. Early in *The Lonely Man of Faith*, Rav Soloveitchik mentions that he wasn't seriously bothered by this issue. But his readership certainly was!

The same is true about belief in God, and the conflict between science and faith. Sure, the Rav mentioned and discussed these matters, but never directly.

These issues – biblical criticism and belief in God – are fully discussed by former British Chief Rabbi Lord Jonathan Sacks in the prodigious works *Crisis and Covenant*[9] and *The Great Partnership*.[10] I remember how my friends and I, who were not religious at the time, waited for the Rav to discuss these matters. But there was total silence. True, in *The Halakhic*

---

7. See Aaron Rakeffet-Rothkoff, "A Note on R. Saul Lieberman and the Rav," *Tradition* 40, no. 4 (2007): 68–74.

8. Walter S. Wurzburger, "Rav Joseph B. Soloveitchik as Posek of Postmodern Orthodoxy," *Tradition* 29, no. 1 (1994): 5–20. See chap. 51 n10.

9. Jonathan Sacks, *Crisis and Covenant: Jewish Thought After the Holocaust* (Manchester, UK: Manchester University Press, 1992), chaps. 7, 8, and 9.

10. Jonathan Sacks, *The Great Partnership: Science, Religion, and the Search for Meaning* (NY: Schocken Books, 2011).

Mind, he does deal with science and faith/philosophy – and in the last chapter with Halacha – but it is far from satisfactory for many secular, searching people. This book, like some of the others, was written in an Orthodox religious context which *a priori* was accepted, but was not convincing to those of us who did not share this point of view.

It is my belief that these topics are more important than the Rav's masterpiece *The Lonely Man of Faith*. I'm not arguing that he should not have written the book. I am only contending that he should have also written major essays or books on these two critical subjects.

*

Coming back to my main argument, here are a few quotations by the Rav:

> Halakhic man received the Torah from Sinai not as a simple recipient but as a creator of worlds, as a partner with the Almighty in the act of creation. The power of creative interpretation (hiddush) is the very foundation of the received tradition. . . .
>
> He [halakhic man] takes up his stand in the midst of the concrete world, his feet planted firmly on the ground of reality, and he looks about and sees, listens and hears, and publicly protests against the oppression of the helpless, the defrauding of the poor, the plight of the orphan. . . . The actualization of the ideals of justice and righteousness is the pillar of fire which halakhic man follows, when he, as a rabbi and teacher in Israel, serves his community. . . . The anguish of the poor, the despair of the helpless and humiliated outweigh many many commandments. . . .
>
> Even the Holy One, blessed be He, has, as it were, handed over His imprimatur, His official seal in Torah matters, to man; it is as if the Creator of the world Himself abides by man's decision and instruction. . .[11]

If so, why was it impossible to accept Rabbi Rackman's opinion that one *has* to see certain rulings by our sages, especially those concerning women, in the context of historical developments? If the Rav would have done so, then, in his own words, the Holy One, blessed be He, would have abided by *his* decision and instruction. The obligation to shape and perfect Hala-

---

11. R. Joseph B. Soloveitchik, *Halakhic Man*, trans. Lawrence Kaplan (Philadelphia: The Jewish Publication Society of America, 1983), 81, 91, 80.

cha increases over history as human beings become more mature. That is the very foundation of *Torah she-Ba'al Peh* (the Oral Law). Why not make use of it and carry that responsibility with pride?

*

I cannot believe that any *aguna* or *mamzer* will find comfort in *The Lonely Man of Faith* when they are forced to live unbearable lives. What is more important? To write beautifully about Halacha's deep concern for the poor, the helpless, and the humiliated, which outweighs "many many commandments," but not to act on it? Or, to actually try to solve the problem of the *aguna*, the *mamzer*, and the *kohen* who can't marry his loved one because she happens to be a convert?

As Rabbi Eliezer Berkovits writes, ". . . the deed is the stuff of which history is made."[12] Deeds, not beautiful abstract ideas!

*

Due to lack of time, I must now conclude my response to you. The literature and opinions on Rav Soloveitchik's halachic stand and philosophy are so numerous that one could write many books on the subject. But I believe that it has already been overdone.

*

I close with the following. You are indeed misinformed about my personal involvement in practical Halacha. To mention only a few examples: Twice, I have personally married a *kohen* with a *giyoret*. In one case, the *giyoret* was also a *gerusha* (divorcee). In these instances, on my own initiative, but together with halachic authorities much greater than I, we proved that the *kohen* was actually not a *kohen*, and that even after a *get* was obtained by that specific woman, it became clear that in fact she was not a *gerusha*, because she was never halachically married. I never openly published our conclusions because we didn't want the couples involved to get hurt. I have had major clashes about these cases with European rabbinates that refused to marry these people.

I have performed several conversions with a private *bet din*, when other *batei din* refused to do so. I have suggested[13] that we allow people to ride bicycles on Shabbat, based on a *psak* (halachic decision) of the Ben Ish

---

12. Eliezer Berkovits, *God, Man, and History: A Jewish Interpretation* (Middle Village, NY: Jonathan David, 1959), 138.
13. See chaps. 38 and 39.

Chai, and have advocated a halachically permitted "Shabbat tram" in Yerushalayim, to enable people to see their parents who live far away. I have argued in favor of opening restaurants on Shabbat for those Israelis who have nowhere to go, where they wouldn't have to pay and where all the laws of Shabbat could be easily observed.[14] An attempt to open such restaurants was blocked by the Rabbanut's threats to remove its *hechsher* (certificate of kashrut) from these restaurants!

I have also advocated for relaxing the "*chumra* of Rabbi Zeira"[15] concerning the duration of *nidda* abstinence, which prevents couples from having relations more frequently, and which can also lead to difficulty in conceiving. This would no doubt encourage many more couples to observe the laws of family purity.[16]

I have suggested that we build "Jewish" cemeteries for children from mixed marriages who are not halachically Jewish, so that they too can have a "Jewish" burial if they so wish.[17] After all, they are of *zera Yisrael* (of Jewish seed, that is, patrilineal descent). For all of these issues, I have strong halachic arguments.

Together with Rabbi Dr. Norman Lamm of Yeshiva University, I have refused to listen to a *psak* by the London Beth Din prohibiting participation in the famous Limmud Conference in England – which hosts close to three thousand attendants – because Reform and Conservative rabbis also teach there. I told the Beth Din that I believed this was a major mistake, since it gives the impression that we Orthodox rabbis are afraid of the Reform and Conservative movements, and that by not contributing we are actively handing over all Limmud participants to these denominations.[18]

---

14. Ibid.

15. The Talmud (*Nidda* 66a, *Berachot* 31a, and *Megilla* 28b) states: "R. Zeira said: The daughters of Israel have undertaken to be so strict with themselves that if they see a drop of blood no bigger than a mustard seed, they wait seven clean days after it." This stringency lengthens the period of abstinence between husband and wife. The biblical law mandates seven days of separation from the onset of the woman's menstrual period, whereas the stringency extended in the Talmud mandates a separation of seven clean days from the *cessation* of the menstrual flow. This was codified as law in *Mishne Torah* (*Hilchot Isurei Biah* 11: 3–4, 9) and *Shulchan Aruch, Yoreh De'ah* 183:1.

16. See Daniel Rosenak, *Le-Hachzir Tahara le-Yoshna* (Tel Aviv: Yediot Aharonot and Chemed, 2011). See also Tsipy Ivry, "Halachic Infertility: Rabbis, Doctors, and the Struggle over Professional Boundaries," *Medical Anthropology* 32, no. 3 (2013): 208–226. See also Rabbi Evan Hoffman, "Dam Tohar: The Forgotten Leniency." To obtain this article, email evanhoffman@gmail.com.

17. See chap. 45.

18. See Nathan Lopes Cardozo, "Why I Love to Teach at Limmud" (Thoughts to Ponder 283), *David Cardozo Academy*, Dec. 8, 2011, https://www.cardozoacademy.org/thoughts-to-ponder/why-i-love-to-teach-at-limmud/.

I don't see myself as a *posek*, although I know a lot about practical Halacha and believe that I'm well informed on the latest developments in the halachic world. I'm not a member of any official rabbinate, but I am very busy suggesting new possibilities, and I have acted and will continue to act on them, even if the rabbinical establishment does not agree with me. It is time to move forward and not be afraid. . .

Thank you again for your letter.

Sincerely,

Nathan Lopes Cardozo

Chapter 54

Second Response by Tanya White

Dear Rabbi Cardozo,

Let me begin by thanking you for your thorough and thoughtful response to my letter. You address many of the points I made and make a convincing argument for some of your assertions, but by no means all. As I mentioned in my previous letter, the complexity and breadth of Rav Soloveitchik's influence, legacy and works have already filled thousands of pages and will continue to do so, hence it is beyond the scope of this correspondence to address all areas of this subject and *Katonti* from being able to offer anything new that has not already been said. There are, however, four points I would like to address with regards to your response.

I: ON THE "IDOLIZATION" OF THE RAV

I believe you are correct to point out that in recent years there has been an "idolization" of the Rav, though again I think you are guilty of your own critique as I shall attempt to demonstrate. As we know, both the secular and Charedi communities suffer from a similar malaise. They both create "molten images." The onset of modernity perpetuated what Nietzsche had already predicted in the nineteenth century, that men would become "gods." As the power of human capabilities has grown exponentially, so too has its inability for self-criticism or allegiance to any external authority other than itself. The arrogance and self-belief in our ability to conquer all has led us to worship our own self-image to the detriment of key virtues such as self-sacrifice, humility, self-restraint and faith. The secular absolutizing of humanity left unchecked leads to nihilism, egocentricity, totalization and metaphoric blindness to anything outside of self; in other words, the ills of society today. In the religious world there exists a parallel situation. The dual threat of modernity and Zionism meant that the ultra-Orthodox communities have had to build walls both internally and externally. Their need to reject "modernish" values led to a system of defensiveness rather than innovation. They rejected the "idolization" of the human, in favor of the "idolization" of the Halacha and the "Gedolim."[1] The definition of idol worship is creating an image that is immune to change. An image that we compartmentalize to suit our own agenda, that we "use," or "manipulate," as the idol worshipers did in ancient times, to achieve our goals.[2] There is no doubt that over the years, as witnessed noticeably in the last few months, there has been a move to the right in so called Modern Orthodox institutions in America. As this process played out, the legacy of the "Rav," the "Gedol Hador," was used to justify the status quo by resisting any calls for change. To this extent I agree that there has been an "idolization" (though I would probably term it obsession rather than idolization) of the Rav, which is the natural result of the shift to the right in certain Modern Orthodox circles. In "idolizing" something or someone, we create a unitary monolithic image of that thing and hence lose its depth and complexity, and herein lies the danger.

The Rav, as witnessed through his writings and by those who knew him first hand, possessed a profoundly complex and often conflicted personality. He was, like our greatest role models, deeply human. This meant he was subject to constraints both personal and political, as furthermore conditioned by the time in which he was living and making decisions. Additionally, his views and personality changed over time (as I argued in my first letter), and hence in the same way that he has been idolized, with his halachic decisions set in stone by the those on the right, I believe through your depiction of the Rav, you have also totalized his legacy as a failure to move Modern Orthodoxy forward in the halachic realm, which is not quite accurate and misses much of its complexity. I quote William Kolbrener (whom you were introducing in your original article) when he says,

---

1. This is seen on a hermeneutic level through the treatment of problematic biblical narratives, such as the refusal to criticize the *Avot*, or David Hamelech for his sin. This has the effect of turning biblical figures into saints as per Christianity, rather than viewing them as human beings (the debate of *Tanach be-Gova Eynayim*). But far more disturbing are the practical implications of this mindset, including the despicable covering up of the rampant incidents of sexual impropriety that are committed by an authority figure in the Charedi world (teacher, father, rabbi), so as not to disillusion anyone of the person's greatness.

2. For a detailed and thoroughgoing discussion of the subject of modern "idolatry," see Moshe Halbertal and Avishai Margalit, *Idolatry*, trans. Naomi Goldblum (Cambridge: Harvard University Press, 2007).

"the attempts of various students and followers to embody Soloveitchik ideals – to manifest that vision in cultural or institutional form – has been the compromise of complexity."[3] He has become, as Kolbrener so correctly posits, a "dichotomous image" acquiring a dual reputation adopted by each belligerent side. Any attempt to oversimplify and polemicize his legacy does it a great injustice – an injustice I believe you too commit.

II: THE ORIGINALITY AND RELEVANCE OF *HALAKHIC MAN*

The Rav wrote and taught on the heels of the greatest crisis for Orthodoxy since the destruction of the Second Temple. The challenge of modernity, which manifested itself in movements such as the Reform and Conservative, coupled with the crisis of faith arising from the Holocaust, meant there was much searching for answers. You argue that as the leading voice for Modern Orthodoxy, the Rav had a responsibility to present a compelling and enriching religious response. Halacha was for many outdated, irrelevant and incongruent with the enticing values of modernity such as autonomy, creativity and self-determination. Furthermore, Christianity's assault on Judaism as being too legalistic (an argument originating with Spinoza and adopted by the Reform movement at the time too), was forefront in the minds of many American Jews. The Rav does respond to some of these challenges, but I believe the Rav did not see himself as defender of Modern Orthodoxy. As I will argue, the Rav's works were not polemical or defensive, designed to "answer" religious dilemmas of the time. They were far more personal and cathartic and in being so naturally addressed some, but not all, of the pressing issues.

What the Rav did in *Halakhic Man* goes far beyond, as you cursorily state, "reading Immanuel Kant in a Jewish religious framework." Its originality stems from its ability to turn the whole halachic process on its head. Instead of "idolizing" Halacha as we mentioned is done in the Charedi circles, the Rav transfers the "authority" of the Halacha to the individual. The "authority" becomes embedded in human creativity as opposed to the system or the Divine.[4] Halakhic Man is neither subdued nor coerced

---

3. William Kolbrener, *The Last Rabbi: Joseph Soloveitchik and Talmudic Tradition* (Bloomington: Indiana University Press, 2016), 127.

4. It is true that the idea of human autonomy as opposed to divine authority is already formulated in early talmudic sources, however this trend became up-surged during the Middle Ages when the halachic system became ever more stagnant and the general religious outlook was one that favored the restraint and suppression of the individual in favor of divine or clerical authority. The enlightenment put an end to this religious oppression but at the same time threatened the foundation of religion. Though there was a renaissance in Jewish thought in the nineteenth and

but rather self-determined and creative. For the first time in the history of modern thought, the inner working of the talmudic personality was brought face to face with the enlightened intellectual, and as it turned out their worlds were not so far apart. This was the innovation in the Rav's work.[5] Halakhic Man in contrast to *homo religiosus* is practical, active and this-worldly, he seeks answers to religious dilemmas in the workings of the real world, not in a transcendent realm. I cannot think of anything more relevant to today's disaffected Israeli youth, both secular and religious (who have never read Kant anyway). The ideas need restating in more accessible and modern terms, but are still highly relevant.

III: THE RAV AND HALACHIC INNOVATION

The central thesis of your article, as I read it, was that you believe Rabbi Soloveitchik should have made greater halachic innovations, which he did not, and hence fails in your eyes as the great leader he is purported to be. I want to offer two different approaches that I believe answer this critique. The first focuses on the practical implementation of halachic decisions and the constraints he was under, the second his overall halachic philosophy.

1. I acknowledge that his halachic decisions were grounded in a more conservative approach than what one may expect based on his theoretical and philosophic writings. However, hindsight is always a wonderful thing. Rav Soloveitchik lived during a tumultuous period, his commitment to Zionism, women's Torah and Talmud learning and co-ed schooling[6] as well as an uncompromising allegiance to modernity, in the face of much opposition, was itself a colossal challenge. Perhaps the time was not ripe for the changes we would have expected him to make; perhaps, as we have already said, he was not an "idol" with whom the gift of hindsight and

---

early twentieth centuries with thinkers such as Buber, Rosensweig, Cohen, no one placed the halachic process in the framework of modernity until Soloveitchik's *Halakhic Man*.

5. As already noted, this response has a superficial air to it. I have presented the Rav's work in a unitary fashion without conceding to its multifarious and often contradictory elements. This is in order to make a point. However, one must acknowledge the argument by Singer and Sokol (David Singer and Moshe Sokol, "Joseph Soloveitchik: Lonely Man of Faith," *Modern Judaism* 2, no. 3 [1982]: 227–272) and more recently by Dov Schwartz (Dov Schwartz, *Religion or Halakha: The Philosophy of Rabbi Joseph B. Soloveitchik* [Leiden: Brill, 2007]), that *Halakhic Man* is simply apologetics, "dressing up Talmudism in neo-Kantian garb," and the counter-response to this by David Hartman, with whom my sympathies lie. It is also prudent to look at chaps. 28 and 29, especially the references to all the leading literature on the subject, in Reuven Ziegler, *Majesty and Humility: The Thought of Rabbi Joseph B. Soloveitchik* (Jerusalem: Urim, 2012).

6. See Seth Farber, *An American Orthodox Dreamer* (Hanover, NH: Brandeis University Press, 2004), chap. 4, where he outlines the novelty of both co-ed schooling and talmudic study for women and shows them to have become the defining feature of Modern Orthodoxy in America. To this, Rav Soloveitchik must be credited.

prophecy was given. He was not to know that his ambivalent response to subjects such as interfaith or intrafaith dialogue, women in the halachic process, status of the *mechitzah* or status of non-Jews, would be misinterpreted or totally revised by some of his students. It seems on some issues the Rav was treading water, waiting to give a definitive ruling in the ripeness of time, which for him never materialized. This *temporization,*[7] perhaps an intentional policy, perhaps not, legitimized the conservative agenda of the more Charedi elements of Modern Orthodoxy, the corollary of which is being felt today, and that does feel like a failing. Though that failing, I believe, is less the Rav's, more the ills of a narrow and parochial mindset typical in certain sectors of Orthodoxy.

You ask me when I think the time may have been ripe for the Rav to make these changes? Despite your contention to the contrary, I believe he did make changes, in your opinion not enough, in my opinion just enough to keep him balancing all the political baggage. You yourself acknowledge that he made attempts to create a *bet din* with Rabbi Saul Lieberman of the JTS, through which perhaps he felt more change could be administered, though it ultimately failed. Those who called for radical halachic change during the 50s and 60s, such as Hartman and Greenberg, were seen as pariahs in certain circles, though now their thought is seen as far less radical. These voices were needed (hence the Rav's private legitimization of many of the projects and views of these personalities[8]) to pave the path for change today; however for the Rav to legitimize such change was perhaps too soon. As he himself quotes in 1945 at the opening of the Maimonides school, "the dreamer of yesterday is often the architect of tomorrow."[9]

2. It may very well be that the reason you fail to understand the Rav on this issue is because you are coming from a totally different starting point. The Rav believed that *psak* follows from whatever the halachic system dictates. It seems to me that your thinking is that the halachic system should follow whatever is necessary for the sake of whatever *psak* is needed for this day and age. Both views may be legitimate, but one cannot be held

---

7. I adopt a word used by Rabbi Yitz Greenberg in an article featured in a forthcoming book on the proceedings of the Oxford Conference entitled *The Road Not Travelled: Modern Orthodoxy and the Work of Rabbi Yitz Greenberg*, quoted with permission of the author.

8. I quote from your response, "The Rav admitted to Rabbi Rackman that he may have been right." Rabbi Greenberg and Rabbi Hartman both suggest the Rav legitimized various actions they took, whilst in public he remained ambivalent. See article in the previous footnote where Rabbi Greenberg expresses a few instances of this, as well as in his book *For the Sake of Heaven and Earth* (Philadelphia: Jewish Publication Society, 2004).

9. Seth Farber, *An American Orthodox Thinker: Rabbi Joseph B. Soloveitchik and Boston's Maimonides School* (Hanover, NH: Brandeis University Press, 2004).

up against the other, for their fundamental view of the halachic system differs fundamentally.

To put it another way, if we take two extreme views of Halacha, on the one side, "Chadash asur min haTorah" of the Chatam Sofer, and "Where there is a Rabbinic will, there is a halakhic way" of Blu Greenberg, while the two of them could argue on a philosophical level which view is more correct, it would be meaningless for them to argue that the other should embrace their specific *psak halacha* since they are coming from such different approaches.

It appears you have more in common with Blu Greenberg while the Rav has more in common with the Chatam Sofer[10] (again this paints an inaccurate black and white picture of the issue that does, however, underscore the point at hand). This is highlighted in the new book *Halakhic Morality*, where amongst other things Soloveitchik writes, "The Halakhic system is basically constant and unalterable." By contrast, he claims that ethics have much more room for reformulation and change. You will surely ask, if this is in fact his "true" view, what about the creativity and innovation as well as the ethical activism that he so clearly advocates in *Halakhic Man*? To that I would reply by saying the following:

1. The *chiddushim* he speaks about were personified by his grandfather Rav Chaim. These were not cases where someone came with a practical halachic question and he wanted to adapt the Halacha to give a certain answer but rather the reverse, where clever learning of texts led to a certain answer that differed from previous understandings. The desired answer was not the driver nor the creative element, rather this was embodied in the exposition itself.

2. Based on the theory that *Halakhic Man* is based on the Rav's father, the Rav's sister tells of how post WWI, there was a huge *aguna* problem on a scale never before experienced, and the Rav's father was active in trying to deal with it by writing letters to the government and rabbis near the front. He found many novel ways to free *agunot* using his utmost halachic creativity, but he "never deviated from the Halacha".[11]

The two differing interpretations I have offered above should leave us in no doubt that your critique of his lack of halachic ingenuity is unfounded.

---

10. I am indebted to Meir Valman for this insightful point, as well as other important points he made in an initial reading of this response.

11. Shulamit Meiselman Soloveitchik, *The Soloveitchik Heritage: A Daughter's Memoir* (Hoboken, NJ: Ktav, 1995), 163.

IV: THE RAV AND ISSUES OF CONCERN

You write:

"I wonder why he never dealt with some extremely important issues that keep many people away from Orthodoxy. Two examples suffice: (1) The issue of *Torah min ha-Shamayim* and biblical criticism; and (2) the matter of belief in God (especially after the Holocaust) and the conflict between science and belief."

At the start of *The Lonely Man of Faith*, the Rav states:

> I have never been seriously troubled by the problem of the Biblical doctrine of creation vis-à-vis the scientific story of evolution at both the cosmic and the organic levels, nor have I been perturbed by the confrontation of the mechanistic interpretation of the human mind with the Biblical spiritual concept of man. I have not been perplexed by the impossibility of fitting the mystery of revelation into the framework of historical empiricism. Moreover, I have not even been troubled by the theories of Biblical criticism which contradict the very foundations upon which the sanctity and integrity of the Scriptures rest. However, while theoretical oppositions and dichotomies have never tormented my thoughts, I could not shake off the disquieting feeling that the practical role of the man of faith within modern society is a very difficult, indeed, a paradoxical one.[12]

For the Rav, the dilemma of science and biblical criticism in regard to the Torah was not as serious a challenge as the role of faith in modern society. For the Rav, the answer to problems of faith come through the "experience" of the religious personality and its development. Though this is not found in *Halakhic Man*, it is certainly expressed in later works such as "U-Bikashtem mi-Sham" and *The Lonely Man of Faith*. It is from these and other places where the Rav describes this intensely loving relationship with the Divine that his thoughts on belief and faith can be inferred. Thus overemphasis on history and texts was not of any concern since the man of faith is impervious to such issues.[13]

Furthermore, your use of Rabbi Jonathan Sacks as an example of some-

---

12. R. Joseph B. Soloveitchik, *The Lonely Man of Faith* (NY: Doubleday, 1992), 7.

13. For an in-depth study on this question and some interesting answers and theories, see Aryeh Sklar, "Rabbi Joseph B. Soloveitchik and the Problem of Biblical Criticism," *Kol Hamevaser*, Nov. 3, 2016.

one who has addressed the issue is imprudent since I believe the inspiration for his thinking on this subject came from Rav Soloveitchik! I would suggest that his approach is based on what he calls the "epistemological pluralism" of the Rav. In an early essay,[14] Rabbi Sacks skillfully analyzes *The Halakhic Mind* and in doing so formulates the Rav's position on science and religion by showing their mutually exclusive realms. This purposeful disintegration allows, he says, for religion to be "presented autonomously, as a cognitive system independent of, but parallel to science."[15] Anyone familiar with Rabbi Sacks will already detect from this the seeds of his thinking on science and religion, expressed so brilliantly and originally in his recent book *The Great Partnership*.

You seem to suggest that because he was great he should have dealt with these important contemporary topics. I think that is the wrong way round. He dealt with what mattered to him in a highly original and unmatched way and because of that he became great. I would argue that that is why he is still so revered. Issues of biblical criticism, science, belief in God tend to come and go, and some of the arguments are only really relevant to a few intellectuals that grasp them in all their details. The Jewish responses to them often look very dated today hundreds of years later or even a few years later in the case of some of the scientific debates. But Rav Soloveitchik's focus on the crisis of faith in modern society and the need for religious experience is probably even more relevant today than when he was alive and touches far more people.

We must concede that Rav Soloveitchik's works were perhaps more a cathartic individual process than a polemic for the public, but it is this that makes them so powerful and compelling. Regarding the Holocaust, it is true the Rav never offered a systematic and complete response; he was not as such a post-Holocaust thinker. In "Kol Dodi Dofek" he indeed grapples with the challenge, but it is integrated into a general discussion of suffering and Zionism, and hence arguably does not provide a satisfactory response for someone looking for something comprehensive.

V: CONCLUSION

You, Rabbi Cardozo, are a radical thinker. As an educator myself, I often use your ideas and thoughts to shake up complacent minds, or present an

---

14. Jonathan Sacks, "Rabbi J.B. Soloveitchik's Early Epistemology: A Review of 'The Halakhic Mind,'" *Tradition* 23, no. 3 (1988): 75–87.

15. Ibid., 77.

idea from a novel perspective. Yours is a much needed voice in a time of reappraisal and revision; the Judaism you champion is authentic and raw. However, acknowledging the couple of occasions you have acted on these ideas, I stand by my original critique that it is the ideas you espouse, as opposed to actions that you take, that defines your position. You are therefore not so far removed from the critique you levy at Rav Soloveitchik. I would like to suggest that Judaism needs bold thinkers more than ever today and it is to this task you have successfully set yourself. Equally, it needs courageous halachic innovation. However, this will take time; it will not and cannot happen overnight. Today in Israel through organizations such as Tzohar and ITIM (the founder of which, Rabbi Seth Farber, was a Yeshiva University graduate and deeply influenced by Rav Soloveitchik's thought) and halachic authoritative personalities such as Rav David Stav, Rav Yuval Cherlow, Rav Benny Lau and Rav Yossi Zvi Rimon, the ethical and ritualistic realm in Halacha is being addressed in a serious and formative way, but there is still a long road ahead.

We are standing at the horizon of a new tomorrow, one that Judaism must be ready to face head-on. I would like to think that Rav Soloveitchik lay the groundwork, but in the end it's all a matter of interpretation, and as long as we keep our minds open to new ways of seeing and resist the temptation to "idolize" even our own ideas, we will fulfill what Chazal state: *Elu V'Elu Divrei Elohim Chaim* – the living breathing God is found in the multiplicity of interpretation and complexity of life – "these and those are the words of the living God."

With best wishes,
Tanya White

*

In the spirit of Bet Hillel, I have given Mrs. White the last word, although I have serious doubts about her arguments. The serious reader of this book will understand why. To my great regret, many of my practical (more radical) halachic suggestions – many more than those mentioned in this book – have been rejected by the rabbinical authorities, including the Modern Orthodox. As such, I cannot do more than suggest them and wait for better days!

Nathan Lopes Cardozo
The David Cardozo Academy, Jerusalem
www.cardozoacademy.org
office@cardozoacademy.org

Index

holding on to time, 206–207
holiness
  achieving, 268–269
  authorities regarding *yayin nesech*, 93
  autonomous religiosity, 63–65, 80
  being in a state of, 120–121
  chosenness of the Jewish people, 241
  conflict between body and soul, 125
  conversion as not about Halacha, 363
  conversion of Ruth, 374–376
  distinction between intent of man vs.
    God, 209–210
  fairness as not deciding factor in
    Halacha, 271
  going off the *derech*, 110
  Halacha and absurdity, 303
  Halacha as legal hairsplitting, 329
  internalizing meaning behind mitzvot,
    127–128
  near collapse of Halacha, 102
  need for spiritual conversions, 395
  new halachic and spiritual criteria for
    conversion, 388
  new world order, 206
  Pan-Halacha, 240
  problem of evil, 268
  prohibition of carrying on Shabbat,
    406
  reason for a Jewish nation, 88
  secular law and Halacha as duties or
    rights, 340–341
  sexuality as measure of, 269–270
  Shabbat as spiritual, 350
  Shabbat violation for sanctification,
    351–352
  spiritual change through physical
    action, 125
  struggle in Halacha between fairness
    and, 263–299
  taking off one's *kippa*, 180
  theology of the halachic loophole, 289
  thoughts of Plato, 104
  Torah as timely, 213
Holland, 41, 181, 222
Holocaust, 158, 267n19, 338n8, 420,
  434, 441, 445–446
Holy of Holies, 209, 351
homosexuality, 175, 238, 258–262
hope only when man is unsettled, moral,
  45
hora'at sha'ah, 78
Huna, Rav, 182
hypocrisy, camouflage, and hiding
  behind the kashrut laws, 402–405
hypocrisy vs. authenticity regarding
  Chanuka, 229–233

I

Ibn Ezra, 263n2
iceberg, questions as only the tip of the,
  202–203
ideal and idyllic, Halacha as, 115–133
ideal Halacha, no, 246–253
ideal vs. reality regarding Jewish status,
  357–360
ideas, encouragement of new Torah,
  176–177
idol worship
  anti-Halacha and Amalek, 242n12, 244
  authorities regarding *yayin nesech*,
    92–93
  breaking point in Jewish history,
    203–204
  conversion of Ruth, 373, 375
  defensive Halacha and the waiting
    mode, 93
  deliberately creating an atmosphere of
    rebellion, 42
  distinction between intent of man vs.
    God, 210
  familiarity as motive behind
    prohibition, 86
  far-fetched halachic arguments, 289
  fighting for a mission, 94
  genius and limitations of R. Joseph B.
    Soloveitchik, 423
  Halacha and absurdity, 306
  Halacha as counterproductive, 90–91
  Halacha as deliberate chaos, 52
  holding on to time, 206–207
  intellectual dishonesty, 40
  intent vs. content, 210
  Ms. White's response to R. Cardozo's
    article about R. Soloveitchik, 426
  ontological view of non-Jews, 87
  prohibition of *yayin nesech*, 84
  protest as motive behind prohibition,
    85, 85n11
  R. Cardozo's response to Ms.
    White regarding article about R.
    Soloveitchik, 432
  R. Soloveitchik and halachic
    innovation, 442
  religious self-deception, 108
  sacrifices as progressive or regressive
    Judaism, 221–222
  sages' responsibility to update Torah,
    295
  tentativeness of science, 148
  Torah as a divine compromise, 291
  Torah as first rebellious text, 95
  treatment of R. Soloveitchik as,
    439–441